You're Rea... WRONG WAY!

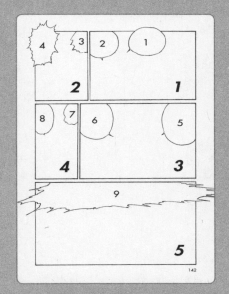

NISEKOI reads from right to left, starting in the upper-right corner. Japanese is read from right to left, meaning that action, sound effects, and word-b... reversed f...

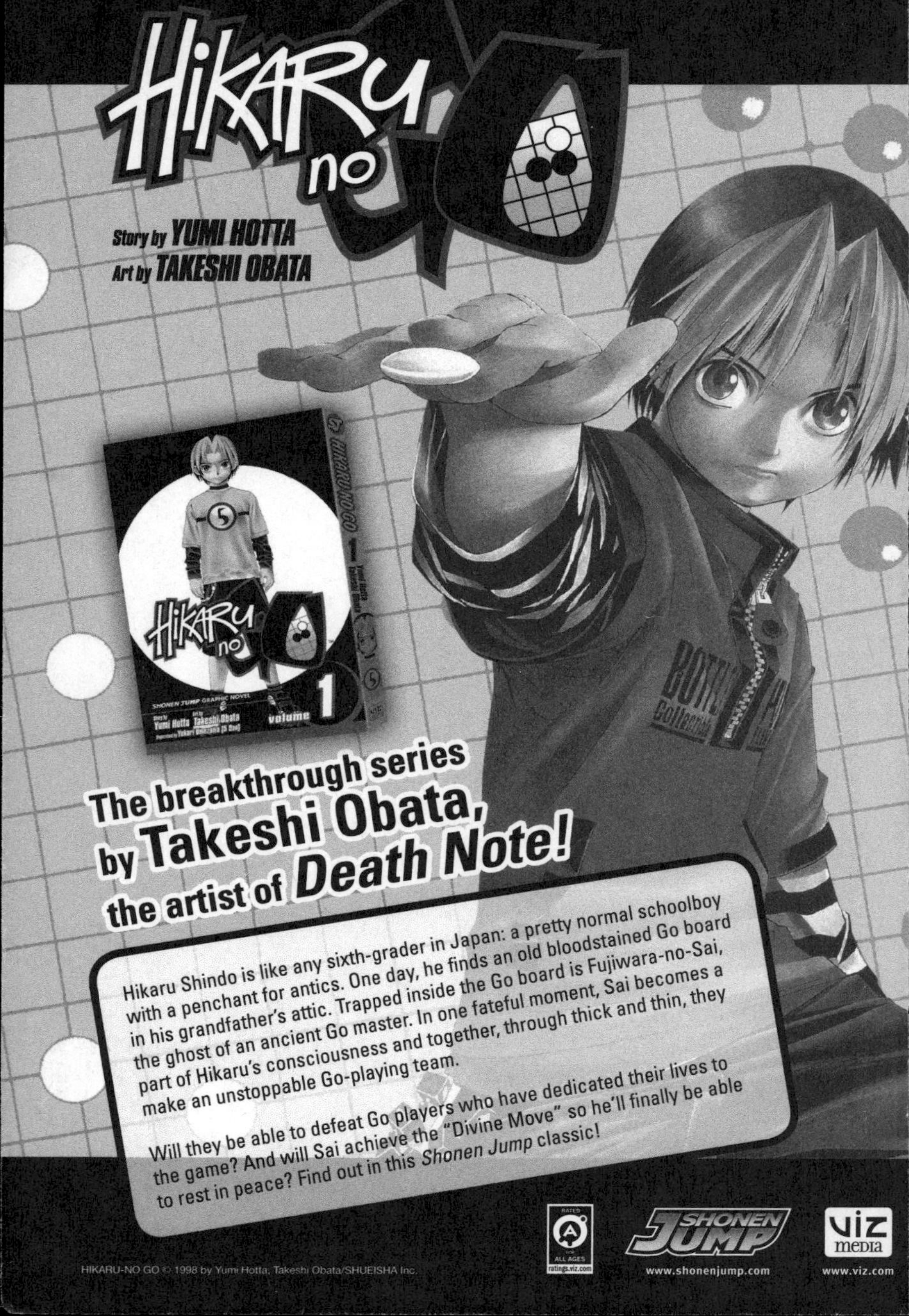
HIKARU no GO
Story by YUMI HOTTA
Art by TAKESHI OBATA
HIKARU no GO
volume 1
The breakthrough series by Takeshi Obata, the artist of Death Note!
Hikaru Shindo is like any sixth-grader in Japan: a pretty normal schoolboy with a penchant for antics. One day, he finds an old bloodstained Go board in his grandfather's attic. Trapped inside the Go board is Fujiwara-no-Sai, the ghost of an ancient Go master. In one fateful moment, Sai becomes a part of Hikaru's consciousness and together, through thick and thin, they make an unstoppable Go-playing team.
Will they be able to defeat Go players who have dedicated their lives to the game? And will Sai achieve the "Divine Move" so he'll finally be able to rest in peace? Find out in this Shonen Jump classic!
RATED A ALL AGES ratings.viz.com
SHONEN JUMP
www.shonenjump.com
VIZ media
www.viz.com
HIKARU-NO GO © 1998 by Yumi Hotta, Takeshi Obata/SHUEISHA Inc.

Raku and Onodera go to a shopping mall together in this volume. Well, I love malls too! No matter what the weather's like, it's a big, comfortable space where you can eat food and treats and shop and have fun all day. I could live in a mall!

Naoshi Komi

I'd happily appear three or four times!

Second time. Nothing wrong with that.

NAOSHI KOMI was born in Kochi Prefecture, Japan, on March 28, 1986. His first serialized work in *Weekly Shonen Jump* was the series *Double Arts*. His current series, *Nisekoi*, is serialized in *Weekly Shonen Jump*.

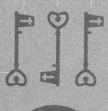

NISEKOI:
False Love
VOLUME 19
SHONEN JUMP Manga Edition

Story and Art by
NAOSHI KOMI

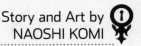

Translation ✐ Camellia Nieh
Touch-Up Art & Lettering ✐ Stephen Dutro
Design ✐ Fawn Lau
Shonen Jump Series Editor ✐ John Bae
Graphic Novel Editor ✐ Amy Yu

Published by VIZ Media, LLC
P.O. Box 77010
San Francisco, CA 94107

10 9 8 7 6 5 4 3 2 1
First printing, January 2017

www.shonenjump.com

www.viz.com

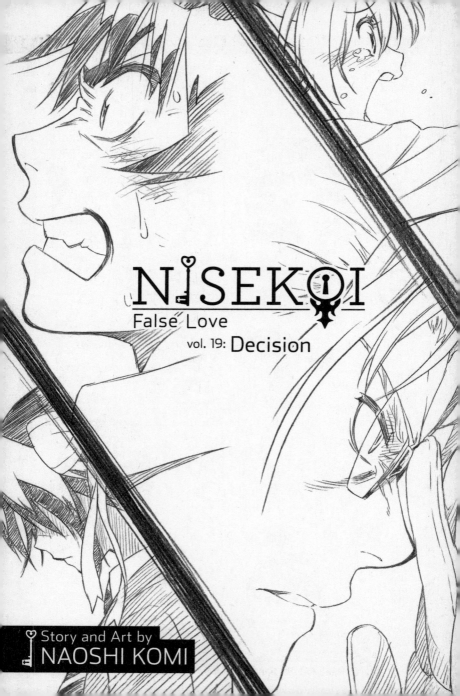

NISEKOI
False Love
vol. 19: Decision

Story and Art by
NAOSHI KOMI

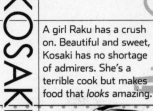

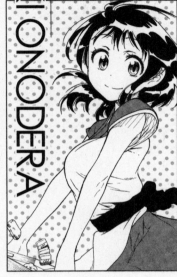

CHITOGE KIRISAKI

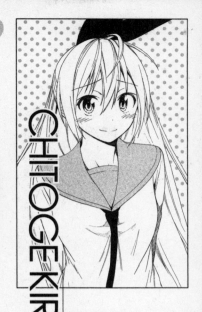

A half-Japanese bombshell with stellar athletic abilities. Short-tempered and violent. Comes from a family of gangsters.

KOSAKI ONODERA

A girl Raku has a crush on. Beautiful and sweet, Kosaki has no shortage of admirers. She's a terrible cook but makes food that *looks* amazing.

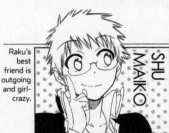

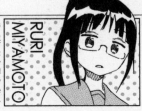

RAKU ICHIJO

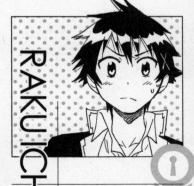

A normal teen whose family happens to be yakuza. Cherishes a pendant given to him by a girl he met ten years ago.

SHU MAIKO

Raku's best friend is outgoing and girl-crazy.

RURI MIYAMOTO

Kosaki's best gal pal. Comes off as aloof, but is actually a devoted and highly intuitive friend.

MARIKA TACHIBANA

Daughter of the chief of police, Marika is Raku's fiancée, according to an agreement made by their fathers—an agreement Marika takes very seriously! Also has a key and remembers making a promise with Raku ten years ago.

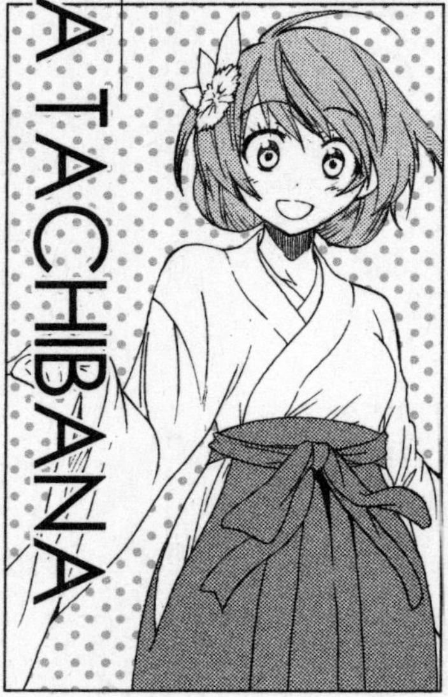

YUI KANAKURA

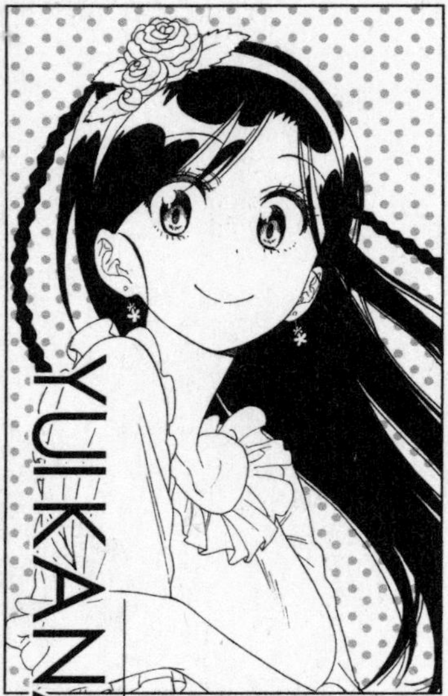

A childhood friend of Raku's, Yui is the head of a Chinese mafia gang and the homeroom teacher of Raku's class at his school. She is currently staying at Raku's house and also has a special key linked to some kind of promise...

CHARACTERS & STORY

Ten years ago, Raku Ichijo made a promise with a girl he loved that they would get married when they met again...and he still treasures the pendant she gave him to seal their pledge.

Thanks to his family's circumstances, Raku has to pretend he's dating Chitoge Kirisaki, the daughter of a rival gangster. Despite their constant spats, Raku and Chitoge manage to fool everyone. Chitoge also has a token from her first love ten years ago—an old key. Meanwhile, Raku's crush, Kosaki, also has a key, as do Marika, the girl Raku's father has arranged for him to marry, and Yui, a childhood friend who's their homeroom teacher. Now, after their school trip, Chitoge is devastated to learn that her family is moving away! What will Raku do?!

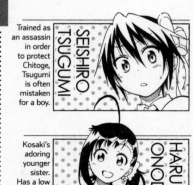

SEISHIRO TSUGUMI

Trained as an assassin in order to protect Chitoge, Tsugumi is often mistaken for a boy.

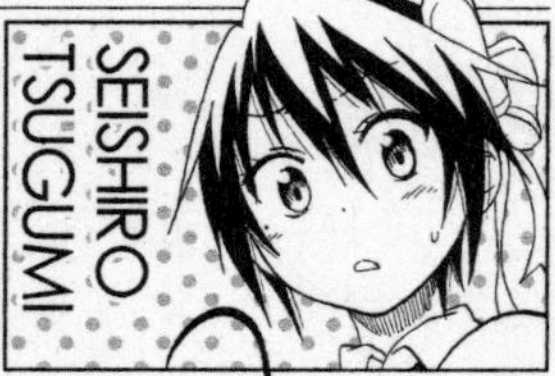

HARU ONODERA

Kosaki's adoring younger sister. Has a low opinion of Raku.

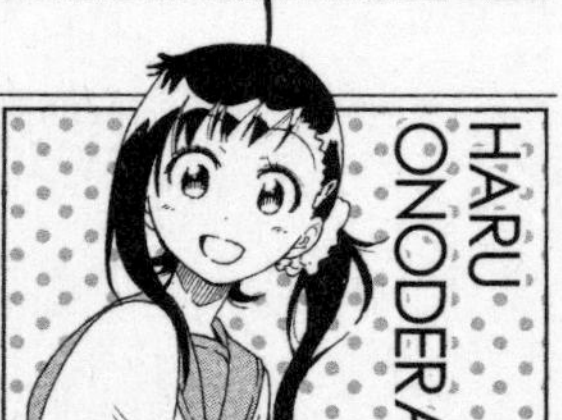

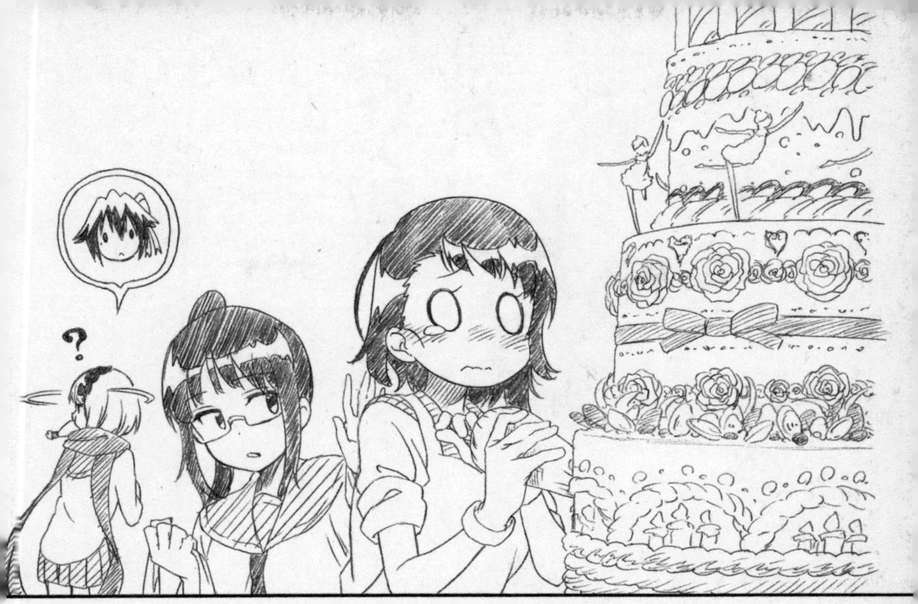

NISEKOI
False Love

vol. 19: Decision

TABLE OF CONTENTS

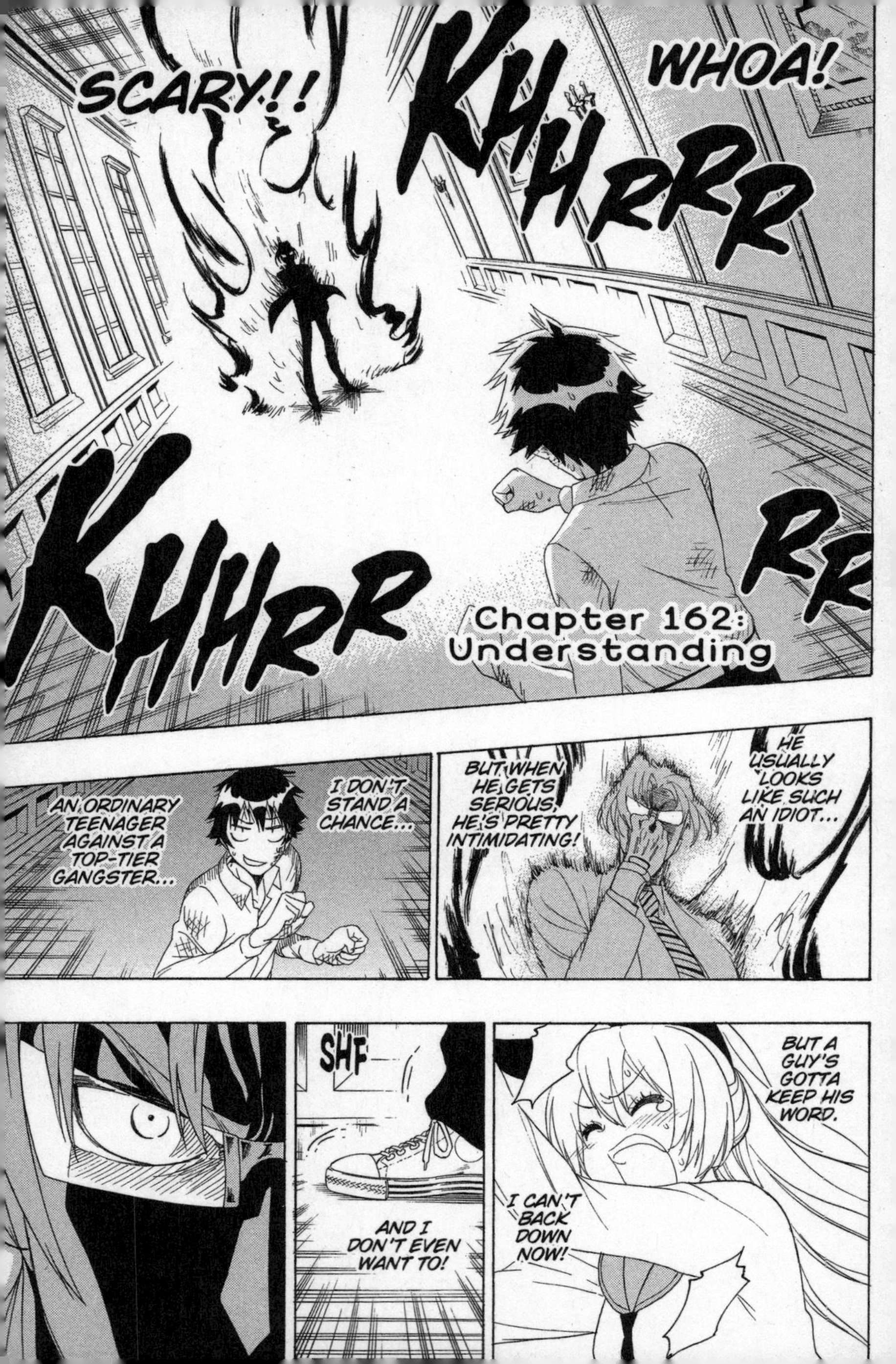
WHOA!
KHHRRR
SCARY!!
KHHRR RR
Chapter 162: Understanding
HE USUALLY LOOKS LIKE SUCH AN IDIOT...
BUT WHEN HE GETS SERIOUS, HE'S PRETTY INTIMIDATING!
I DON'T STAND A CHANCE...
AN ORDINARY TEENAGER AGAINST A TOP-TIER GANGSTER...
BUT A GUY'S GOTTA KEEP HIS WORD.
I CAN'T BACK DOWN NOW!
SHF
AND I DON'T EVEN WANT TO!

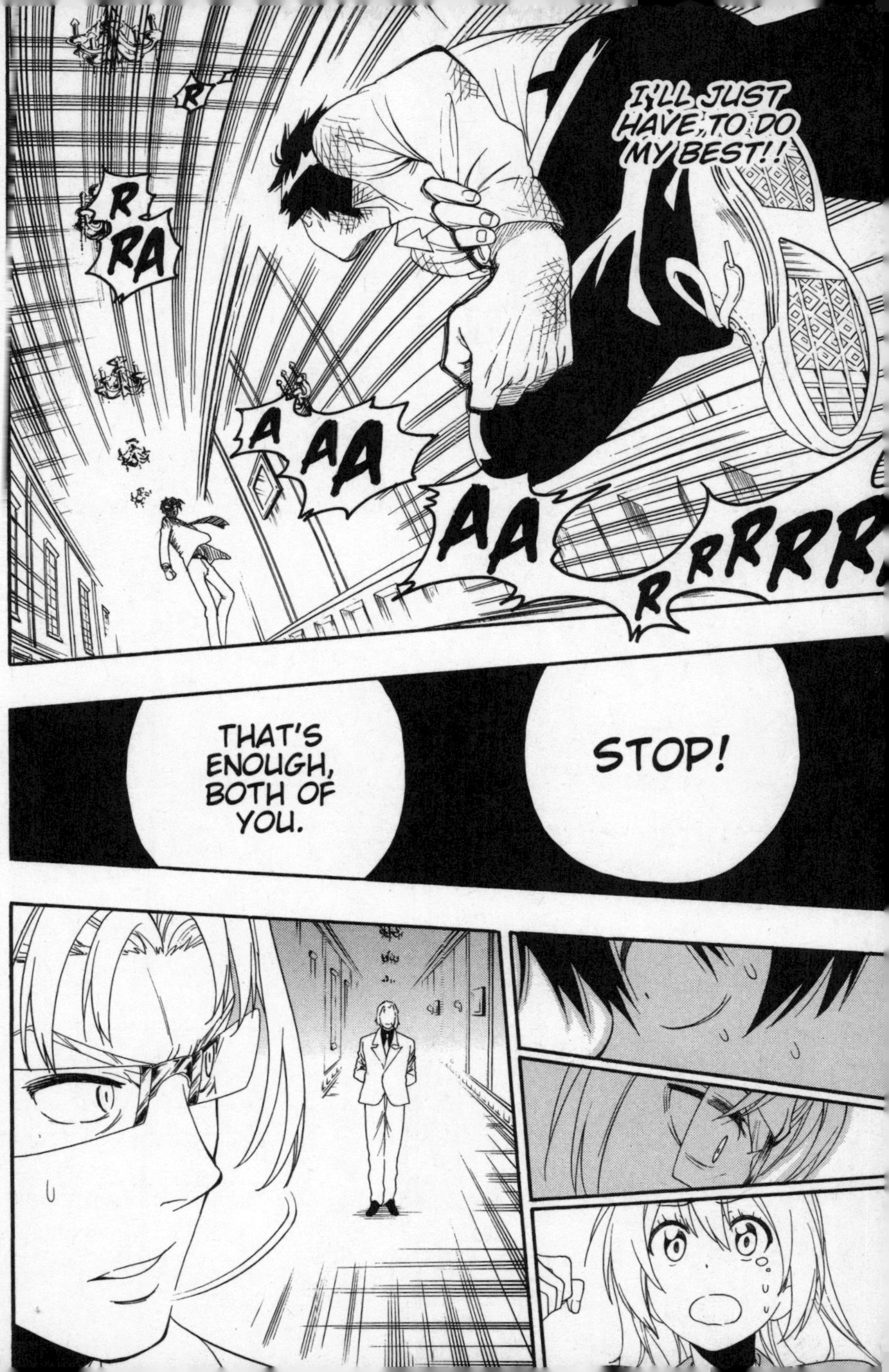
I'LL JUST HAVE TO DO MY BEST!!
R
RRA
AAAAA
RRRRRR
STOP!
THAT'S ENOUGH, BOTH OF YOU.

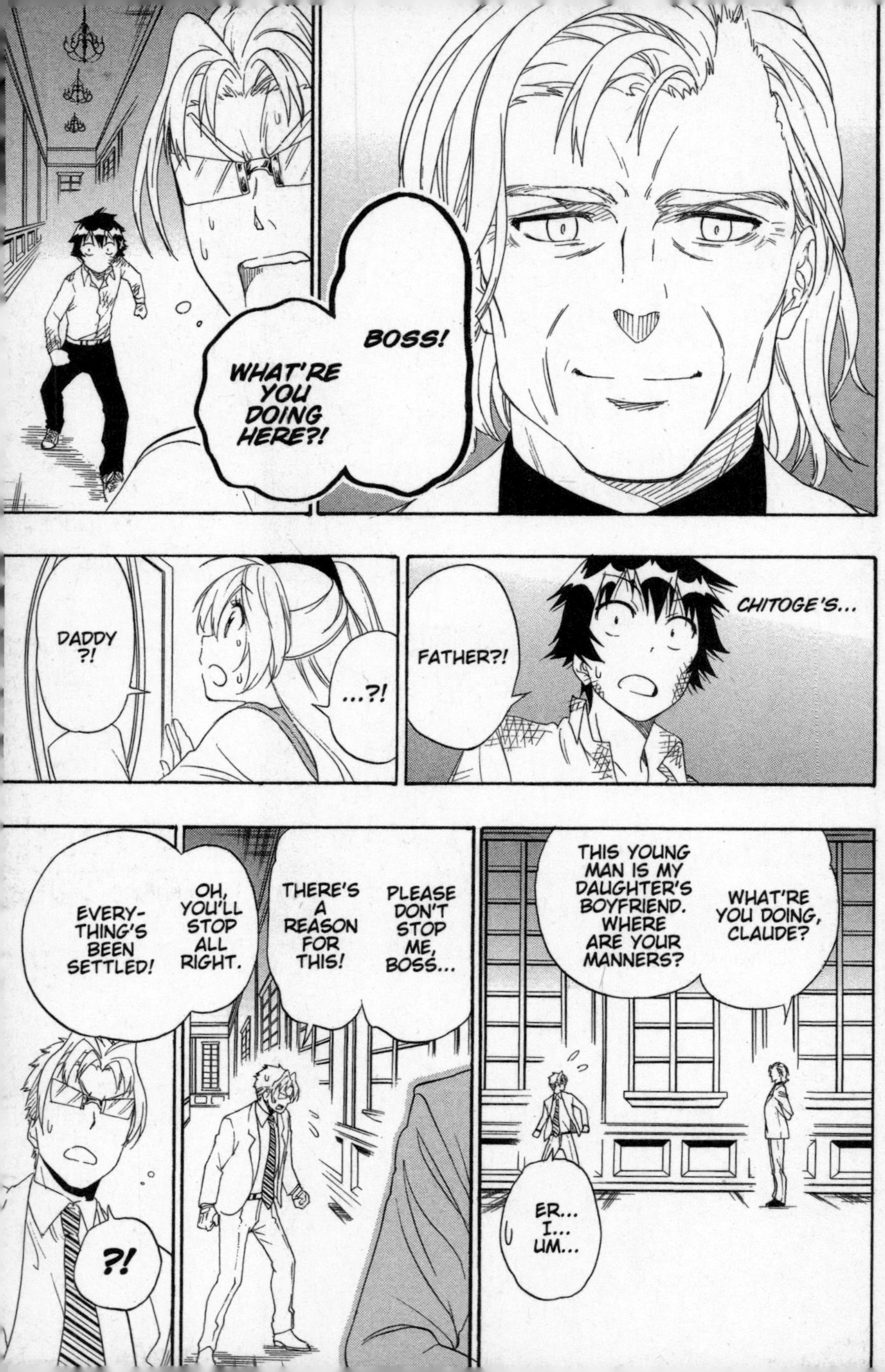
BOSS! WHAT'RE YOU DOING HERE?!
CHITOGE'S...
FATHER?!
...?!
DADDY?!
WHAT'RE YOU DOING, CLAUDE?
THIS YOUNG MAN IS MY DAUGHTER'S BOYFRIEND. WHERE ARE YOUR MANNERS?
ER... I... UM...
PLEASE DON'T STOP ME, BOSS...
THERE'S A REASON FOR THIS!
OH, YOU'LL STOP ALL RIGHT.
EVERYTHING'S BEEN SETTLED!
?!

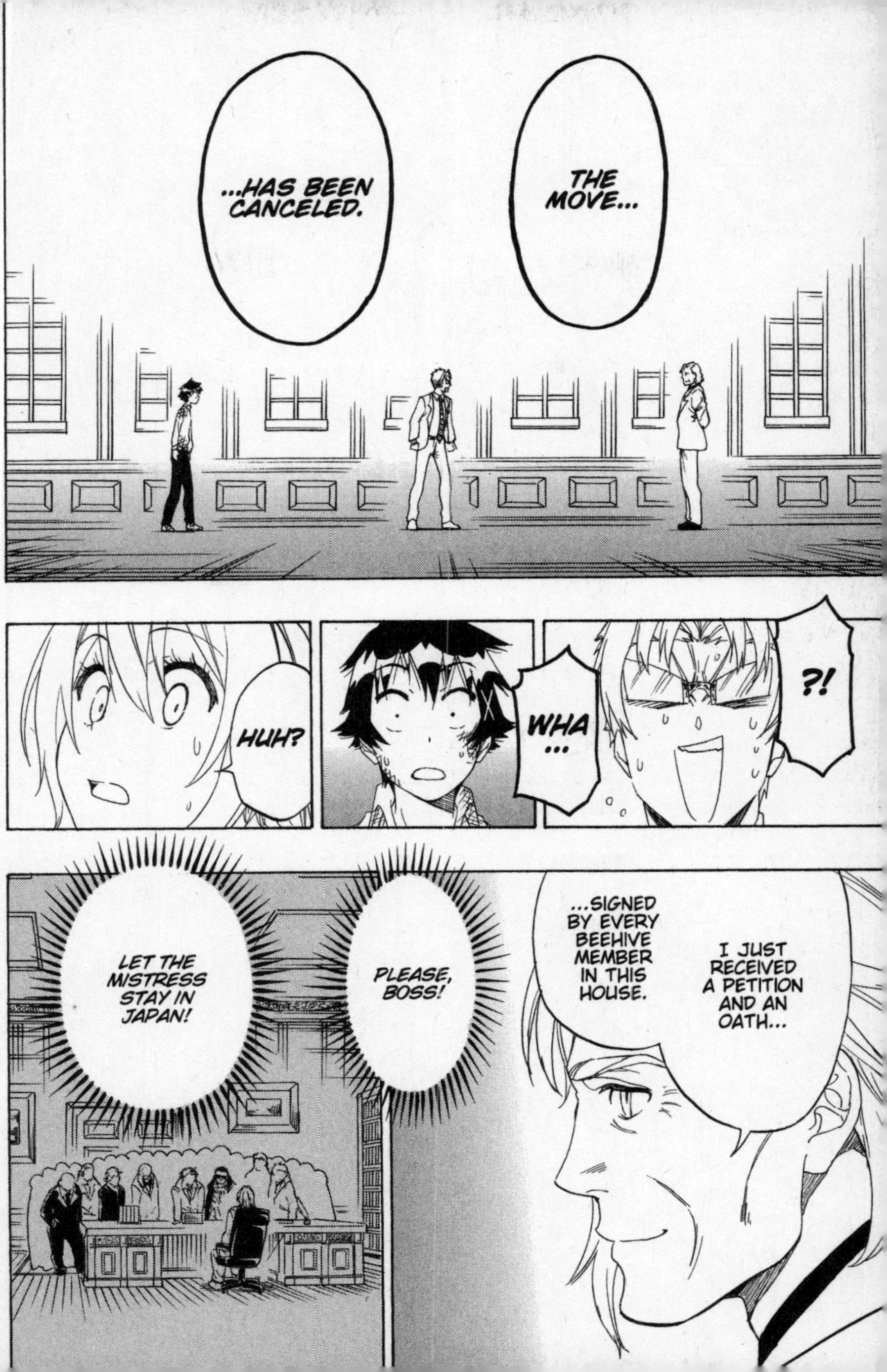
THE MOVE...
...HAS BEEN CANCELED.
?!
WHA ...
HUH?
I JUST RECEIVED A PETITION AND AN OATH...
...SIGNED BY EVERY BEEHIVE MEMBER IN THIS HOUSE.
PLEASE, BOSS!
LET THE MISTRESS STAY IN JAPAN!

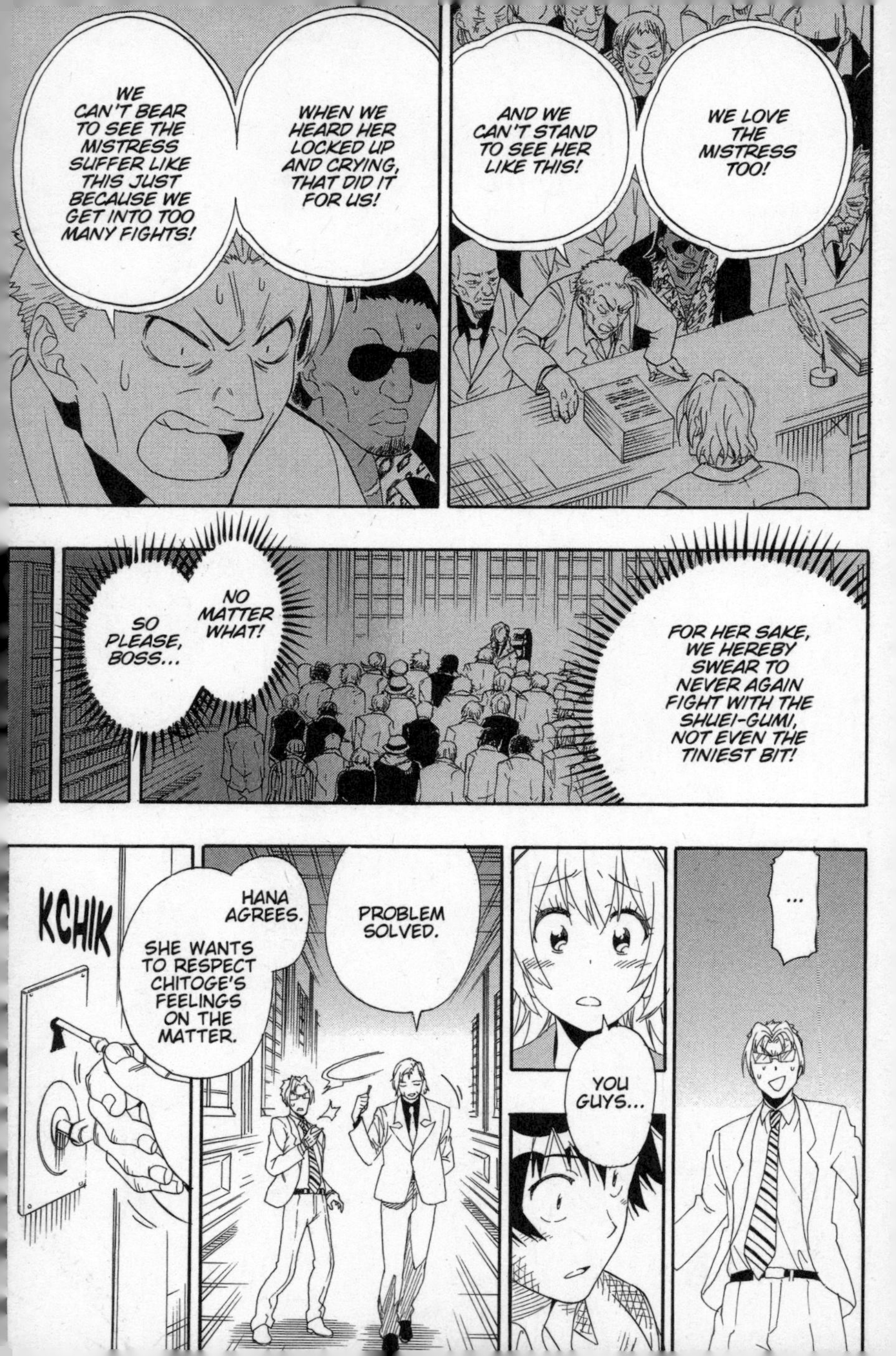
WE LOVE THE MISTRESS TOO!
AND WE CAN'T STAND TO SEE HER LIKE THIS!
WHEN WE HEARD HER LOCKED UP AND CRYING, THAT DID IT FOR US!
WE CAN'T BEAR TO SEE THE MISTRESS SUFFER LIKE THIS JUST BECAUSE WE GET INTO TOO MANY FIGHTS!
FOR HER SAKE, WE HEREBY SWEAR TO NEVER AGAIN FIGHT WITH THE SHUEI-GUMI, NOT EVEN THE TINIEST BIT!
SO PLEASE, BOSS... NO MATTER WHAT!
...
YOU GUYS...
PROBLEM SOLVED.
HANA AGREES. SHE WANTS TO RESPECT CHITOGE'S FEELINGS ON THE MATTER.
KCHIK

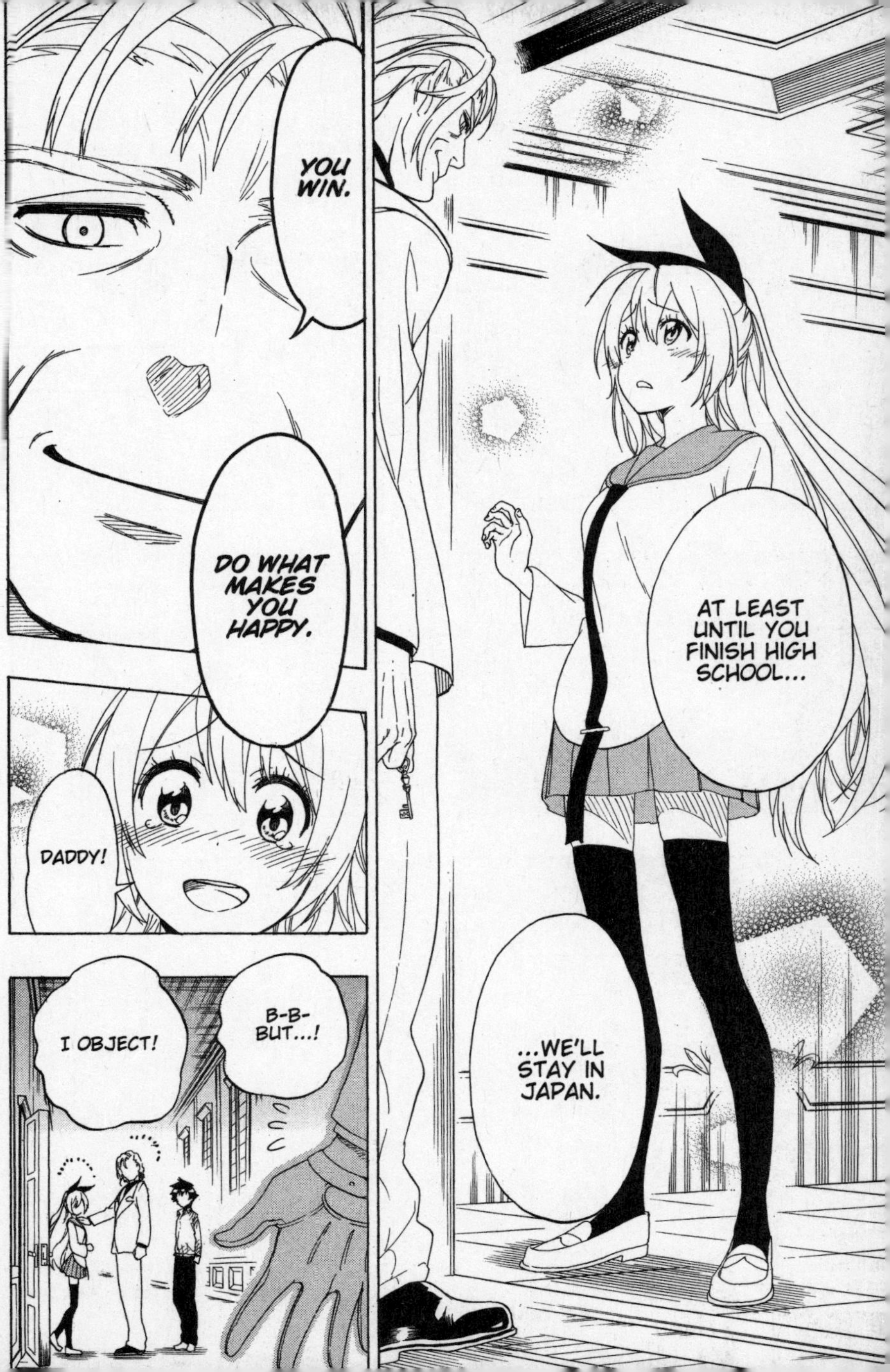
AT LEAST UNTIL YOU FINISH HIGH SCHOOL...
...WE'LL STAY IN JAPAN.
YOU WIN.
DO WHAT MAKES YOU HAPPY.
DADDY!
B-B-BUT...!
I OBJECT!

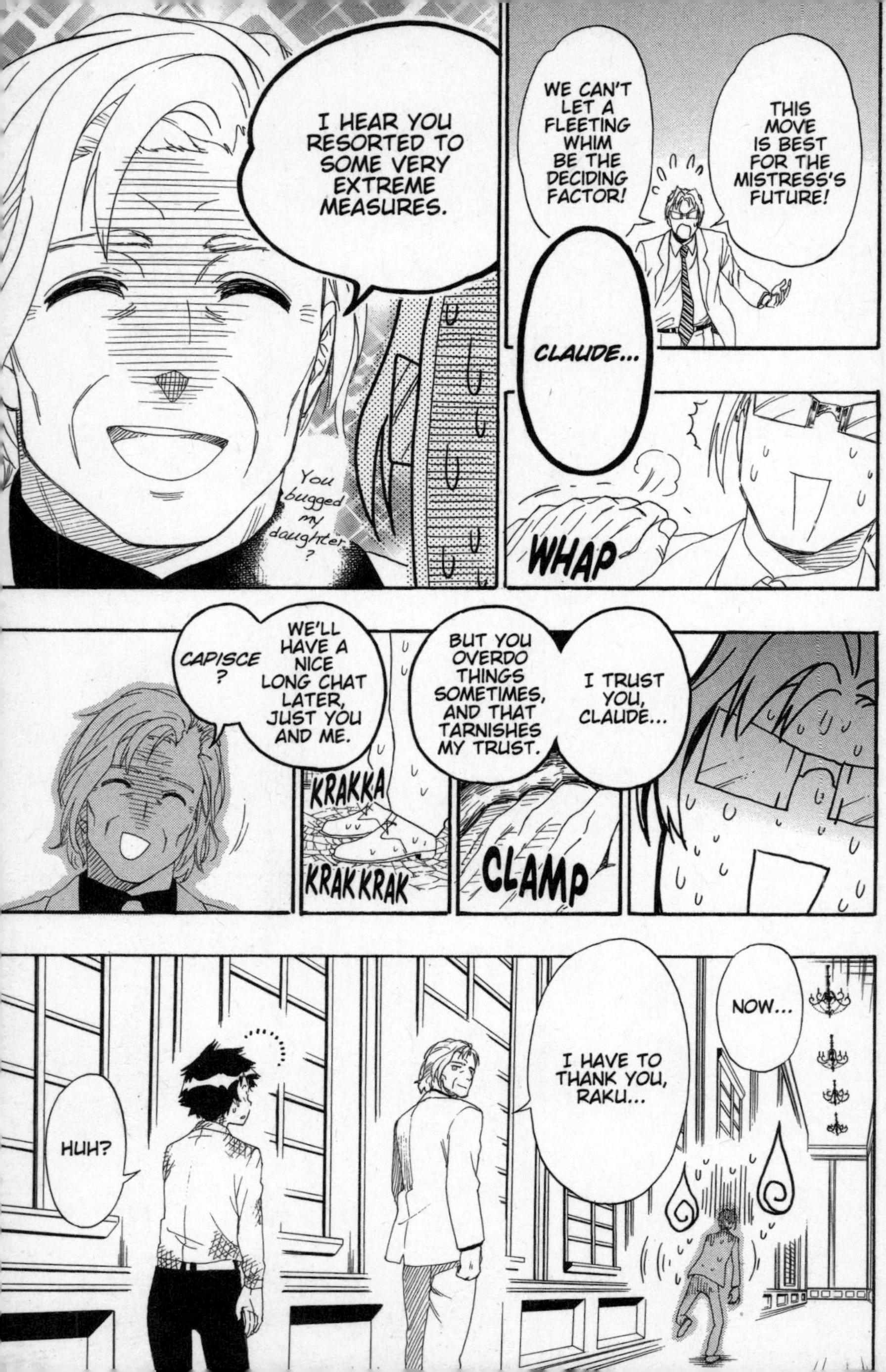

THIS MOVE IS BEST FOR THE MISTRESS'S FUTURE!
WE CAN'T LET A FLEETING WHIM BE THE DECIDING FACTOR!
CLAUDE...
WHAP
I HEAR YOU RESORTED TO SOME VERY EXTREME MEASURES.
You bugged my daughter?
I TRUST YOU, CLAUDE...
BUT YOU OVERDO THINGS SOMETIMES, AND THAT TARNISHES MY TRUST.
CLAMP
KRAKKA
KRAKKRAK
WE'LL HAVE A NICE LONG CHAT LATER, JUST YOU AND ME.
CAPISCE?
NOW...
I HAVE TO THANK YOU, RAKU...
HUH?

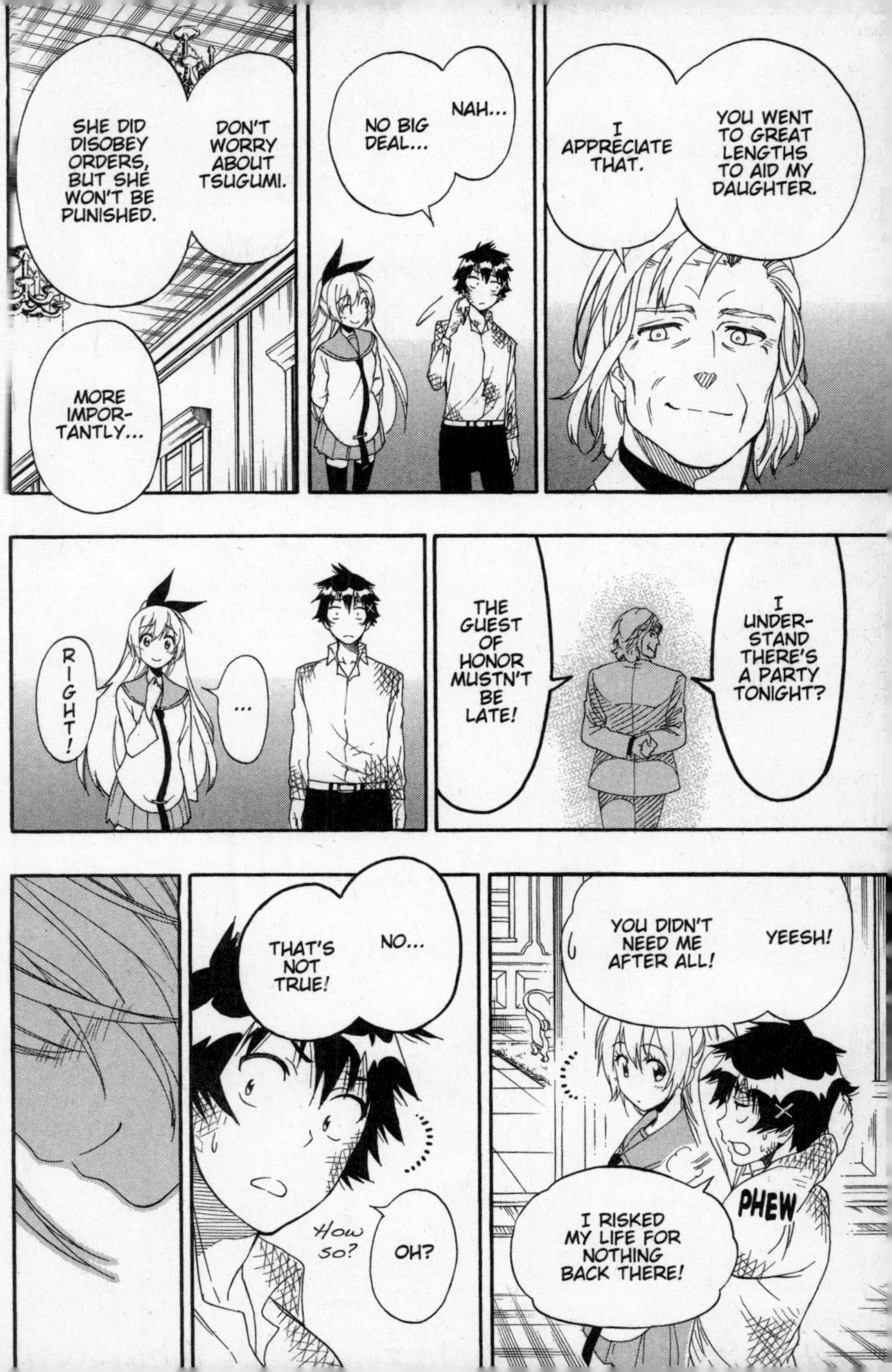

YOU WENT TO GREAT LENGTHS TO AID MY DAUGHTER.
I APPRECIATE THAT.
NAH...
NO BIG DEAL...
DON'T WORRY ABOUT TSUGUMI.
SHE DID DISOBEY ORDERS, BUT SHE WON'T BE PUNISHED.
MORE IMPORTANTLY...
I UNDERSTAND THERE'S A PARTY TONIGHT?
THE GUEST OF HONOR MUSTN'T BE LATE!
...
RIGHT!
YEESH!
YOU DIDN'T NEED ME AFTER ALL!
PHEW
I RISKED MY LIFE FOR NOTHING BACK THERE!
NO...
THAT'S NOT TRUE!
OH?
How so?

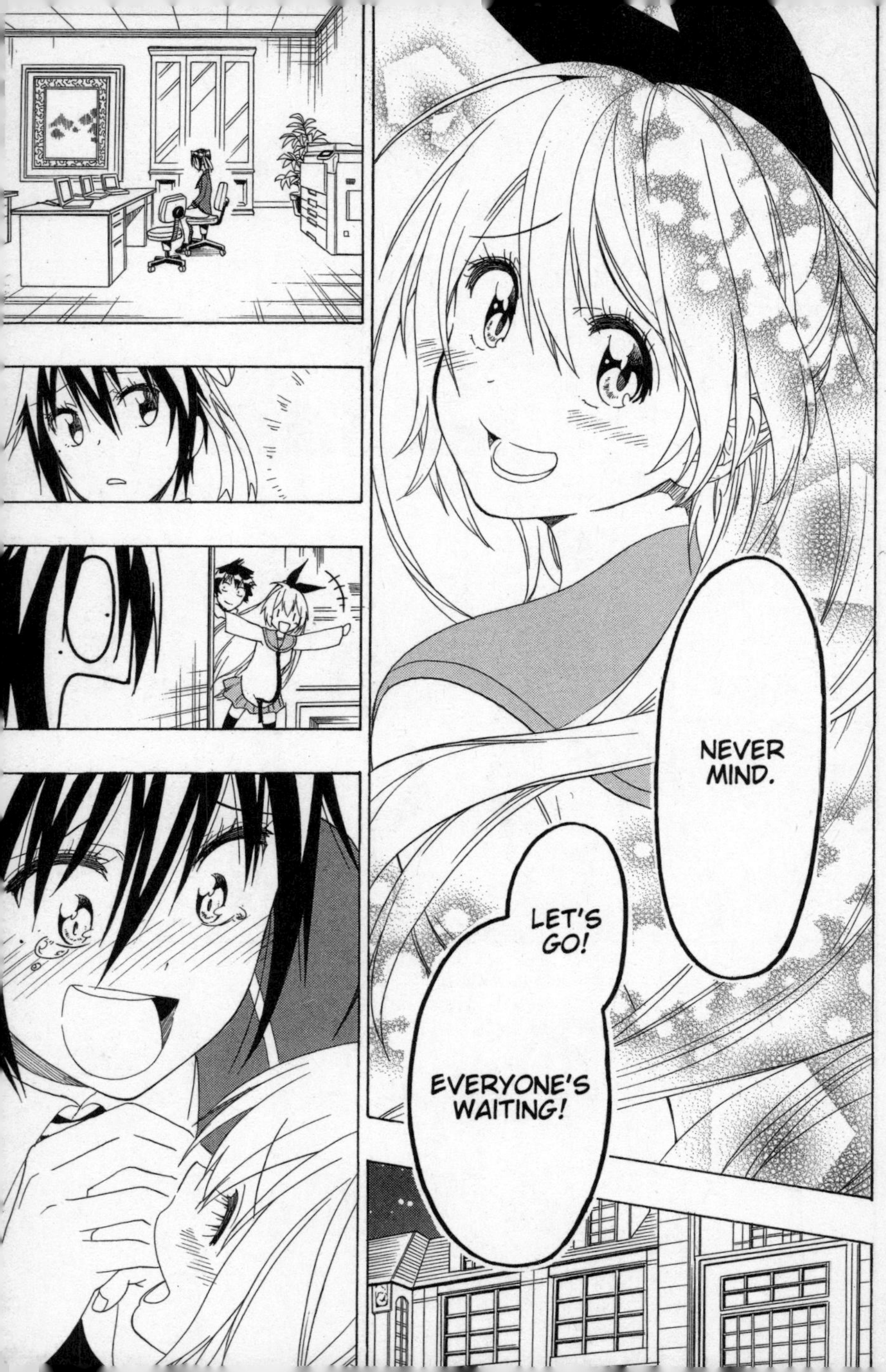
NEVER MIND.
LET'S GO!
EVERYONE'S WAITING!

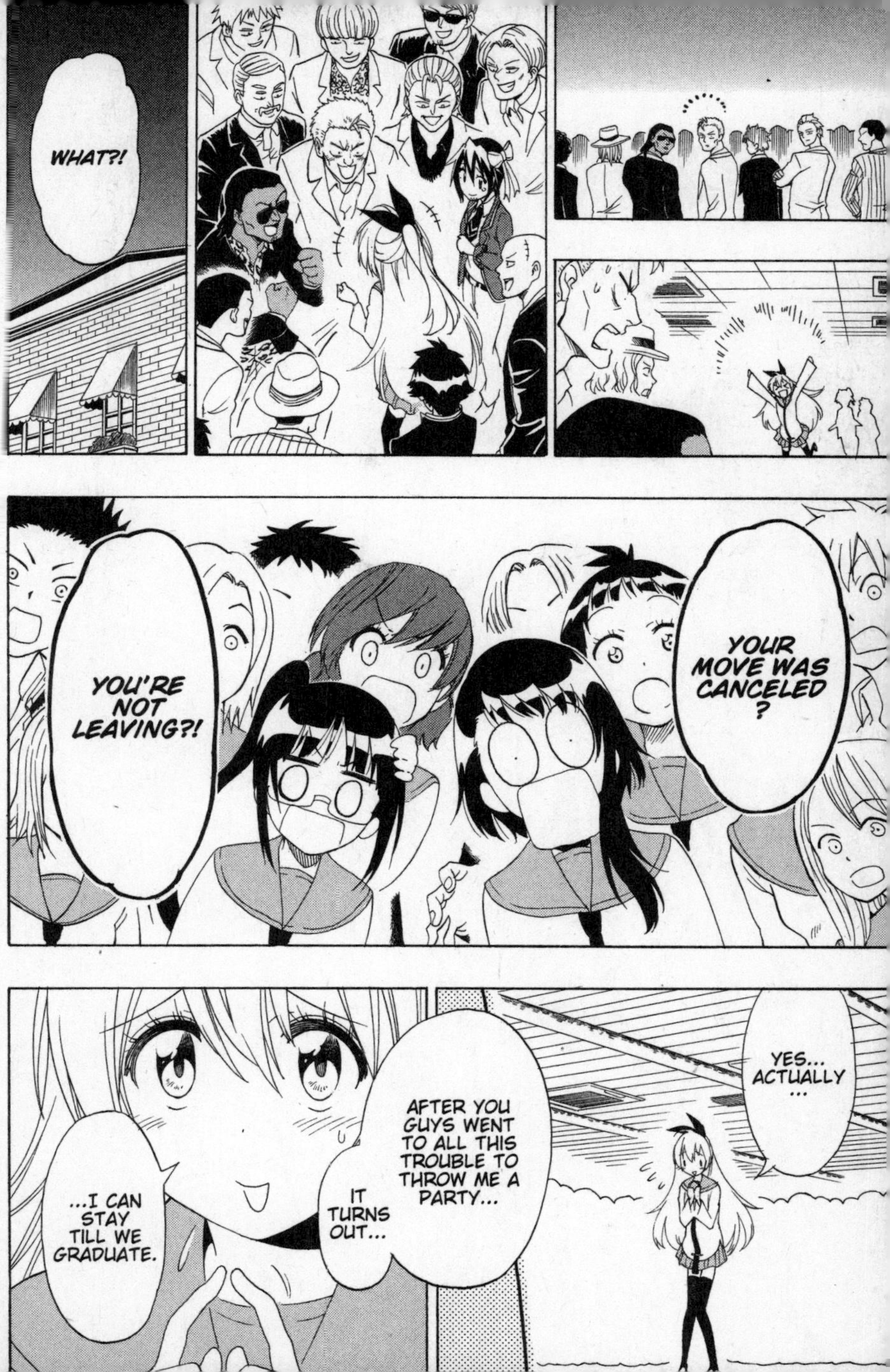
WHAT?!
YOUR MOVE WAS CANCELED?
YOU'RE NOT LEAVING?!
YES... ACTUALLY...
AFTER YOU GUYS WENT TO ALL THIS TROUBLE TO THROW ME A PARTY...
IT TURNS OUT...
...I CAN STAY TILL WE GRADUATE.

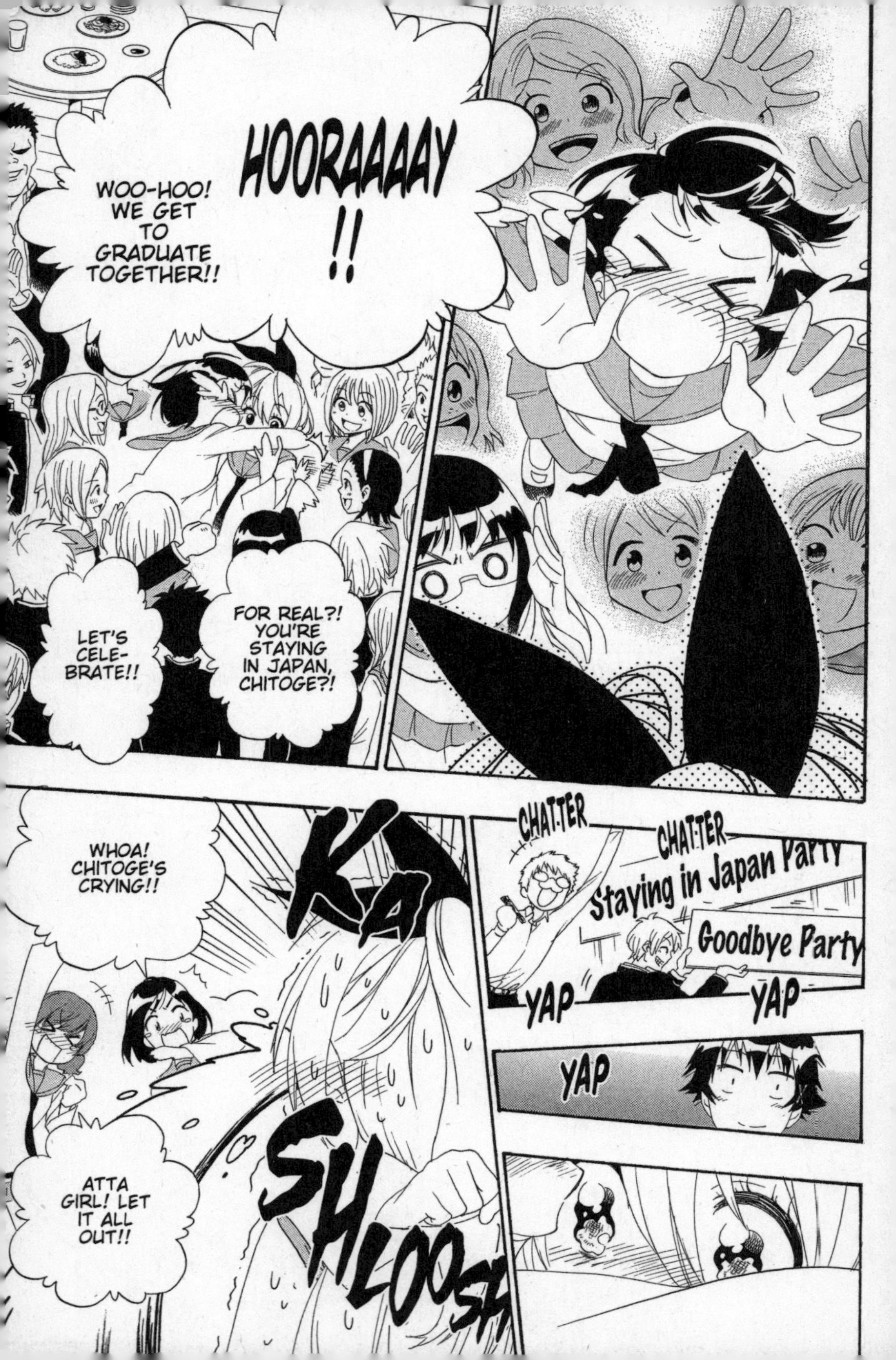
HOORAAAY!!
WOO-HOO! WE GET TO GRADUATE TOGETHER!!
FOR REAL?! YOU'RE STAYING IN JAPAN, CHITOGE?!
LET'S CELEBRATE!!
CHATTER
CHATTER
Staying in Japan Party
Goodbye Party
YAP
YAP
YAP
KA
WHOA! CHITOGE'S CRYING!!
SHLOOSH
ATTA GIRL! LET IT ALL OUT!!

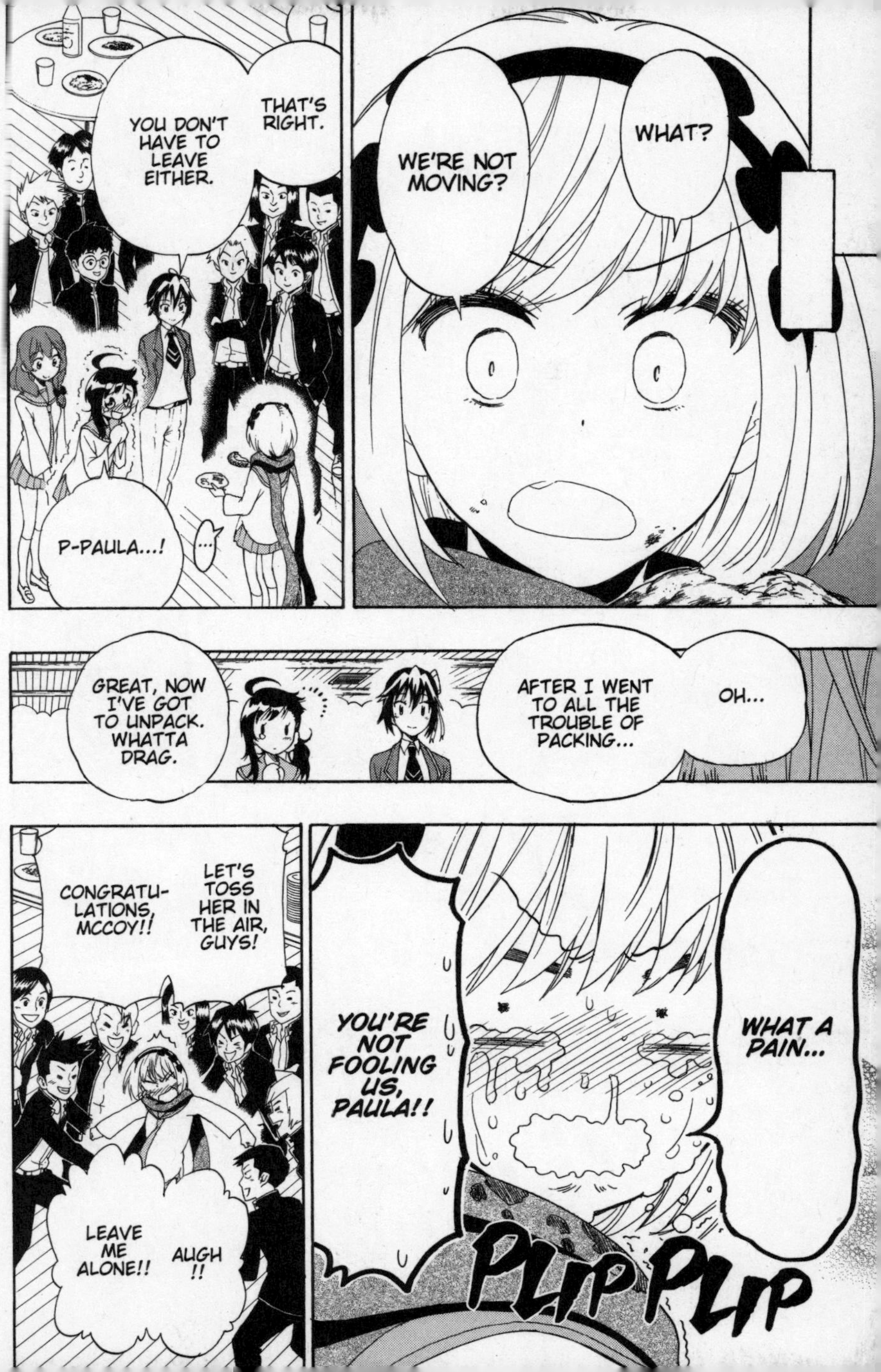
WHAT?
WE'RE NOT MOVING?
THAT'S RIGHT.
YOU DON'T HAVE TO LEAVE EITHER.
...
P-PAULA...!
OH...
AFTER I WENT TO ALL THE TROUBLE OF PACKING...
GREAT, NOW I'VE GOT TO UNPACK. WHATTA DRAG.
WHAT A PAIN...
YOU'RE NOT FOOLING US, PAULA!!
PLIP PLIP
LET'S TOSS HER IN THE AIR, GUYS!
CONGRATULATIONS, MCCOY!!
AUGH!!
LEAVE ME ALONE!!

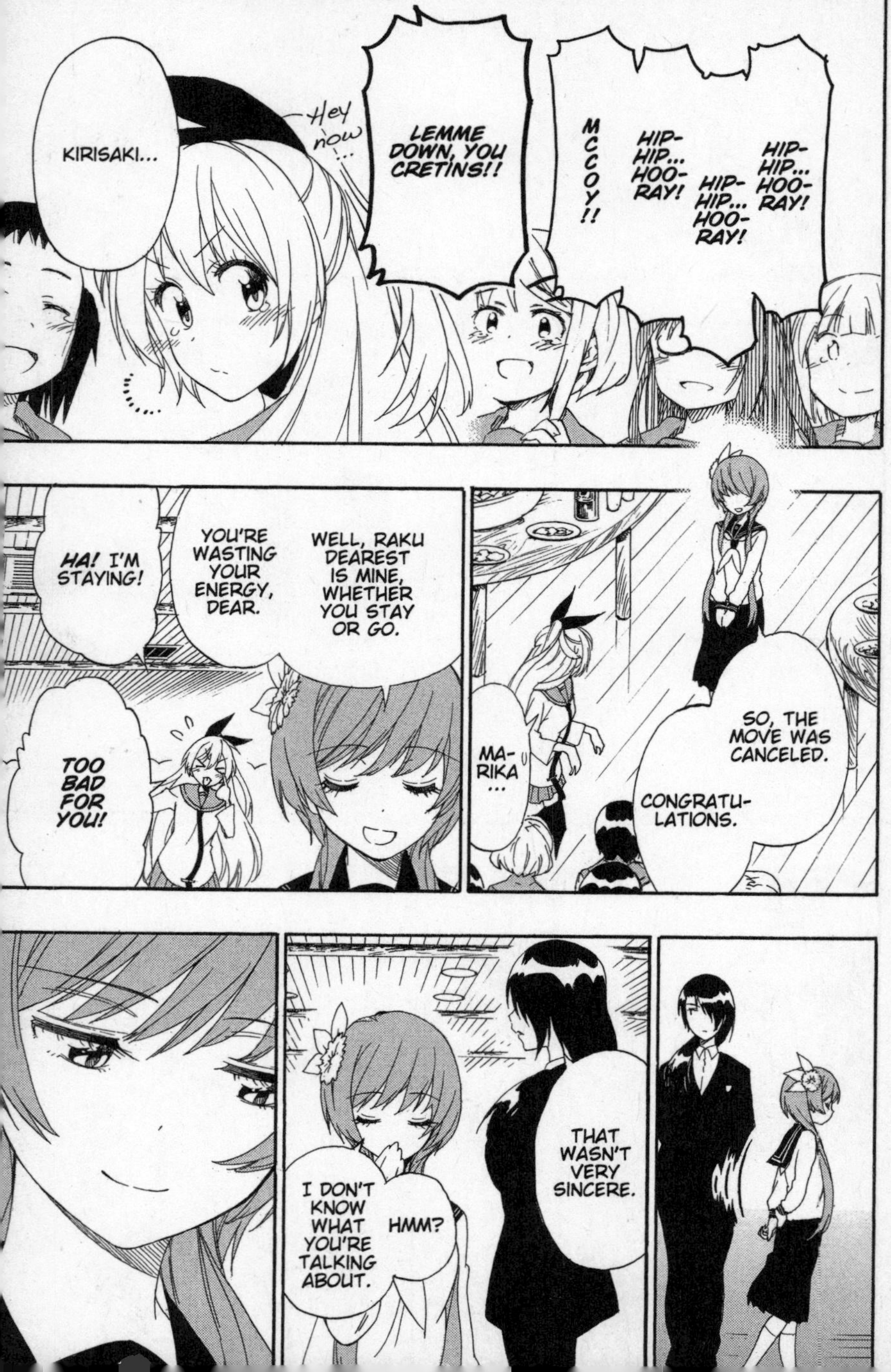
HIP-HIP... HOO-RAY!
HIP-HIP... HOO-RAY!
HIP-HIP... HOO-RAY!
MCCOY!!
LEMME DOWN, YOU CRETINS!!
Hey now...
KIRISAKI...
SO, THE MOVE WAS CANCELED.
CONGRATU-LATIONS.
MA-RIKA...
WELL, RAKU DEAREST IS MINE, WHETHER YOU STAY OR GO.
YOU'RE WASTING YOUR ENERGY, DEAR.
HA! I'M STAYING!
TOO BAD FOR YOU!
THAT WASN'T VERY SINCERE.
HMM?
I DON'T KNOW WHAT YOU'RE TALKING ABOUT.

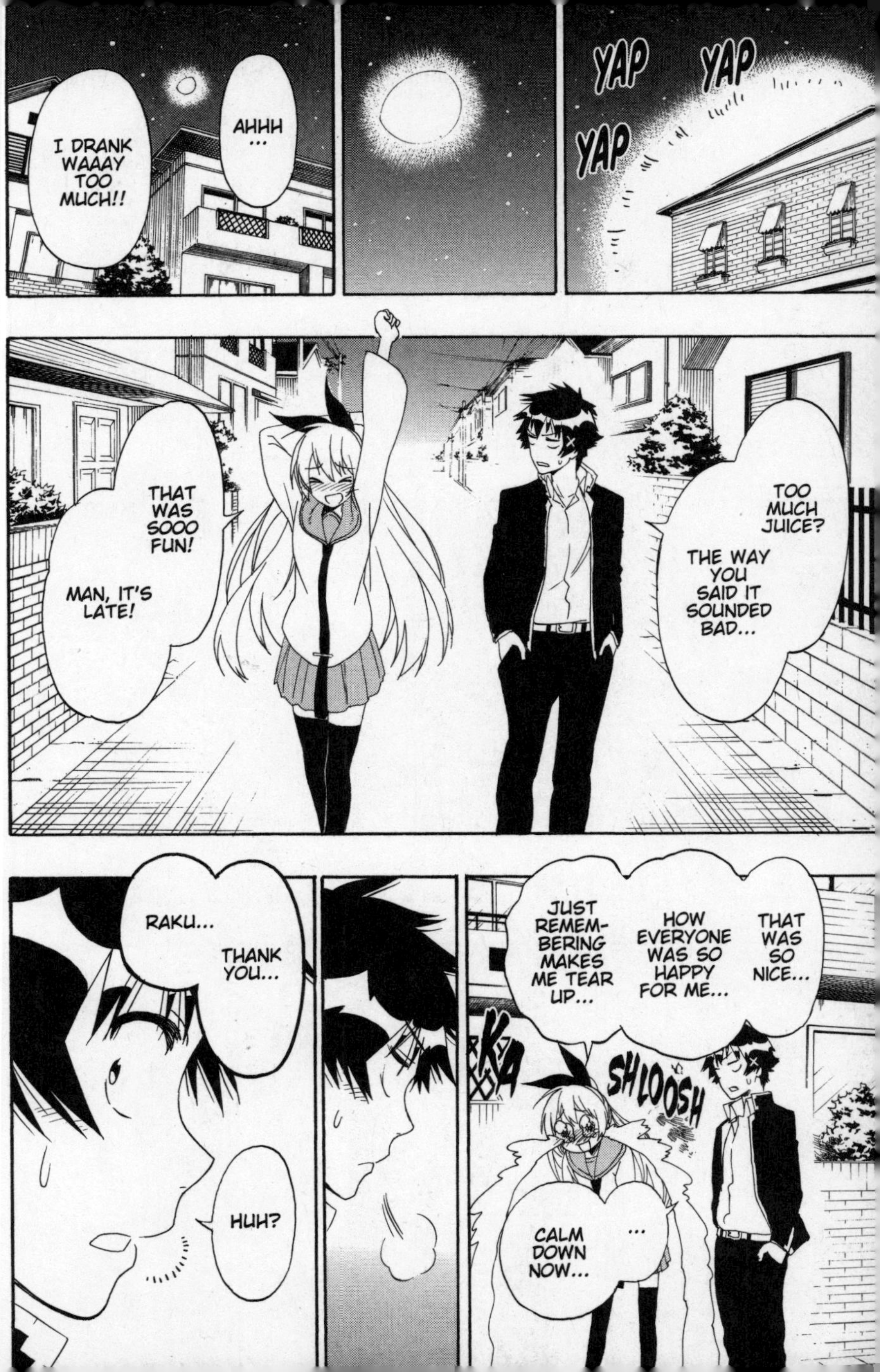
YAP YAP
YAP
AHHH...
I DRANK WAAAY TOO MUCH!!
THAT WAS SOOO FUN!
MAN, IT'S LATE!
TOO MUCH JUICE?
THE WAY YOU SAID IT SOUNDED BAD...
THAT WAS SO NICE...
HOW EVERYONE WAS SO HAPPY FOR ME...
JUST REMEMBERING MAKES ME TEAR UP...
KA
SHLOOSH
...
CALM DOWN NOW...
RAKU...
THANK YOU...
HUH?

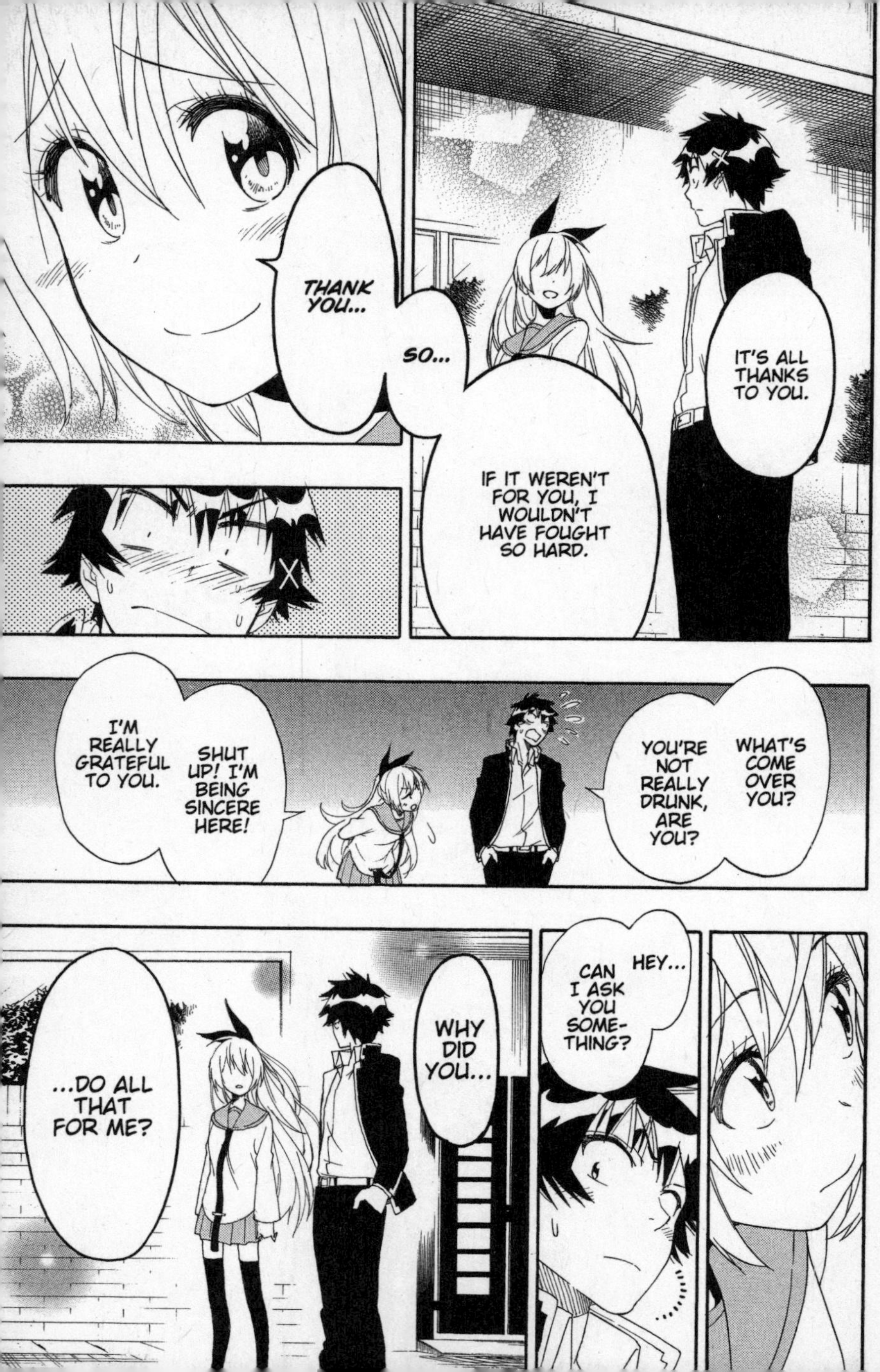
IT'S ALL THANKS TO YOU.
IF IT WEREN'T FOR YOU, I WOULDN'T HAVE FOUGHT SO HARD.
SO...
THANK YOU...
WHAT'S COME OVER YOU?
YOU'RE NOT REALLY DRUNK, ARE YOU?
SHUT UP! I'M BEING SINCERE HERE!
I'M REALLY GRATEFUL TO YOU.
HEY...
CAN I ASK YOU SOME-THING?
WHY DID YOU...
...DO ALL THAT FOR ME?

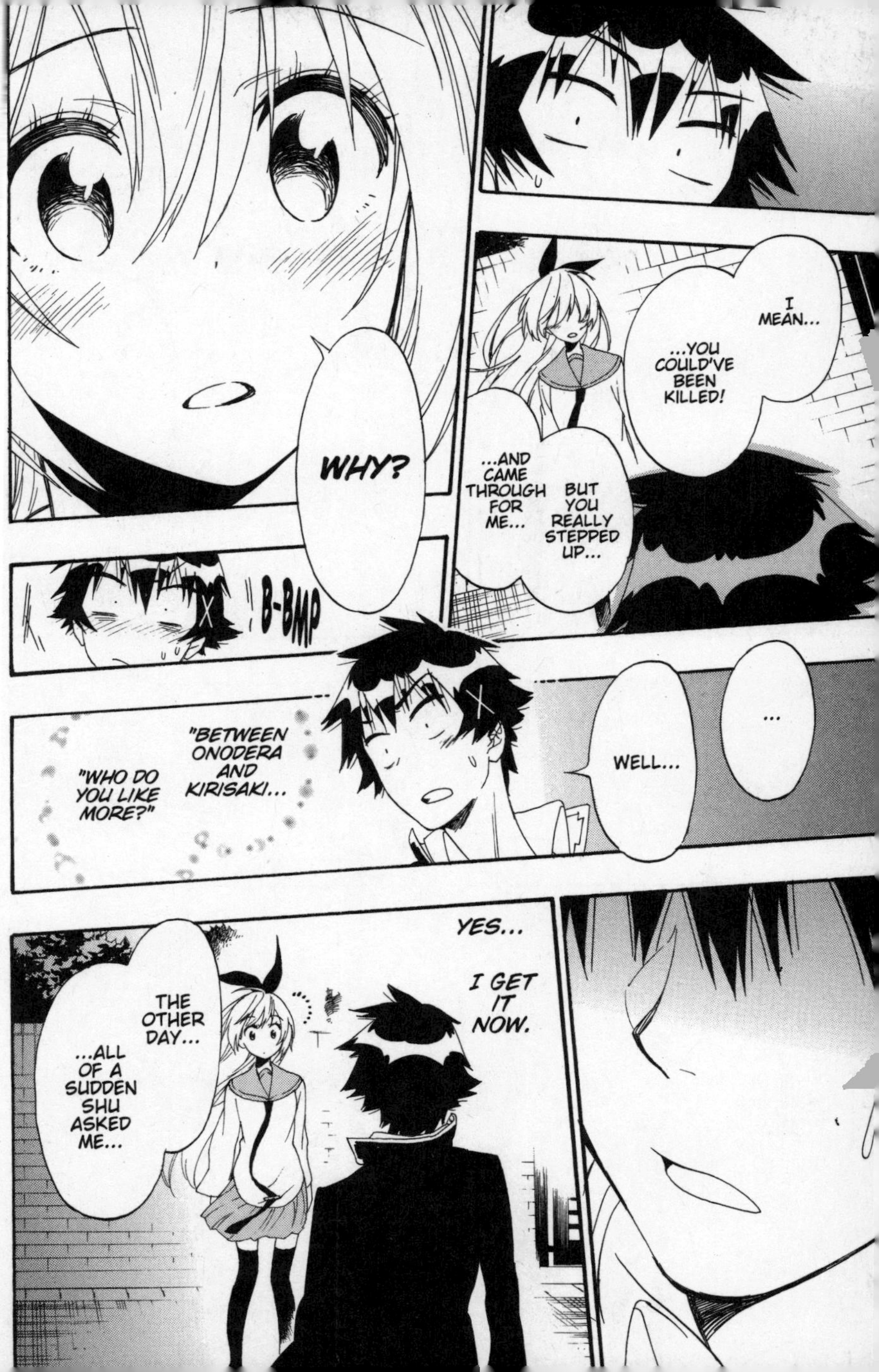
I MEAN...
...YOU COULD'VE BEEN KILLED!
BUT YOU REALLY STEPPED UP...
...AND CAME THROUGH FOR ME...
WHY?
B-BMP
...
WELL...
"BETWEEN ONODERA AND KIRISAKI...
"WHO DO YOU LIKE MORE?"
YES...
I GET IT NOW.
THE OTHER DAY...
...ALL OF A SUDDEN SHU ASKED ME...

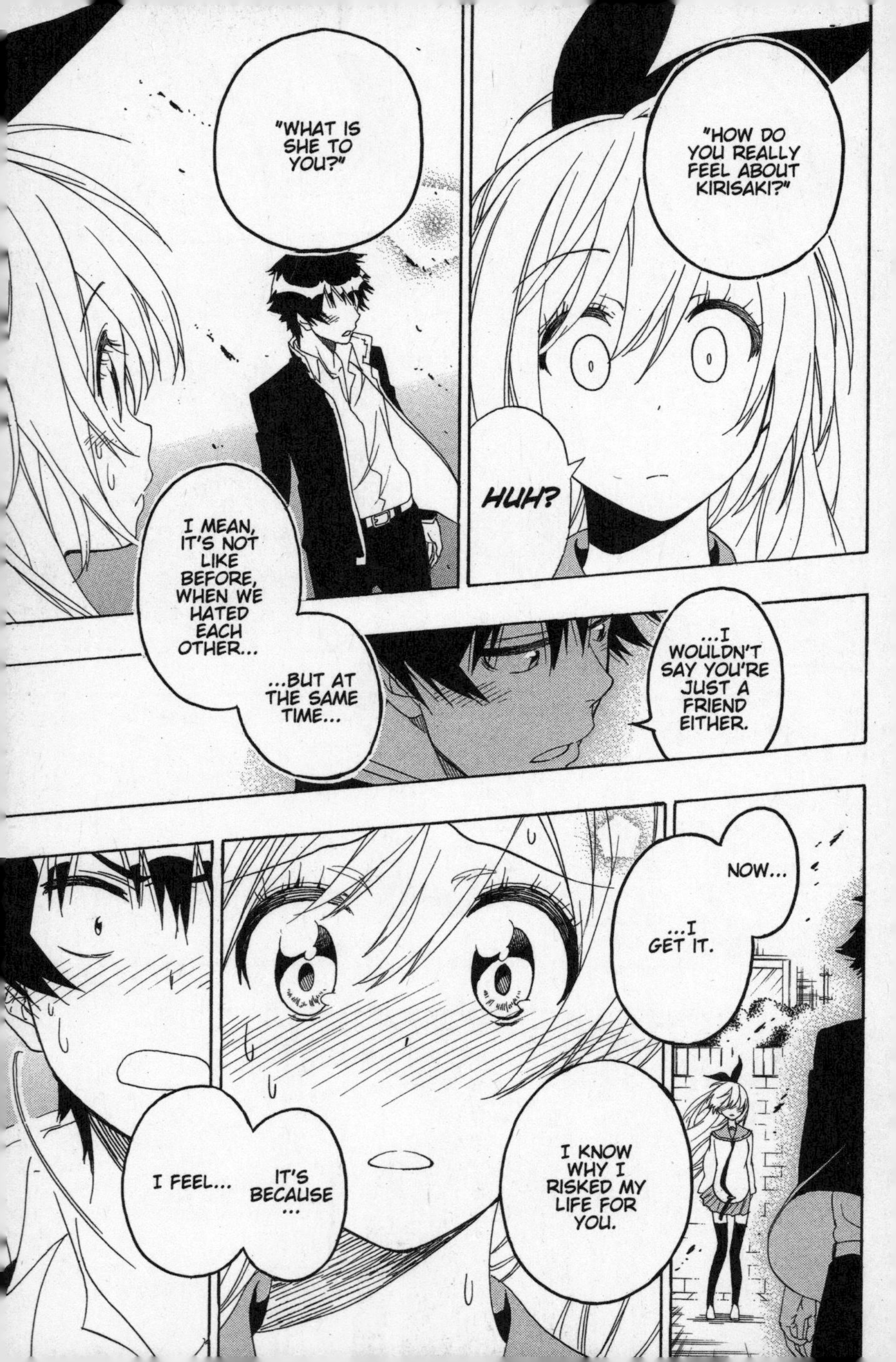
"HOW DO YOU REALLY FEEL ABOUT KIRISAKI?"
HUH?
"WHAT IS SHE TO YOU?"
I MEAN, IT'S NOT LIKE BEFORE, WHEN WE HATED EACH OTHER...
...BUT AT THE SAME TIME...
...I WOULDN'T SAY YOU'RE JUST A FRIEND EITHER.
NOW... ...I GET IT.
I KNOW WHY I RISKED MY LIFE FOR YOU.
IT'S BECAUSE... I FEEL...

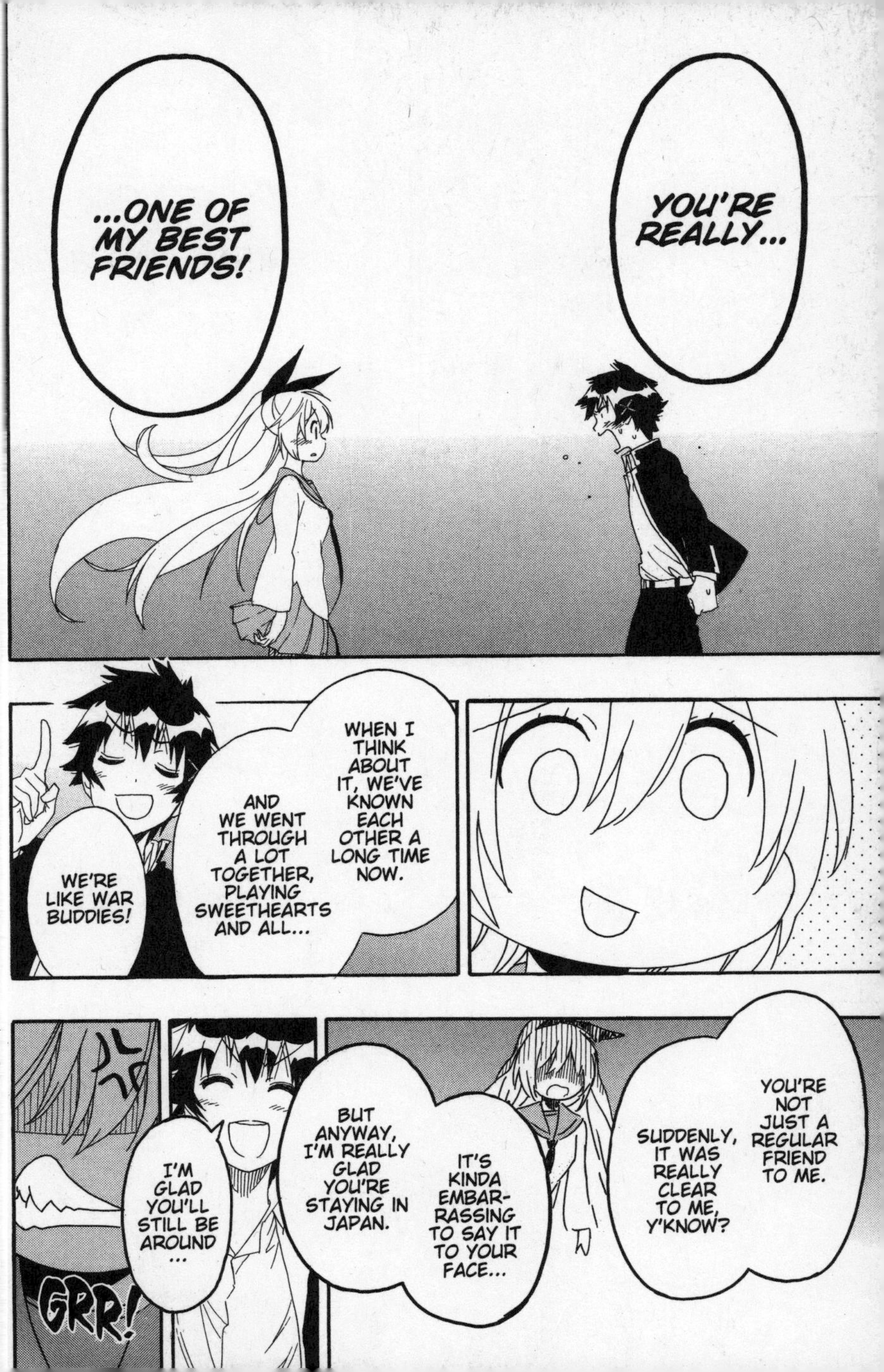
YOU'RE REALLY...
...ONE OF MY BEST FRIENDS!
WHEN I THINK ABOUT IT, WE'VE KNOWN EACH OTHER A LONG TIME NOW.
AND WE WENT THROUGH A LOT TOGETHER, PLAYING SWEETHEARTS AND ALL...
WE'RE LIKE WAR BUDDIES!
YOU'RE NOT JUST A REGULAR FRIEND TO ME.
SUDDENLY, IT WAS REALLY CLEAR TO ME, Y'KNOW?
IT'S KINDA EMBARRASSING TO SAY IT TO YOUR FACE...
BUT ANYWAY, I'M REALLY GLAD YOU'RE STAYING IN JAPAN.
I'M GLAD YOU'LL STILL BE AROUND...
GRR!

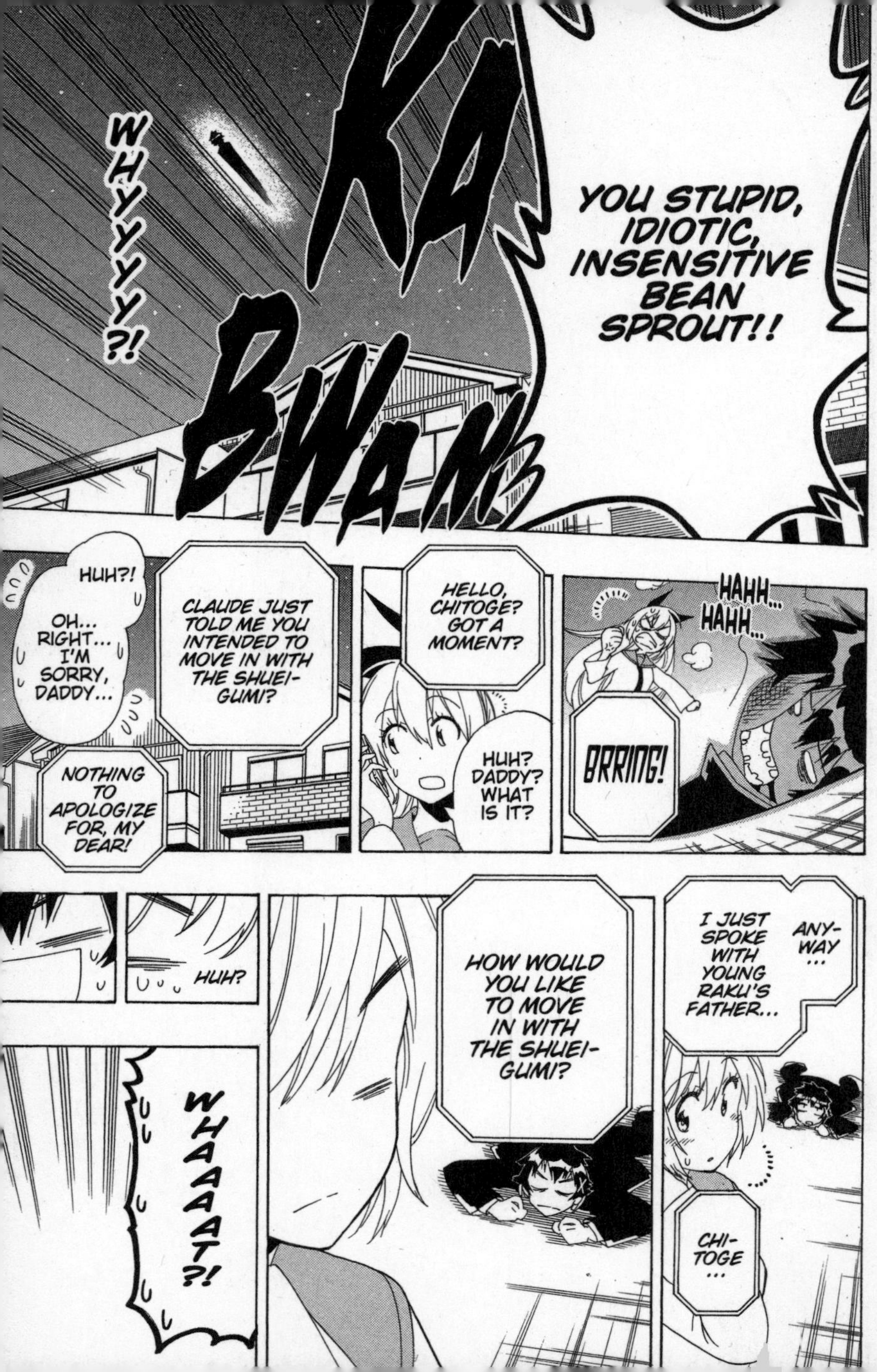
YOU STUPID, IDIOTIC, INSENSITIVE BEAN SPROUT!!
KA BWAM
WHYYYYY?!
HAHH... HAHH...
BRRING!
HELLO, CHITOGE? GOT A MOMENT?
HUH? DADDY? WHAT IS IT?
CLAUDE JUST TOLD ME YOU INTENDED TO MOVE IN WITH THE SHUEI-GUMI?
HUH?!
OH... RIGHT... I'M SORRY, DADDY...
NOTHING TO APOLOGIZE FOR, MY DEAR!
ANYWAY...
I JUST SPOKE WITH YOUNG RAKU'S FATHER...
CHITOGE...
HOW WOULD YOU LIKE TO MOVE IN WITH THE SHUEI-GUMI?
HUH?
WHAAAAT?!

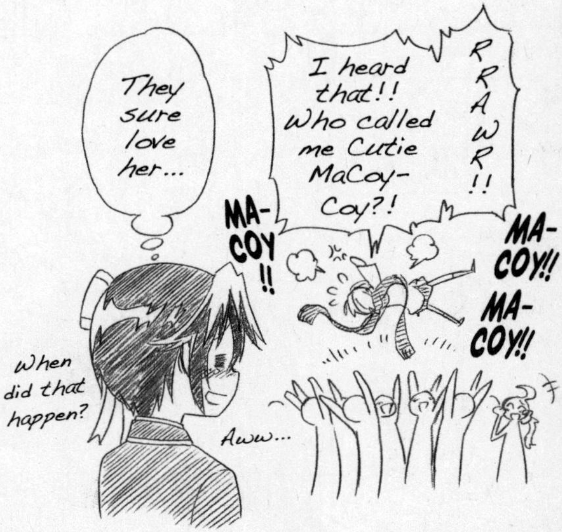
RRAWR!!
I heard that!! Who called me Cutie MaCoy-Coy?!
They sure love her...
MA-COY!!
MA-COY!!
MA-COY!!
Aww...
When did that happen?

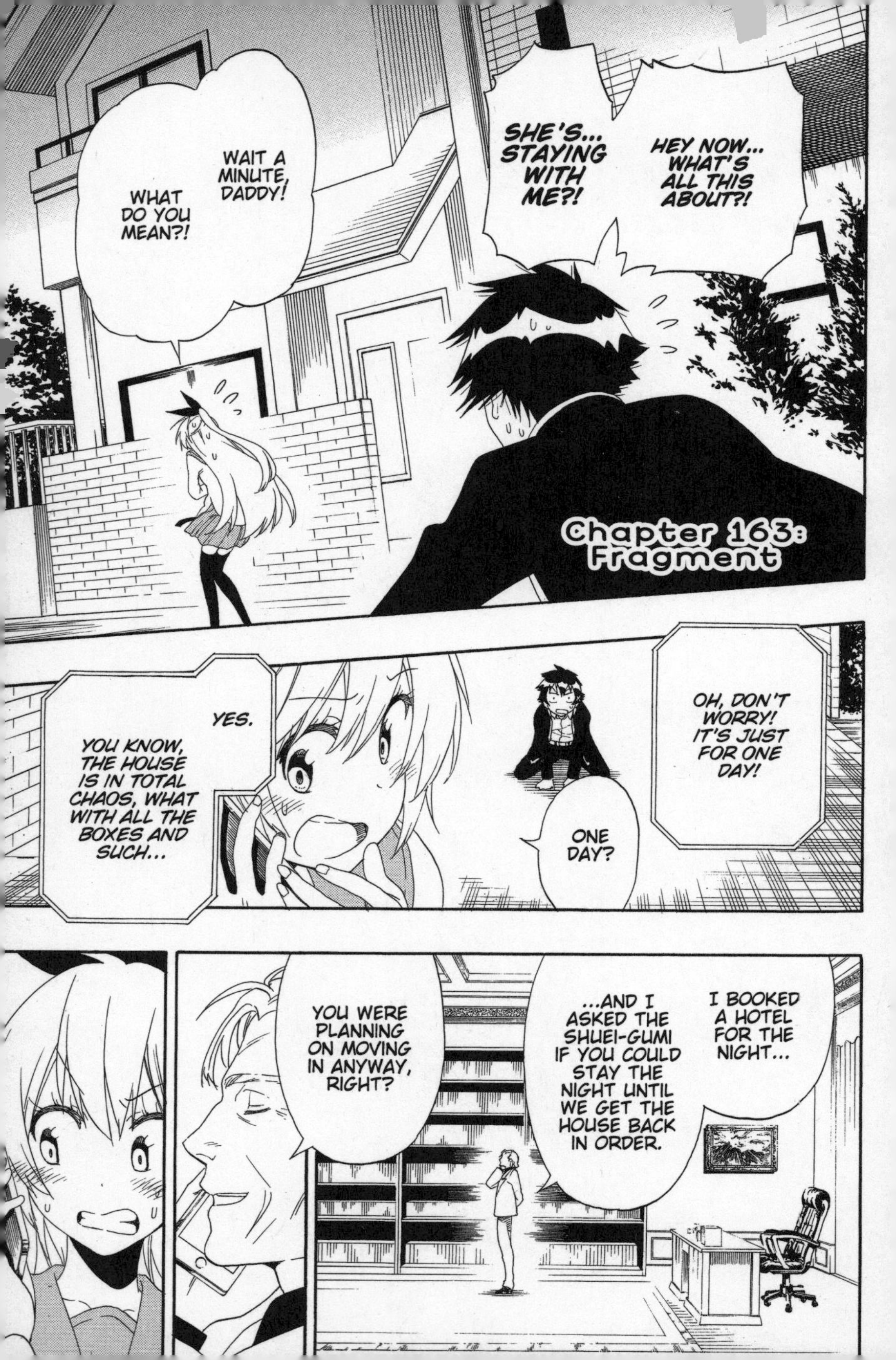
HEY NOW... WHAT'S ALL THIS ABOUT?!
SHE'S... STAYING WITH ME?!
WAIT A MINUTE, DADDY!
WHAT DO YOU MEAN?!
Chapter 163: Fragment
OH, DON'T WORRY! IT'S JUST FOR ONE DAY!
ONE DAY?
YES.
YOU KNOW, THE HOUSE IS IN TOTAL CHAOS, WHAT WITH ALL THE BOXES AND SUCH...
I BOOKED A HOTEL FOR THE NIGHT...
...AND I ASKED THE SHUEI-GUMI IF YOU COULD STAY THE NIGHT UNTIL WE GET THE HOUSE BACK IN ORDER.
YOU WERE PLANNING ON MOVING IN ANYWAY, RIGHT?

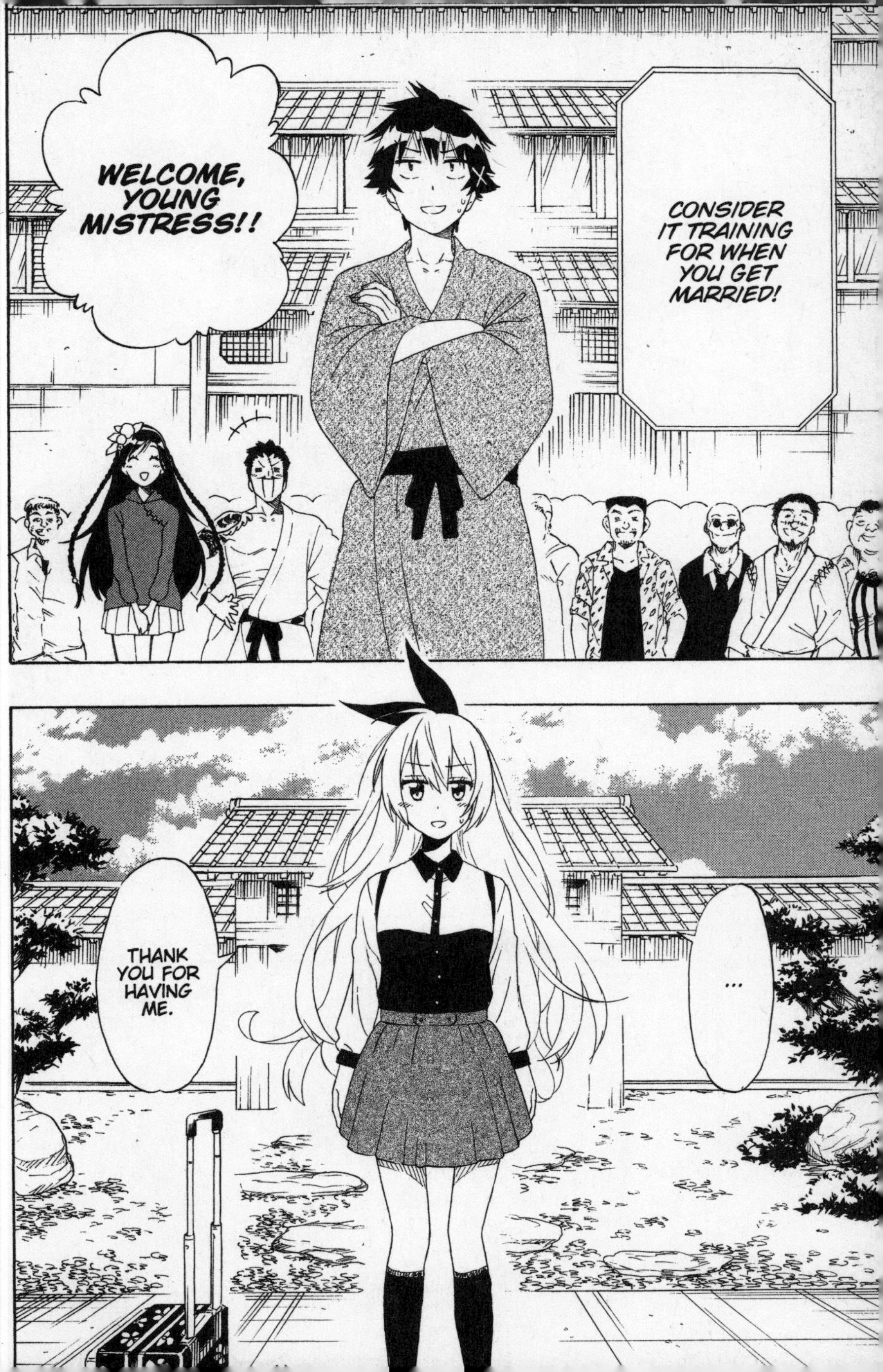
CONSIDER IT TRAINING FOR WHEN YOU GET MARRIED!
WELCOME, YOUNG MISTRESS!!
...
THANK YOU FOR HAVING ME.

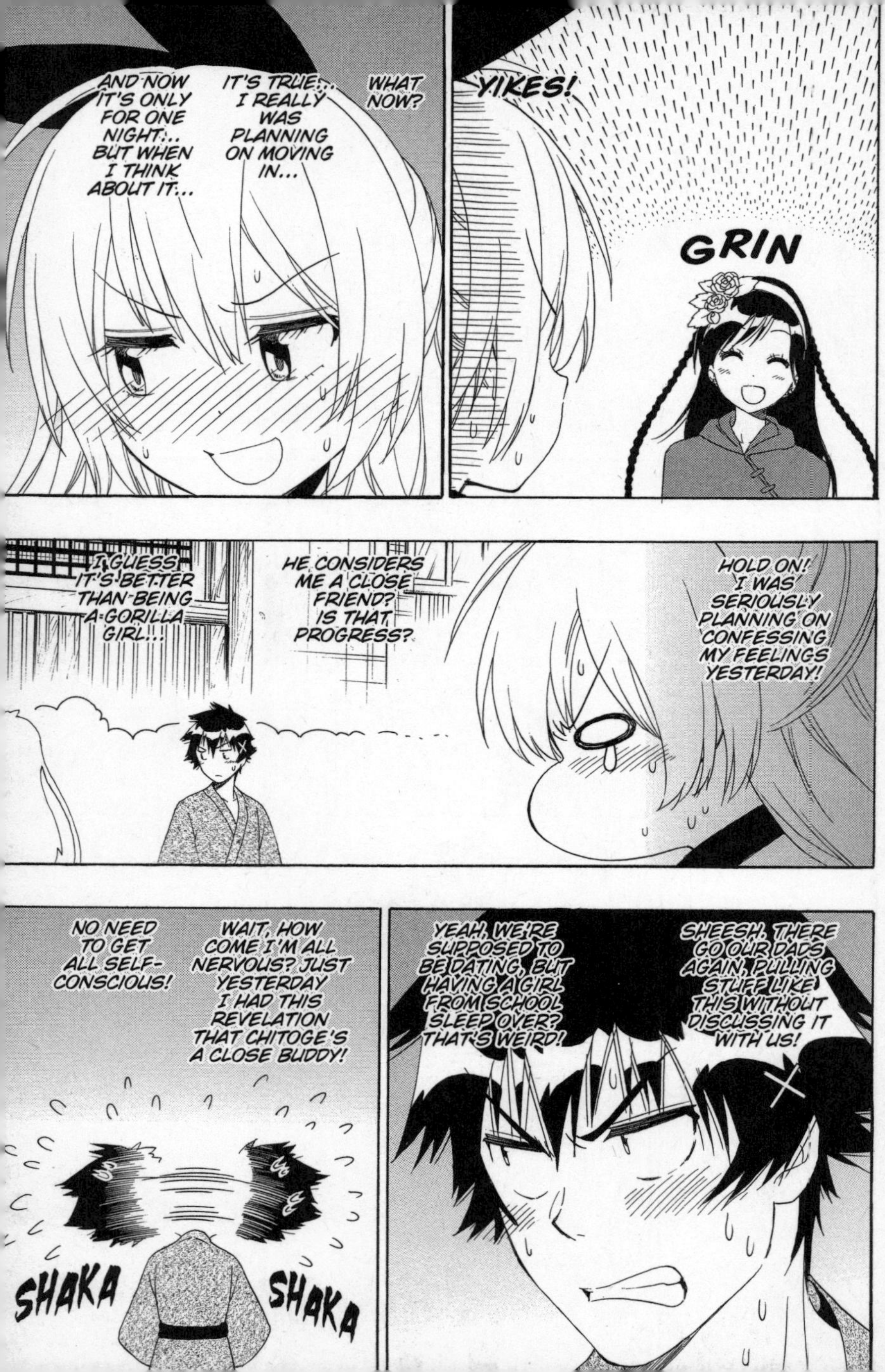
YIKES!
GRIN
WHAT NOW?
IT'S TRUE... I REALLY WAS PLANNING ON MOVING IN...
AND NOW IT'S ONLY FOR ONE NIGHT... BUT WHEN I THINK ABOUT IT...
HOLD ON! I WAS SERIOUSLY PLANNING ON CONFESSING MY FEELINGS YESTERDAY!
HE CONSIDERS ME A CLOSE FRIEND? IS THAT PROGRESS?
I GUESS IT'S BETTER THAN BEING A GORILLA GIRL...
SHEESH. THERE GO OUR DADS AGAIN, PULLING STUFF LIKE THIS WITHOUT DISCUSSING IT WITH US!
YEAH, WE'RE SUPPOSED TO BE DATING, BUT HAVING A GIRL FROM SCHOOL SLEEP OVER? THAT'S WEIRD!
WAIT, HOW COME I'M ALL NERVOUS? JUST YESTERDAY I HAD THIS REVELATION THAT CHITOGE'S A CLOSE BUDDY!
NO NEED TO GET ALL SELF-CONSCIOUS!
SHAKA
SHAKA

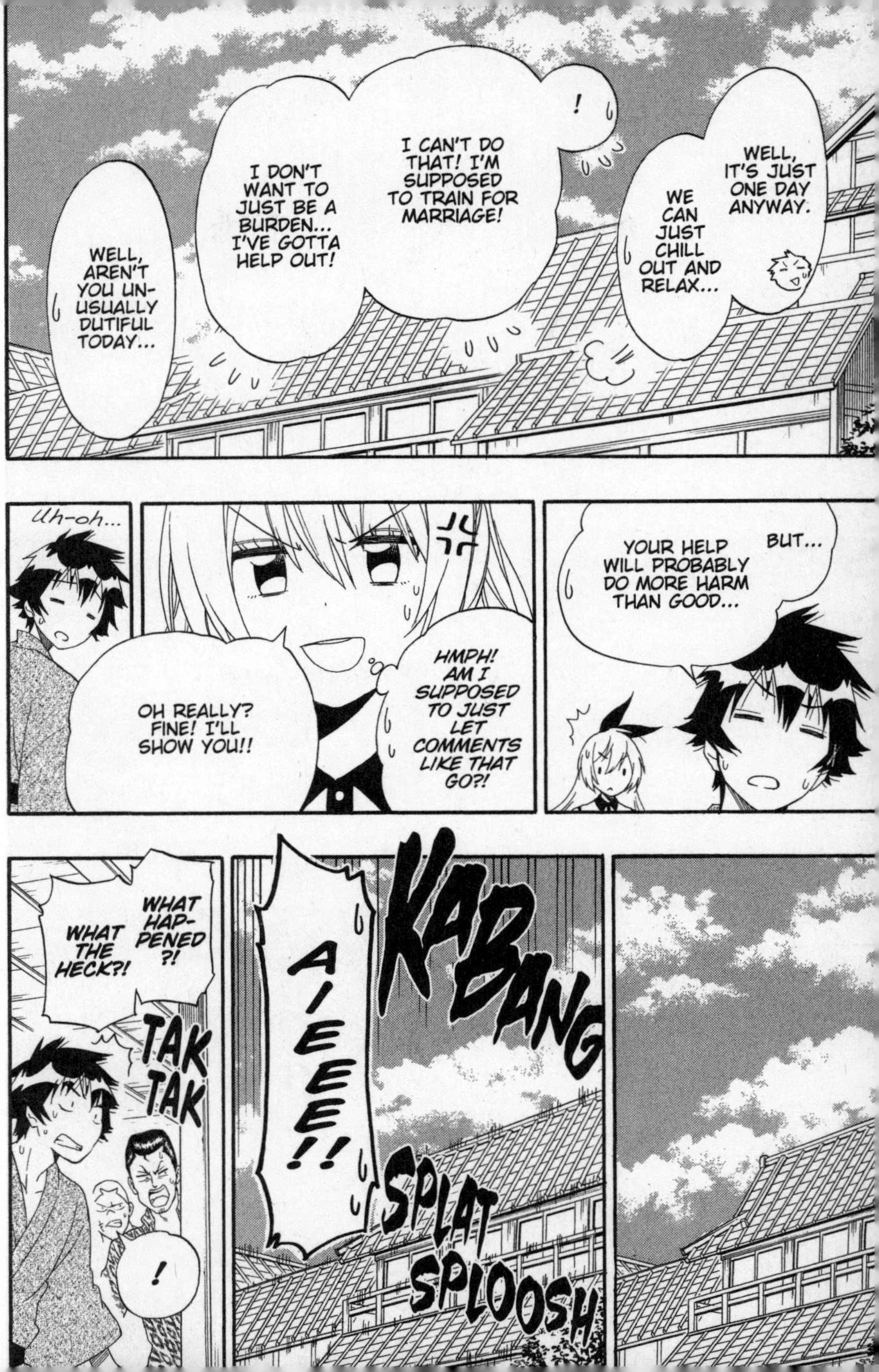
WELL, IT'S JUST ONE DAY ANYWAY.
WE CAN JUST CHILL OUT AND RELAX...
!
I CAN'T DO THAT! I'M SUPPOSED TO TRAIN FOR MARRIAGE!
I DON'T WANT TO JUST BE A BURDEN... I'VE GOTTA HELP OUT!
WELL, AREN'T YOU UN-USUALLY DUTIFUL TODAY...
BUT...
YOUR HELP WILL PROBABLY DO MORE HARM THAN GOOD...
HMPH! AM I SUPPOSED TO JUST LET COMMENTS LIKE THAT GO?!
OH REALLY? FINE! I'LL SHOW YOU!!
Uh-oh...
KABANG
AIEEEE!!
SPLAT
SPLOOSH
WHAT HAP-PENED?!
WHAT THE HECK?!
TAK TAK
!

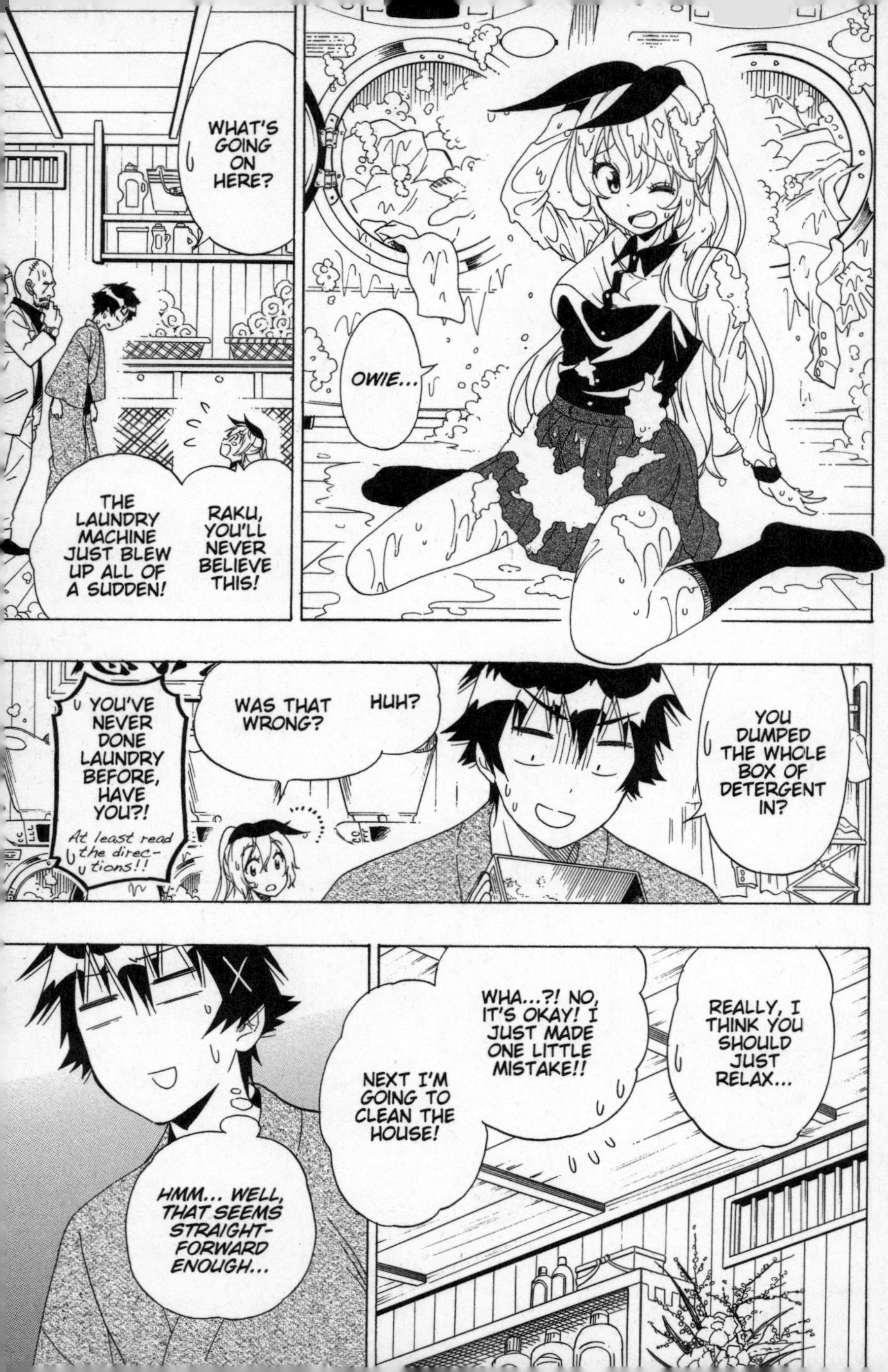
OWIE...
WHAT'S GOING ON HERE?
RAKU, YOU'LL NEVER BELIEVE THIS!
THE LAUNDRY MACHINE JUST BLEW UP ALL OF A SUDDEN!
YOU DUMPED THE WHOLE BOX OF DETERGENT IN?
HUH?
WAS THAT WRONG?
YOU'VE NEVER DONE LAUNDRY BEFORE, HAVE YOU?!
At least read the direc-tions!!
REALLY, I THINK YOU SHOULD JUST RELAX...
WHA...?! NO, IT'S OKAY! I JUST MADE ONE LITTLE MISTAKE!!
NEXT I'M GOING TO CLEAN THE HOUSE!
HMM... WELL, THAT SEEMS STRAIGHT-FORWARD ENOUGH...

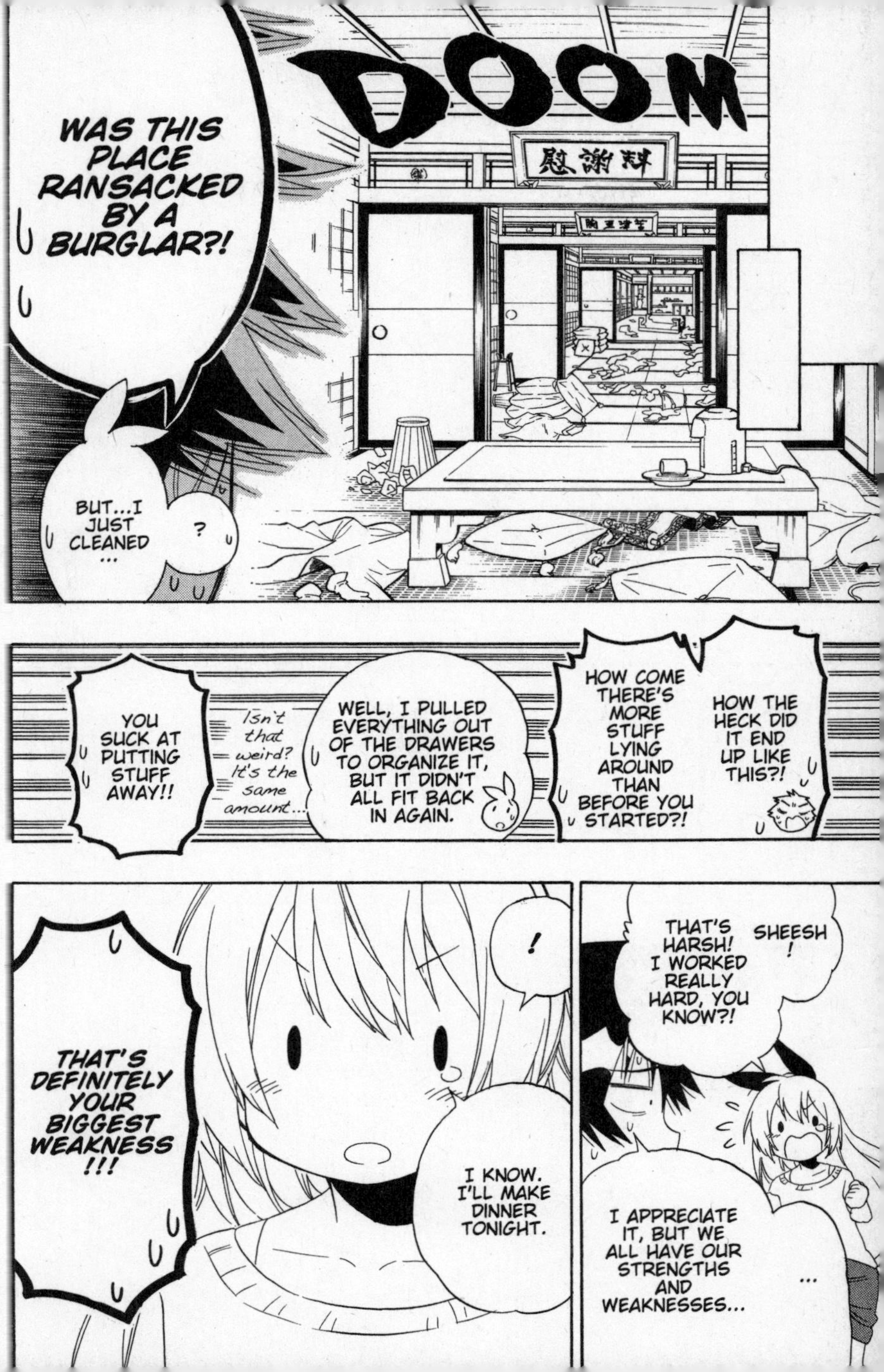

DOOM
WAS THIS PLACE RANSACKED BY A BURGLAR?!
?
BUT...I JUST CLEANED ...
HOW THE HECK DID IT END UP LIKE THIS?!
HOW COME THERE'S MORE STUFF LYING AROUND THAN BEFORE YOU STARTED?!
WELL, I PULLED EVERYTHING OUT OF THE DRAWERS TO ORGANIZE IT, BUT IT DIDN'T ALL FIT BACK IN AGAIN.
Isn't that weird? It's the same amount...
YOU SUCK AT PUTTING STUFF AWAY!!
SHEESH!
THAT'S HARSH! I WORKED REALLY HARD, YOU KNOW?!
...
I APPRECIATE IT, BUT WE ALL HAVE OUR STRENGTHS AND WEAKNESSES...
THAT'S DEFINITELY YOUR BIGGEST WEAKNESS!!!
!
I KNOW. I'LL MAKE DINNER TONIGHT.

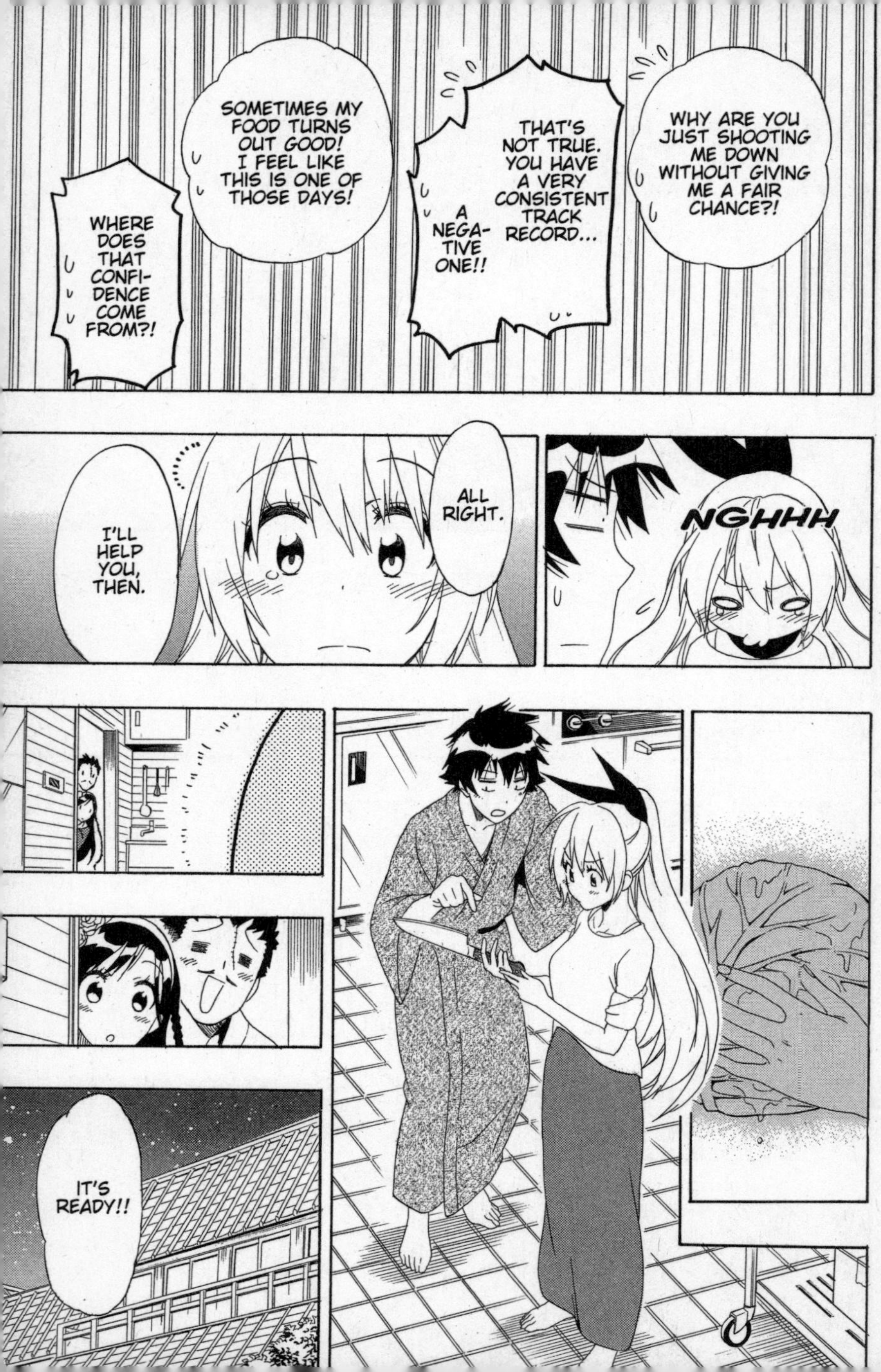
WHY ARE YOU JUST SHOOTING ME DOWN WITHOUT GIVING ME A FAIR CHANCE?!
THAT'S NOT TRUE. YOU HAVE A VERY CONSISTENT TRACK RECORD...
A NEGATIVE ONE!!
SOMETIMES MY FOOD TURNS OUT GOOD! I FEEL LIKE THIS IS ONE OF THOSE DAYS!
WHERE DOES THAT CONFIDENCE COME FROM?!
NGHHH
ALL RIGHT.
I'LL HELP YOU, THEN.
IT'S READY!!

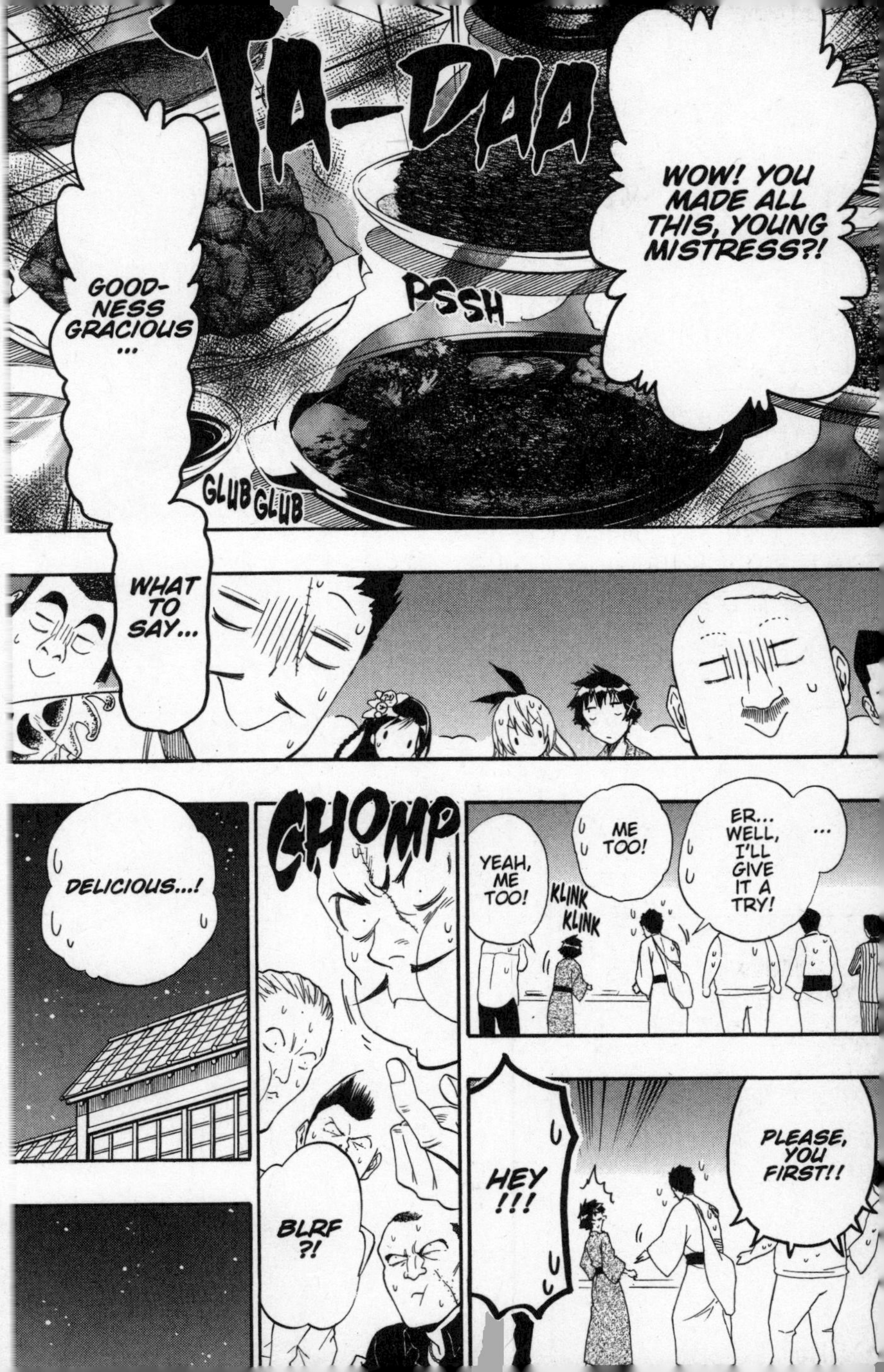
TA-DAA
WOW! YOU MADE ALL THIS, YOUNG MISTRESS?!
PSSH
GOODNESS GRACIOUS...
GLUB GLUB
WHAT TO SAY...
...
ER... WELL, I'LL GIVE IT A TRY!
ME TOO!
YEAH, ME TOO!
KLINK KLINK
PLEASE, YOU FIRST!!
HEY!!!
CHOMP
BLRF?!
DELICIOUS...!

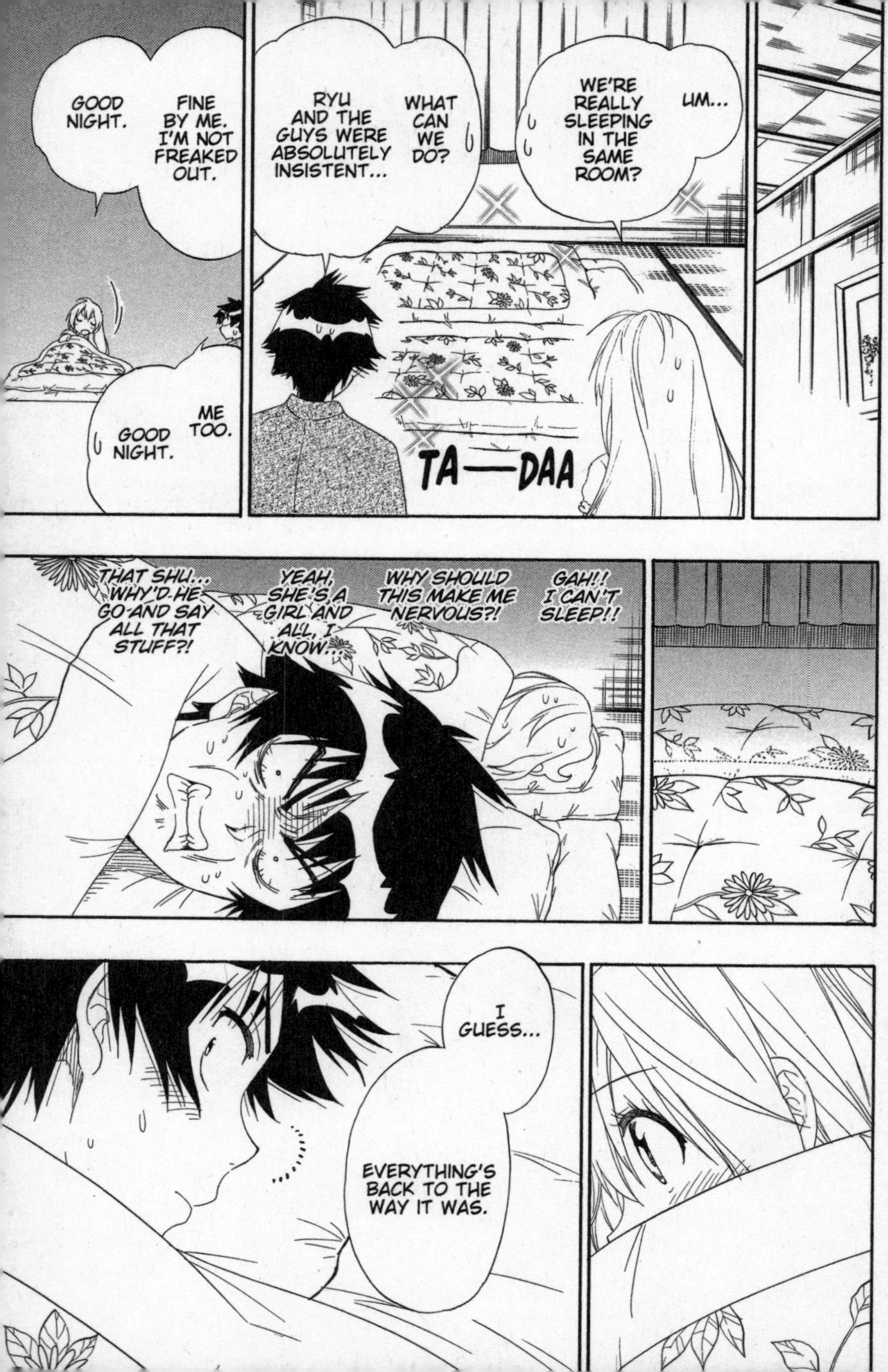
UM...
WE'RE REALLY SLEEPING IN THE SAME ROOM?
WHAT CAN WE DO?
RYU AND THE GUYS WERE ABSOLUTELY INSISTENT...
TA—DAA
FINE BY ME. I'M NOT FREAKED OUT.
GOOD NIGHT.
ME TOO.
GOOD NIGHT.
GAH!! I CAN'T SLEEP!!
WHY SHOULD THIS MAKE ME NERVOUS?!
YEAH, SHE'S A GIRL AND ALL, I KNOW...
THAT SHU... WHY'D HE GO AND SAY ALL THAT STUFF?!
I GUESS...
EVERYTHING'S BACK TO THE WAY IT WAS.
...

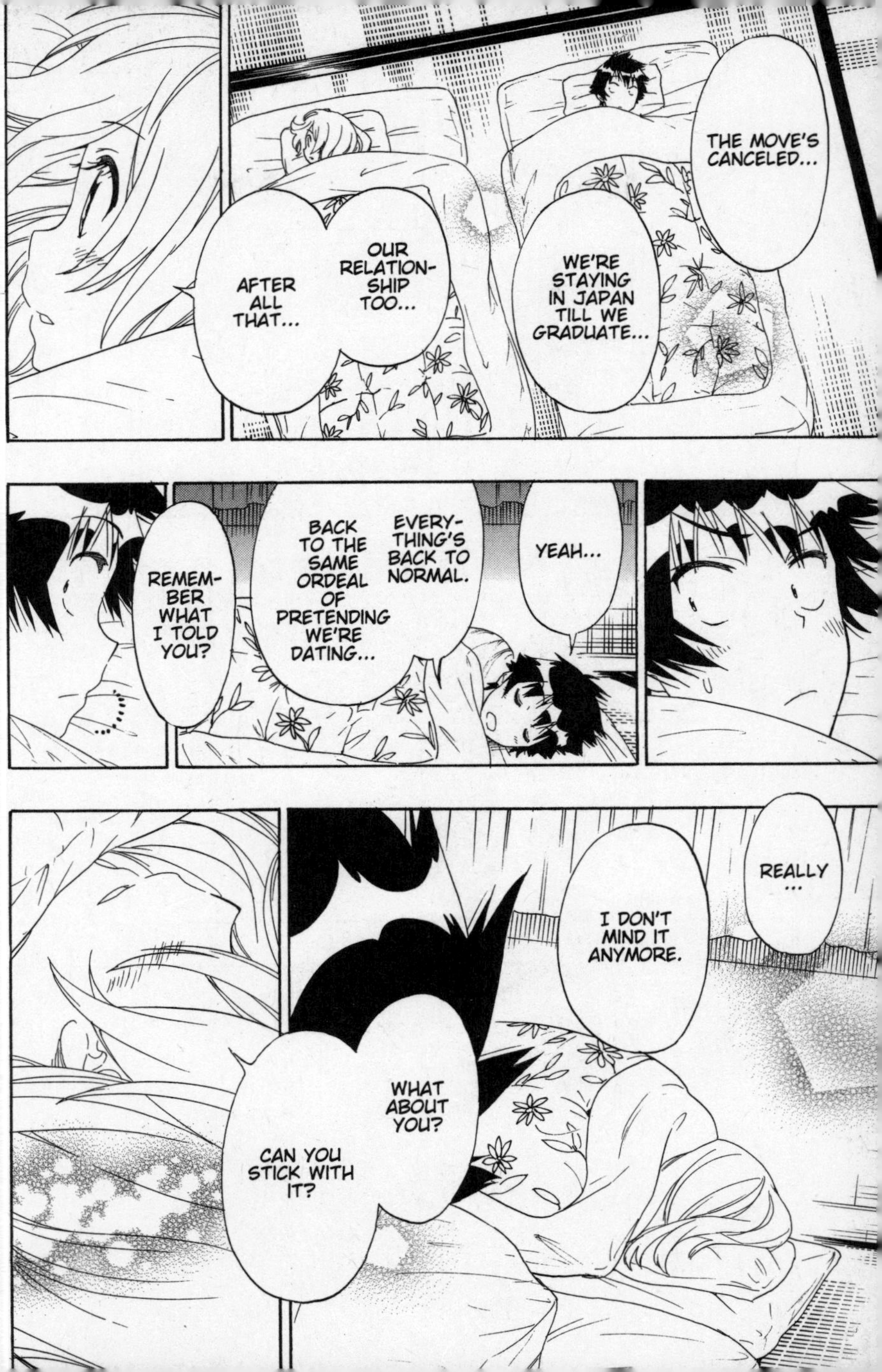
THE MOVE'S CANCELED...
WE'RE STAYING IN JAPAN TILL WE GRADUATE...
OUR RELATIONSHIP TOO...
AFTER ALL THAT...
YEAH...
EVERYTHING'S BACK TO NORMAL.
BACK TO THE SAME ORDEAL OF PRETENDING WE'RE DATING...
REMEMBER WHAT I TOLD YOU?
REALLY ...
I DON'T MIND IT ANYMORE.
WHAT ABOUT YOU?
CAN YOU STICK WITH IT?

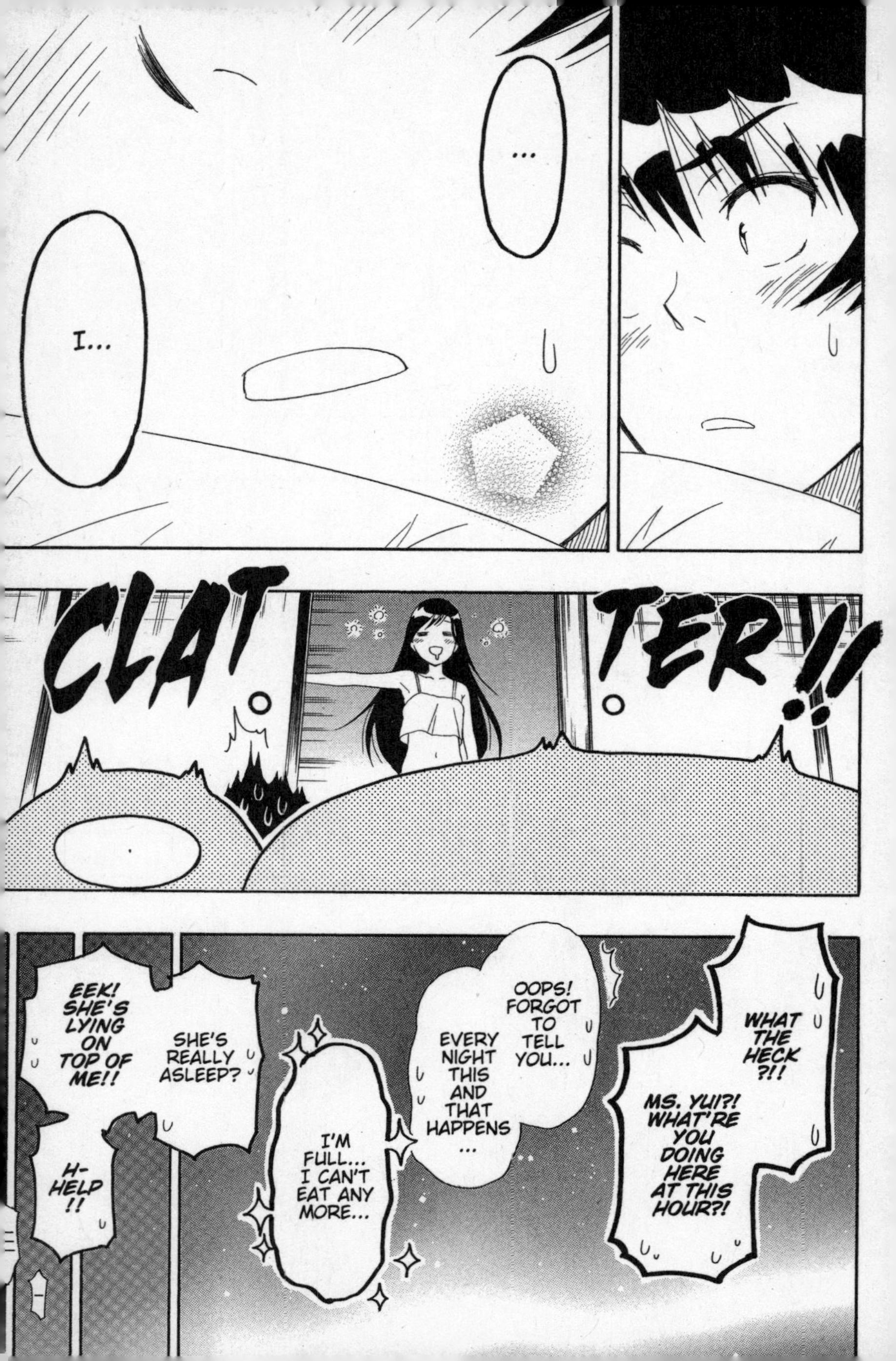
...
I...
CLATTER!!
WHAT THE HECK?!!
MS. YUI?! WHAT'RE YOU DOING HERE AT THIS HOUR?!
OOPS! FORGOT TO TELL YOU...
EVERY NIGHT THIS AND THAT HAPPENS...
I'M FULL... I CAN'T EAT ANY MORE...
SHE'S REALLY ASLEEP?
EEK! SHE'S LYING ON TOP OF ME!!
H-HELP!!

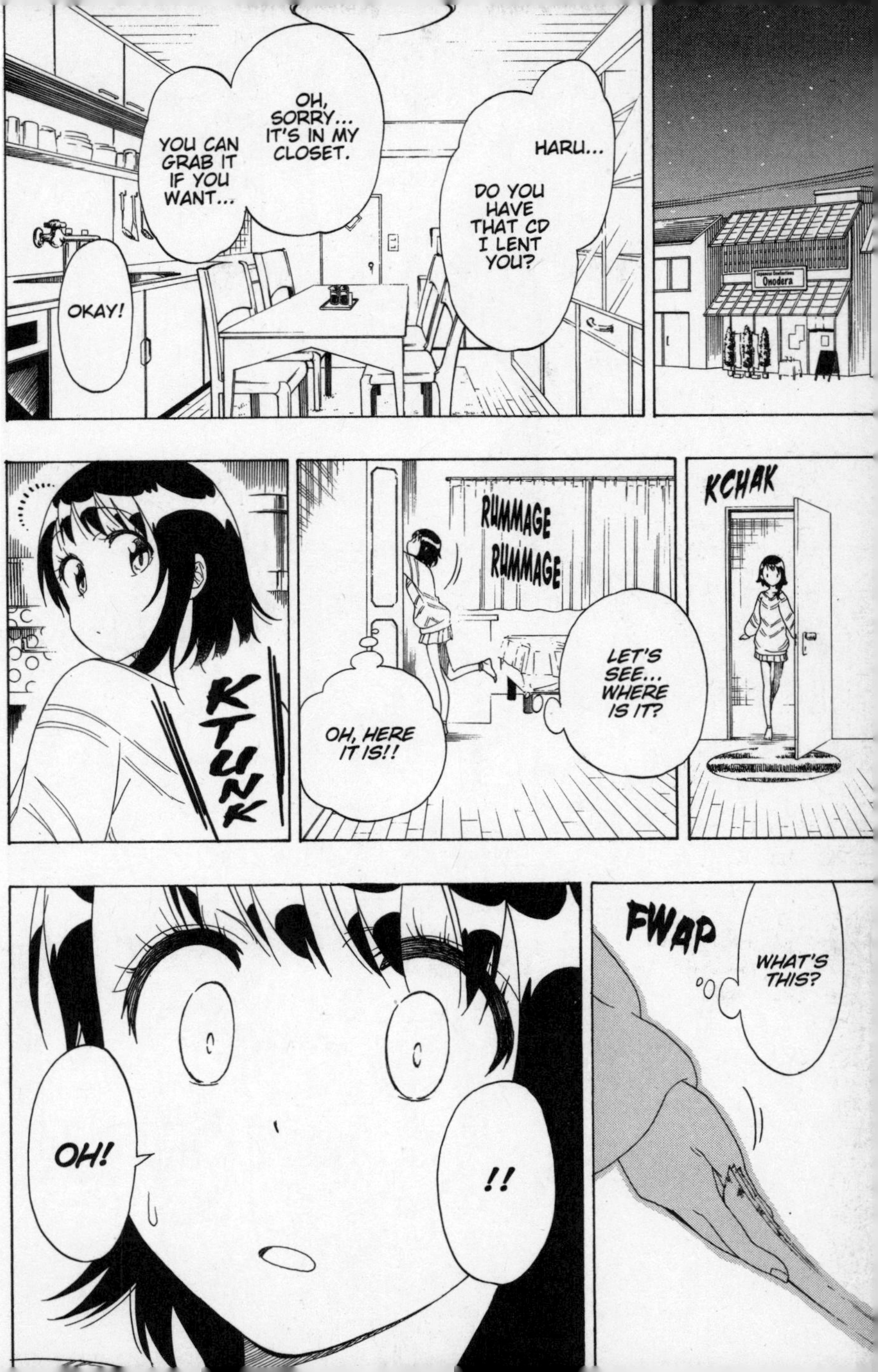
HARU...
DO YOU HAVE THAT CD I LENT YOU?
OH, SORRY... IT'S IN MY CLOSET.
YOU CAN GRAB IT IF YOU WANT...
OKAY!
KCHAK
RUMMAGE RUMMAGE
LET'S SEE... WHERE IS IT?
OH, HERE IT IS!!
KTUNK
FWAP
WHAT'S THIS?
!!
OH!

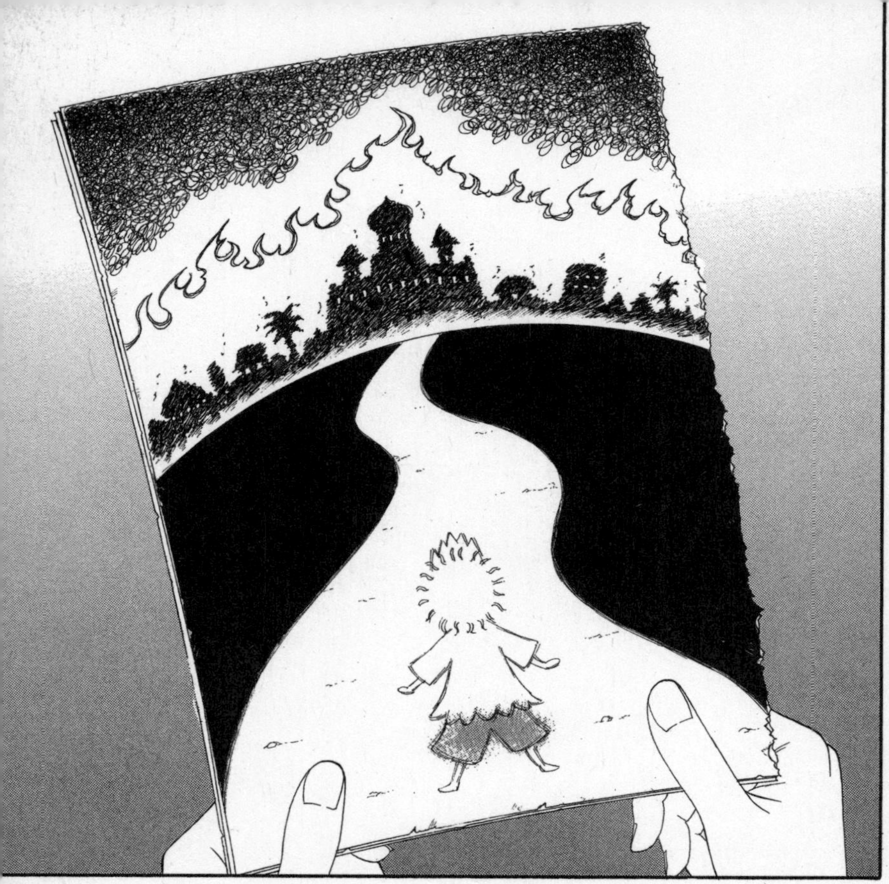

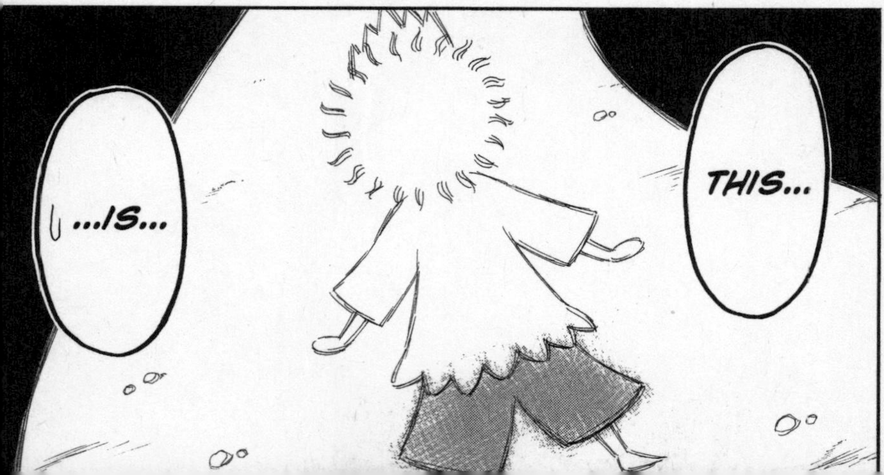
THIS...
...IS...

☆ Doing Laundry ☆

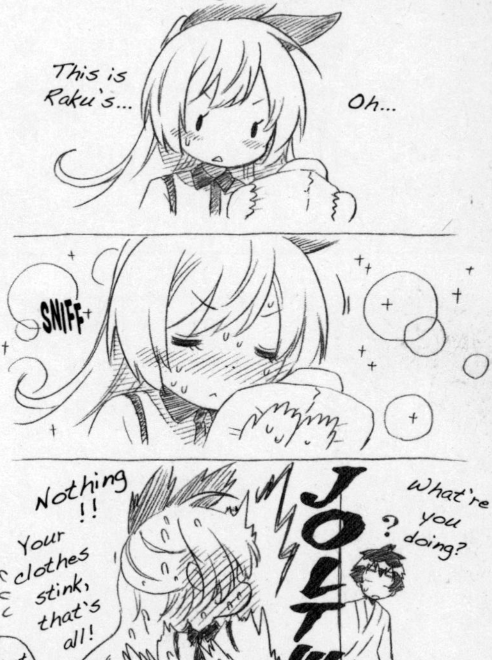

Oh...
This is Raku's...
SNIFF
What're you doing?
?
JOLT!!!
Nothing!!
Your clothes stink, that's all!
What?!

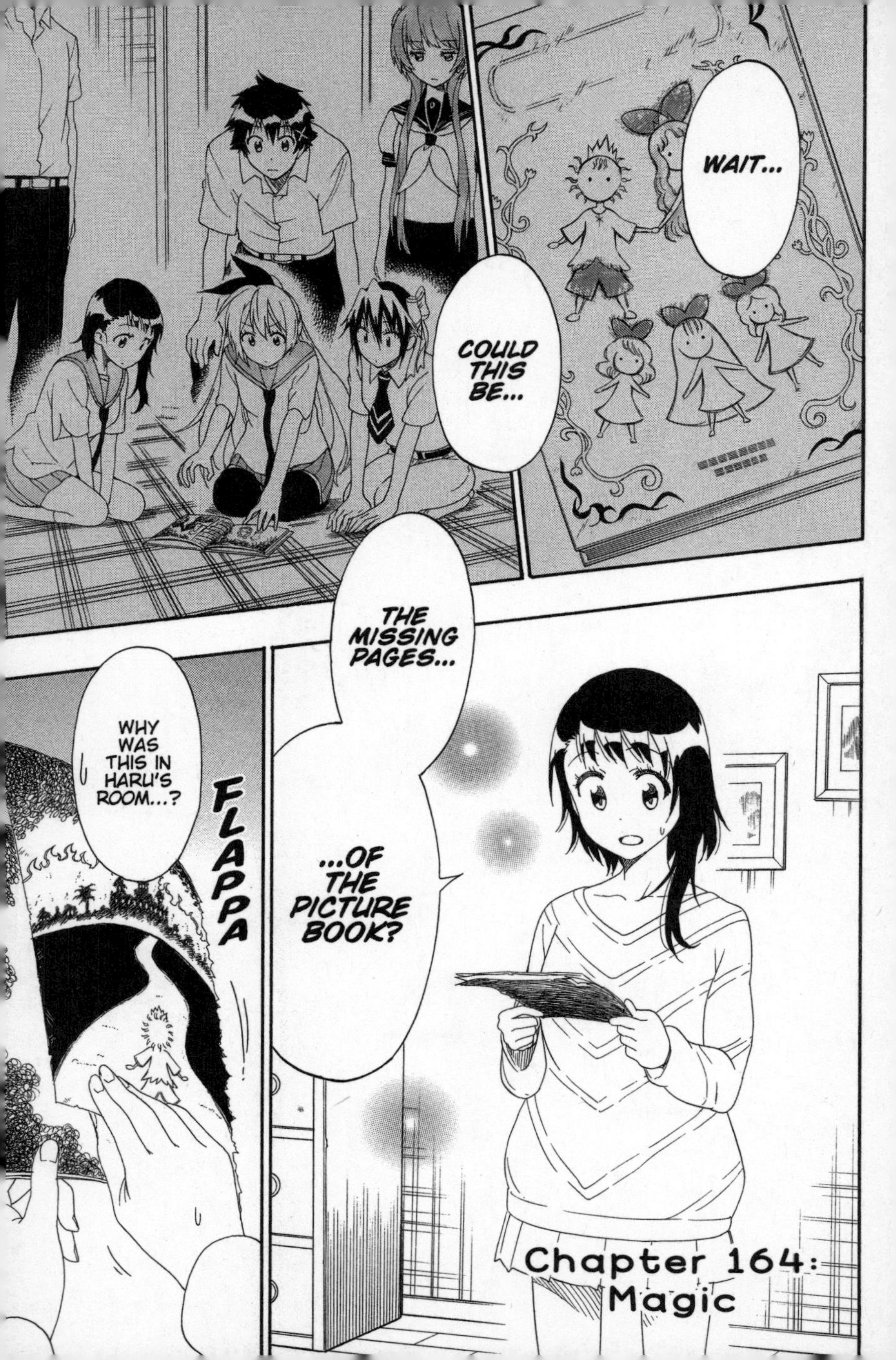
WAIT...
COULD THIS BE...
THE MISSING PAGES...
...OF THE PICTURE BOOK?
Chapter 164: Magic
WHY WAS THIS IN HARU'S ROOM...?
FLAPPA

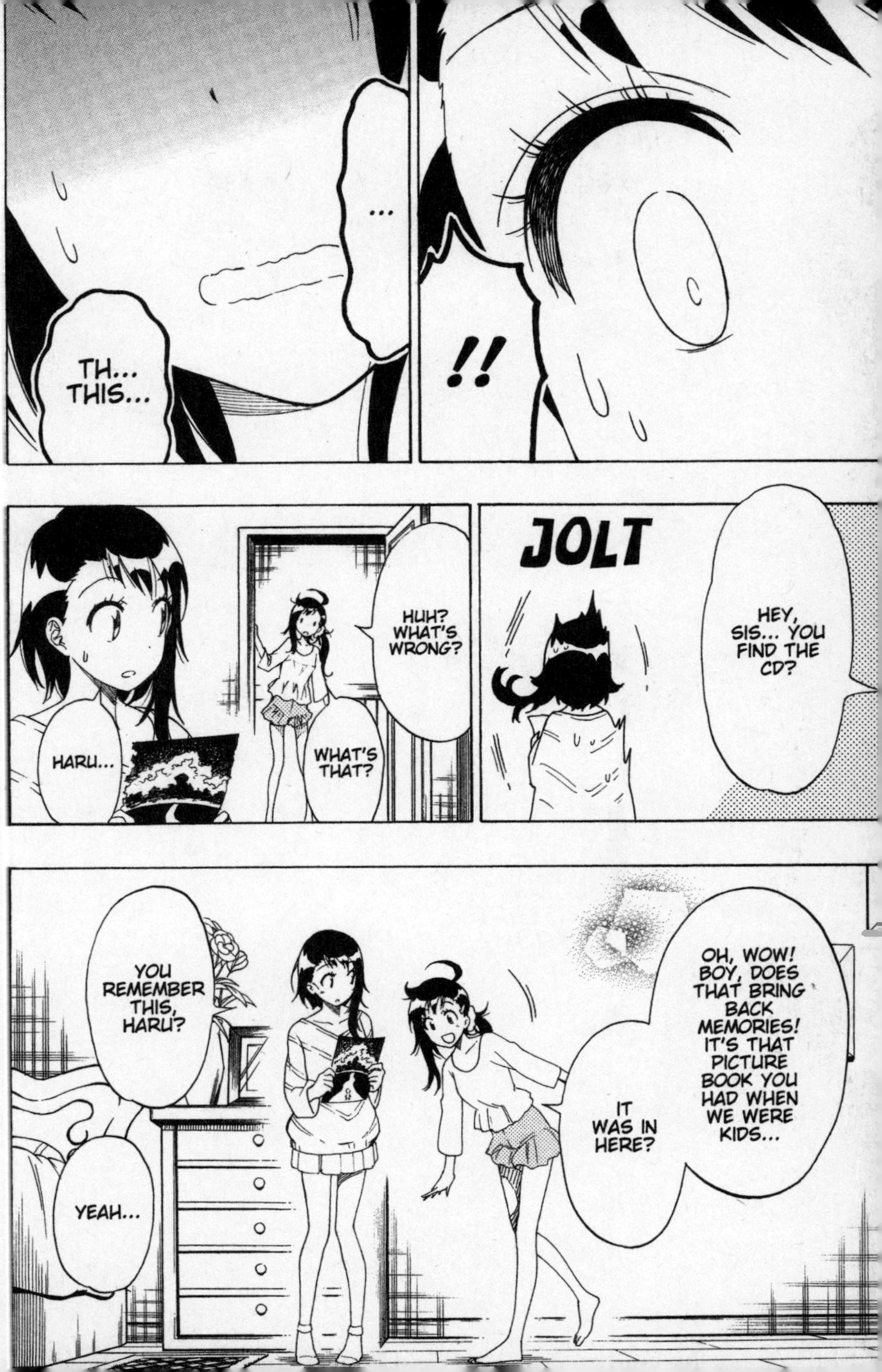
!!
...
TH... THIS...
HEY, SIS... YOU FIND THE CD?
JOLT
HUH? WHAT'S WRONG?
WHAT'S THAT?
HARU...
OH, WOW! BOY, DOES THAT BRING BACK MEMORIES! IT'S THAT PICTURE BOOK YOU HAD WHEN WE WERE KIDS...
IT WAS IN HERE?
YOU REMEMBER THIS, HARU?
YEAH...

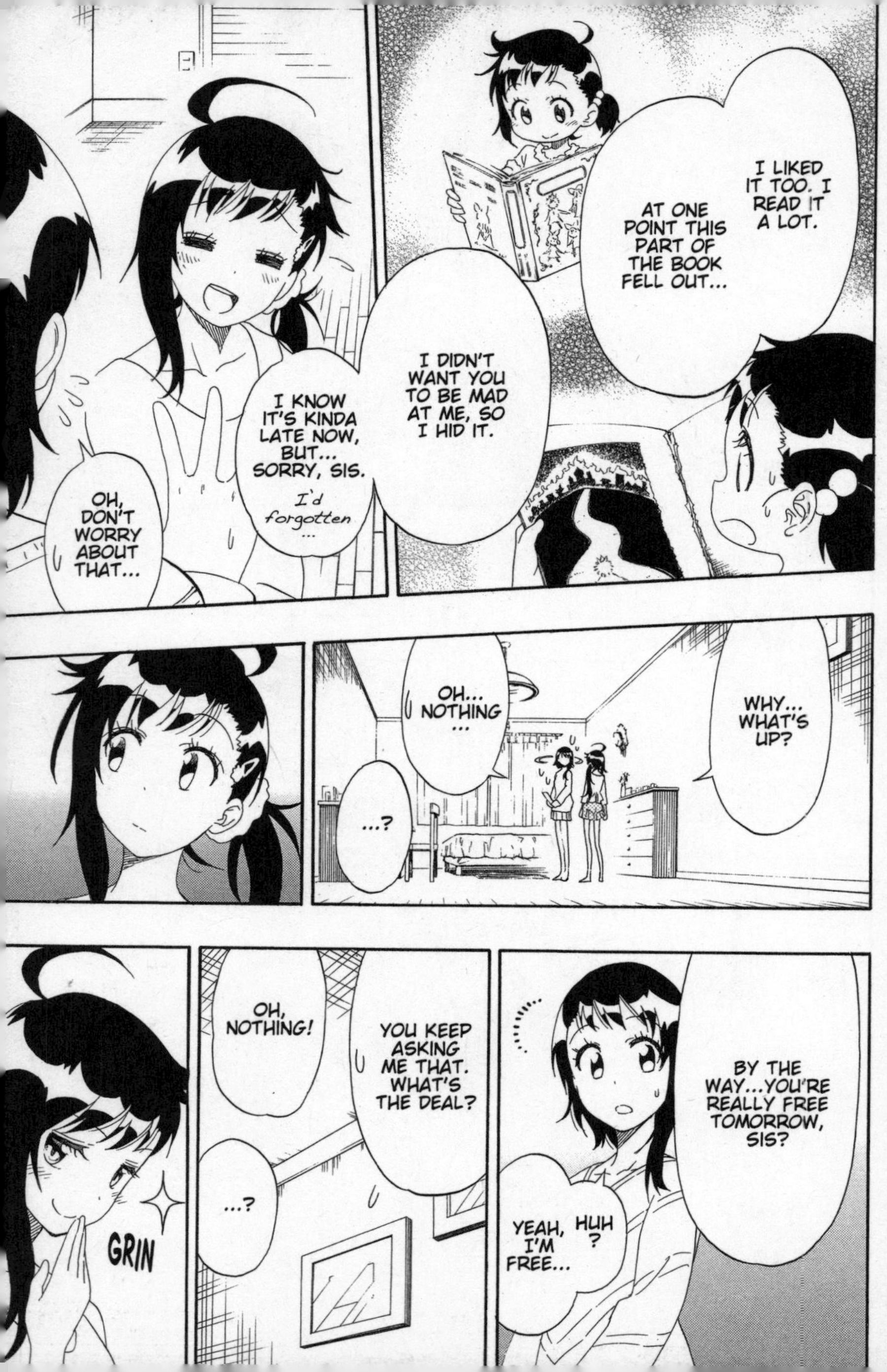
I LIKED IT TOO. I READ IT A LOT.
AT ONE POINT THIS PART OF THE BOOK FELL OUT...
I DIDN'T WANT YOU TO BE MAD AT ME, SO I HID IT.
I KNOW IT'S KINDA LATE NOW, BUT... SORRY, SIS.
I'd forgotten ...
OH, DON'T WORRY ABOUT THAT...
WHY... WHAT'S UP?
OH... NOTHING ...
...?
BY THE WAY...YOU'RE REALLY FREE TOMORROW, SIS?
HUH ?
YEAH, I'M FREE...
YOU KEEP ASKING ME THAT. WHAT'S THE DEAL?
OH, NOTHING!
...?
GRIN

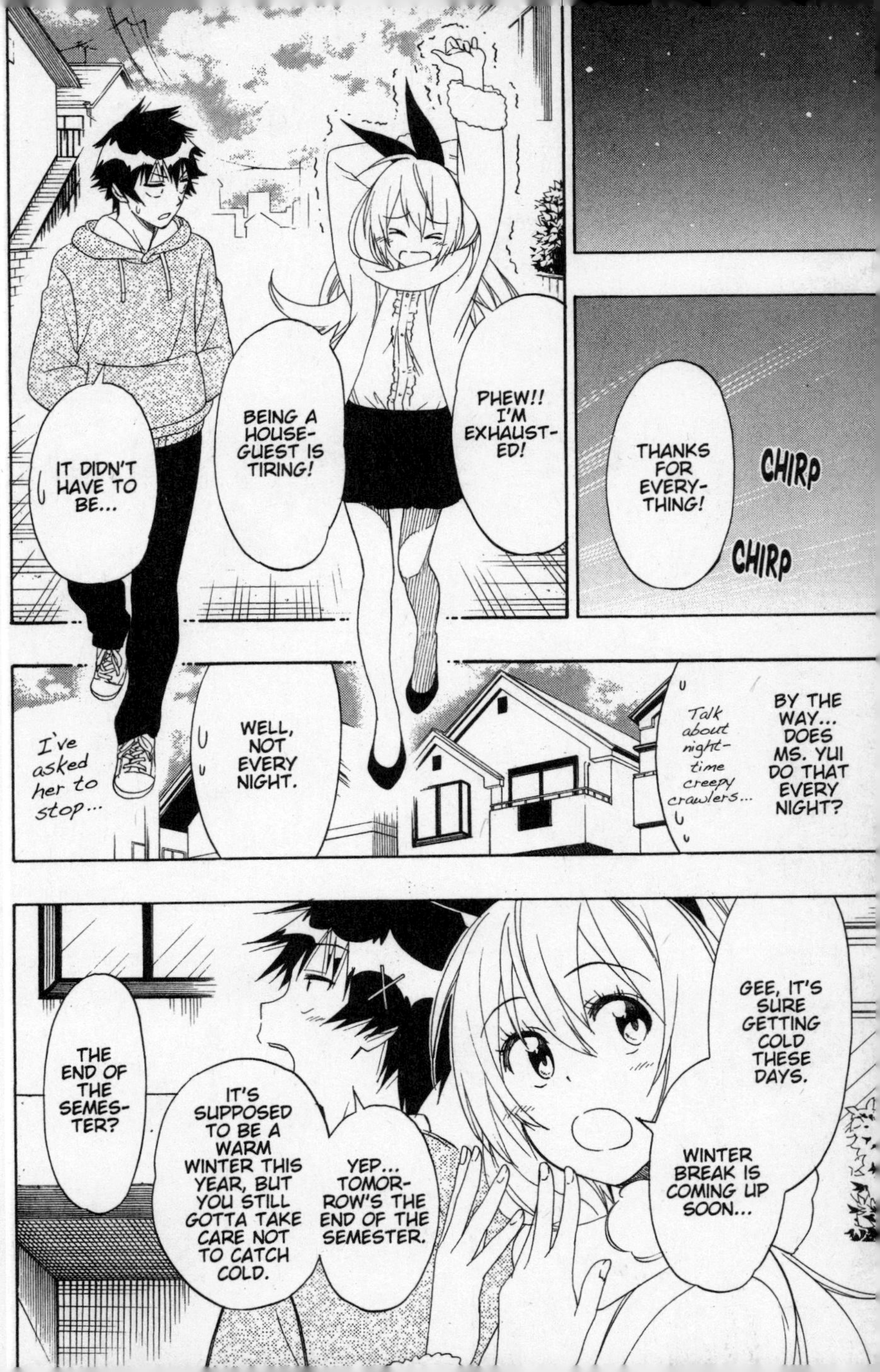
THANKS FOR EVERYTHING!
CHIRP
CHIRP
PHEW!! I'M EXHAUSTED!
BEING A HOUSE-GUEST IS TIRING!
IT DIDN'T HAVE TO BE...
BY THE WAY... DOES MS. YUI DO THAT EVERY NIGHT?
Talk about night-time creepy crawlers...
WELL, NOT EVERY NIGHT.
I've asked her to stop...
GEE, IT'S SURE GETTING COLD THESE DAYS.
IT'S SUPPOSED TO BE A WARM WINTER THIS YEAR, BUT YOU STILL GOTTA TAKE CARE NOT TO CATCH COLD.
WINTER BREAK IS COMING UP SOON...
THE END OF THE SEMESTER?
YEP... TOMORROW'S THE END OF THE SEMESTER.

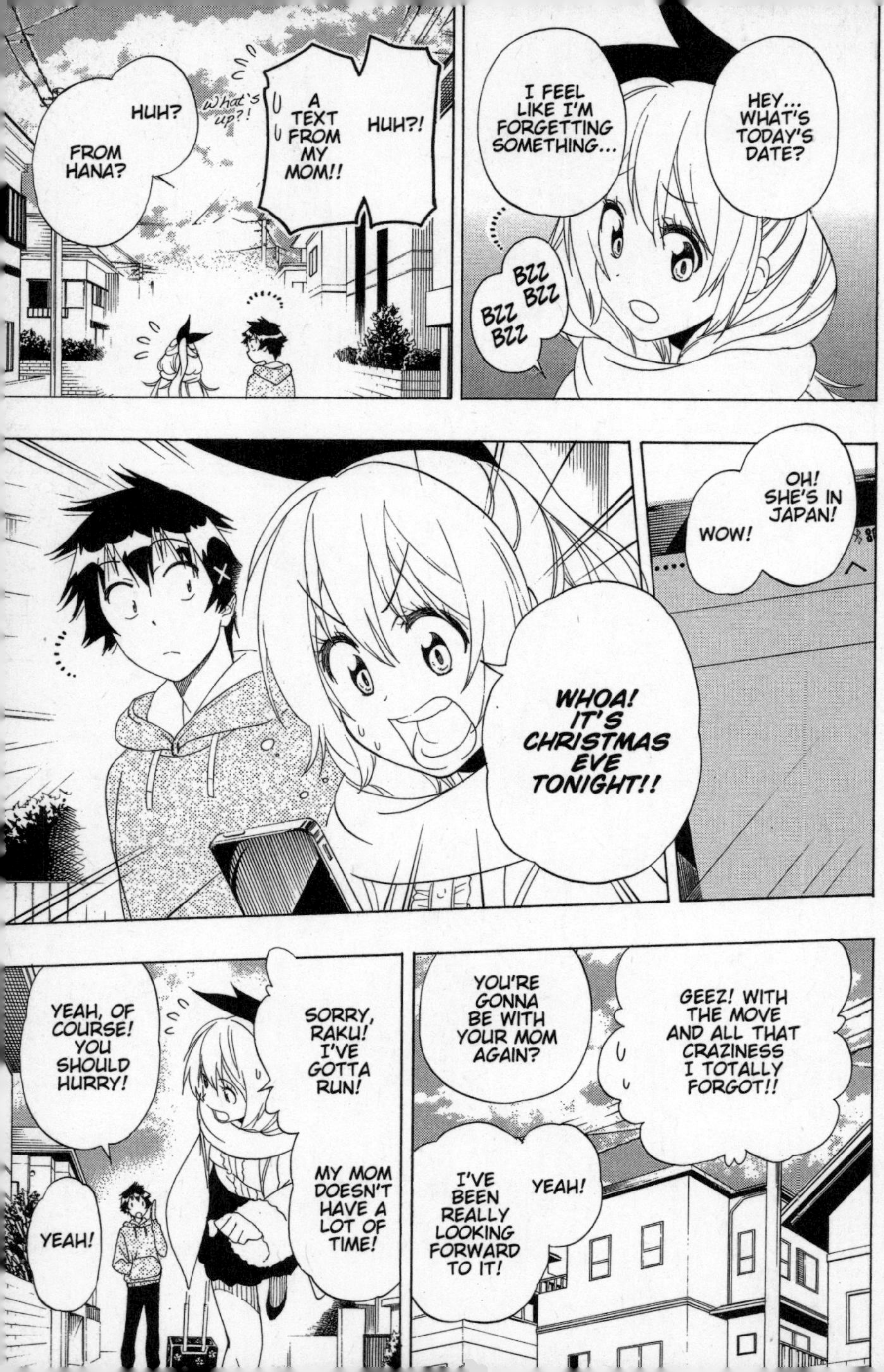
HEY... WHAT'S TODAY'S DATE?
I FEEL LIKE I'M FORGETTING SOMETHING...
BZZ BZZ BZZ BZZ
HUH?!
A TEXT FROM MY MOM!!
What's up?!
HUH? FROM HANA?
OH! SHE'S IN JAPAN!
WOW!
WHOA! IT'S CHRISTMAS EVE TONIGHT!!
GEEZ! WITH THE MOVE AND ALL THAT CRAZINESS I TOTALLY FORGOT!!
YOU'RE GONNA BE WITH YOUR MOM AGAIN?
YEAH!
I'VE BEEN REALLY LOOKING FORWARD TO IT!
SORRY, RAKU! I'VE GOTTA RUN!
YEAH, OF COURSE! YOU SHOULD HURRY!
MY MOM DOESN'T HAVE A LOT OF TIME!
YEAH!

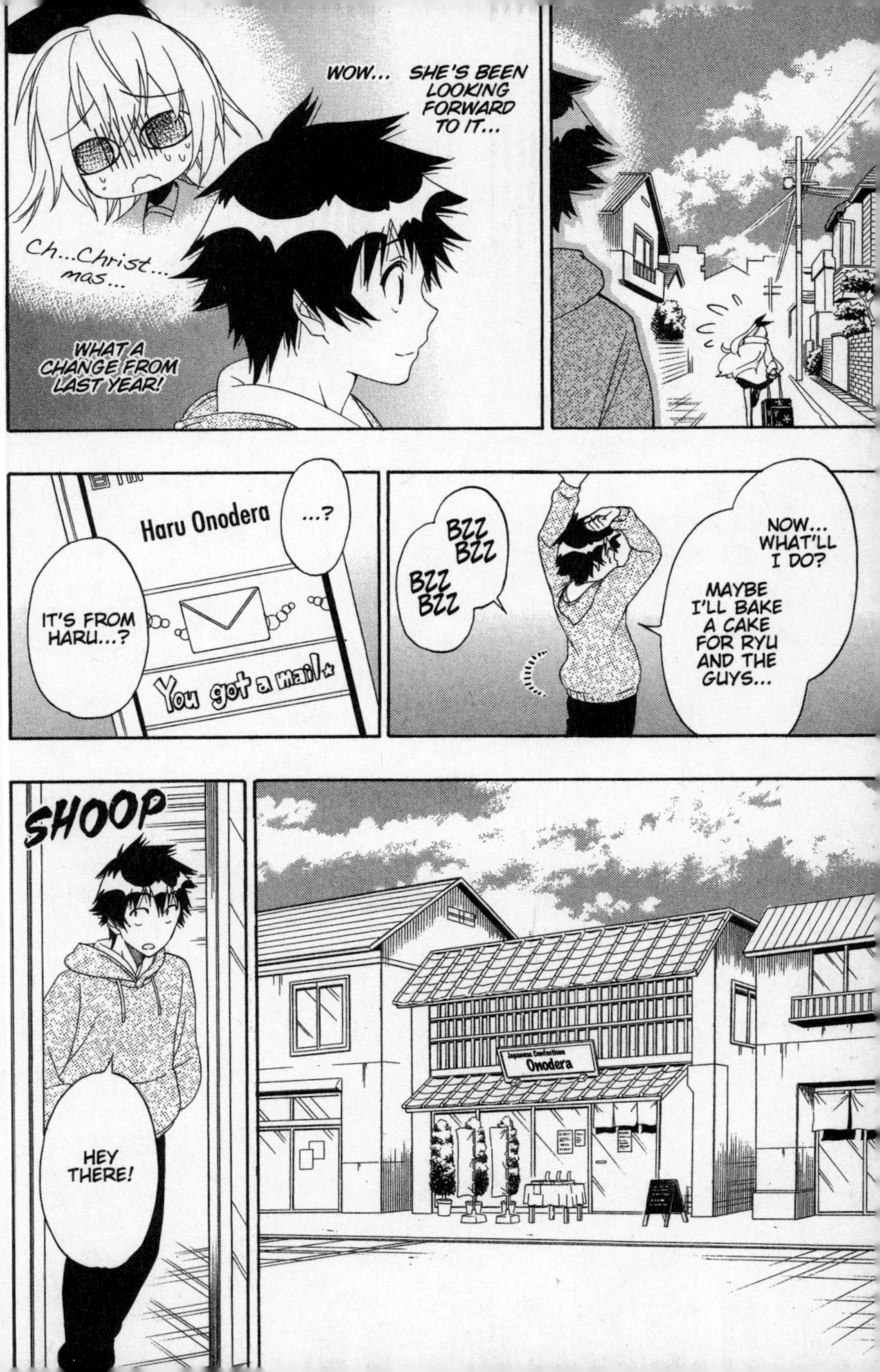
WOW... SHE'S BEEN LOOKING FORWARD TO IT...
Ch...Christ...mas...
WHAT A CHANGE FROM LAST YEAR!
NOW... WHAT'LL I DO?
MAYBE I'LL BAKE A CAKE FOR RYU AND THE GUYS...
BZZ BZZ
BZZ BZZ
...?
Haru Onodera
You got a mail★
IT'S FROM HARU...?
Japanese Confections
Onodera
SHOOP
HEY THERE!

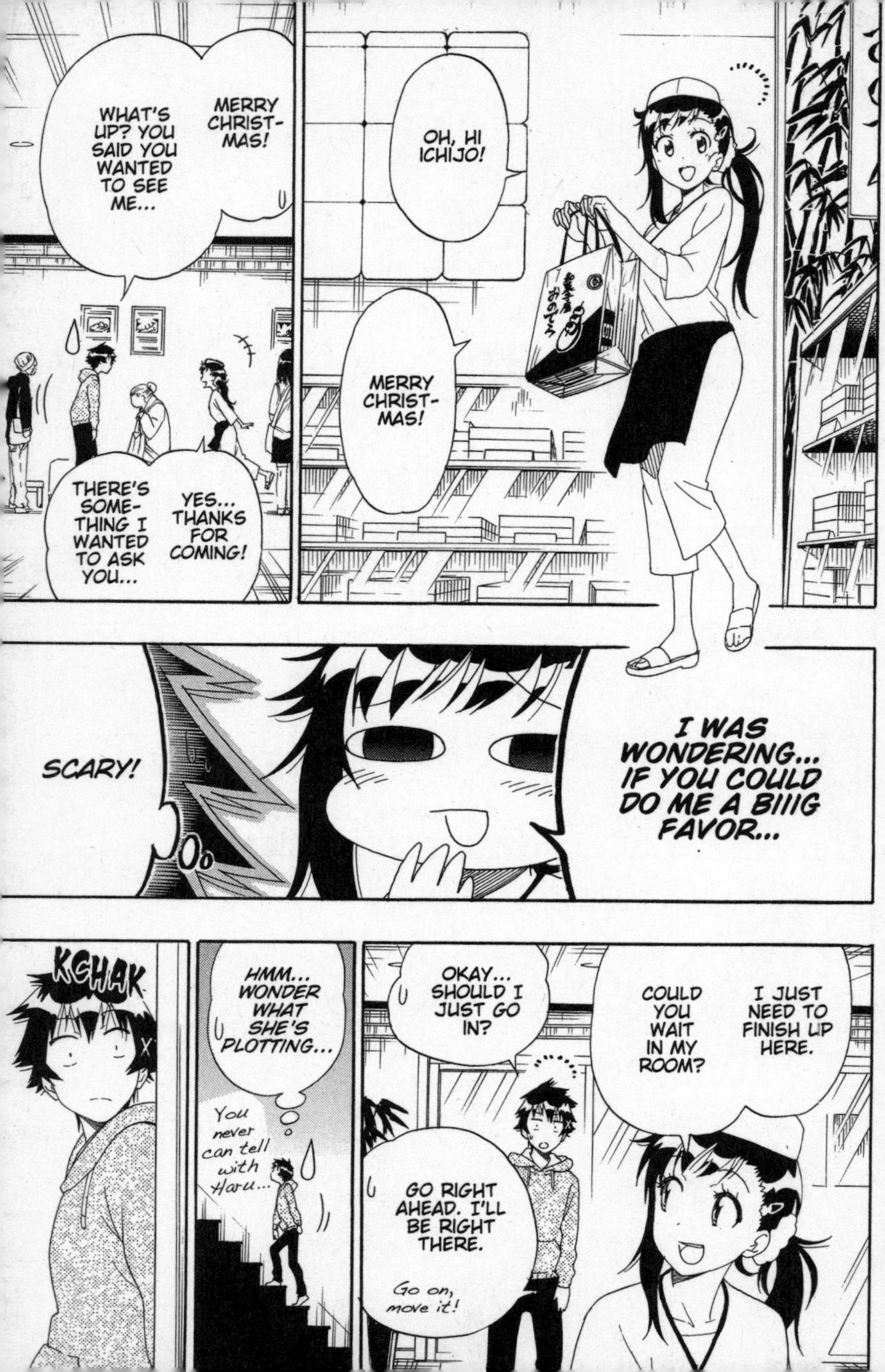
OH, HI ICHIJO!
MERRY CHRISTMAS!
MERRY CHRISTMAS!
WHAT'S UP? YOU SAID YOU WANTED TO SEE ME...
YES... THANKS FOR COMING!
THERE'S SOMETHING I WANTED TO ASK YOU...
I WAS WONDERING... IF YOU COULD DO ME A BIIIG FAVOR...
SCARY!
I JUST NEED TO FINISH UP HERE.
COULD YOU WAIT IN MY ROOM?
OKAY... SHOULD I JUST GO IN?
GO RIGHT AHEAD. I'LL BE RIGHT THERE.
Go on, move it!
HMM... WONDER WHAT SHE'S PLOTTING...
You never can tell with Haru...
KCHAK

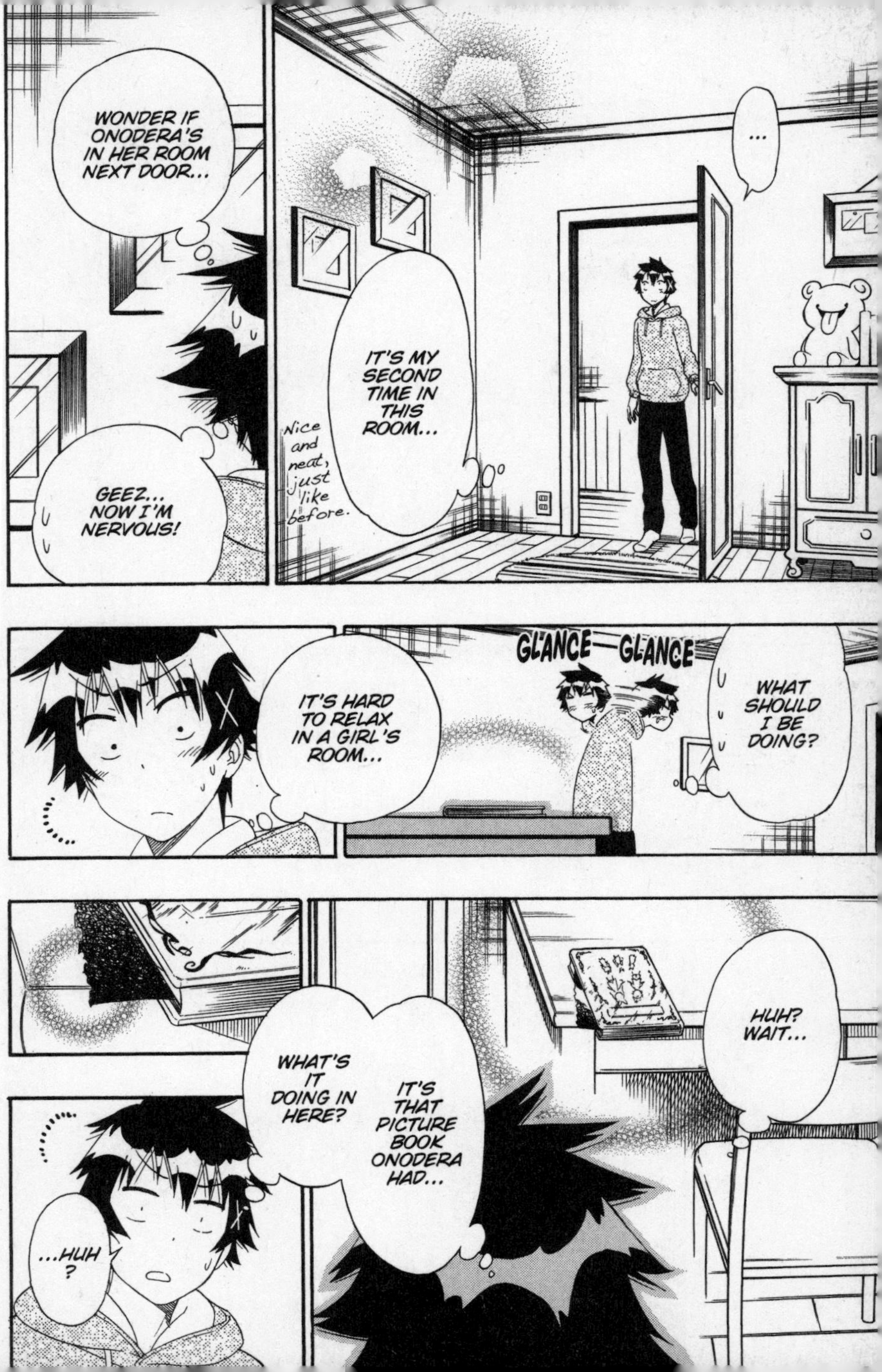
...
IT'S MY SECOND TIME IN THIS ROOM...
Nice and neat, just like before.
WONDER IF ONODERA'S IN HER ROOM NEXT DOOR...
GEEZ... NOW I'M NERVOUS!
GLANCE GLANCE
WHAT SHOULD I BE DOING?
IT'S HARD TO RELAX IN A GIRL'S ROOM...
HUH? WAIT...
IT'S THAT PICTURE BOOK ONODERA HAD...
WHAT'S IT DOING IN HERE?
...HUH?

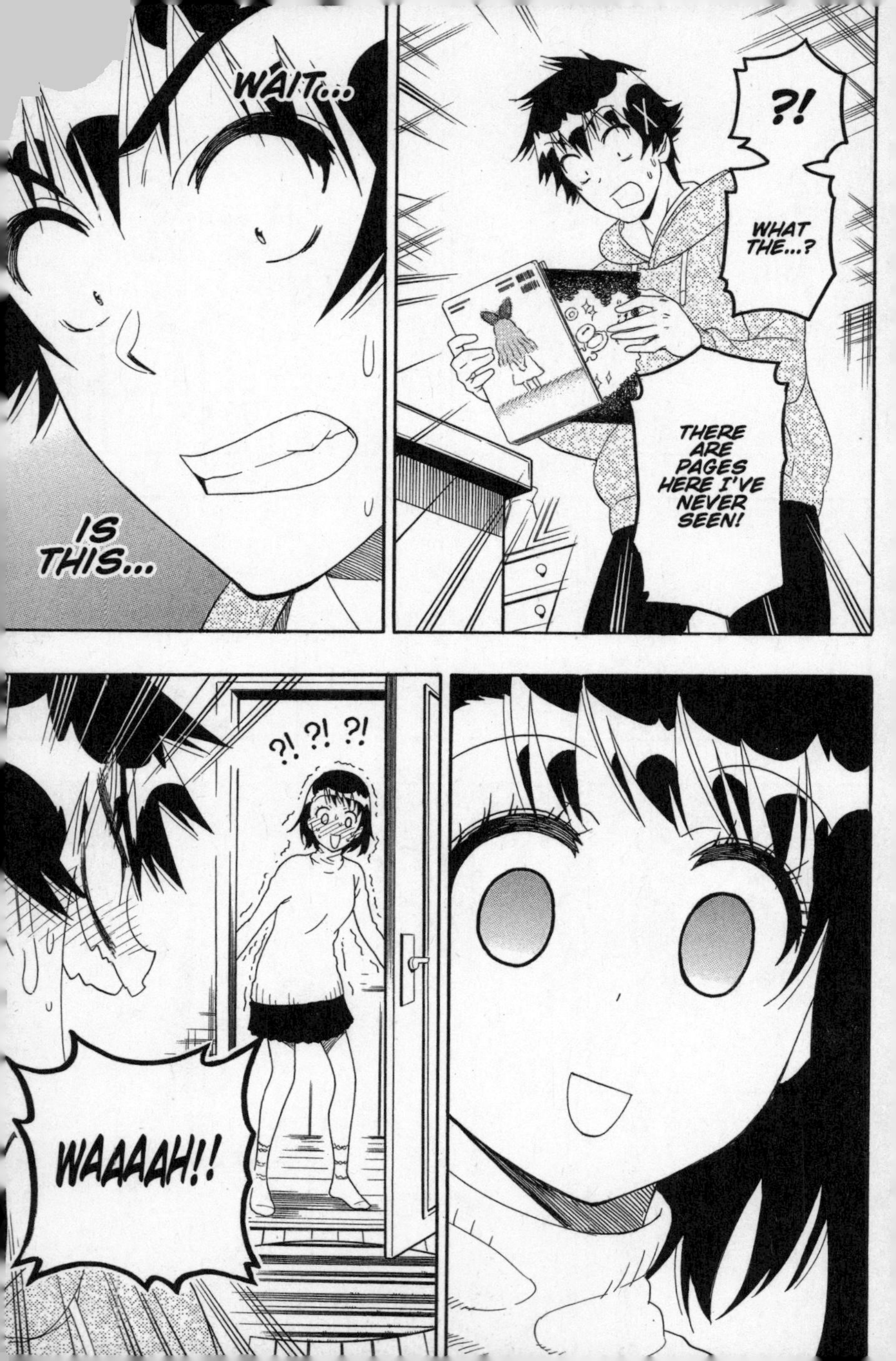
?!
WHAT THE...?
THERE ARE PAGES HERE I'VE NEVER SEEN!
WAIT...
IS THIS...
?! ?! ?!
WAAAAH!!

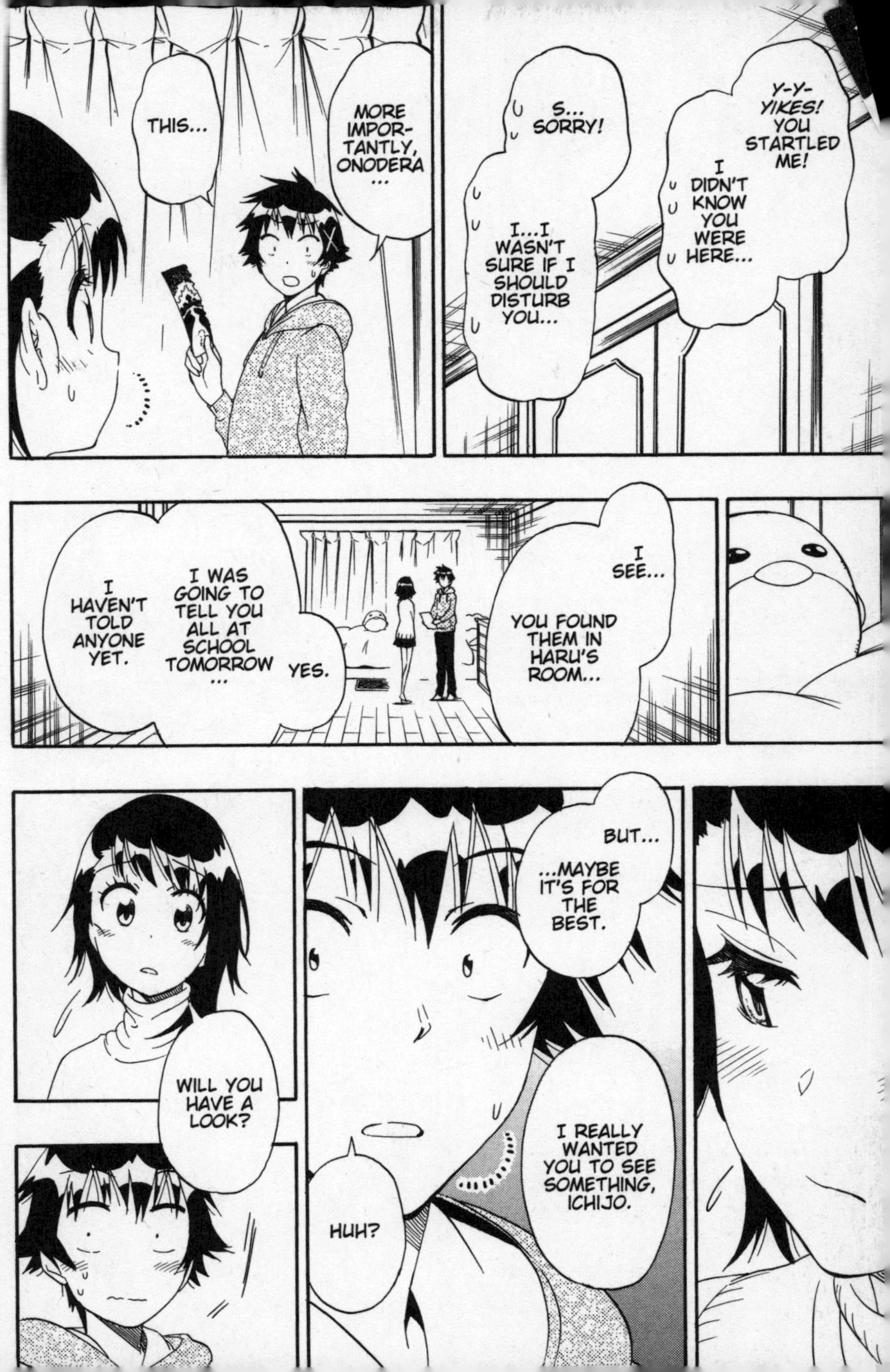

Y-Y-YIKES! YOU STARTLED ME!
I DIDN'T KNOW YOU WERE HERE...
S... SORRY!
I...I WASN'T SURE IF I SHOULD DISTURB YOU...
MORE IMPORTANTLY, ONODERA...
THIS...
I SEE...
YOU FOUND THEM IN HARU'S ROOM...
YES.
I WAS GOING TO TELL YOU ALL AT SCHOOL TOMORROW...
I HAVEN'T TOLD ANYONE YET.
BUT...
...MAYBE IT'S FOR THE BEST.
I REALLY WANTED YOU TO SEE SOMETHING, ICHIJO.
HUH?
WILL YOU HAVE A LOOK?

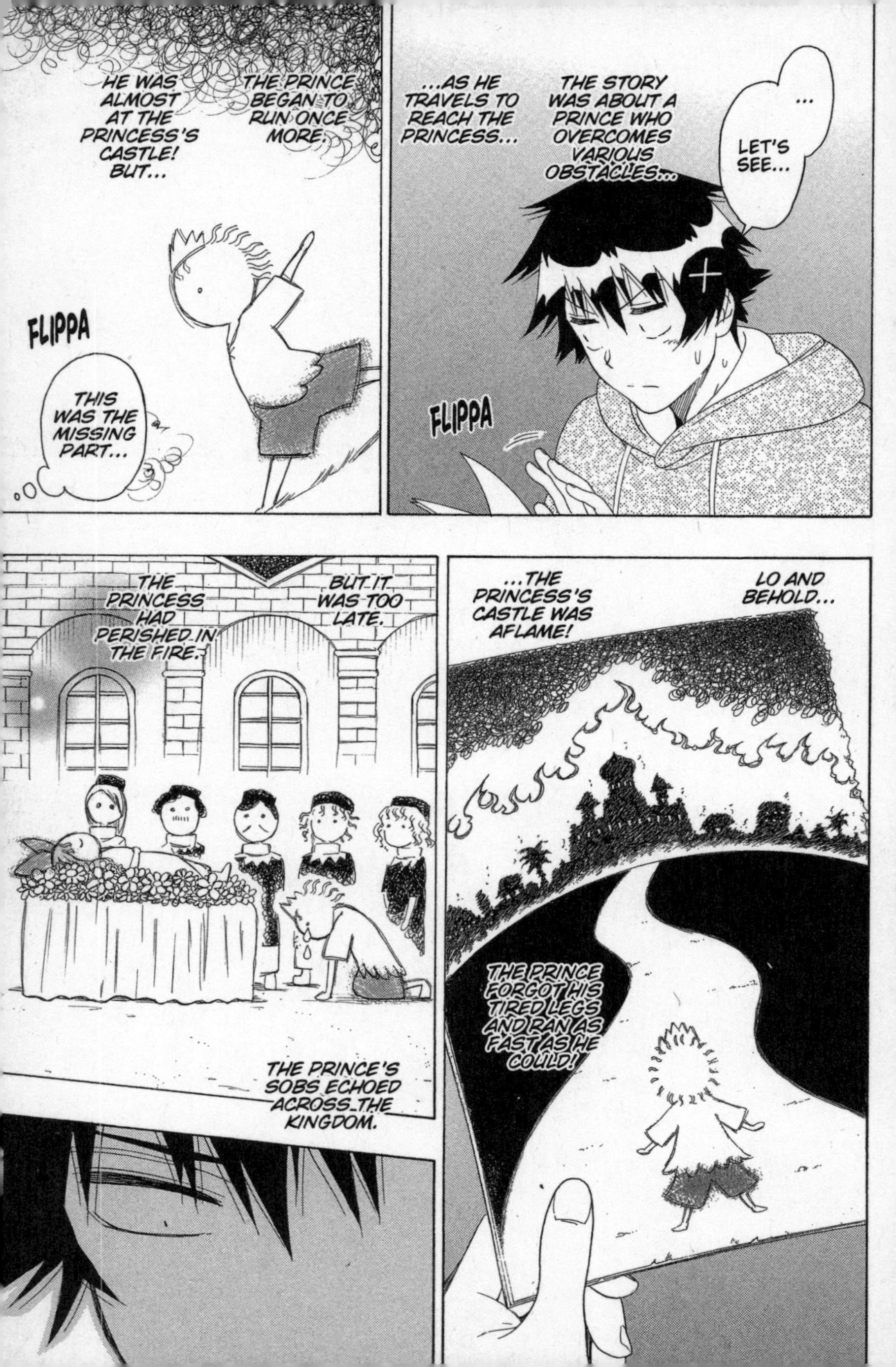
...
LET'S SEE...
THE STORY WAS ABOUT A PRINCE WHO OVERCOMES VARIOUS OBSTACLES...
...AS HE TRAVELS TO REACH THE PRINCESS...
FLIPPA
THE PRINCE BEGAN TO RUN ONCE MORE.
HE WAS ALMOST AT THE PRINCESS'S CASTLE! BUT...
FLIPPA
THIS WAS THE MISSING PART...
LO AND BEHOLD...
...THE PRINCESS'S CASTLE WAS AFLAME!
THE PRINCE FORGOT HIS TIRED LEGS AND RAN AS FAST AS HE COULD!
BUT IT WAS TOO LATE.
THE PRINCESS HAD PERISHED IN THE FIRE.
THE PRINCE'S SOBS ECHOED ACROSS THE KINGDOM.

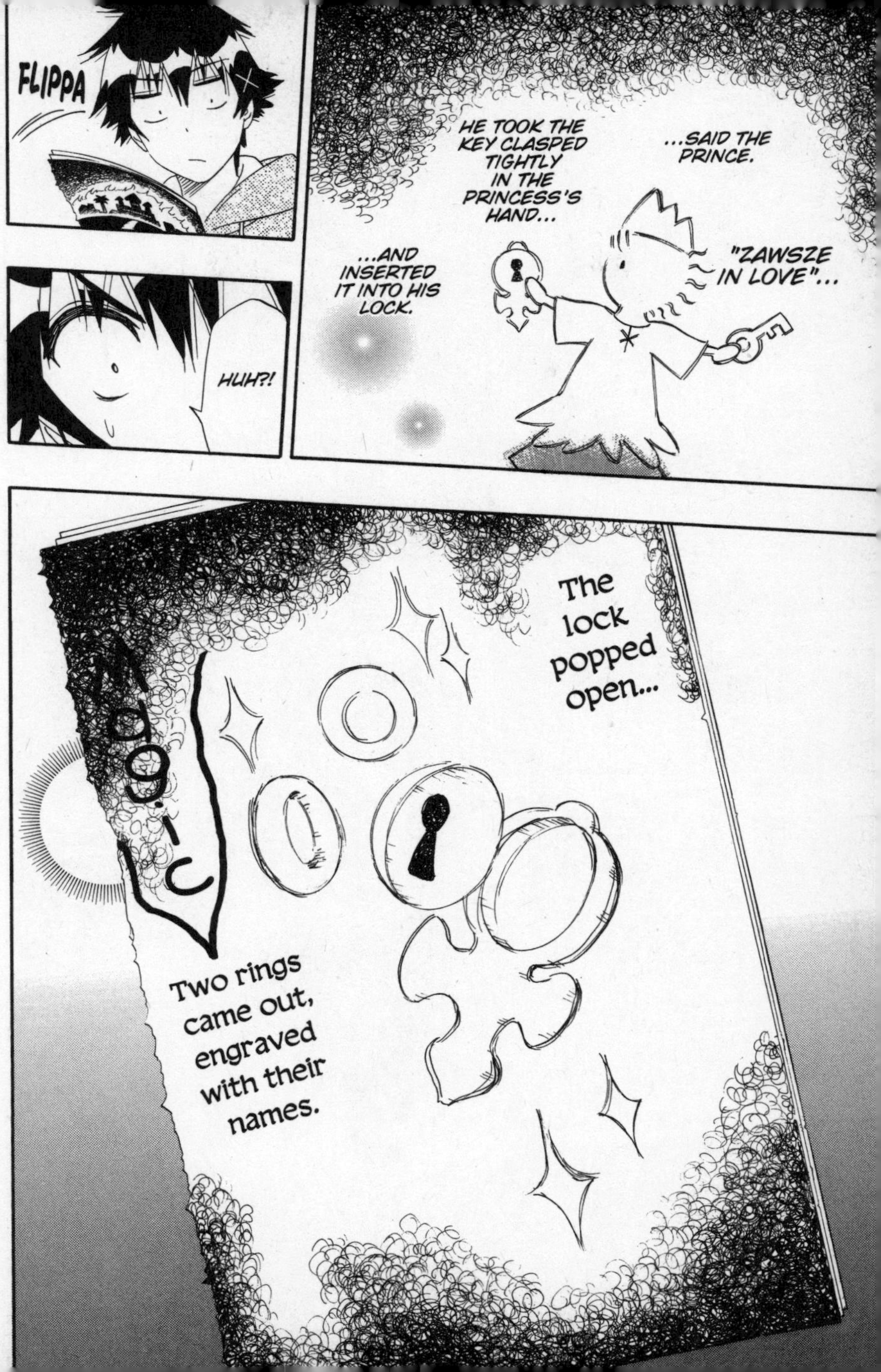
"ZAWSZE IN LOVE"...
...SAID THE PRINCE.
HE TOOK THE KEY CLASPED TIGHTLY IN THE PRINCESS'S HAND...
...AND INSERTED IT INTO HIS LOCK.
FLIPPA
HUH?!
The lock popped open...
Magic
Two rings came out, engraved with their names.

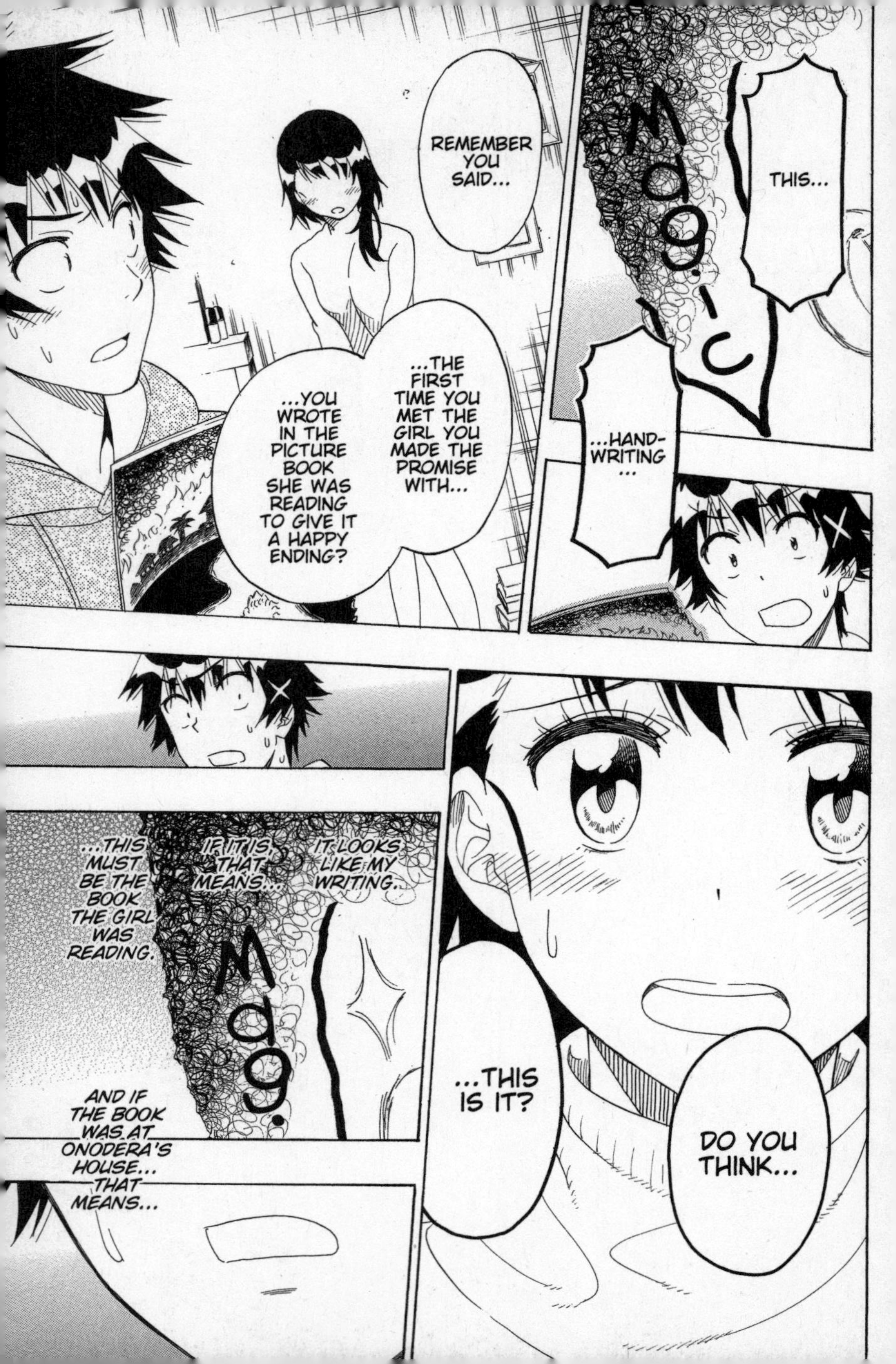
THIS...
...HAND-WRITING...
REMEMBER YOU SAID...
...THE FIRST TIME YOU MET THE GIRL YOU MADE THE PROMISE WITH...
...YOU WROTE IN THE PICTURE BOOK SHE WAS READING TO GIVE IT A HAPPY ENDING?
DO YOU THINK...
...THIS IS IT?
IT LOOKS LIKE MY WRITING.
IF IT IS, THAT MEANS...
...THIS MUST BE THE BOOK THE GIRL WAS READING.
AND IF THE BOOK WAS AT ONODERA'S HOUSE... THAT MEANS...

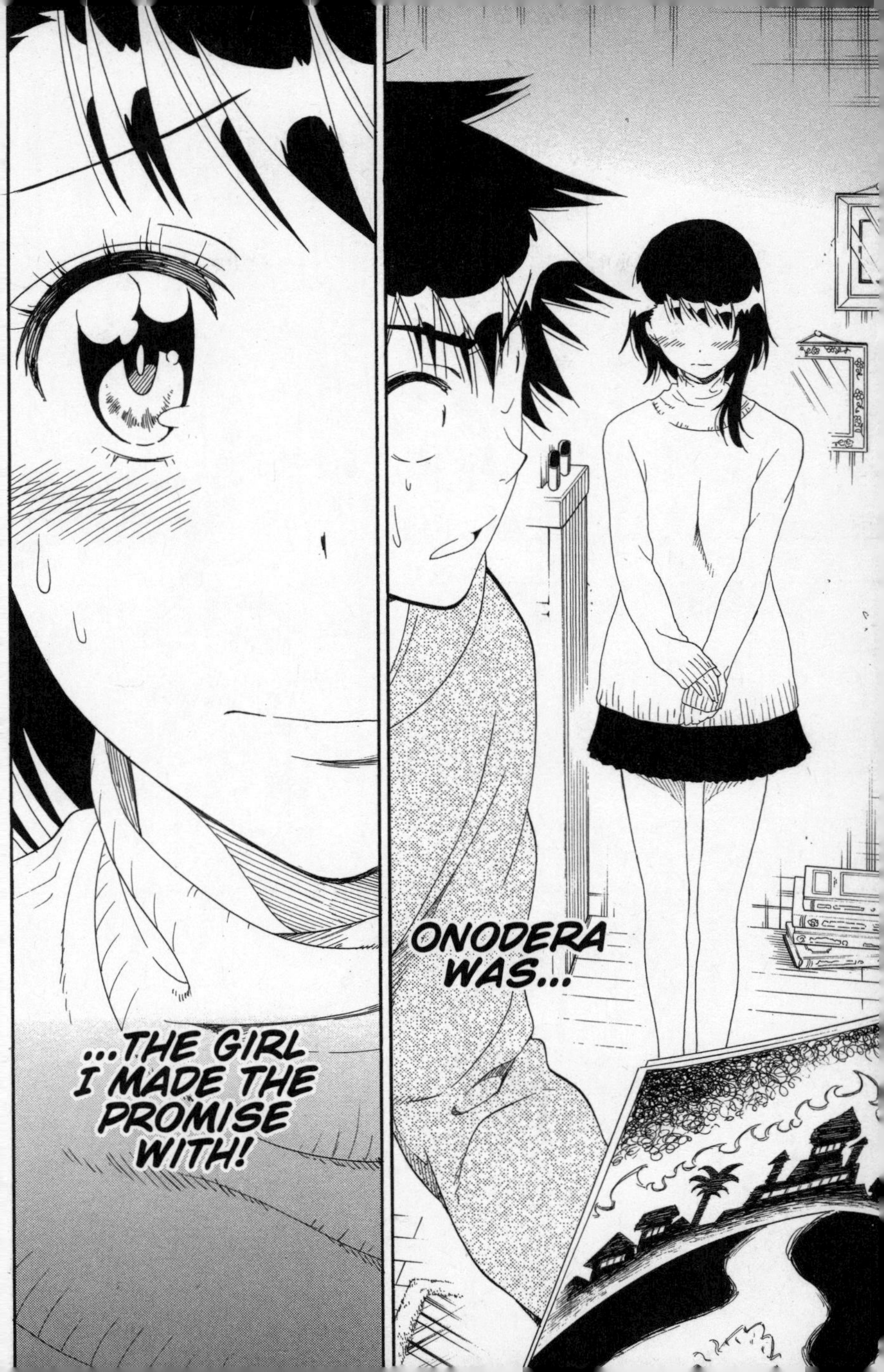
ONODERA WAS...
...THE GIRL I MADE THE PROMISE WITH!

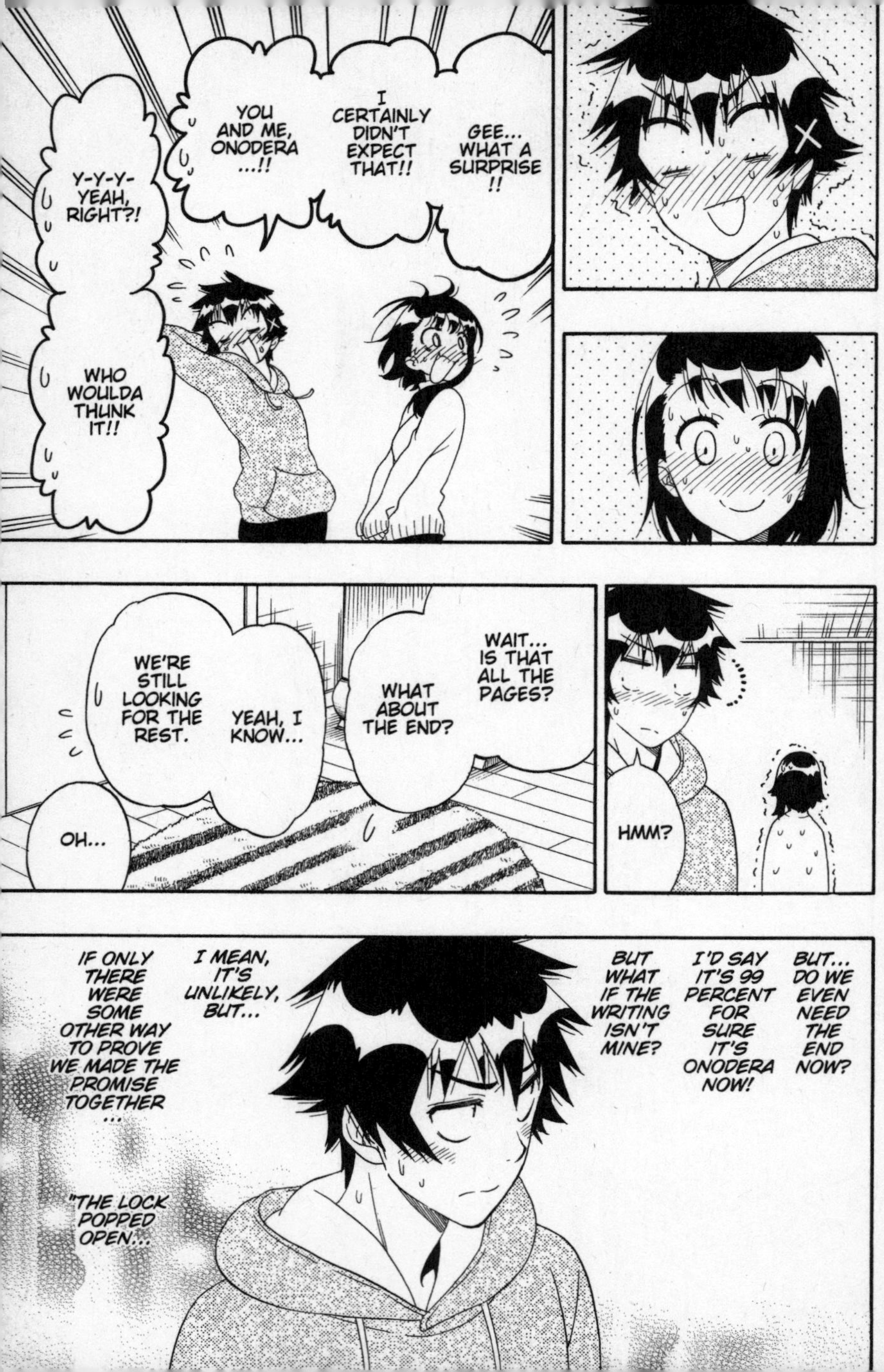
GEE... WHAT A SURPRISE!!
I CERTAINLY DIDN'T EXPECT THAT!!
YOU AND ME, ONODERA...!!
Y-Y-Y-YEAH, RIGHT?!
WHO WOULDA THUNK IT!!
HMM?
WAIT... IS THAT ALL THE PAGES?
WHAT ABOUT THE END?
YEAH, I KNOW...
WE'RE STILL LOOKING FOR THE REST.
OH...
BUT... DO WE EVEN NEED THE END NOW?
I'D SAY IT'S 99 PERCENT FOR SURE IT'S ONODERA NOW!
BUT WHAT IF THE WRITING ISN'T MINE?
I MEAN, IT'S UNLIKELY, BUT...
IF ONLY THERE WERE SOME OTHER WAY TO PROVE WE MADE THE PROMISE TOGETHER...
"THE LOCK POPPED OPEN...

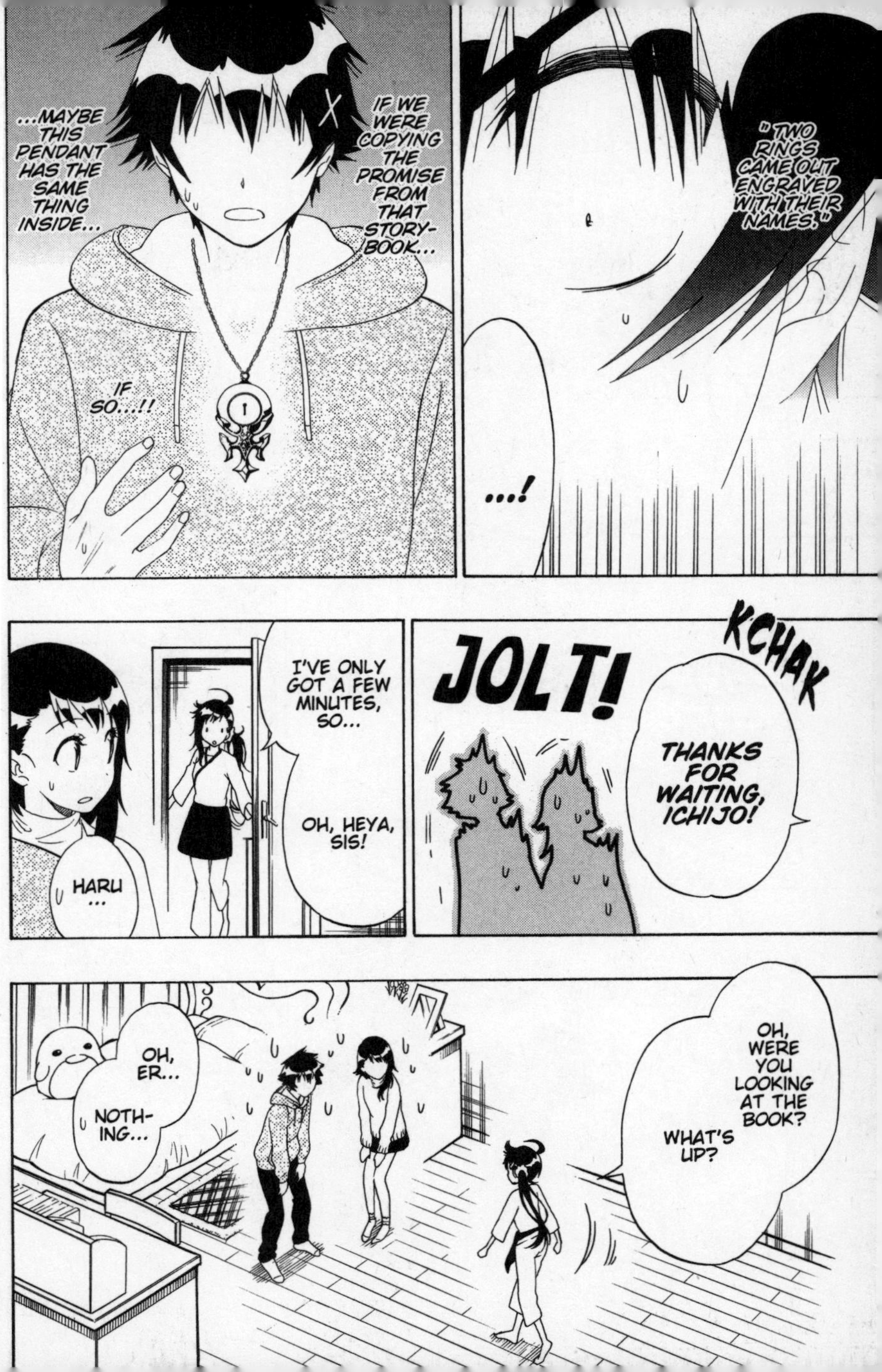
"TWO RINGS CAME OUT ENGRAVED WITH THEIR NAMES."
...!
IF WE WERE COPYING THE PROMISE FROM THAT STORY-BOOK...
...MAYBE THIS PENDANT HAS THE SAME THING INSIDE...
IF SO...!!
KCHAK
JOLT!
THANKS FOR WAITING, ICHIJO!
I'VE ONLY GOT A FEW MINUTES, SO...
OH, HEYA, SIS!
HARU...
OH, WERE YOU LOOKING AT THE BOOK?
WHAT'S UP?
OH, ER...
NOTHING...

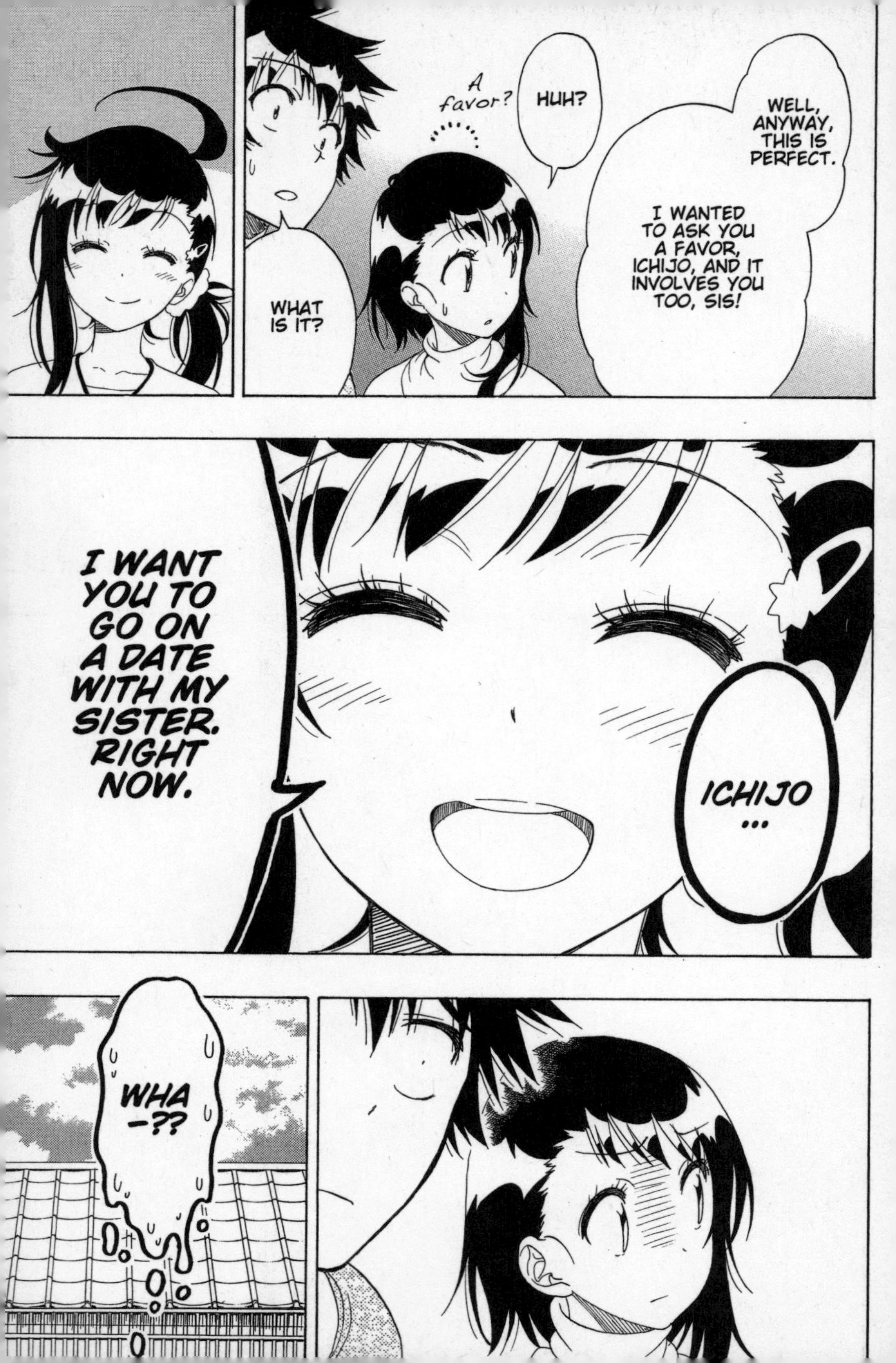
WELL, ANYWAY, THIS IS PERFECT.
I WANTED TO ASK YOU A FAVOR, ICHIJO, AND IT INVOLVES YOU TOO, SIS!
HUH?
A favor?
WHAT IS IT?
ICHIJO...
I WANT YOU TO GO ON A DATE WITH MY SISTER. RIGHT NOW.
WHA-??

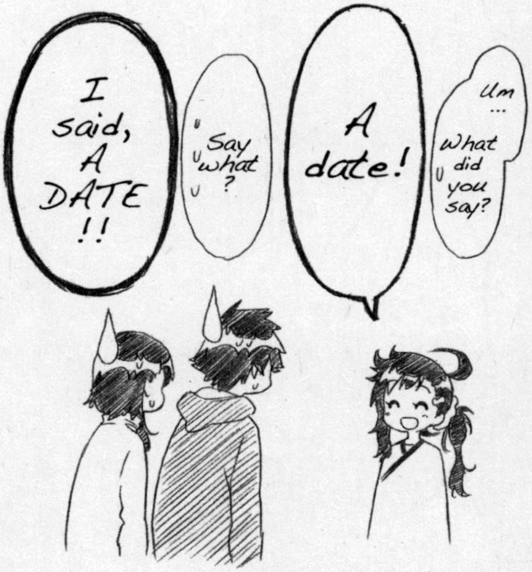
Um... What did you say?
A date!
Say what?
I said, A DATE!!

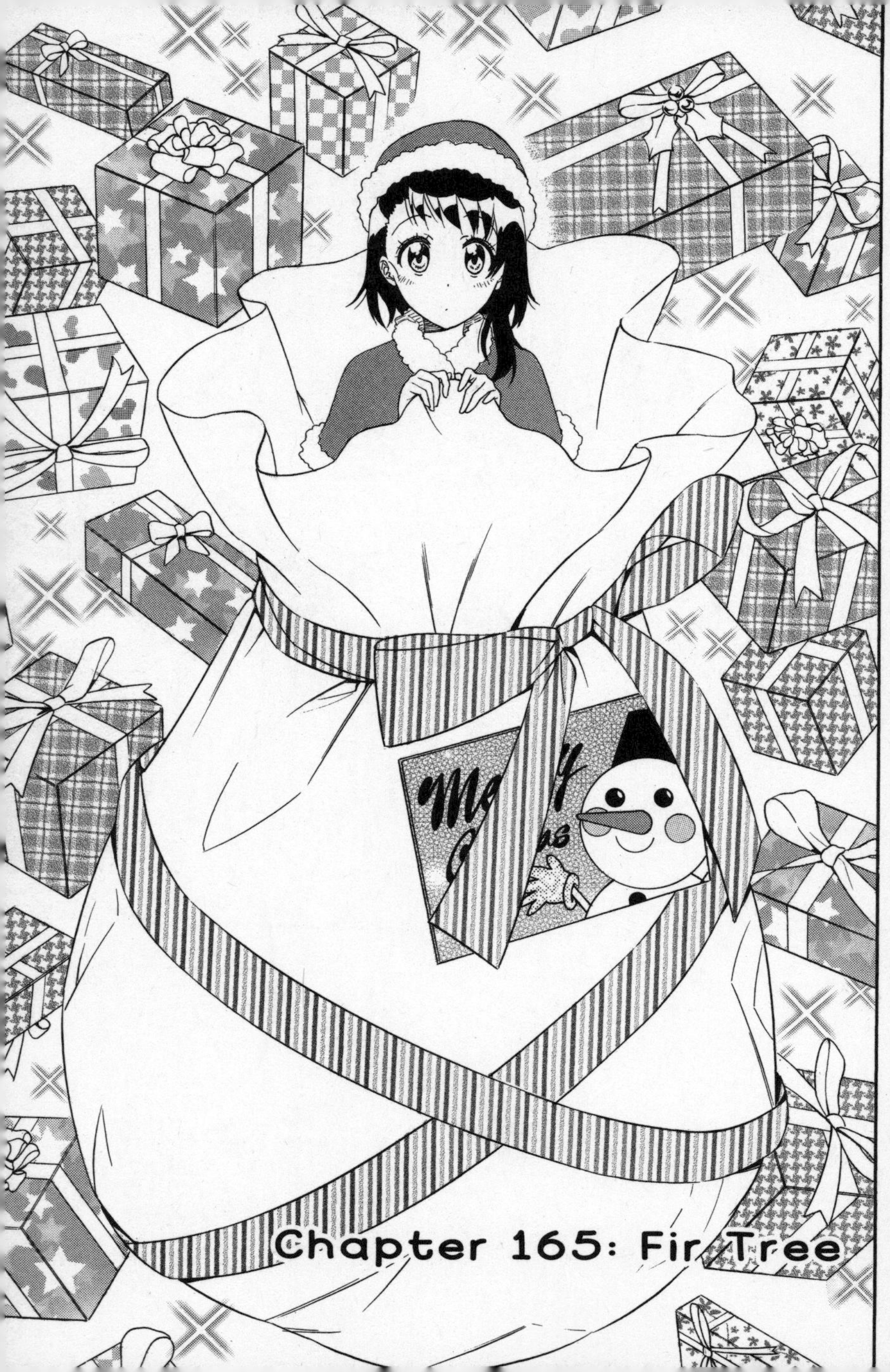
Chapter 165: Fir Tree

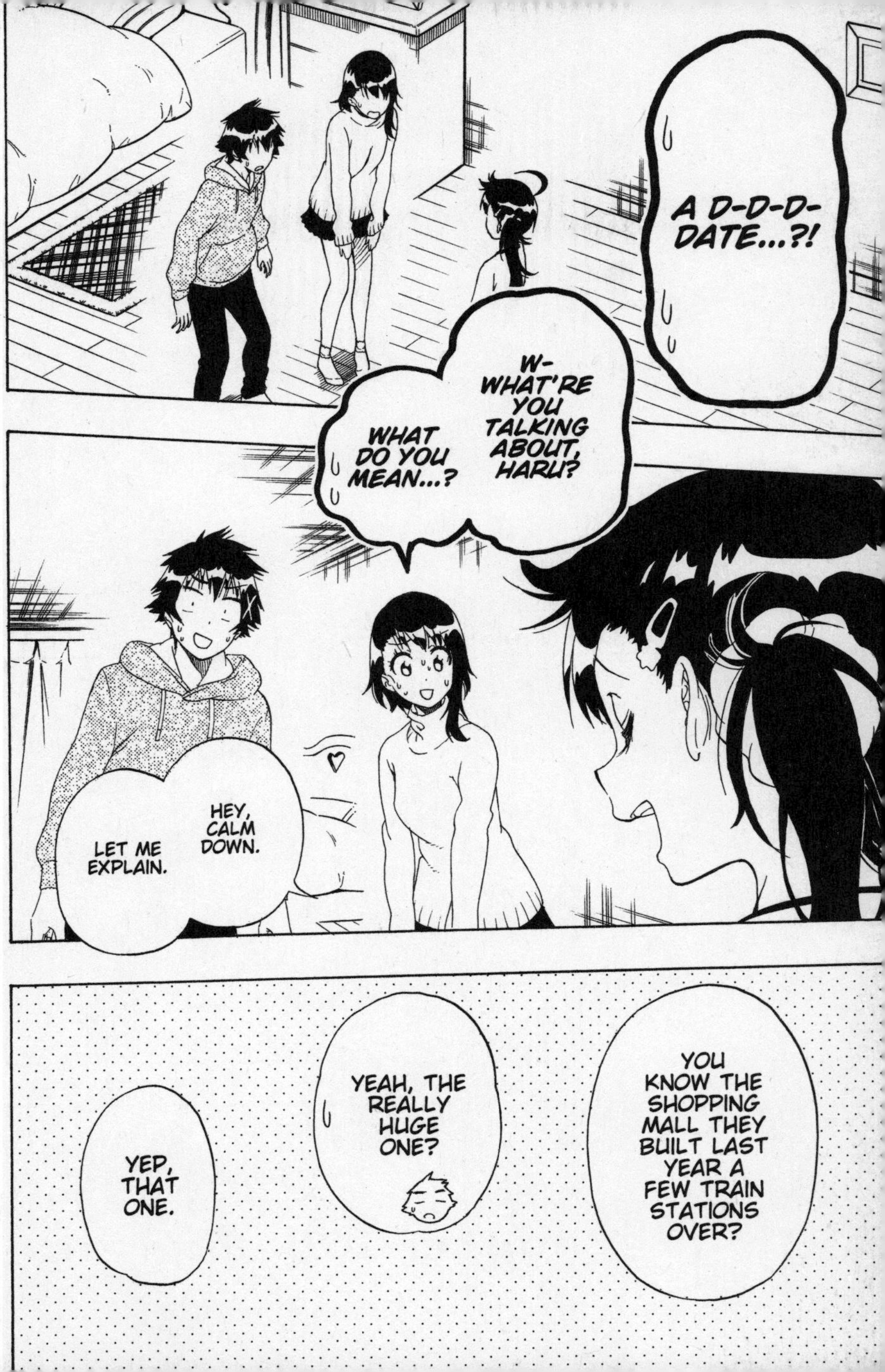
A D-D-D-DATE...?!
W-WHAT'RE YOU TALKING ABOUT, HARU?
WHAT DO YOU MEAN...?
HEY, CALM DOWN.
LET ME EXPLAIN.
YOU KNOW THE SHOPPING MALL THEY BUILT LAST YEAR A FEW TRAIN STATIONS OVER?
YEAH, THE REALLY HUGE ONE?
YEP, THAT ONE.

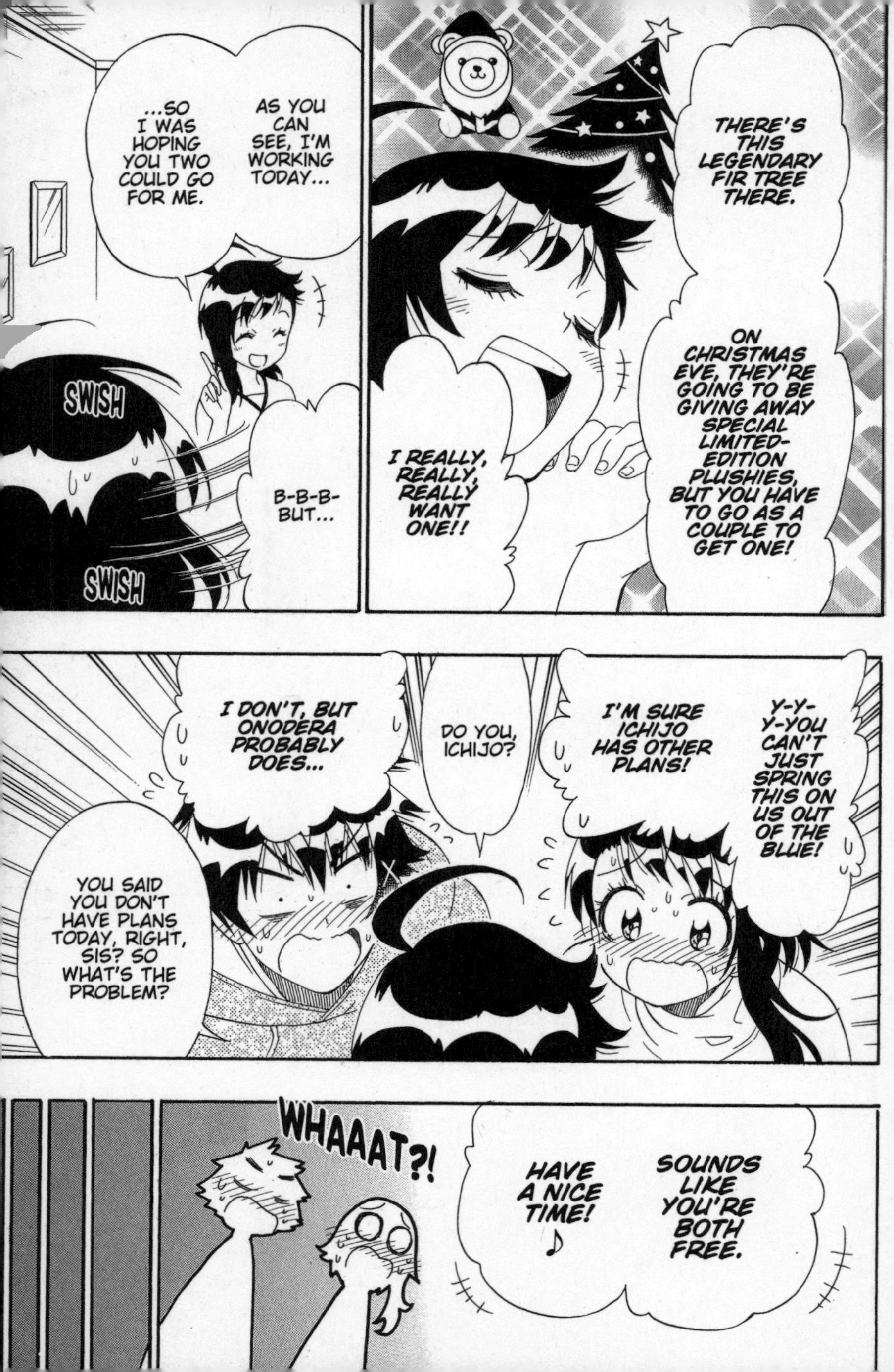
THERE'S THIS LEGENDARY FIR TREE THERE.
ON CHRISTMAS EVE, THEY'RE GOING TO BE GIVING AWAY SPECIAL LIMITED-EDITION PLUSHIES, BUT YOU HAVE TO GO AS A COUPLE TO GET ONE!
I REALLY, REALLY, REALLY WANT ONE!!
AS YOU CAN SEE, I'M WORKING TODAY...
...SO I WAS HOPING YOU TWO COULD GO FOR ME.
SWISH
B-B-B-BUT...
SWISH
Y-Y-Y-YOU CAN'T JUST SPRING THIS ON US OUT OF THE BLUE!
I'M SURE ICHIJO HAS OTHER PLANS!
DO YOU, ICHIJO?
I DON'T, BUT ONODERA PROBABLY DOES...
YOU SAID YOU DON'T HAVE PLANS TODAY, RIGHT, SIS? SO WHAT'S THE PROBLEM?
SOUNDS LIKE YOU'RE BOTH FREE.
HAVE A NICE TIME! ♪
WHAAAT?!

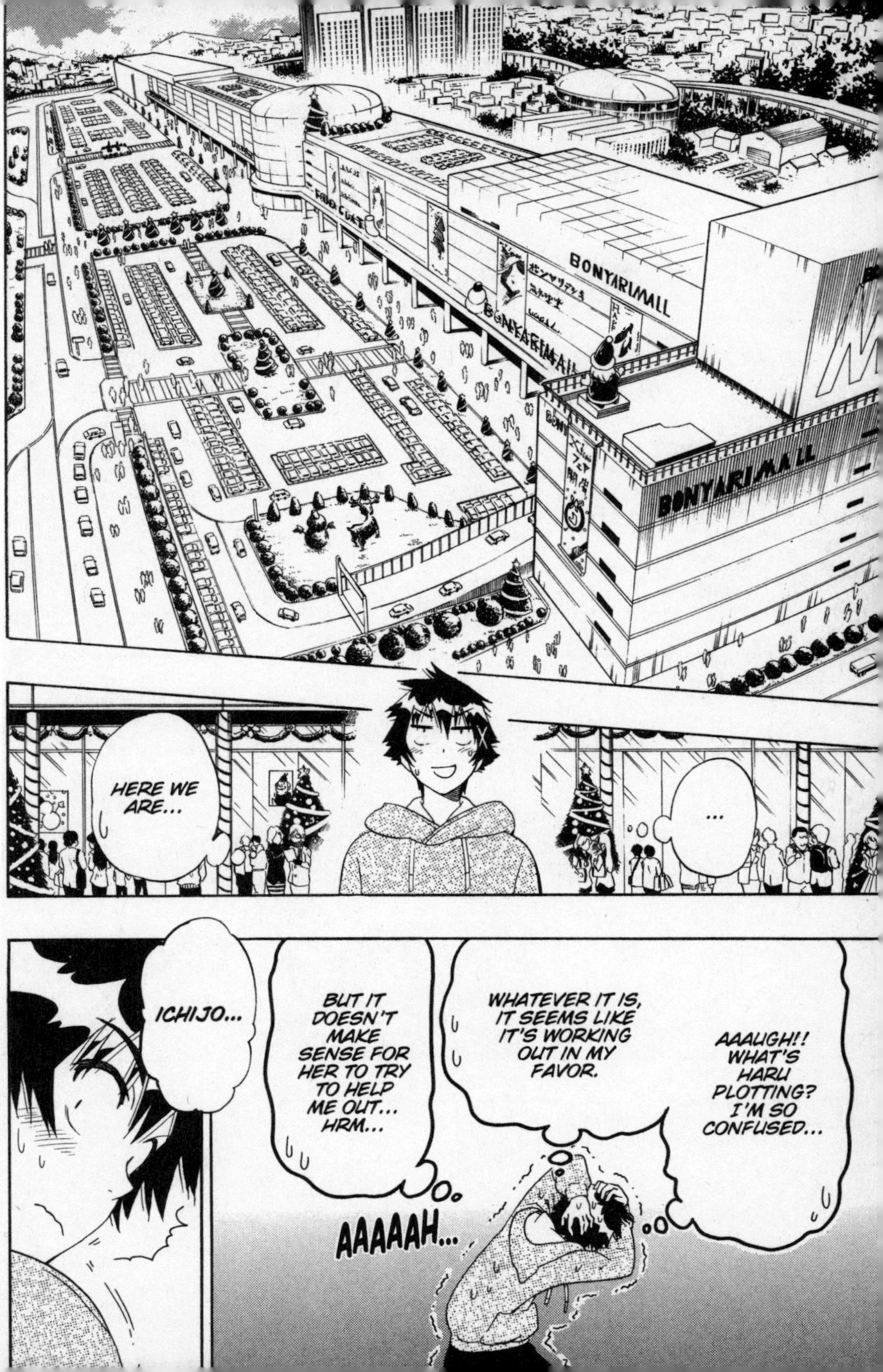
BONYARIMALL
BONYARIMALL
BONYARIMALL
...
HERE WE ARE...
AAAUGH!! WHAT'S HARU PLOTTING? I'M SO CONFUSED...
WHATEVER IT IS, IT SEEMS LIKE IT'S WORKING OUT IN MY FAVOR.
BUT IT DOESN'T MAKE SENSE FOR HER TO TRY TO HELP ME OUT... HRM...
AAAAAH...
ICHIJO...

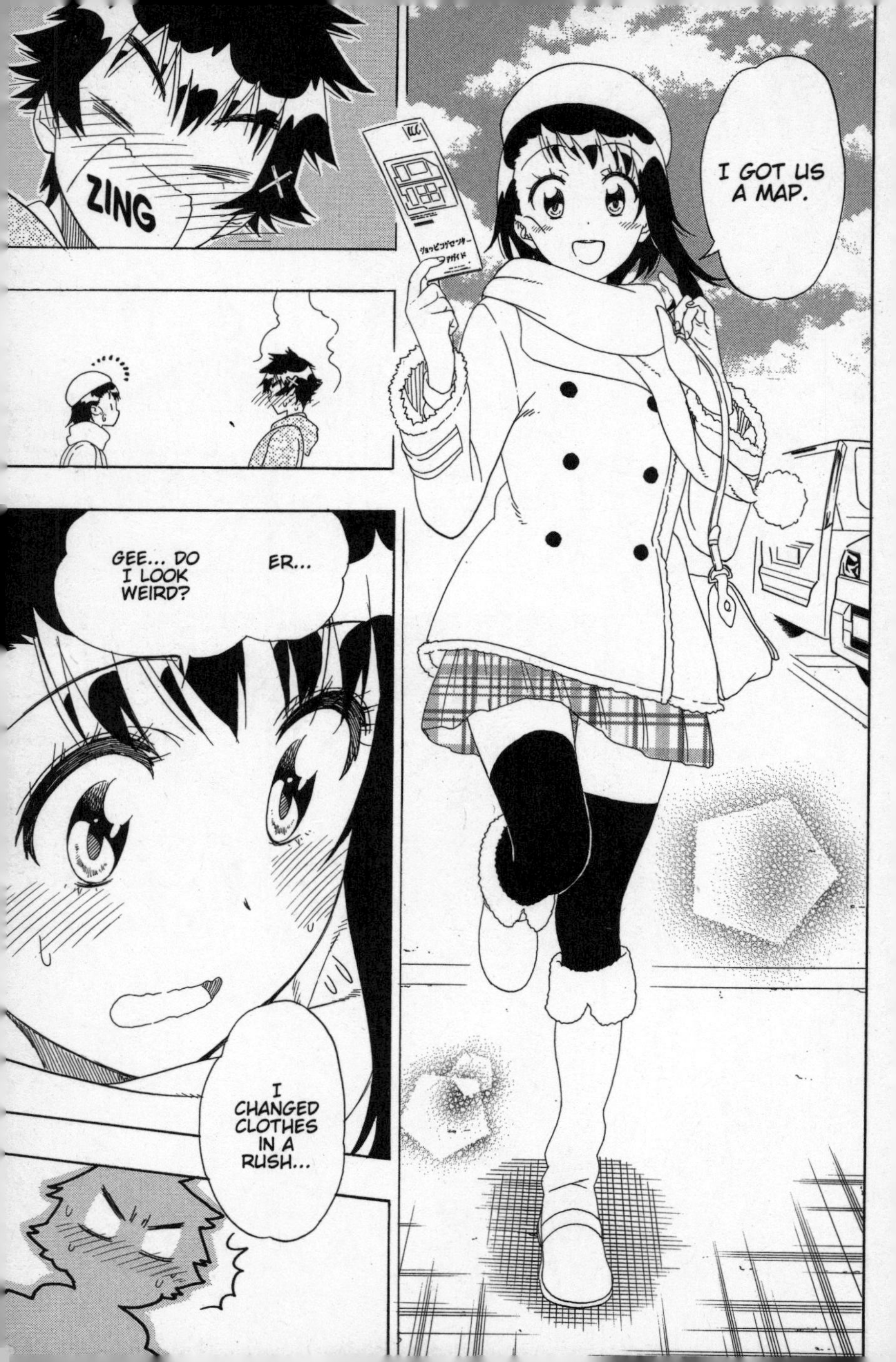
I GOT US A MAP.
ZING
ER...
GEE... DO I LOOK WEIRD?
I CHANGED CLOTHES IN A RUSH...

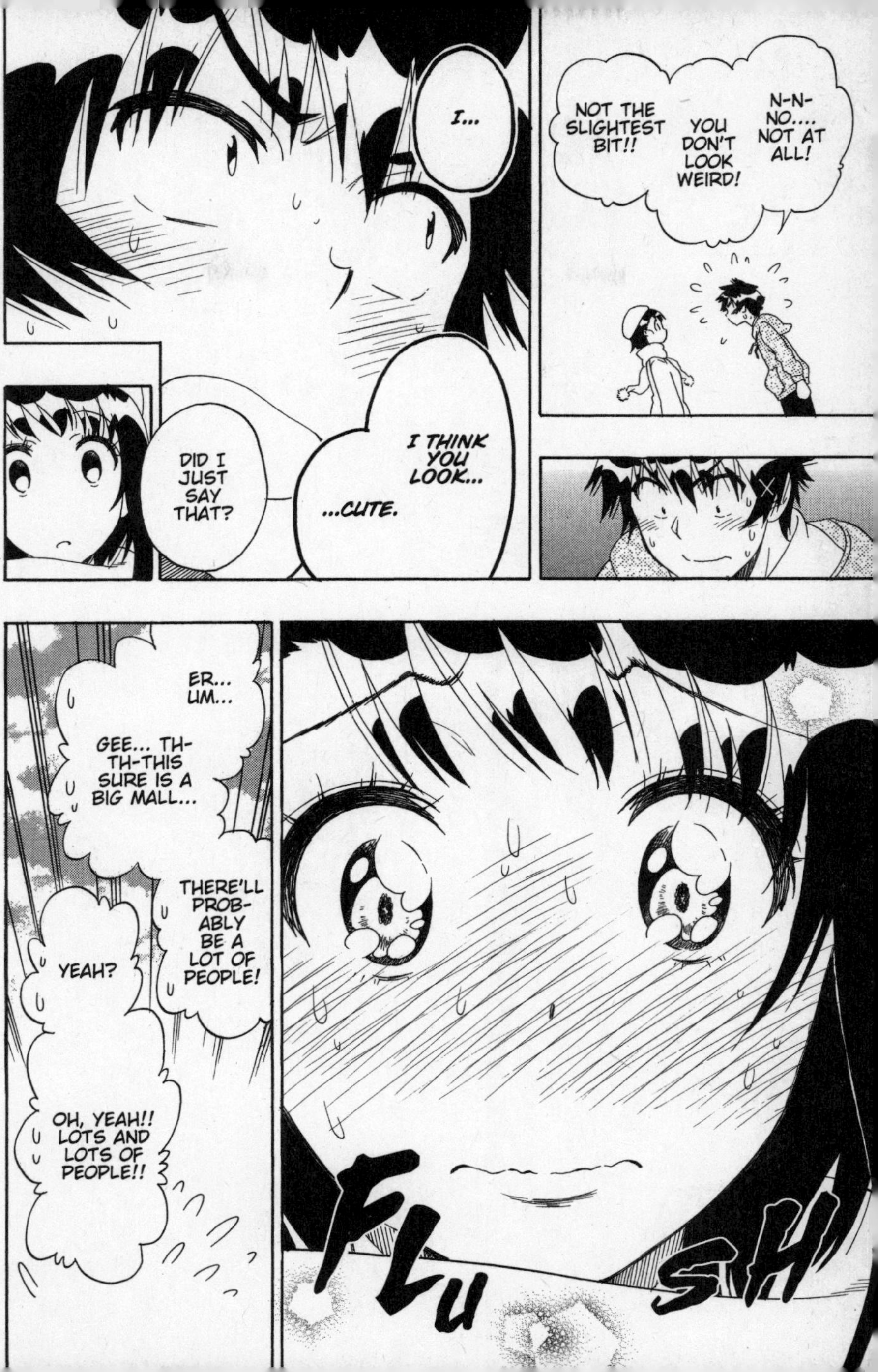
N-N-NO.... NOT AT ALL!
YOU DON'T LOOK WEIRD!
NOT THE SLIGHTEST BIT!!
I...
I THINK YOU LOOK...
...CUTE.
DID I JUST SAY THAT?
FLUSH
ER... UM...
GEE... TH-TH-THIS SURE IS A BIG MALL...
THERE'LL PROBABLY BE A LOT OF PEOPLE!
YEAH?
OH, YEAH!! LOTS AND LOTS OF PEOPLE!!

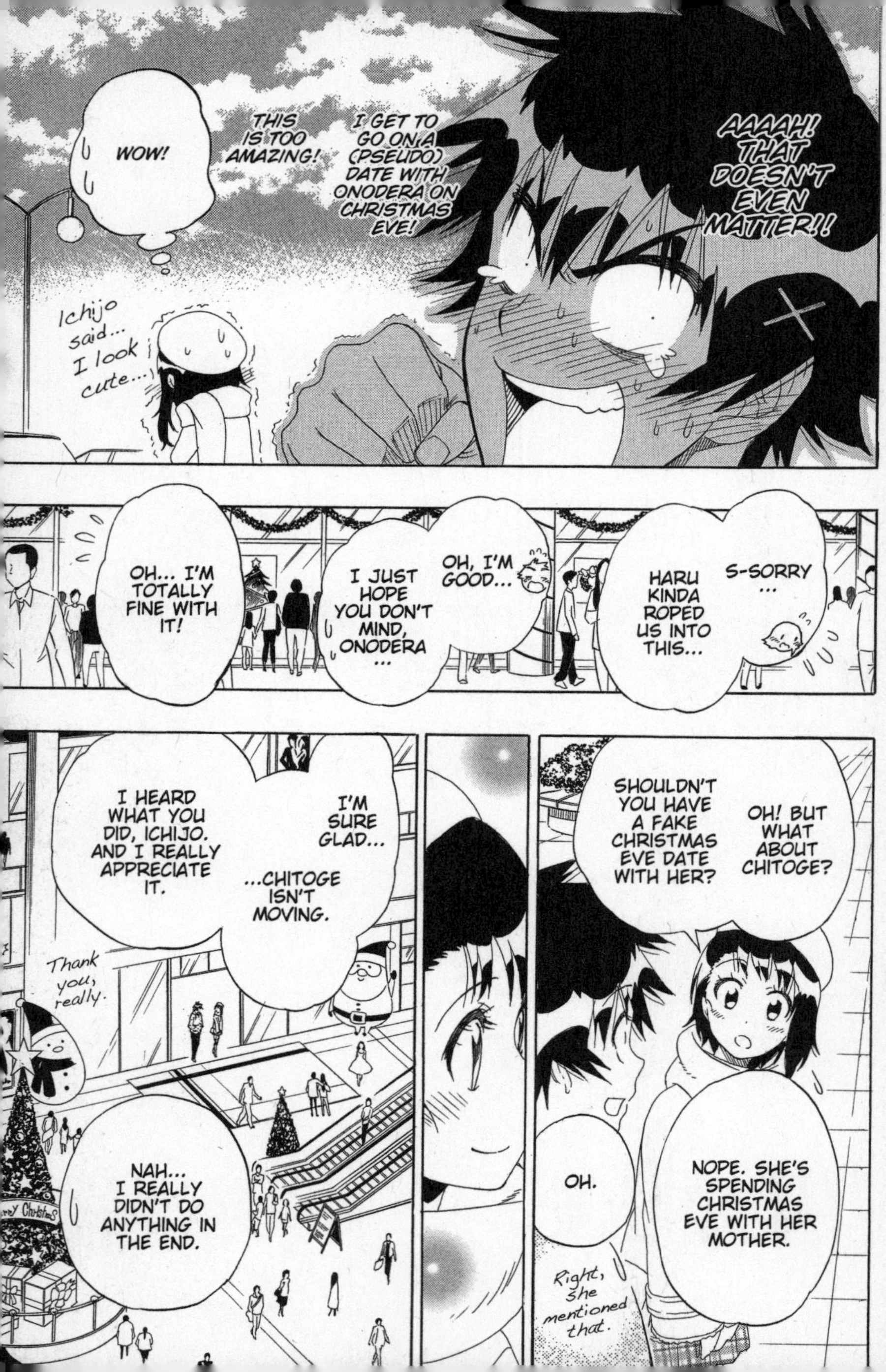
AAAAH! THAT DOESN'T EVEN MATTER!!
I GET TO GO ON A (PSEUDO) DATE WITH ONODERA ON CHRISTMAS EVE!
THIS IS TOO AMAZING!
WOW!
Ichijo said... I look cute...
S-SORRY ...
HARU KINDA ROPED US INTO THIS...
OH, I'M GOOD...
I JUST HOPE YOU DON'T MIND, ONODERA ...
OH... I'M TOTALLY FINE WITH IT!
OH! BUT WHAT ABOUT CHITOGE?
SHOULDN'T YOU HAVE A FAKE CHRISTMAS EVE DATE WITH HER?
NOPE. SHE'S SPENDING CHRISTMAS EVE WITH HER MOTHER.
OH.
Right, she mentioned that.
I'M SURE GLAD...
...CHITOGE ISN'T MOVING.
I HEARD WHAT YOU DID, ICHIJO. AND I REALLY APPRECIATE IT.
Thank you, really.
NAH... I REALLY DIDN'T DO ANYTHING IN THE END.

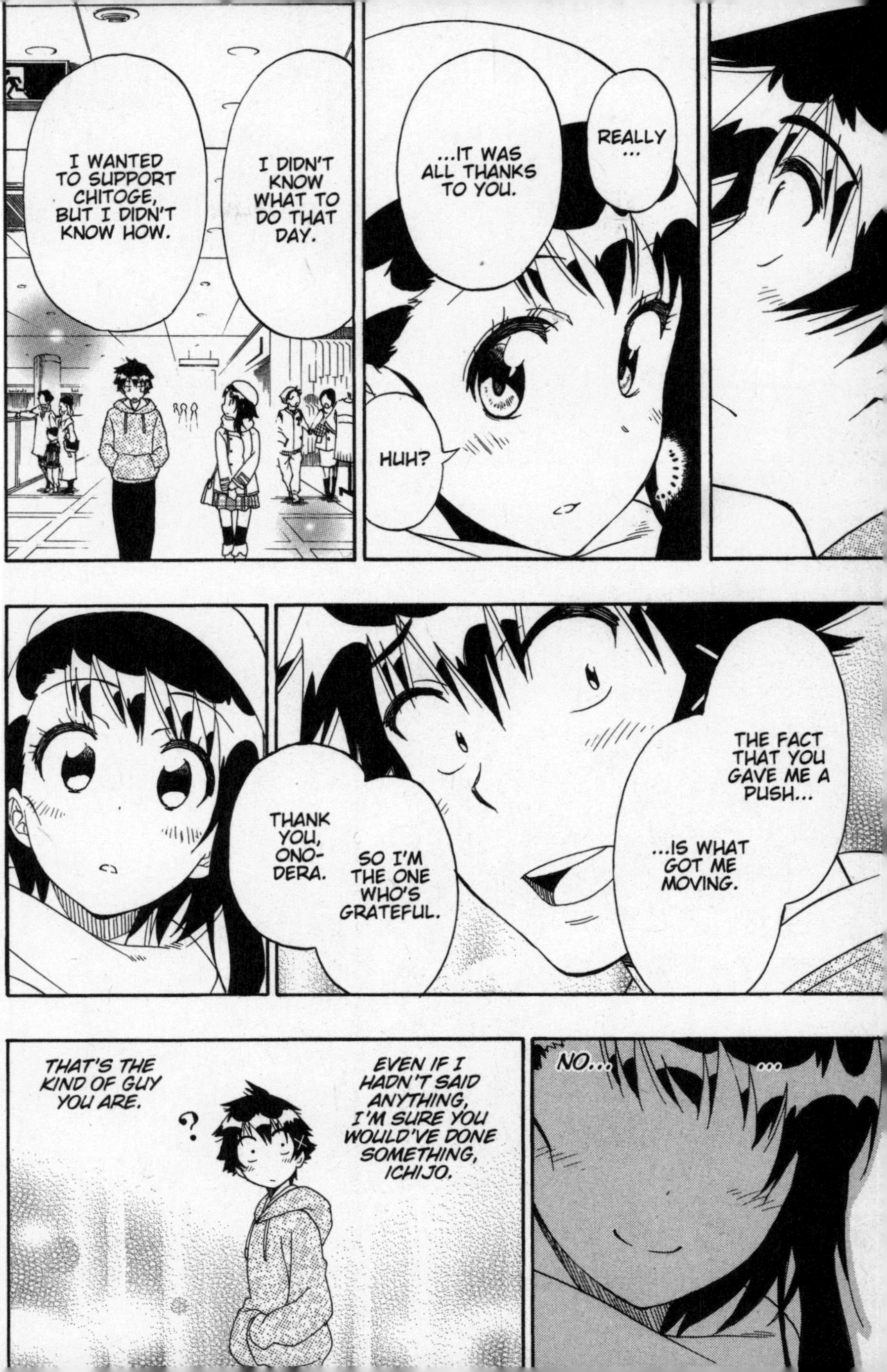
REALLY...
...IT WAS ALL THANKS TO YOU.
HUH?
I DIDN'T KNOW WHAT TO DO THAT DAY.
I WANTED TO SUPPORT CHITOGE, BUT I DIDN'T KNOW HOW.
THE FACT THAT YOU GAVE ME A PUSH...
...IS WHAT GOT ME MOVING.
SO I'M THE ONE WHO'S GRATEFUL.
THANK YOU, ONO-DERA.
...
NO...
EVEN IF I HADN'T SAID ANYTHING, I'M SURE YOU WOULD'VE DONE SOMETHING, ICHIJO.
THAT'S THE KIND OF GUY YOU ARE.
?

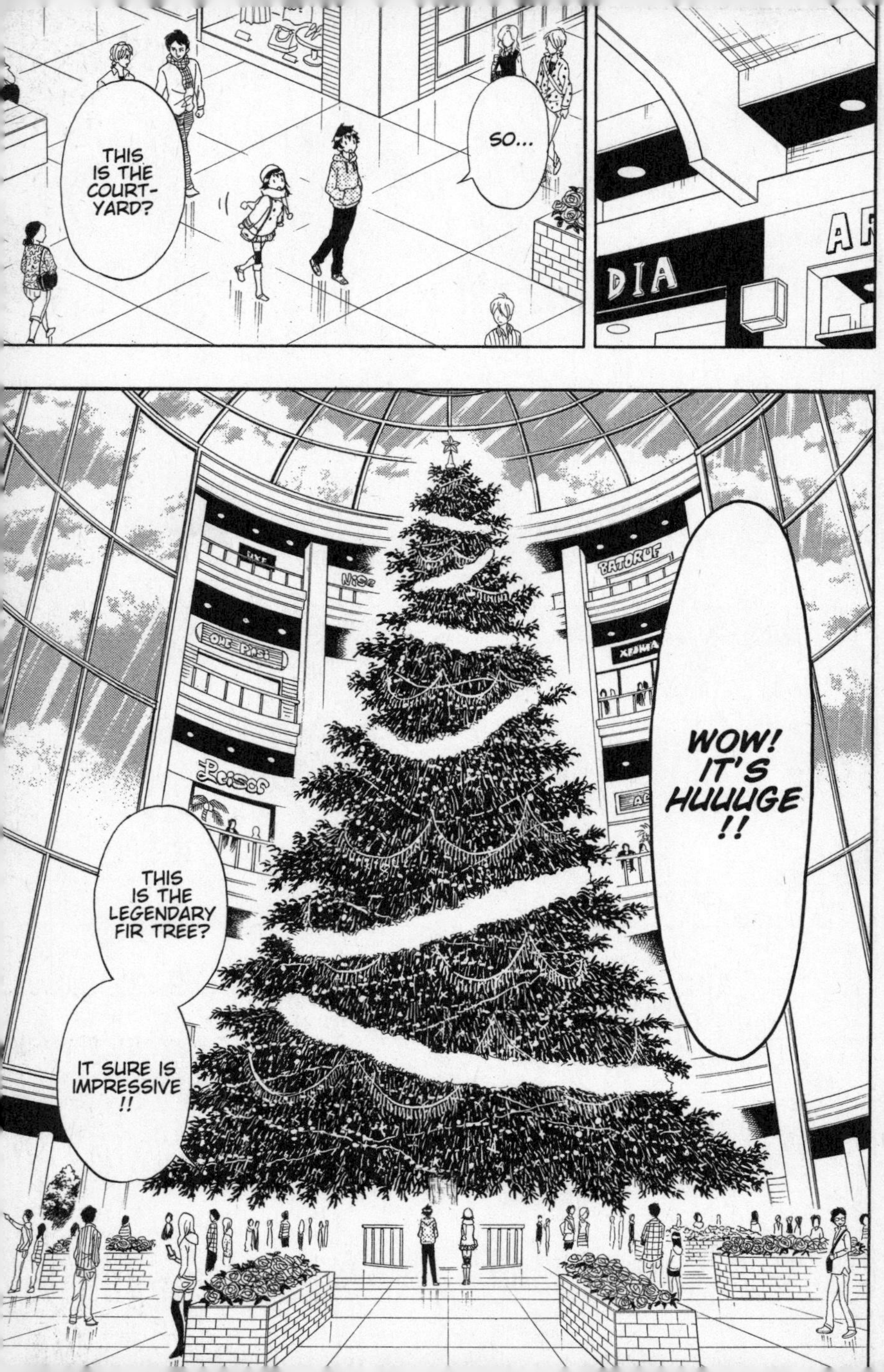
DIA
SO...
THIS IS THE COURT-YARD?
WOW! IT'S HUUUGE !!
THIS IS THE LEGENDARY FIR TREE?
IT SURE IS IMPRESSIVE !!

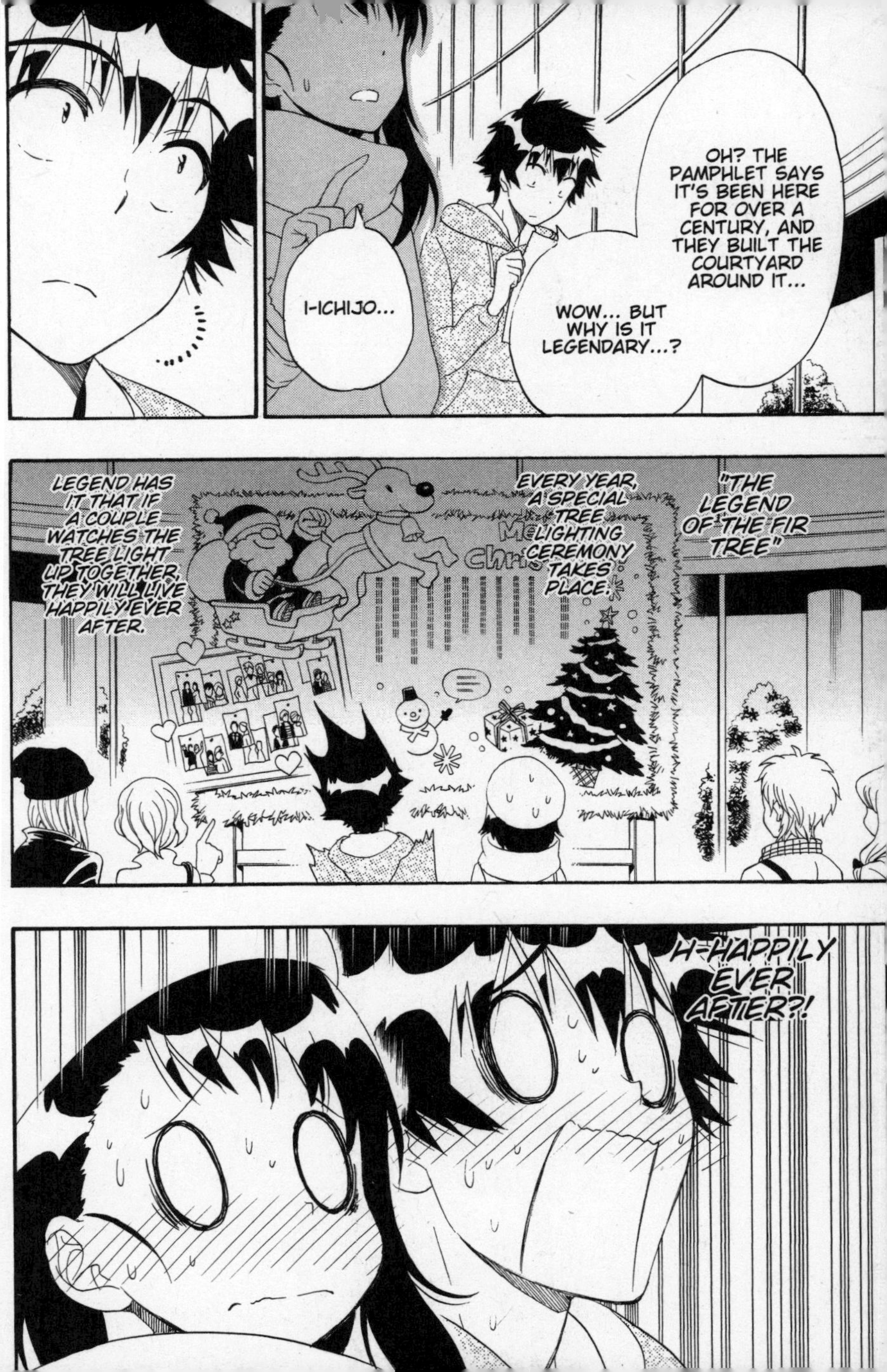
OH? THE PAMPHLET SAYS IT'S BEEN HERE FOR OVER A CENTURY, AND THEY BUILT THE COURTYARD AROUND IT...
WOW... BUT WHY IS IT LEGENDARY...?
I-ICHIJO...
"THE LEGEND OF THE FIR TREE"
EVERY YEAR, A SPECIAL TREE LIGHTING CEREMONY TAKES PLACE.
LEGEND HAS IT THAT IF A COUPLE WATCHES THE TREE LIGHT UP TOGETHER, THEY WILL LIVE HAPPILY EVER AFTER.
H-HAPPILY EVER AFTER?!

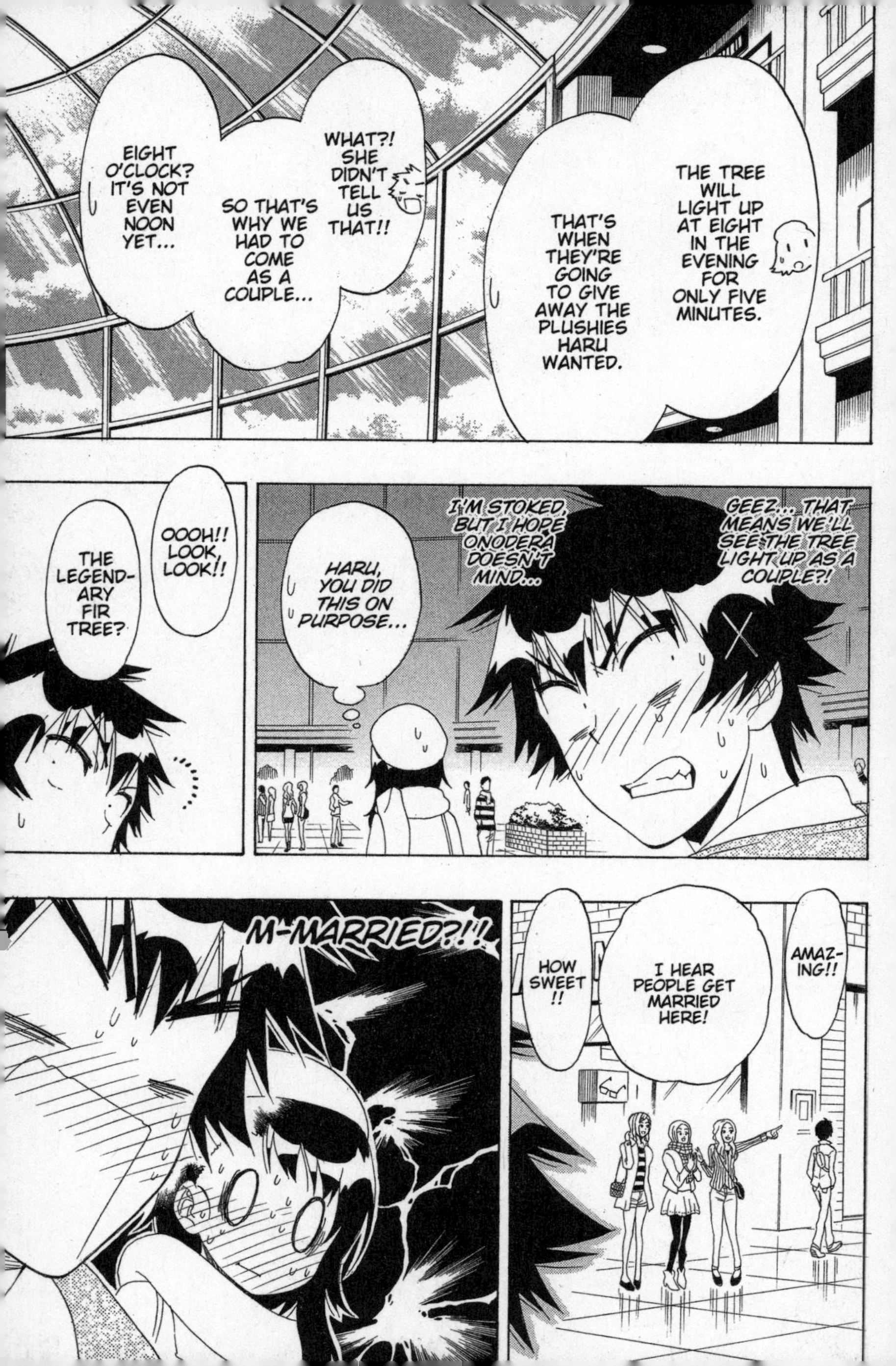
THE TREE WILL LIGHT UP AT EIGHT IN THE EVENING FOR ONLY FIVE MINUTES.
THAT'S WHEN THEY'RE GOING TO GIVE AWAY THE PLUSHIES HARU WANTED.
WHAT?! SHE DIDN'T TELL US THAT!!
SO THAT'S WHY WE HAD TO COME AS A COUPLE...
EIGHT O'CLOCK? IT'S NOT EVEN NOON YET...
GEEZ... THAT MEANS WE'LL SEE THE TREE LIGHT UP AS A COUPLE?!
I'M STOKED, BUT I HOPE ONODERA DOESN'T MIND...
HARU, YOU DID THIS ON PURPOSE...
OOOH!! LOOK, LOOK!!
THE LEGENDARY FIR TREE?
AMAZ-ING!!
I HEAR PEOPLE GET MARRIED HERE!
HOW SWEET!!
M-MARRIED?!!

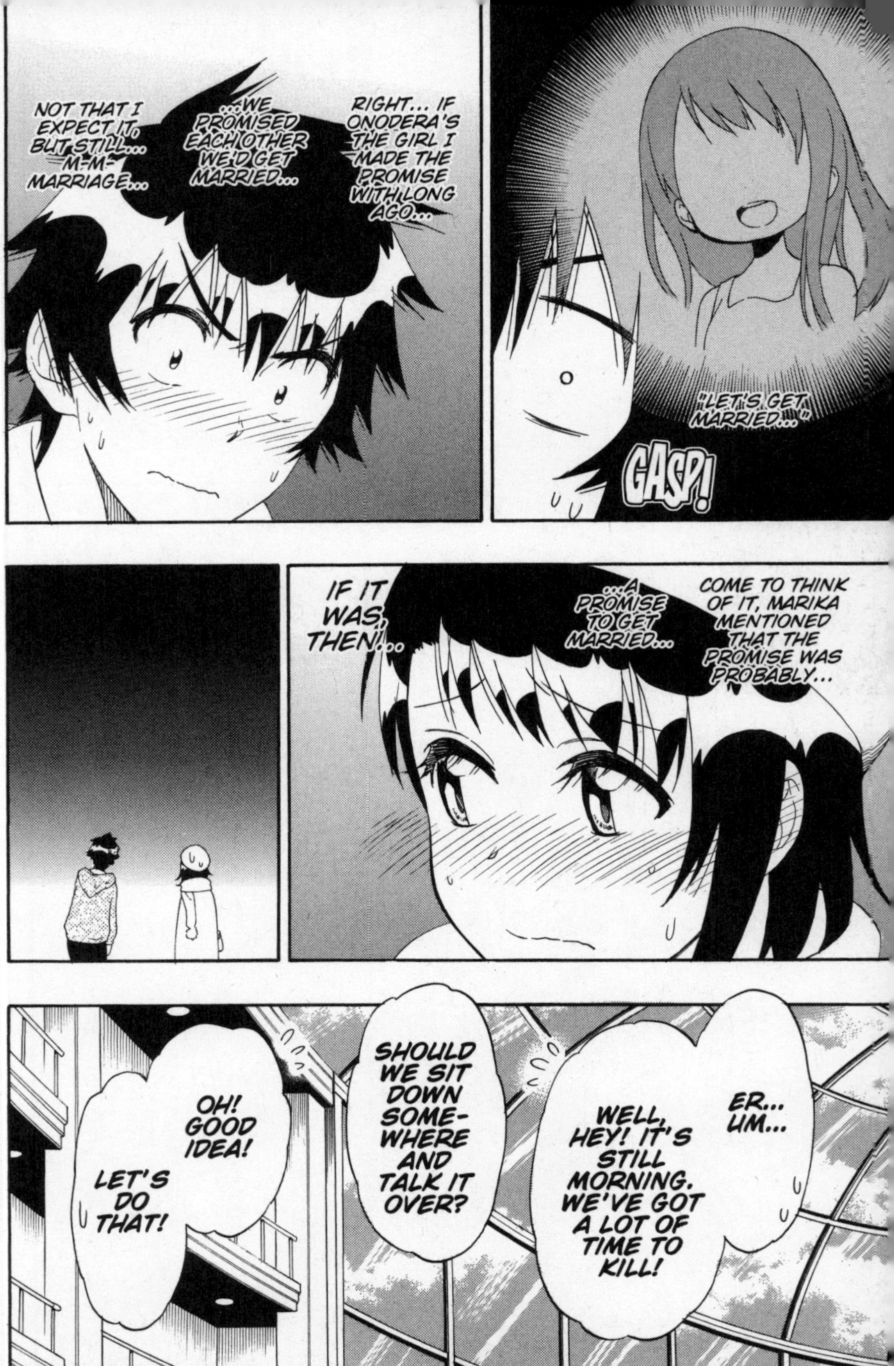
"LET'S GET MARRIED..."
GASP!
RIGHT... IF ONODERA'S THE GIRL I MADE THE PROMISE WITH LONG AGO...
...WE PROMISED EACH OTHER WE'D GET MARRIED...
NOT THAT I EXPECT IT, BUT STILL... M-M-MARRIAGE...
COME TO THINK OF IT, MARIKA MENTIONED THAT THE PROMISE WAS PROBABLY...
...A PROMISE TO GET MARRIED...
IF IT WAS, THEN!...
ER... UM...
WELL, HEY! IT'S STILL MORNING. WE'VE GOT A LOT OF TIME TO KILL!
SHOULD WE SIT DOWN SOME-WHERE AND TALK IT OVER?
OH! GOOD IDEA!
LET'S DO THAT!

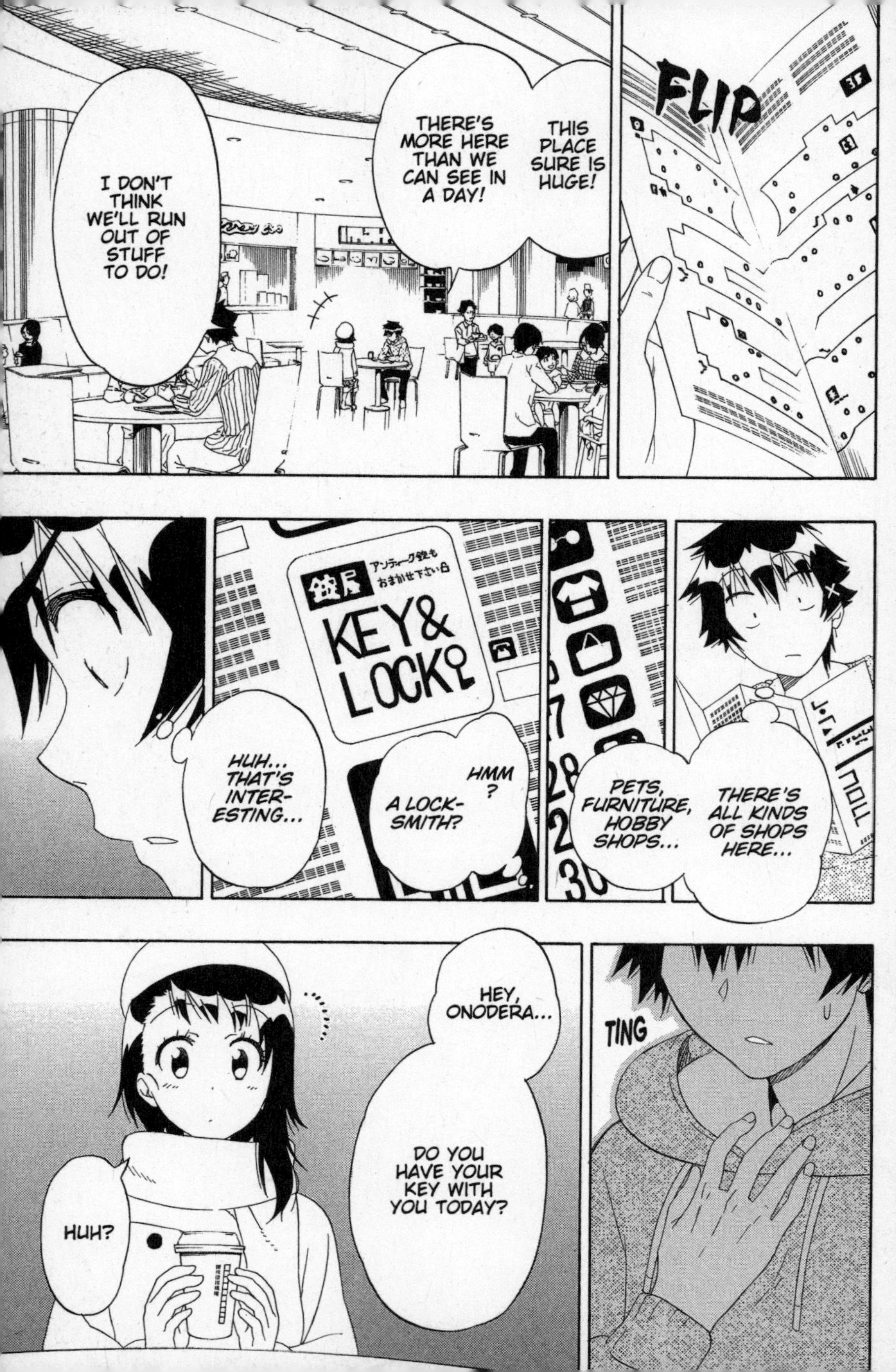
FLIP
THIS PLACE SURE IS HUGE!
THERE'S MORE HERE THAN WE CAN SEE IN A DAY!
I DON'T THINK WE'LL RUN OUT OF STUFF TO DO!
THERE'S ALL KINDS OF SHOPS HERE...
PETS, FURNITURE, HOBBY SHOPS...
KEY& LOCK
HMM?
A LOCKSMITH?
HUH... THAT'S INTERESTING...
TING
HEY, ONODERA...
DO YOU HAVE YOUR KEY WITH YOU TODAY?
HUH?

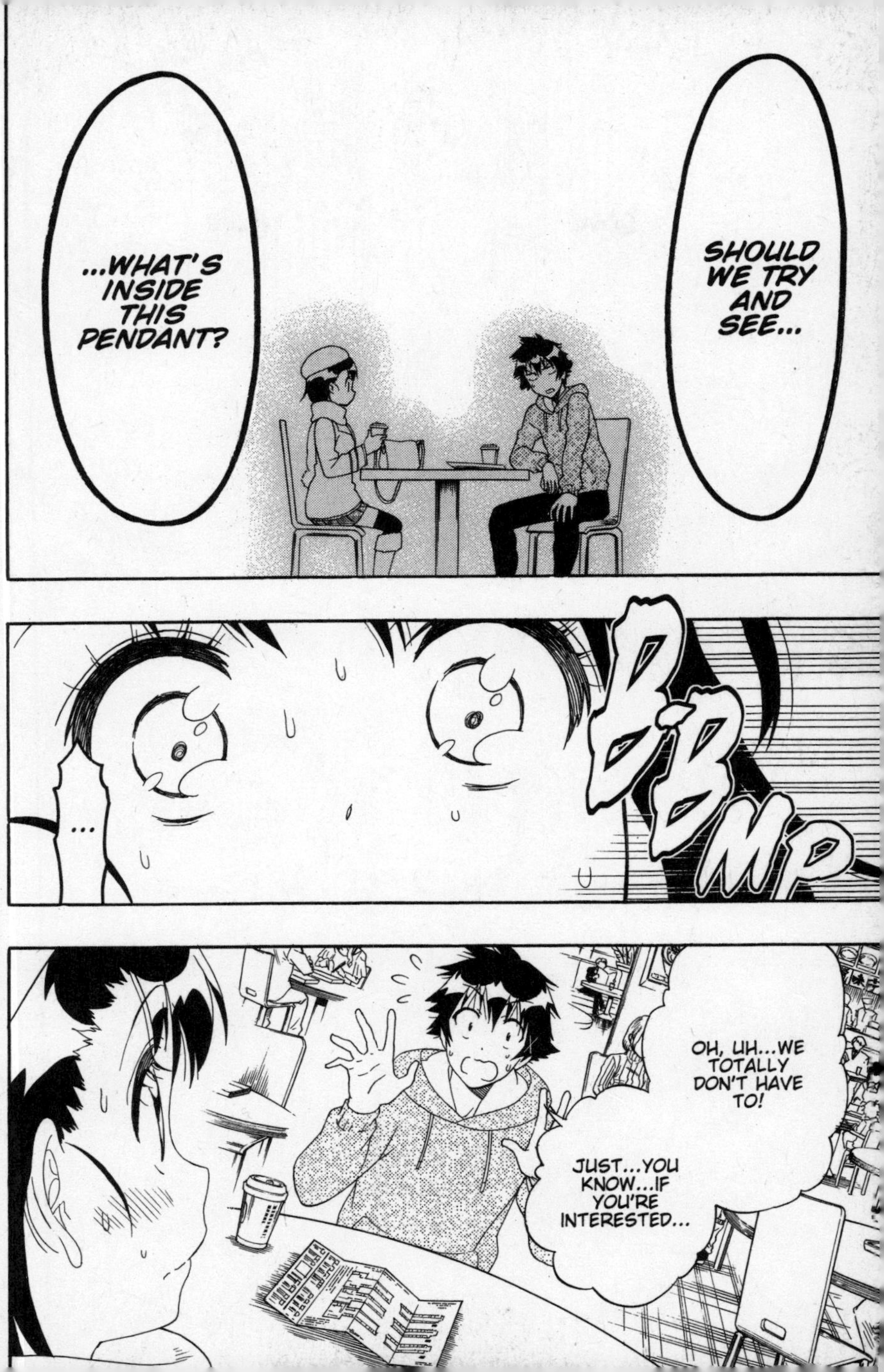

SHOULD WE TRY AND SEE...
...WHAT'S INSIDE THIS PENDANT?
BBMP
...
OH, UH...WE TOTALLY DON'T HAVE TO!
JUST...YOU KNOW...IF YOU'RE INTERESTED...

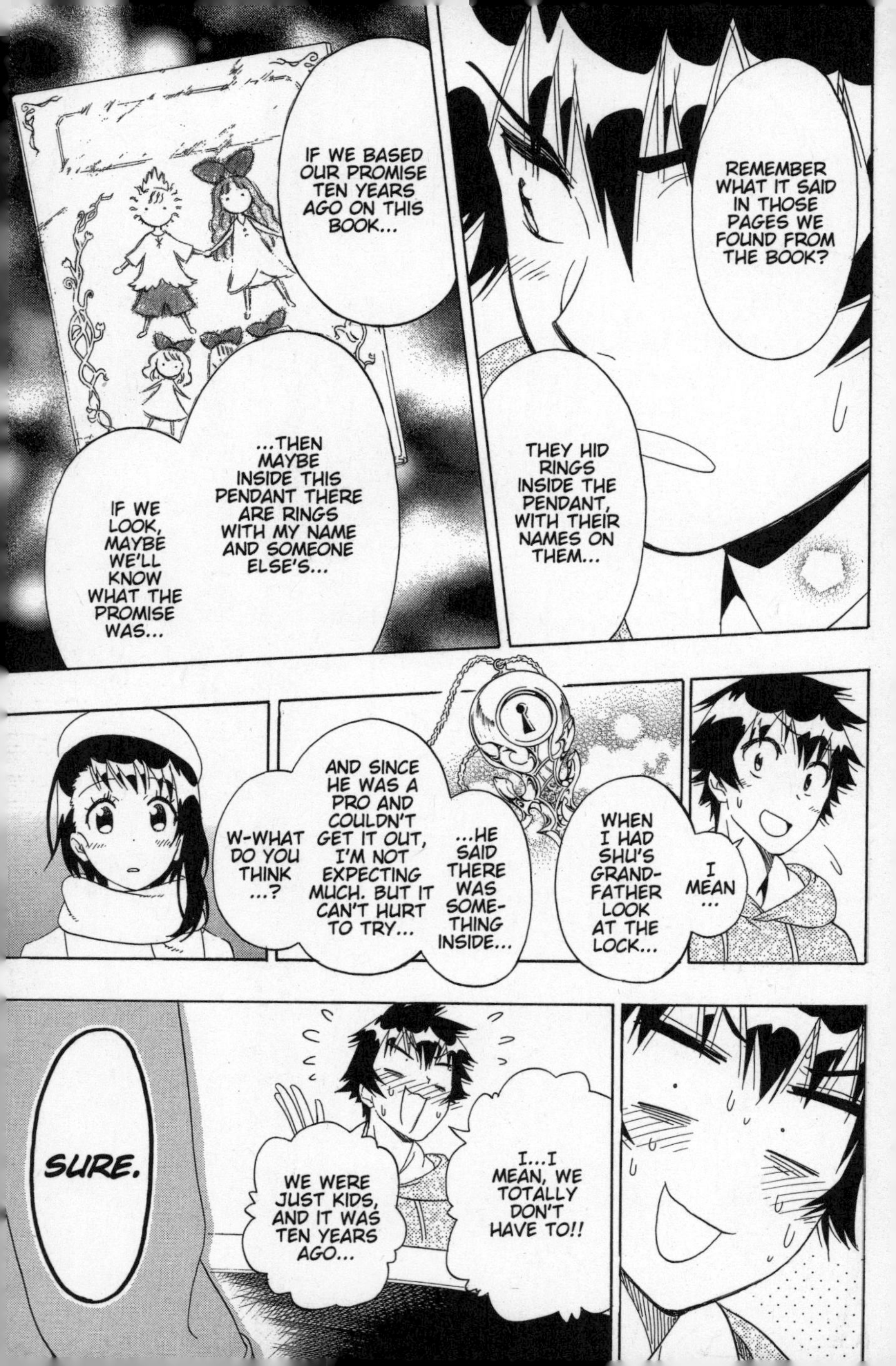
REMEMBER WHAT IT SAID IN THOSE PAGES WE FOUND FROM THE BOOK?
THEY HID RINGS INSIDE THE PENDANT, WITH THEIR NAMES ON THEM...
IF WE BASED OUR PROMISE TEN YEARS AGO ON THIS BOOK...
...THEN MAYBE INSIDE THIS PENDANT THERE ARE RINGS WITH MY NAME AND SOMEONE ELSE'S...
IF WE LOOK, MAYBE WE'LL KNOW WHAT THE PROMISE WAS...
I MEAN...
WHEN I HAD SHU'S GRANDFATHER LOOK AT THE LOCK...
...HE SAID THERE WAS SOMETHING INSIDE...
AND SINCE HE WAS A PRO AND COULDN'T GET IT OUT, I'M NOT EXPECTING MUCH. BUT IT CAN'T HURT TO TRY...
W-WHAT DO YOU THINK...?
I...I MEAN, WE TOTALLY DON'T HAVE TO!!
WE WERE JUST KIDS, AND IT WAS TEN YEARS AGO...
SURE.

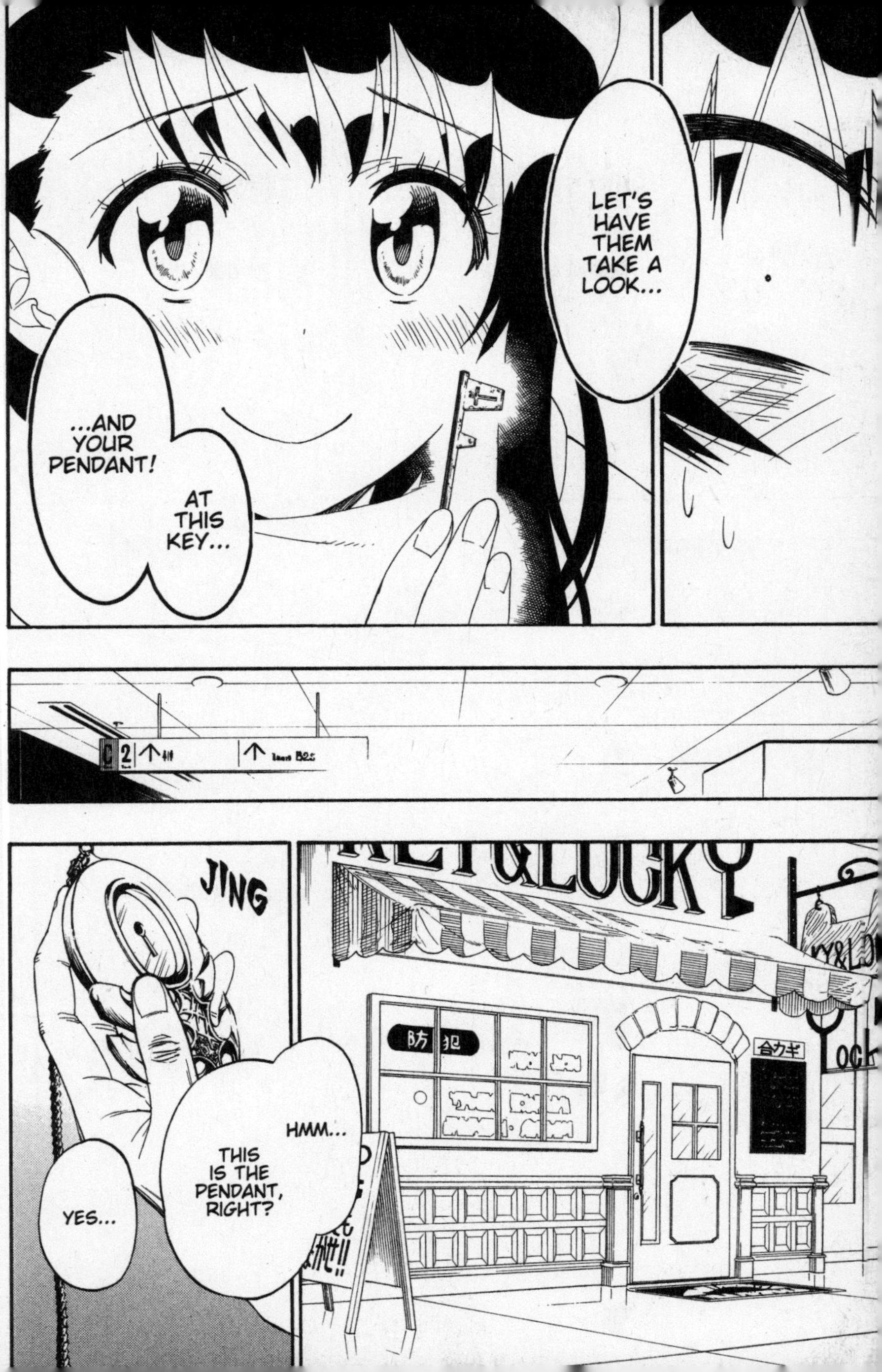
LET'S HAVE THEM TAKE A LOOK...
AT THIS KEY...
...AND YOUR PENDANT!
防犯
合カギ
JING
HMM...
THIS IS THE PENDANT, RIGHT?
YES...

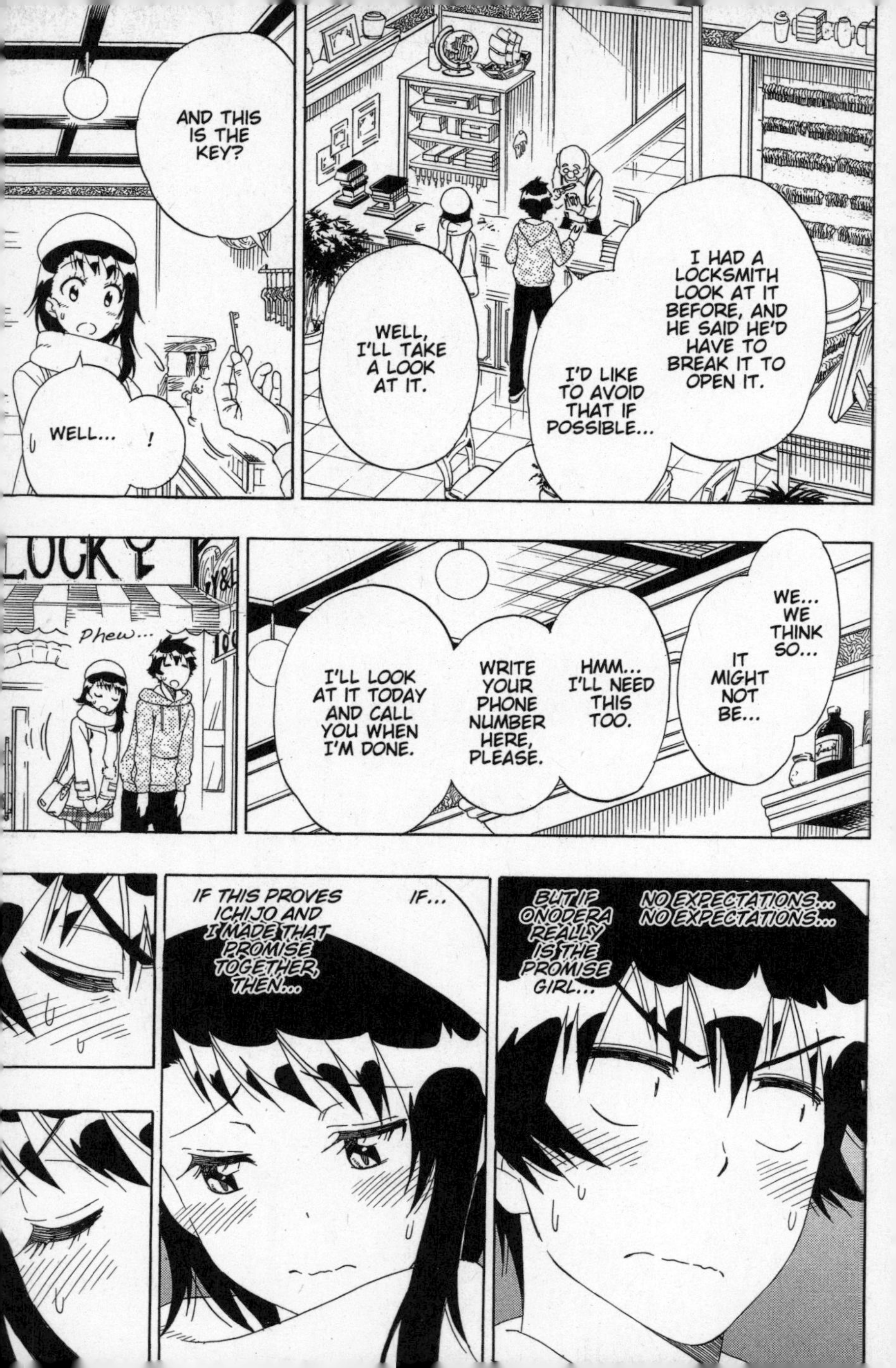
I HAD A LOCKSMITH LOOK AT IT BEFORE, AND HE SAID HE'D HAVE TO BREAK IT TO OPEN IT.
I'D LIKE TO AVOID THAT IF POSSIBLE...
WELL, I'LL TAKE A LOOK AT IT.
AND THIS IS THE KEY?
WELL... !
WE... WE THINK SO...
IT MIGHT NOT BE...
HMM... I'LL NEED THIS TOO.
WRITE YOUR PHONE NUMBER HERE, PLEASE.
I'LL LOOK AT IT TODAY AND CALL YOU WHEN I'M DONE.
LOCK
Phew...
NO EXPECTATIONS... NO EXPECTATIONS...
BUT IF ONODERA REALLY IS THE PROMISE GIRL...
IF...
IF THIS PROVES ICHIJO AND I MADE THAT PROMISE TOGETHER, THEN...

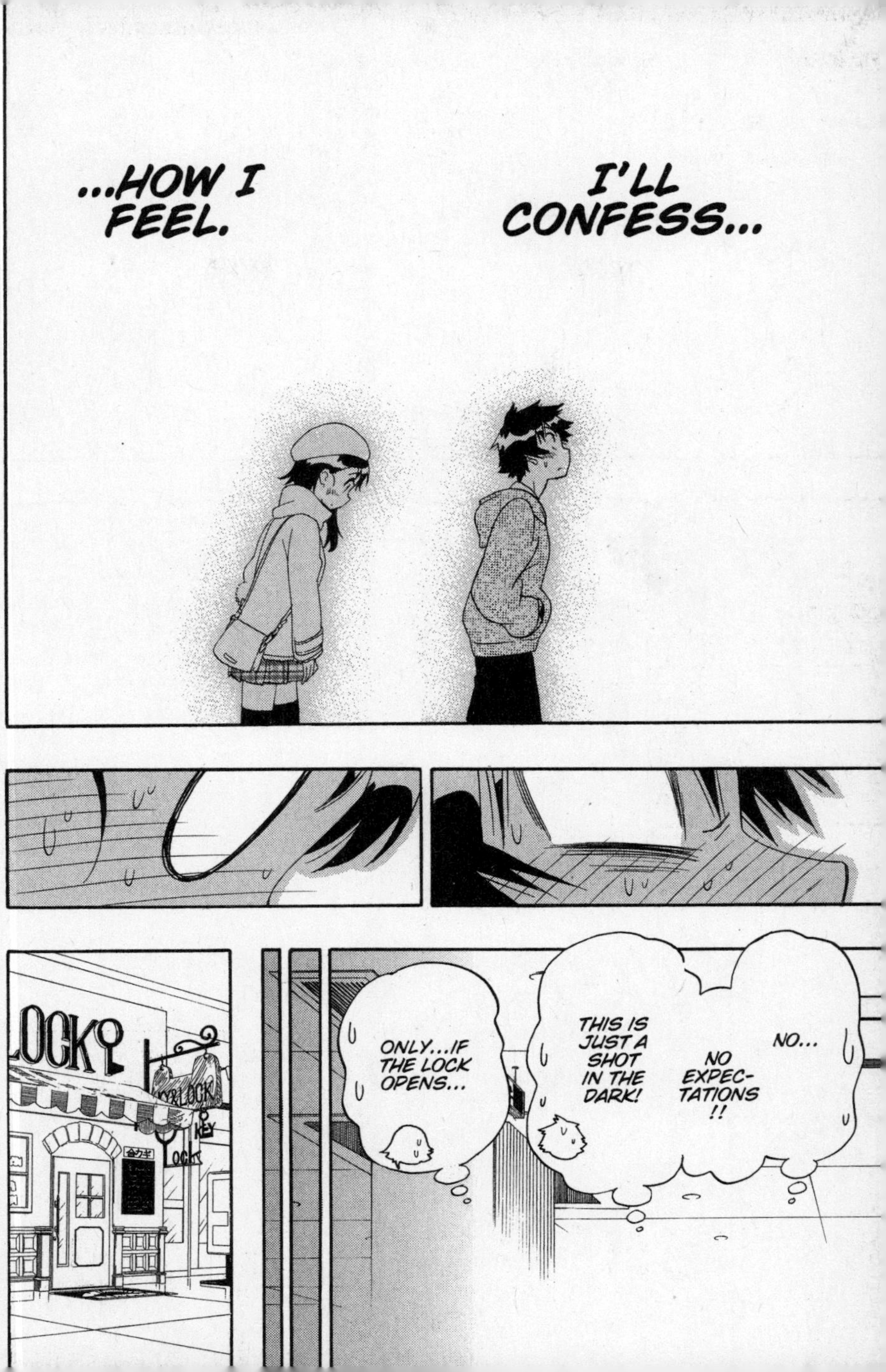
I'LL CONFESS...
...HOW I FEEL.
NO...
NO EXPECTATIONS!!
THIS IS JUST A SHOT IN THE DARK!
ONLY...IF THE LOCK OPENS...
LOCK
KEY
合カギ

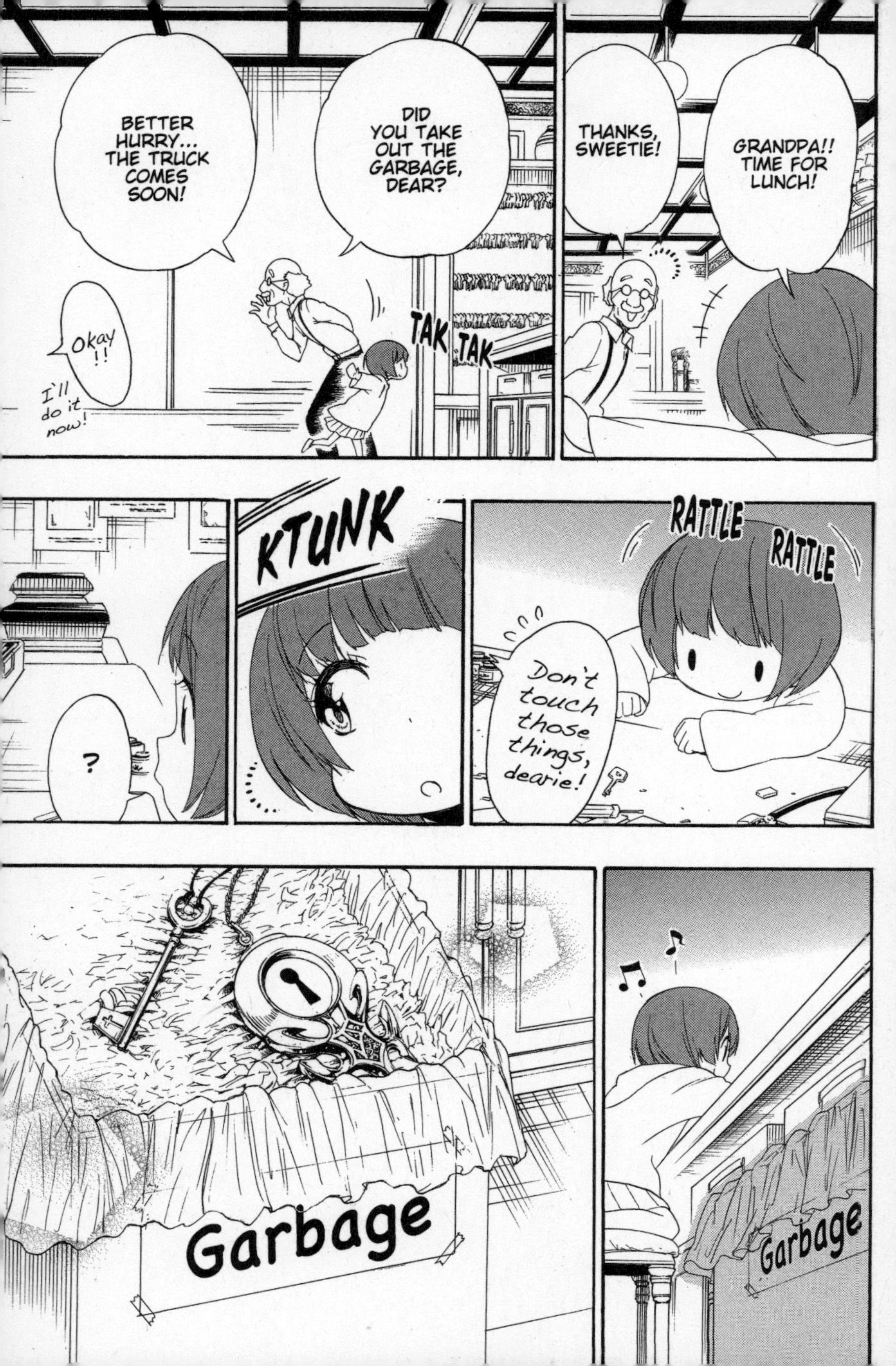
GRANDPA!! TIME FOR LUNCH!
THANKS, SWEETIE!
DID YOU TAKE OUT THE GARBAGE, DEAR?
BETTER HURRY... THE TRUCK COMES SOON!
TAK TAK
Okay!!
I'll do it now!
RATTLE RATTLE
Don't touch those things, dearie!
KTUNK
?
Garbage
Garbage

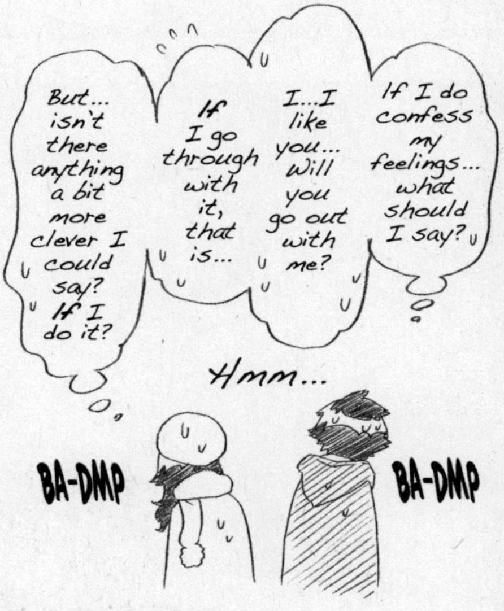
If I do confess my feelings... what should I say?
I...I like you... Will you go out with me?
If I go through with it, that is...
But... isn't there anything a bit more clever I could say? If I do it?
Hmm...
BA-DMP
BA-DMP

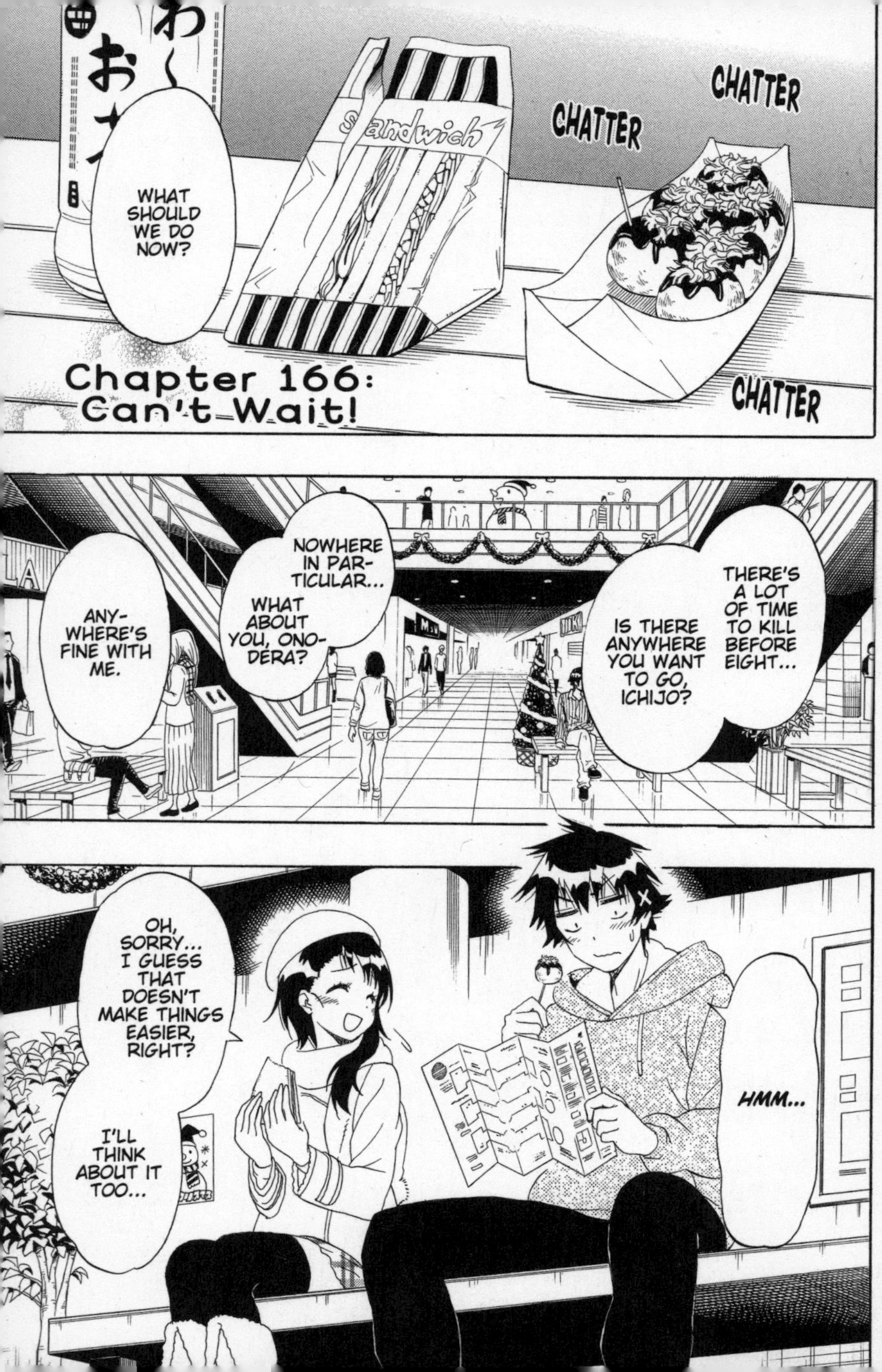
CHATTER
CHATTER
CHATTER
WHAT SHOULD WE DO NOW?
Chapter 166: Can't Wait!
THERE'S A LOT OF TIME TO KILL BEFORE EIGHT...
IS THERE ANYWHERE YOU WANT TO GO, ICHIJO?
NOWHERE IN PAR-TICULAR...
WHAT ABOUT YOU, ONO-DERA?
ANY-WHERE'S FINE WITH ME.
HMM...
OH, SORRY... I GUESS THAT DOESN'T MAKE THINGS EASIER, RIGHT?
I'LL THINK ABOUT IT TOO...

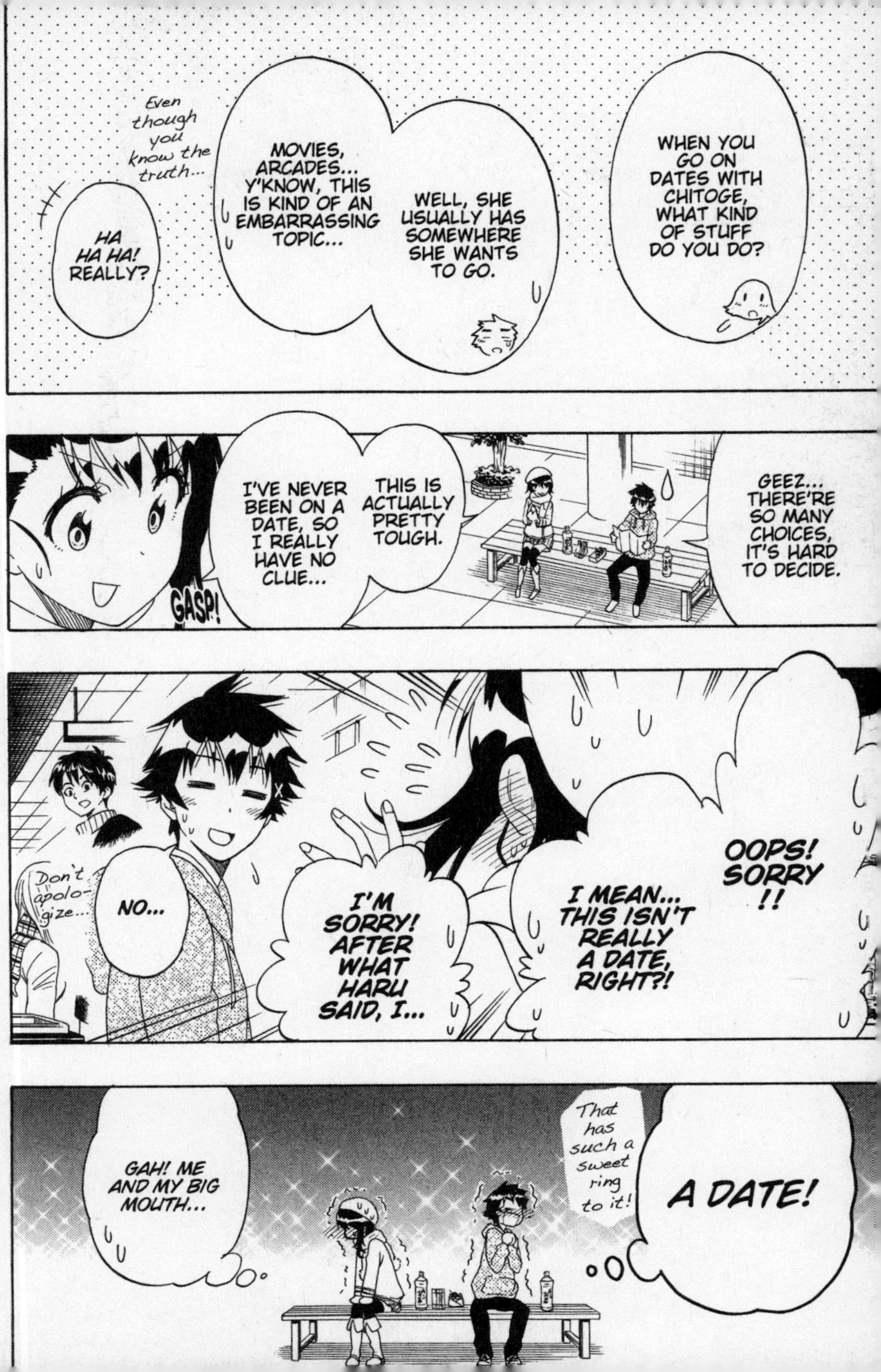

WHEN YOU GO ON DATES WITH CHITOGE, WHAT KIND OF STUFF DO YOU DO?
WELL, SHE USUALLY HAS SOMEWHERE SHE WANTS TO GO.
MOVIES, ARCADES... Y'KNOW, THIS IS KIND OF AN EMBARRASSING TOPIC...
Even though you know the truth...
HA HA HA! REALLY?
GEEZ... THERE'RE SO MANY CHOICES, IT'S HARD TO DECIDE.
THIS IS ACTUALLY PRETTY TOUGH.
I'VE NEVER BEEN ON A DATE, SO I REALLY HAVE NO CLUE...
GASP!
OOPS! SORRY!!
I MEAN... THIS ISN'T REALLY A DATE, RIGHT?!
I'M SORRY! AFTER WHAT HARU SAID, I...
NO...
Don't apologize...
A DATE!
That has such a sweet ring to it!
GAH! ME AND MY BIG MOUTH...

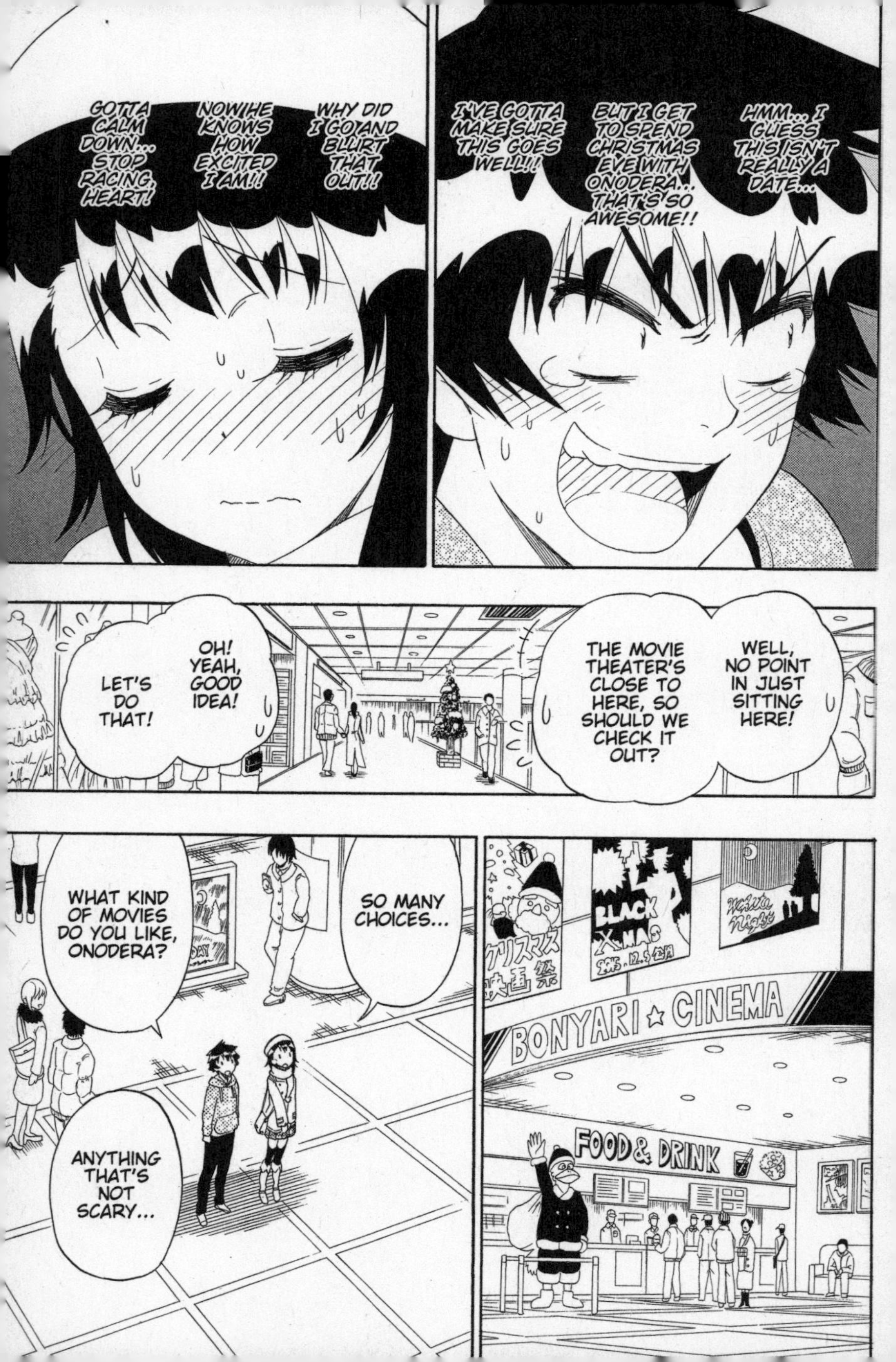
HMM... I GUESS THIS ISN'T REALLY A DATE...
BUT I GET TO SPEND CHRISTMAS EVE WITH ONODERA... THAT'S SO AWESOME!!
I'VE GOTTA MAKE SURE THIS GOES WELL!!
WHY DID I GO AND BLURT THAT OUT!!
NOW HE KNOWS HOW EXCITED I AM!!
GOTTA CALM DOWN... STOP RACING, HEART!
WELL, NO POINT IN JUST SITTING HERE!
THE MOVIE THEATER'S CLOSE TO HERE, SO SHOULD WE CHECK IT OUT?
OH! YEAH, GOOD IDEA!
LET'S DO THAT!
クリスマス映画祭
BLACK
BONYARI ☆ CINEMA
FOOD & DRINK
SO MANY CHOICES...
WHAT KIND OF MOVIES DO YOU LIKE, ONODERA?
ANYTHING THAT'S NOT SCARY...

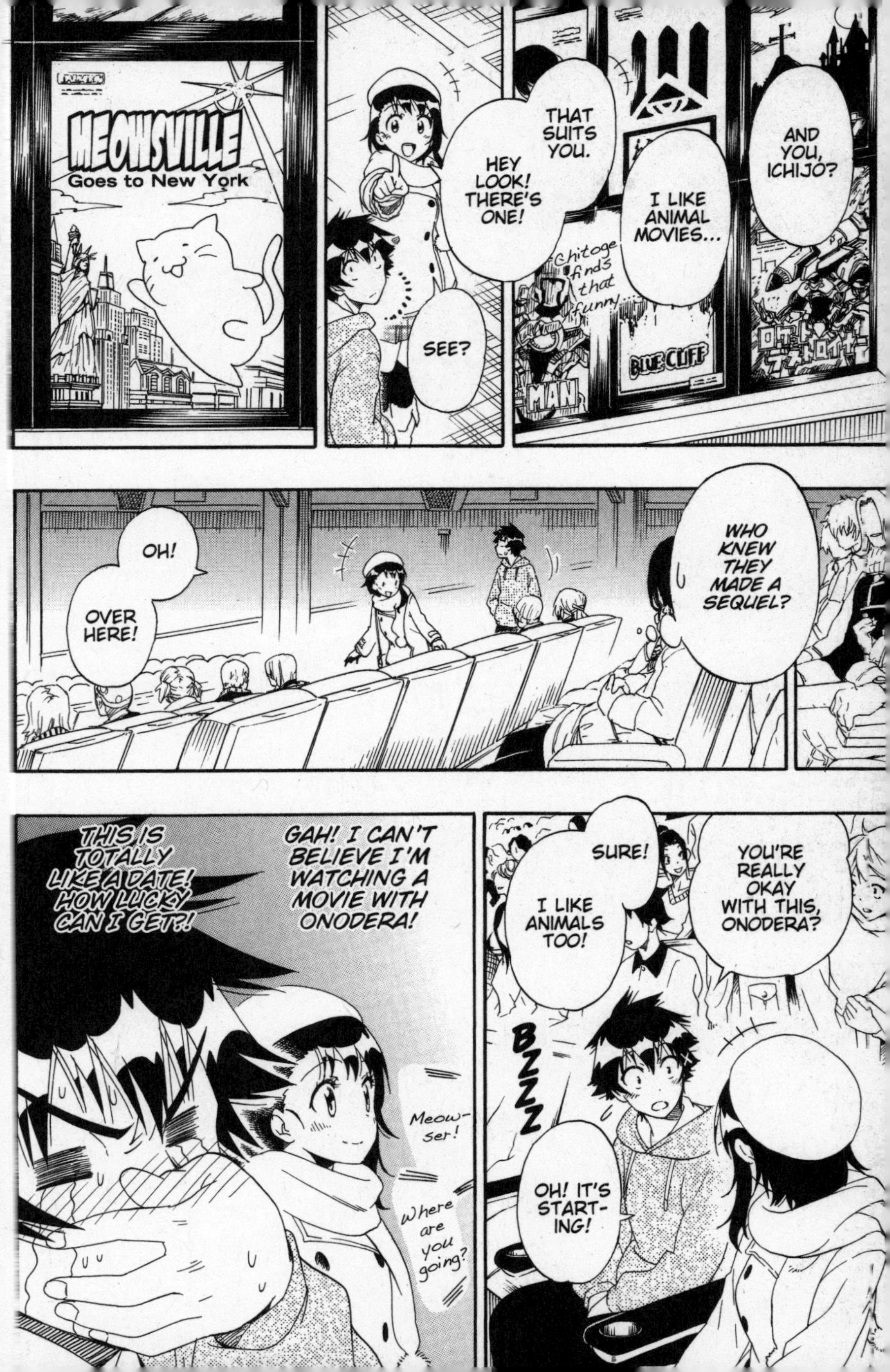
AND YOU, ICHIJO?
I LIKE ANIMAL MOVIES...
THAT SUITS YOU.
Chitoge finds that funny...
BLUE CLIFF
MAN
HEY LOOK! THERE'S ONE!
SEE?
MEOWSVILLE
Goes to New York
WHO KNEW THEY MADE A SEQUEL?
OH!
OVER HERE!
YOU'RE REALLY OKAY WITH THIS, ONODERA?
SURE!
I LIKE ANIMALS TOO!
BZZZ
OH! IT'S STARTING!
GAH! I CAN'T BELIEVE I'M WATCHING A MOVIE WITH ONODERA!
THIS IS TOTALLY LIKE A DATE! HOW LUCKY CAN I GET?!
Meowser!
Where are you going?

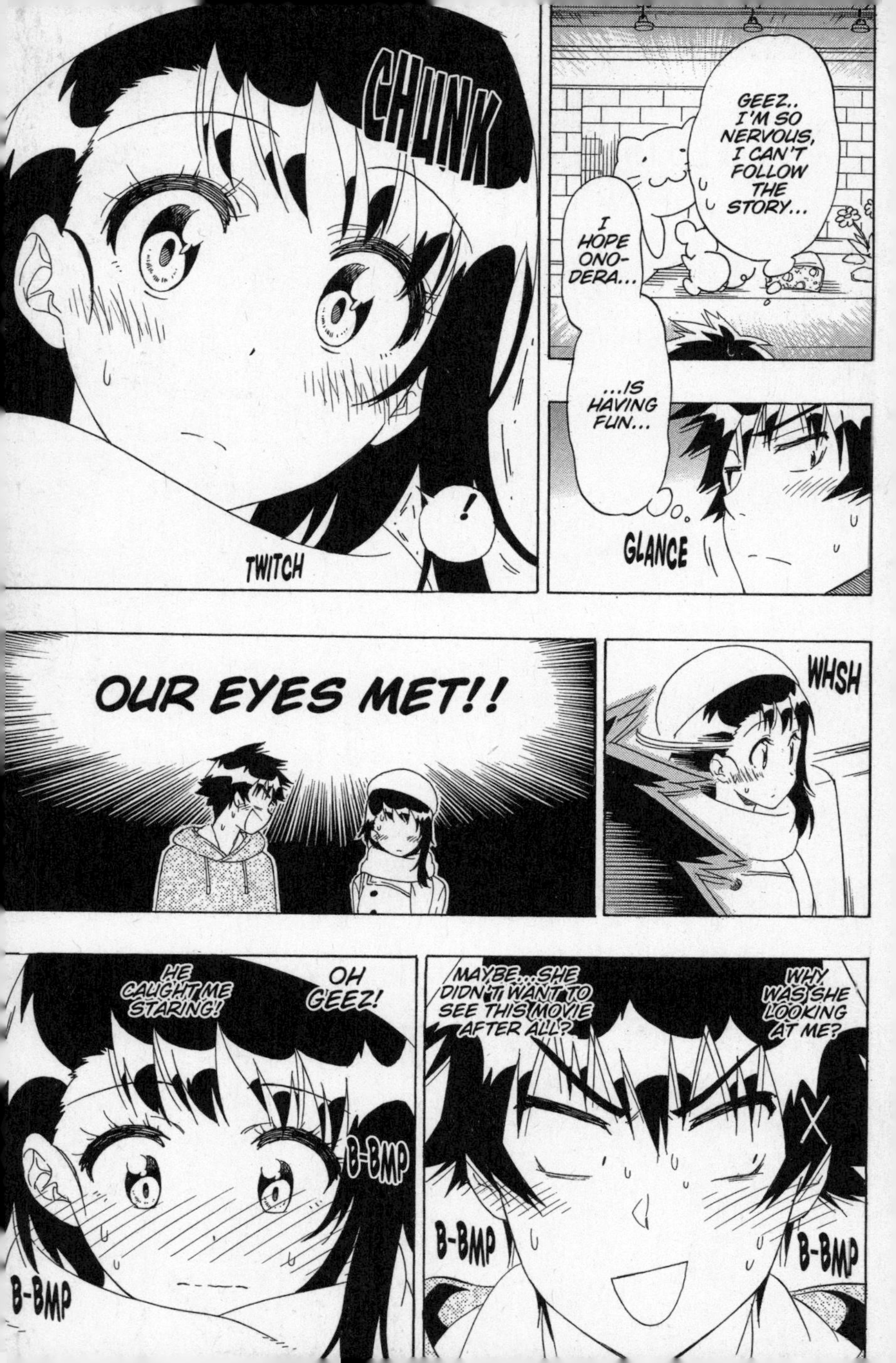
GEEZ.. I'M SO NERVOUS, I CAN'T FOLLOW THE STORY...
I HOPE ONO-DERA...
...IS HAVING FUN...
GLANCE
CHUNK
!
TWITCH
WHSH
OUR EYES MET!!
WHY WAS SHE LOOKING AT ME?
MAYBE... SHE DIDN'T WANT TO SEE THIS MOVIE AFTER ALL?
B-BMP
B-BMP
OH GEEZ!
HE CAUGHT ME STARING!
B-BMP
B-BMP

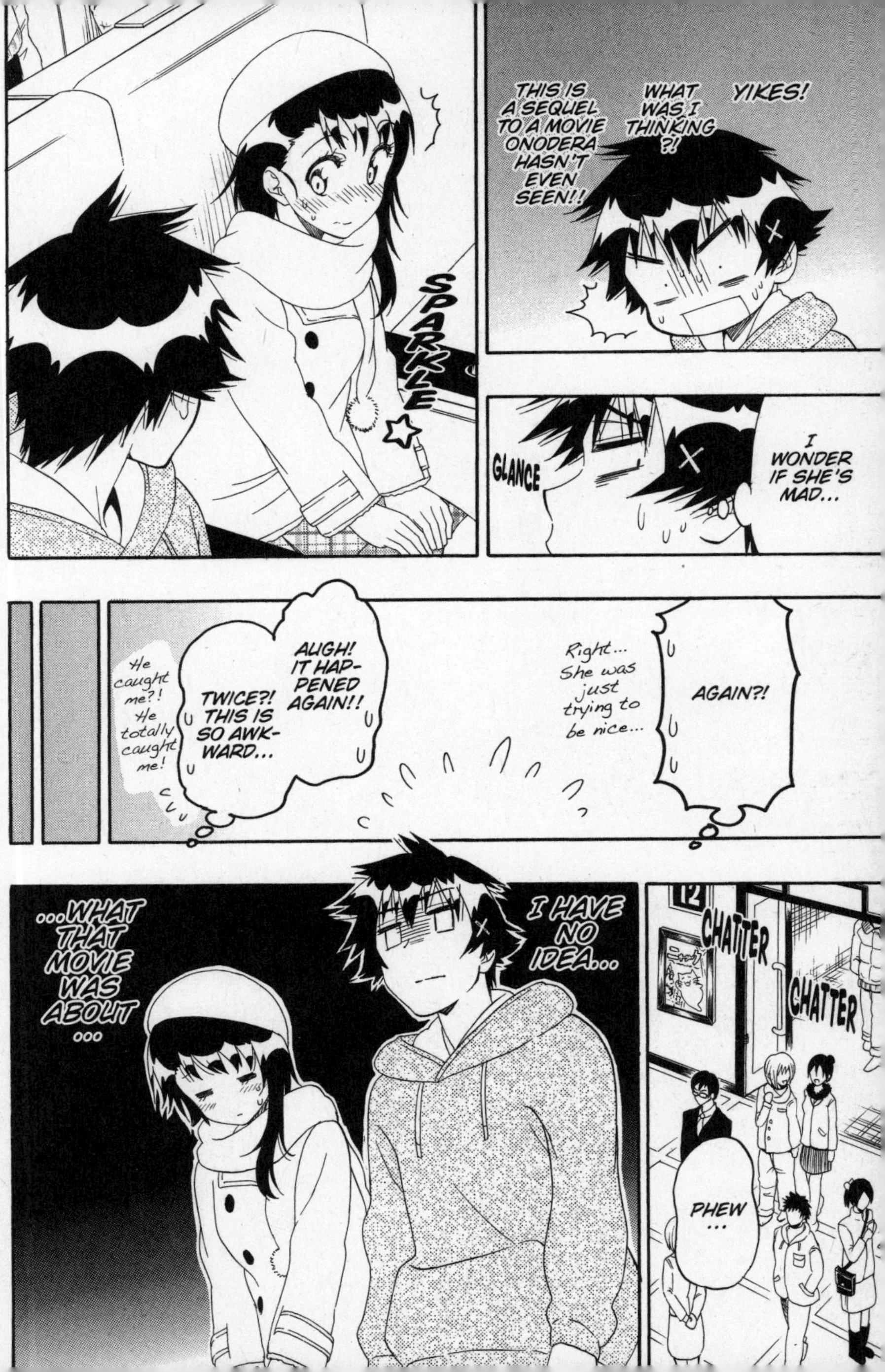
YIKES!
WHAT WAS I THINKING?!
THIS IS A SEQUEL TO A MOVIE ONODERA HASN'T EVEN SEEN!!
I WONDER IF SHE'S MAD...
GLANCE
SPARKLE
AGAIN?!
Right... She was just trying to be nice...
AUGH! IT HAPPENED AGAIN!!
TWICE?! THIS IS SO AWKWARD...
He caught me?! He totally caught me!
CHATTER
CHATTER
PHEW...
I HAVE NO IDEA...
...WHAT THAT MOVIE WAS ABOUT...

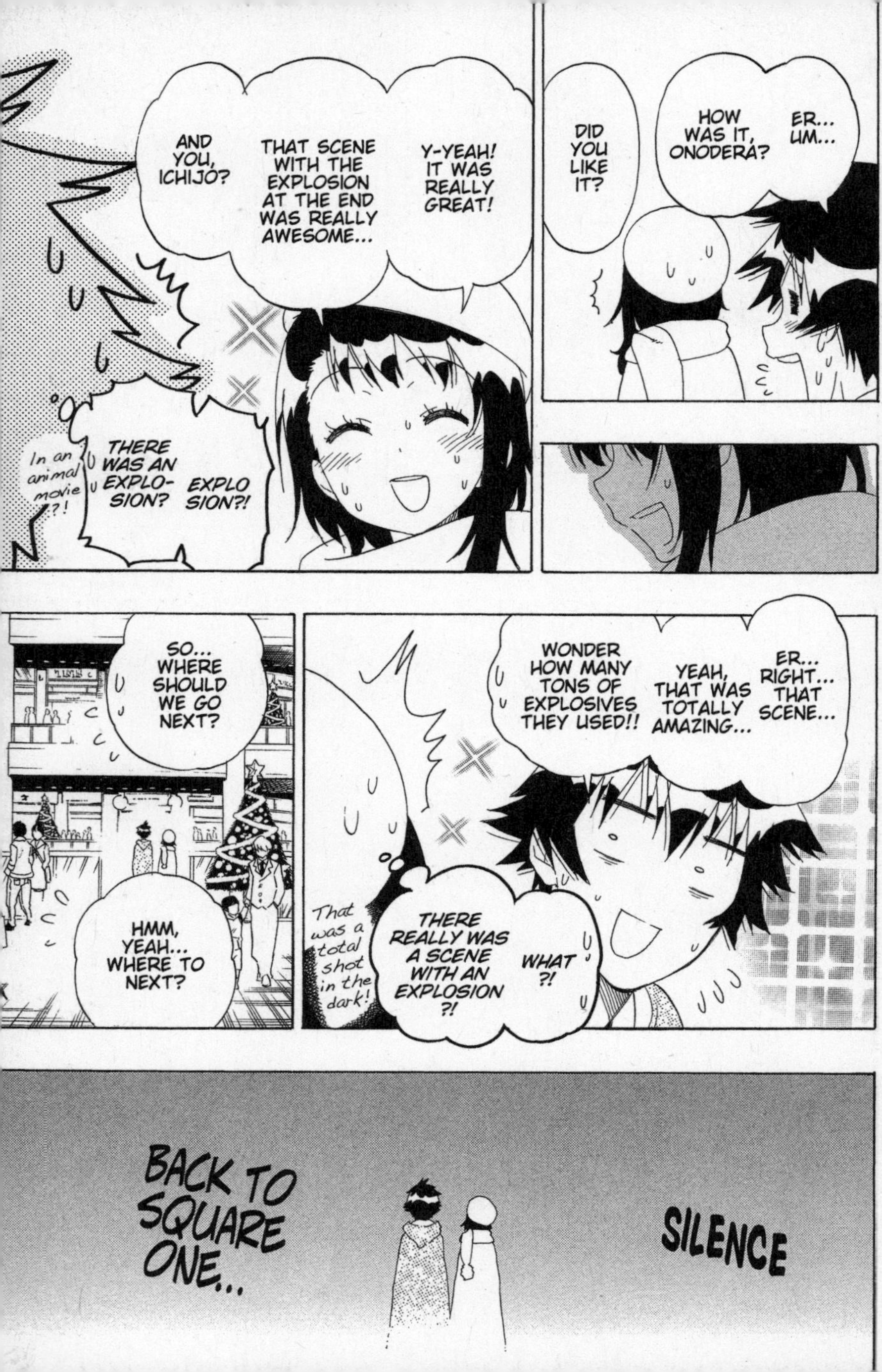

ER... UM...
HOW WAS IT, ONODERA?
DID YOU LIKE IT?
Y-YEAH! IT WAS REALLY GREAT!
THAT SCENE WITH THE EXPLOSION AT THE END WAS REALLY AWESOME...
AND YOU, ICHIJO?
EXPLOSION?!
THERE WAS AN EXPLOSION?
In an animal movie?!
ER... RIGHT... THAT SCENE...
YEAH, THAT WAS TOTALLY AMAZING...
WONDER HOW MANY TONS OF EXPLOSIVES THEY USED!!
WHAT?!
THERE REALLY WAS A SCENE WITH AN EXPLOSION?!
That was a total shot in the dark!
SO... WHERE SHOULD WE GO NEXT?
HMM, YEAH... WHERE TO NEXT?
SILENCE
BACK TO SQUARE ONE...

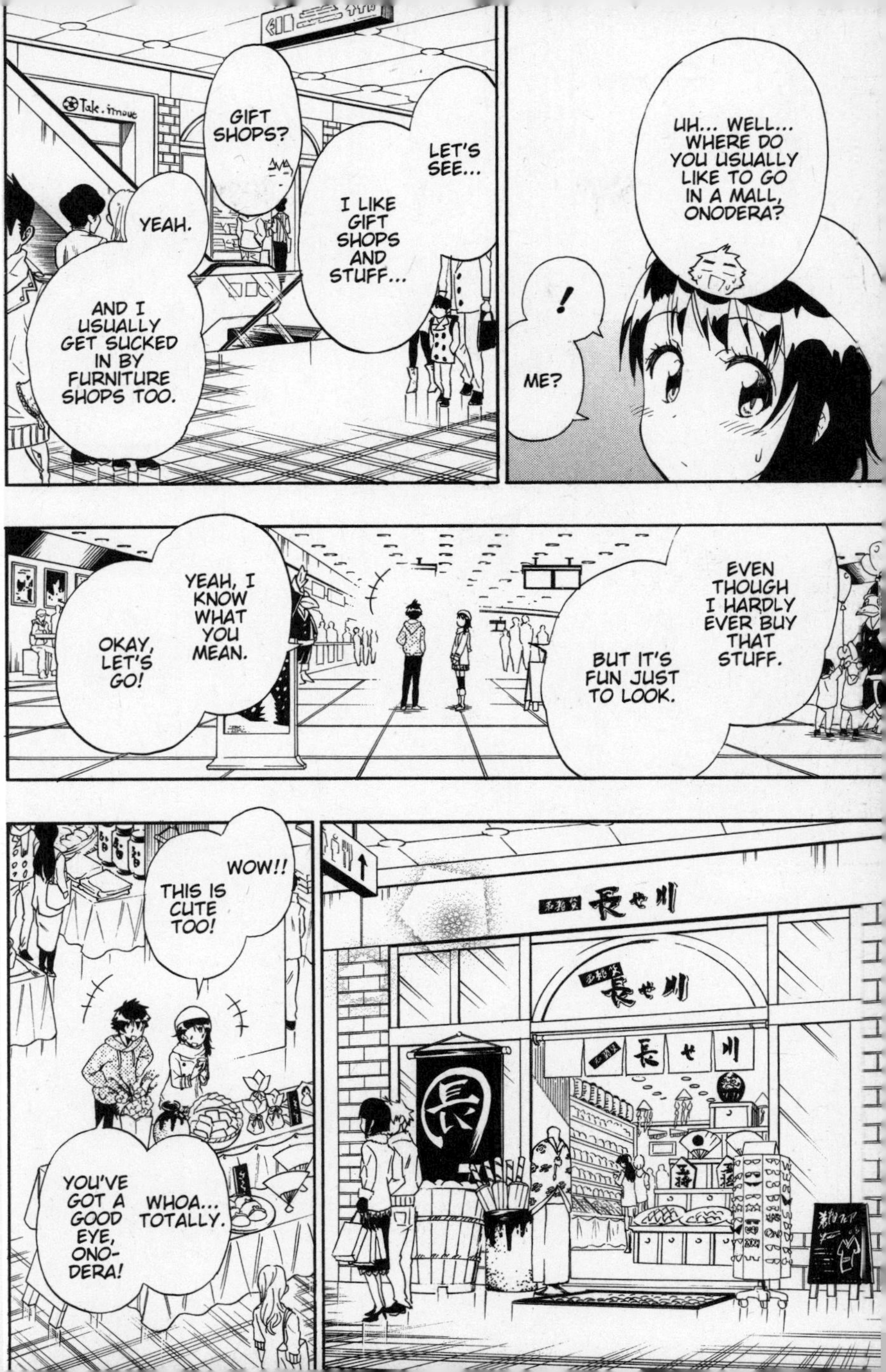
UH... WELL... WHERE DO YOU USUALLY LIKE TO GO IN A MALL, ONODERA?
!
ME?
LET'S SEE...
I LIKE GIFT SHOPS AND STUFF...
GIFT SHOPS?
YEAH.
AND I USUALLY GET SUCKED IN BY FURNITURE SHOPS TOO.
EVEN THOUGH I HARDLY EVER BUY THAT STUFF.
BUT IT'S FUN JUST TO LOOK.
YEAH, I KNOW WHAT YOU MEAN.
OKAY, LET'S GO!
WOW!!
THIS IS CUTE TOO!
WHOA... TOTALLY.
YOU'VE GOT A GOOD EYE, ONODERA!

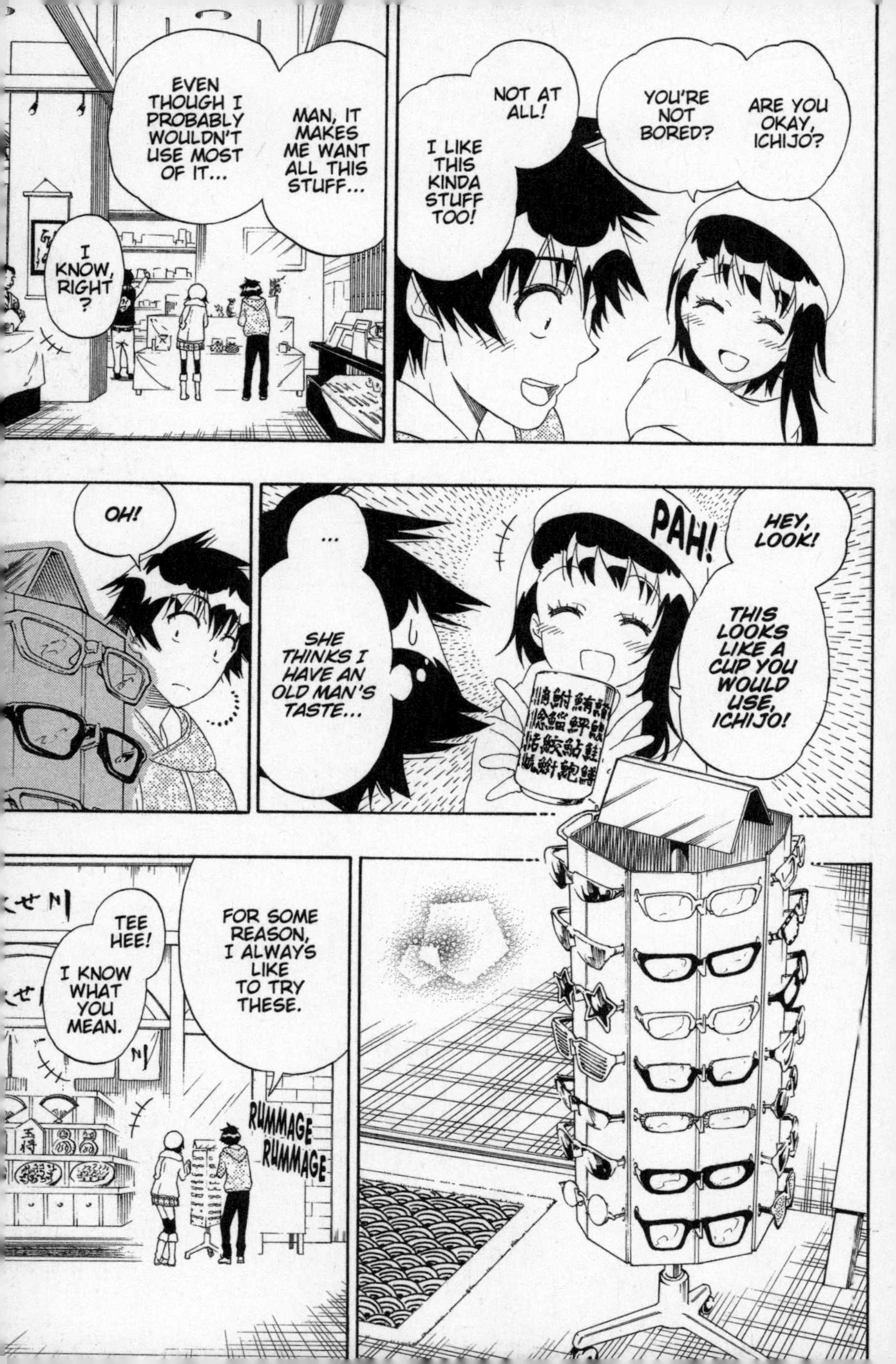
ARE YOU OKAY, ICHIJO?
YOU'RE NOT BORED?
NOT AT ALL!
I LIKE THIS KINDA STUFF TOO!
MAN, IT MAKES ME WANT ALL THIS STUFF...
EVEN THOUGH I PROBABLY WOULDN'T USE MOST OF IT...
I KNOW, RIGHT?
PAH!
HEY, LOOK!
THIS LOOKS LIKE A CUP YOU WOULD USE, ICHIJO!
...
SHE THINKS I HAVE AN OLD MAN'S TASTE...
OH!
FOR SOME REASON, I ALWAYS LIKE TO TRY THESE.
TEE HEE!
I KNOW WHAT YOU MEAN.
RUMMAGE RUMMAGE

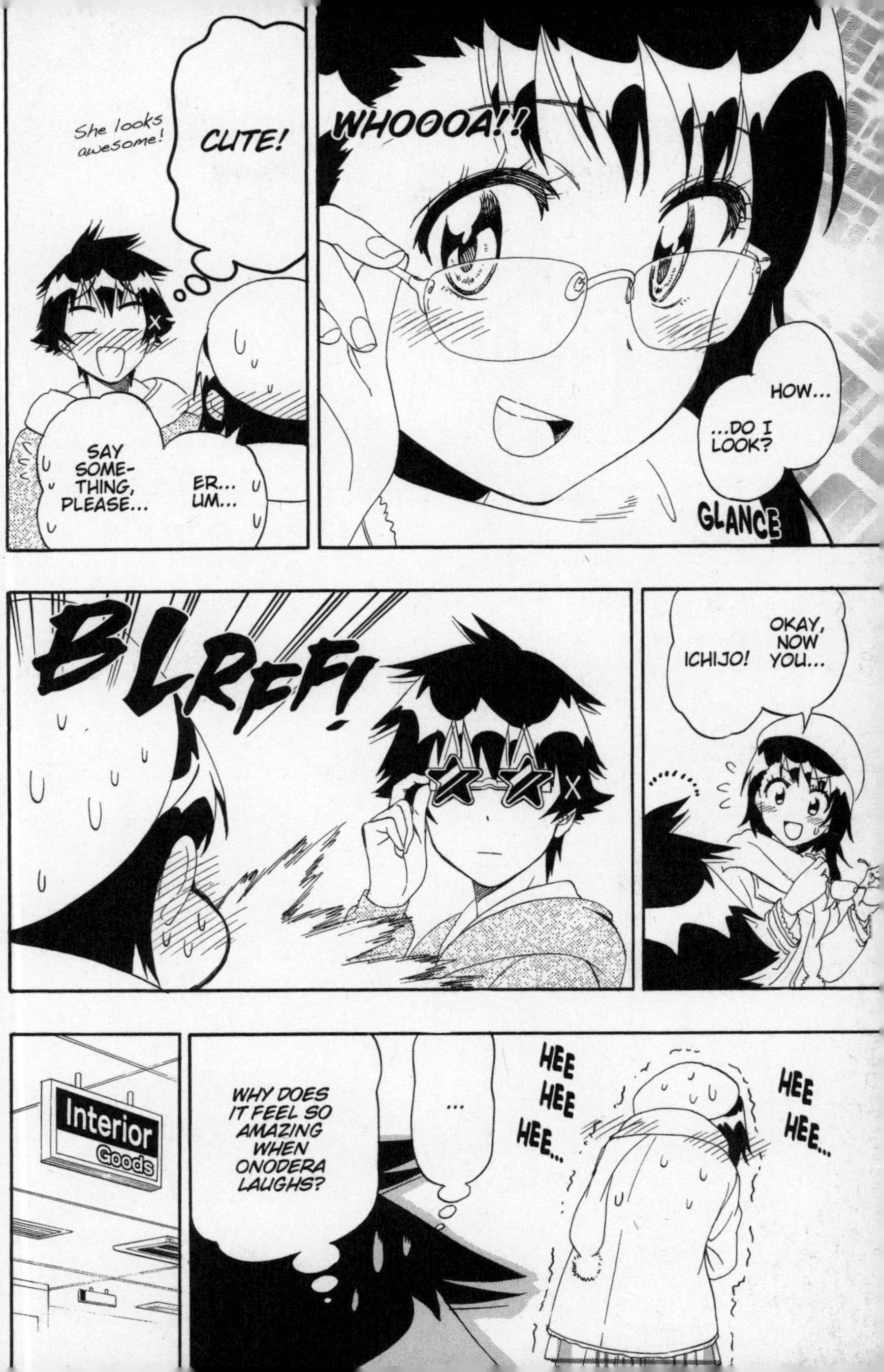
HOW...
...DO I LOOK?
GLANCE
WHOOOA!!
CUTE!
She looks awesome!
ER... UM...
SAY SOME-THING, PLEASE...
OKAY, NOW YOU...
ICHIJO!
......
BLRFF!
HEE HEE...
HEE HEE HEE...
...
WHY DOES IT FEEL SO AMAZING WHEN ONODERA LAUGHS?
Interior
Goods

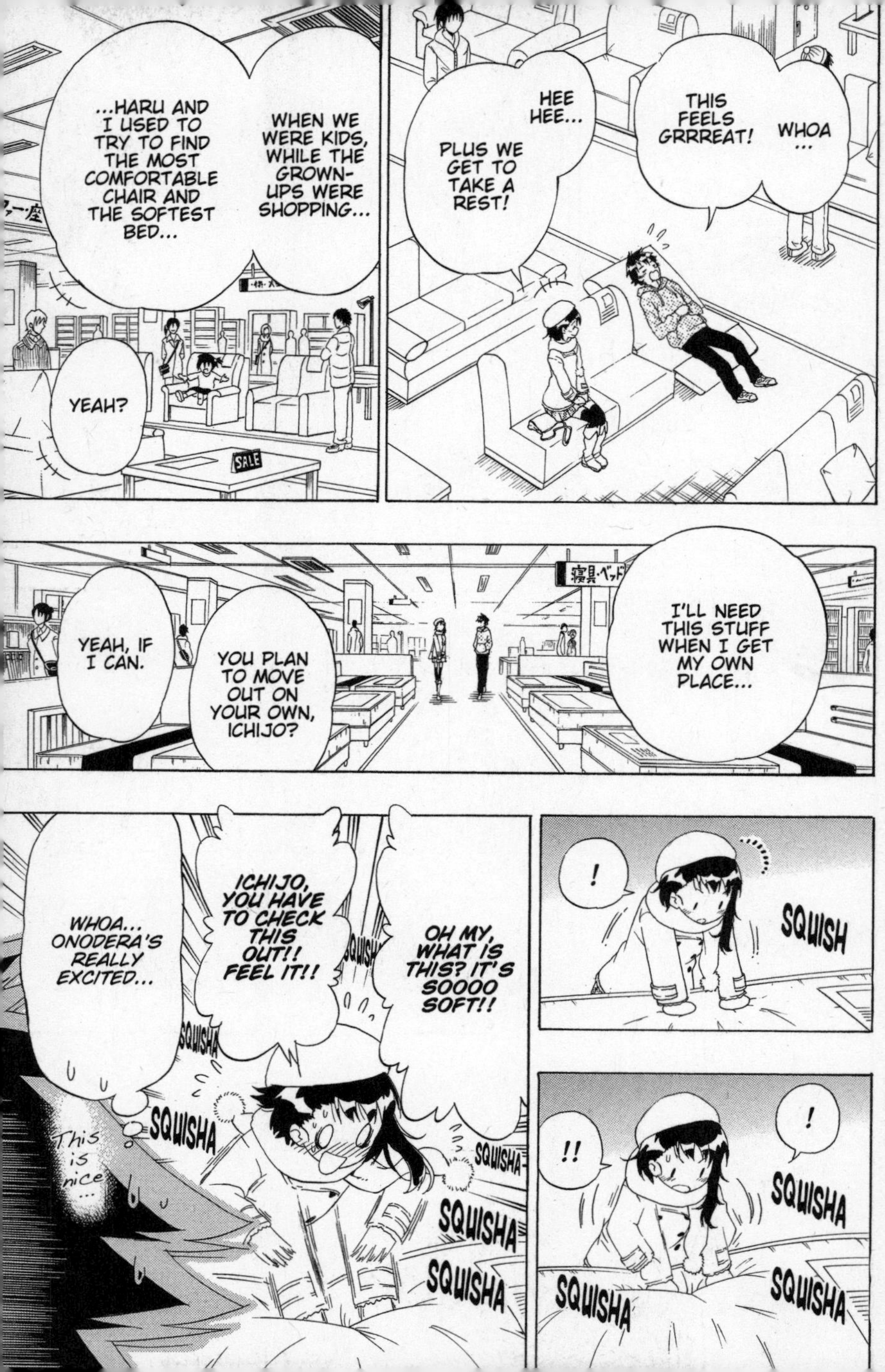
WHOA ...
THIS FEELS GRRREAT!
HEE HEE...
PLUS WE GET TO TAKE A REST!
WHEN WE WERE KIDS, WHILE THE GROWN-UPS WERE SHOPPING...
...HARU AND I USED TO TRY TO FIND THE MOST COMFORTABLE CHAIR AND THE SOFTEST BED...
SALE
YEAH?
I'LL NEED THIS STUFF WHEN I GET MY OWN PLACE...
YOU PLAN TO MOVE OUT ON YOUR OWN, ICHIJO?
YEAH, IF I CAN.
!
SQUISH
!
!!
SQUISHA
SQUISHA
SQUISHA
OH MY, WHAT IS THIS? IT'S SOOOO SOFT!!
ICHIJO, YOU HAVE TO CHECK THIS OUT!! FEEL IT!!
SQUISH
WHOA... ONODERA'S REALLY EXCITED...
SQUISHA
SQUISHA
SQUISHA
SQUISHA
SQUISHA
This is nice...

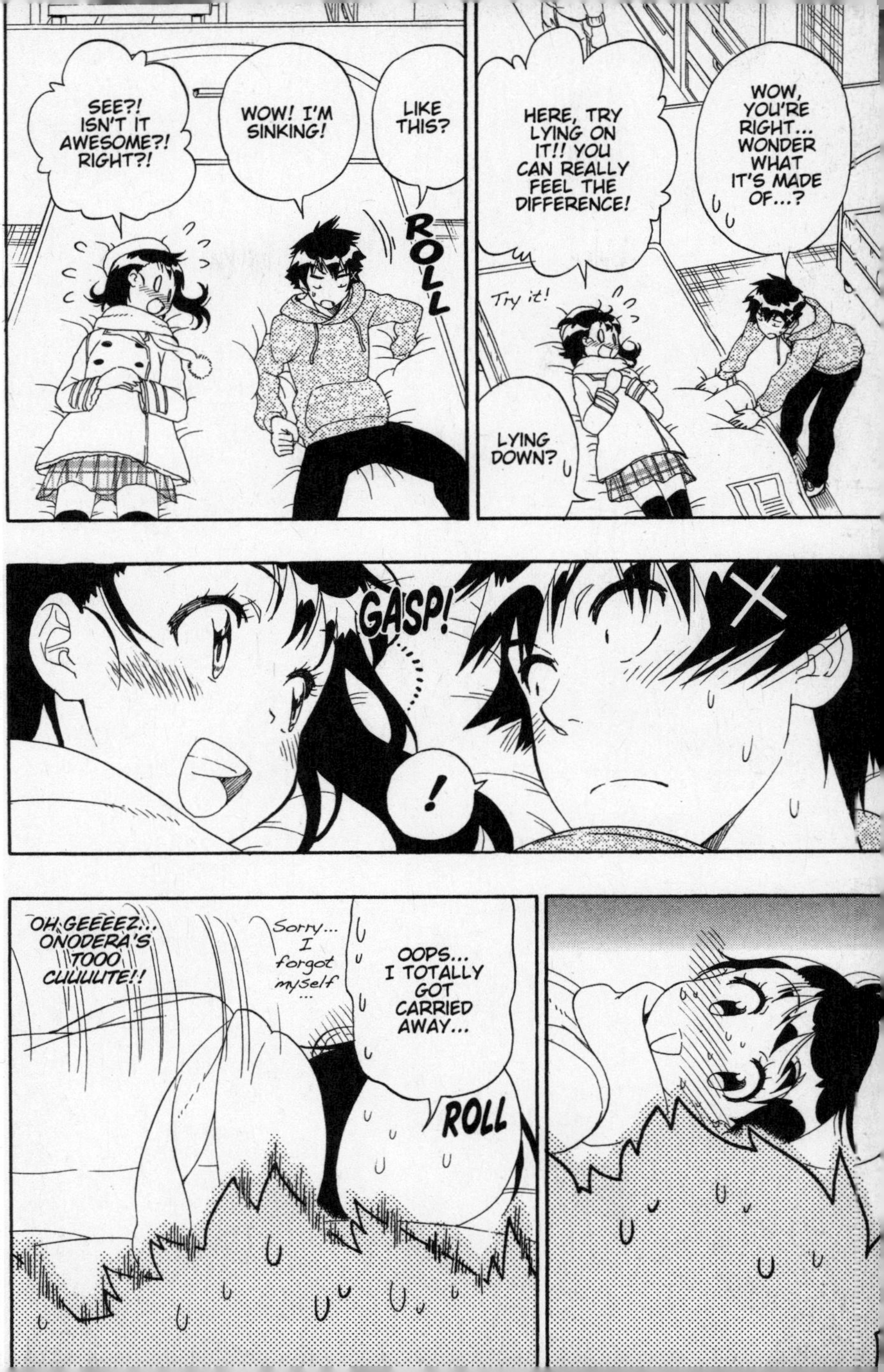
WOW, YOU'RE RIGHT... WONDER WHAT IT'S MADE OF...?
HERE, TRY LYING ON IT!! YOU CAN REALLY FEEL THE DIFFERENCE!
Try it!
LYING DOWN?
LIKE THIS?
ROLL
WOW! I'M SINKING!
SEE?! ISN'T IT AWESOME?! RIGHT?!
GASP!
!
OOPS... I TOTALLY GOT CARRIED AWAY...
ROLL
Sorry... I forgot myself...
OH GEEEEZ... ONODERA'S TOOO CUUUUTE!!

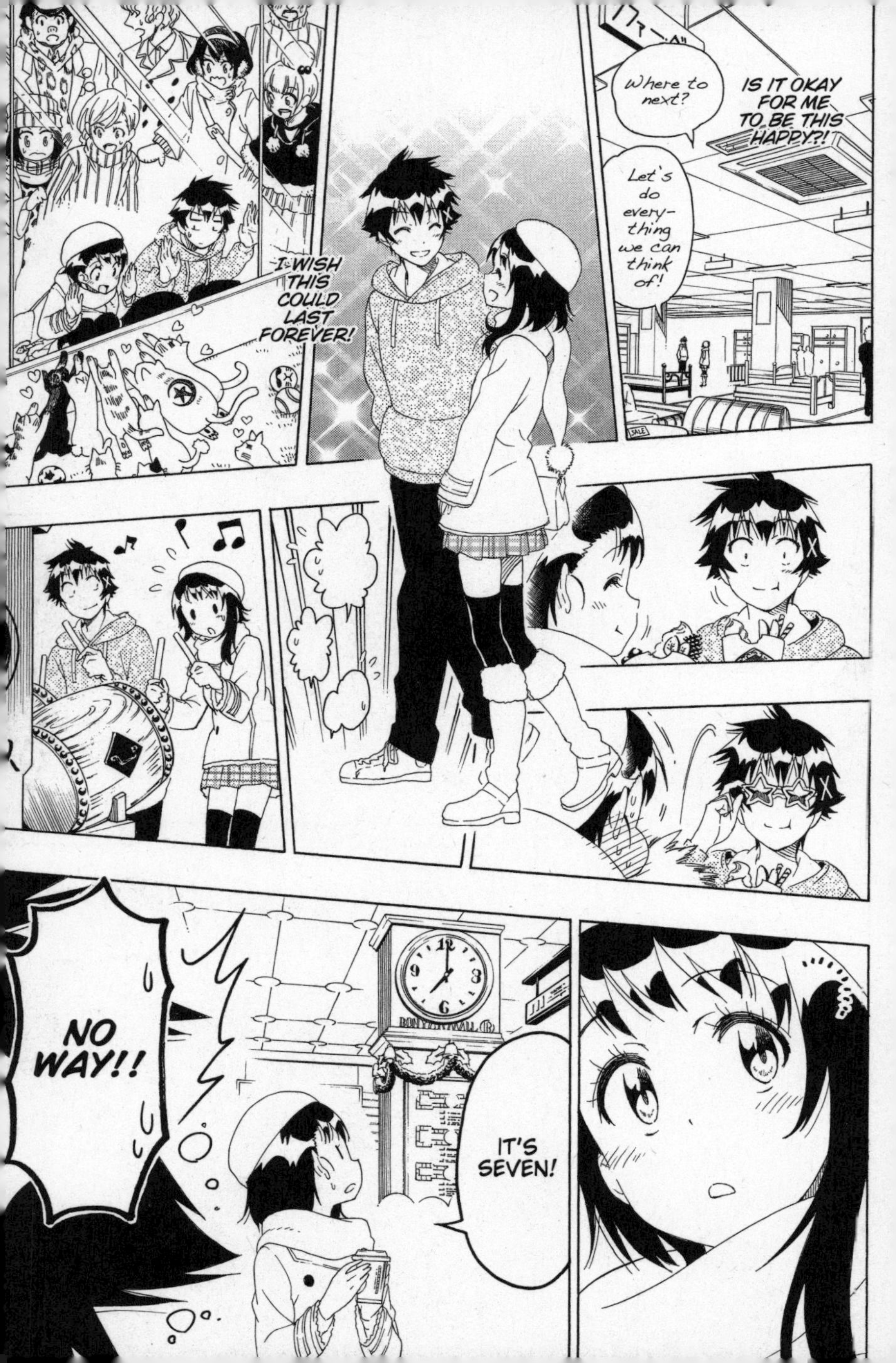
IS IT OKAY FOR ME TO BE THIS HAPPY?!
Where to next?
Let's do every-thing we can think of!
I WISH THIS COULD LAST FOREVER!
IT'S SEVEN!
NO WAY!!

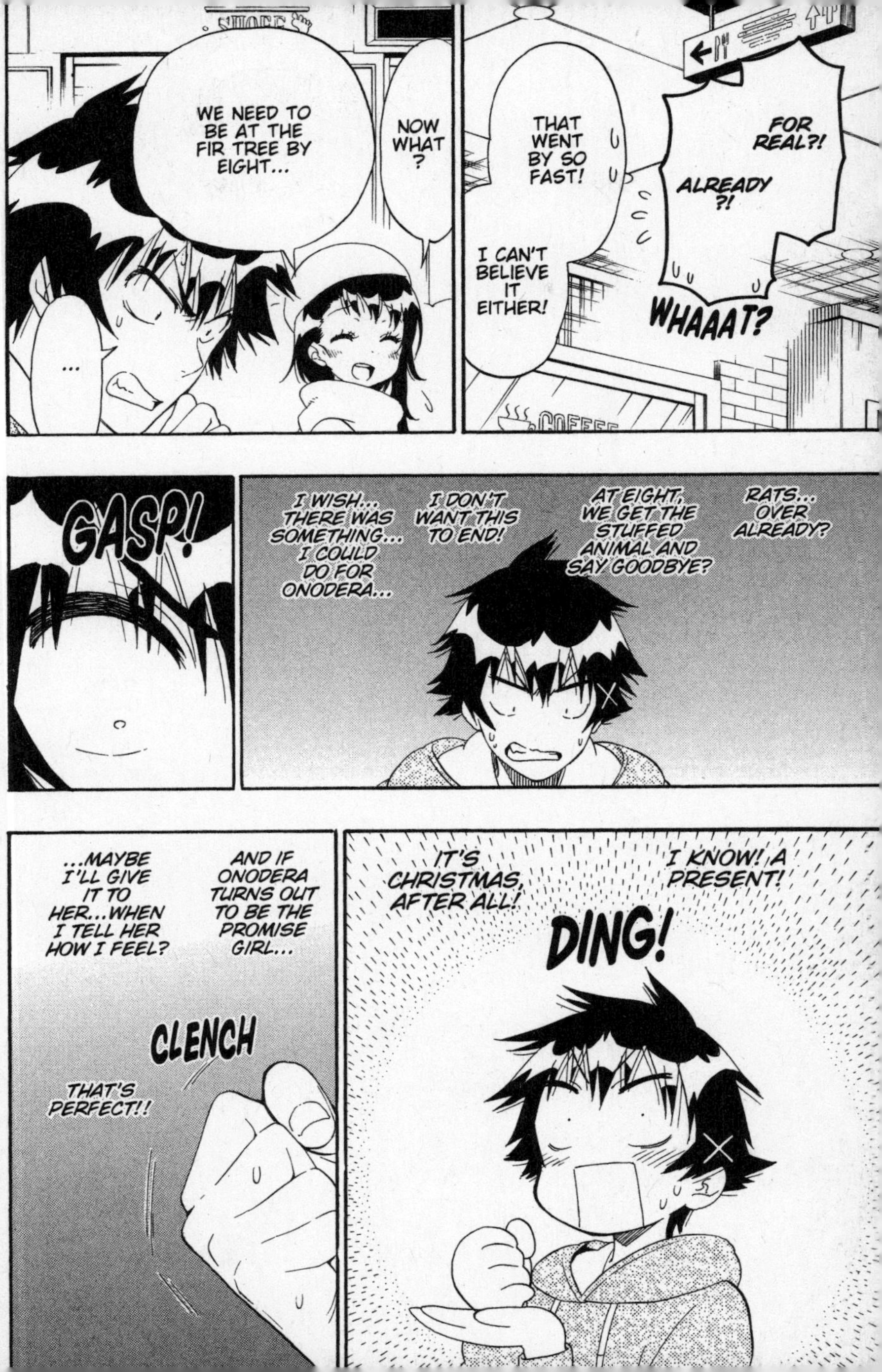
FOR REAL?!
ALREADY ?!
THAT WENT BY SO FAST!
I CAN'T BELIEVE IT EITHER!
WHAAAT?
NOW WHAT ?
WE NEED TO BE AT THE FIR TREE BY EIGHT...
...
RATS... OVER ALREADY?
AT EIGHT, WE GET THE STUFFED ANIMAL AND SAY GOODBYE?
I DON'T WANT THIS TO END!
I WISH... THERE WAS SOMETHING... I COULD DO FOR ONODERA...
GASP!
I KNOW! A PRESENT!
IT'S CHRISTMAS, AFTER ALL!
DING!
AND IF ONODERA TURNS OUT TO BE THE PROMISE GIRL...
...MAYBE I'LL GIVE IT TO HER...WHEN I TELL HER HOW I FEEL?
CLENCH
THAT'S PERFECT!!

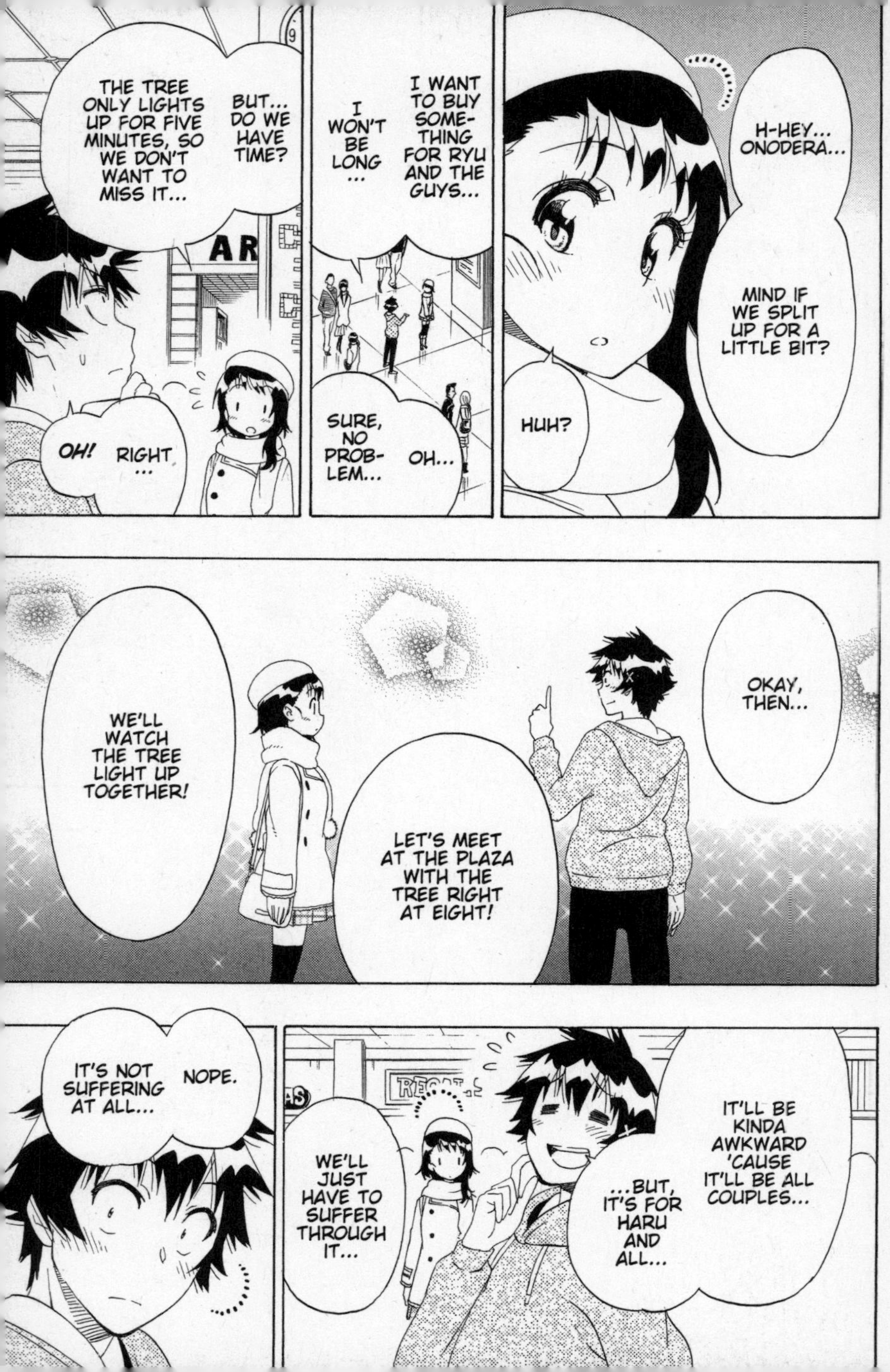
H-HEY... ONODERA...
MIND IF WE SPLIT UP FOR A LITTLE BIT?
HUH?
I WANT TO BUY SOME-THING FOR RYU AND THE GUYS...
I WON'T BE LONG...
OH...
SURE, NO PROB-LEM...
BUT... DO WE HAVE TIME?
THE TREE ONLY LIGHTS UP FOR FIVE MINUTES, SO WE DON'T WANT TO MISS IT...
RIGHT...
OH!
OKAY, THEN...
LET'S MEET AT THE PLAZA WITH THE TREE RIGHT AT EIGHT!
WE'LL WATCH THE TREE LIGHT UP TOGETHER!
IT'LL BE KINDA AWKWARD 'CAUSE IT'LL BE ALL COUPLES...
...BUT, IT'S FOR HARU AND ALL...
WE'LL JUST HAVE TO SUFFER THROUGH IT...
NOPE.
IT'S NOT SUFFERING AT ALL...

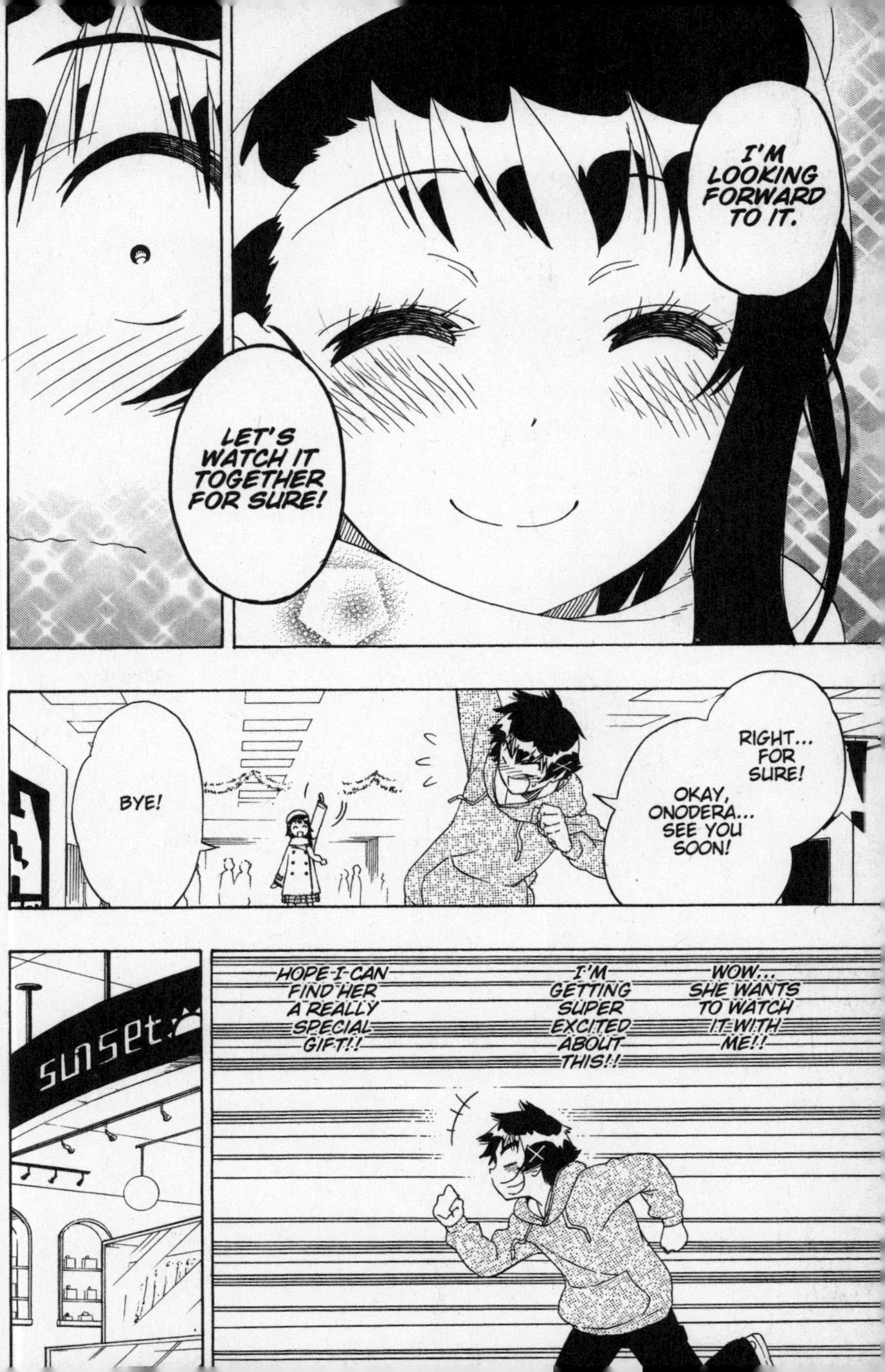
I'M LOOKING FORWARD TO IT.
LET'S WATCH IT TOGETHER FOR SURE!
RIGHT... FOR SURE!
OKAY, ONODERA... SEE YOU SOON!
BYE!
WOW... SHE WANTS TO WATCH IT WITH ME!!
I'M GETTING SUPER EXCITED ABOUT THIS!!
HOPE I CAN FIND HER A REALLY SPECIAL GIFT!!
sunset

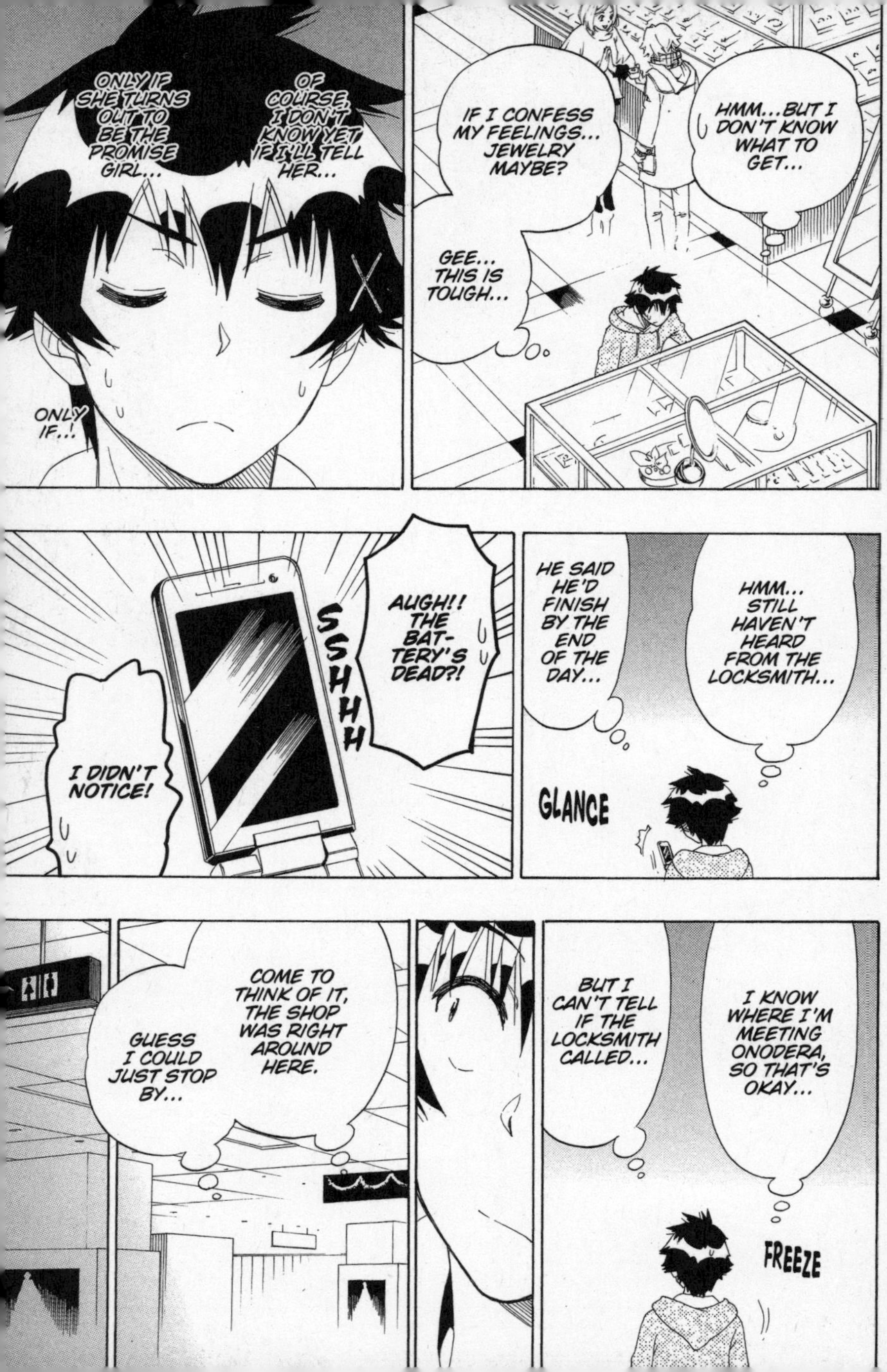
HMM...BUT I DON'T KNOW WHAT TO GET...
IF I CONFESS MY FEELINGS... JEWELRY MAYBE?
GEE... THIS IS TOUGH...
OF COURSE, I DON'T KNOW YET IF I'LL TELL HER...
ONLY IF SHE TURNS OUT TO BE THE PROMISE GIRL...
ONLY IF..!
HMM... STILL HAVEN'T HEARD FROM THE LOCKSMITH...
HE SAID HE'D FINISH BY THE END OF THE DAY...
GLANCE
AUGH!! THE BAT-TERY'S DEAD?!
SSHHHH
I DIDN'T NOTICE!
I KNOW WHERE I'M MEETING ONODERA, SO THAT'S OKAY...
BUT I CAN'T TELL IF THE LOCKSMITH CALLED...
FREEZE
COME TO THINK OF IT, THE SHOP WAS RIGHT AROUND HERE.
GUESS I COULD JUST STOP BY...

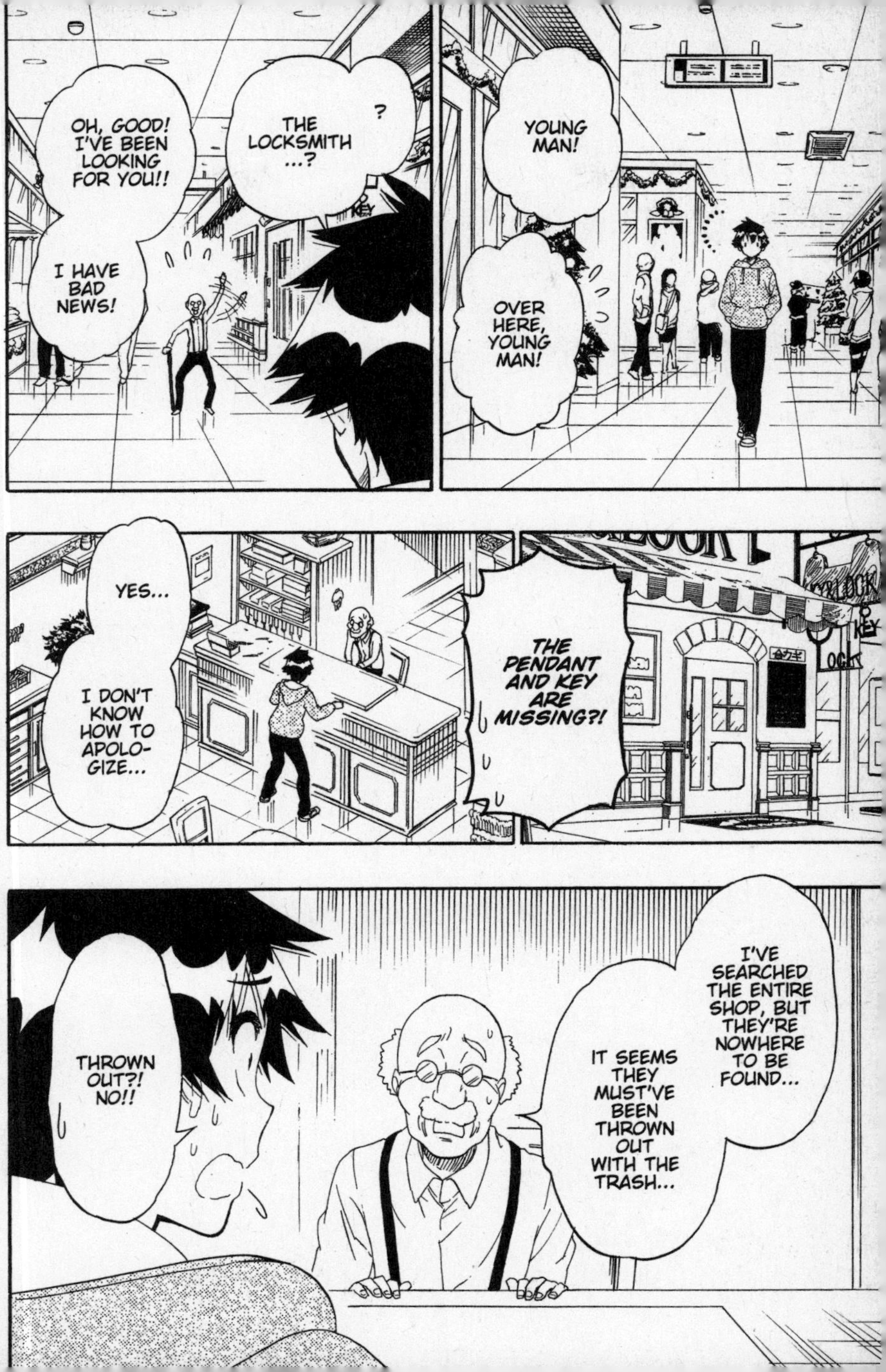
YOUNG MAN!
OVER HERE, YOUNG MAN!
THE LOCKSMITH ...?
OH, GOOD! I'VE BEEN LOOKING FOR YOU!!
I HAVE BAD NEWS!
THE PENDANT AND KEY ARE MISSING?!
YES...
I DON'T KNOW HOW TO APOLO-GIZE...
I'VE SEARCHED THE ENTIRE SHOP, BUT THEY'RE NOWHERE TO BE FOUND...
IT SEEMS THEY MUST'VE BEEN THROWN OUT WITH THE TRASH...
THROWN OUT?! NO!!

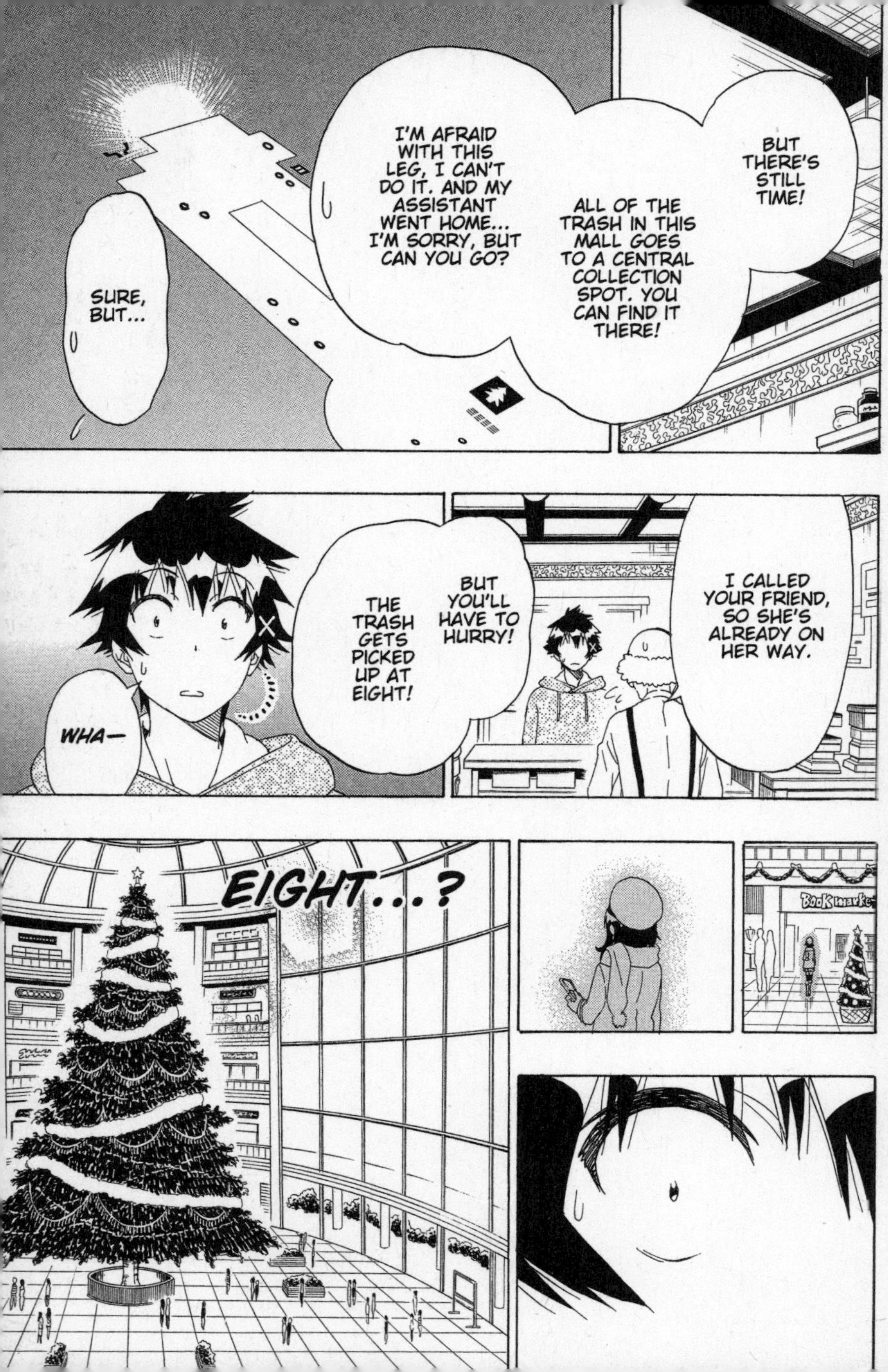
BUT THERE'S STILL TIME!
ALL OF THE TRASH IN THIS MALL GOES TO A CENTRAL COLLECTION SPOT. YOU CAN FIND IT THERE!
I'M AFRAID WITH THIS LEG, I CAN'T DO IT. AND MY ASSISTANT WENT HOME... I'M SORRY, BUT CAN YOU GO?
SURE, BUT...
I CALLED YOUR FRIEND, SO SHE'S ALREADY ON HER WAY.
BUT YOU'LL HAVE TO HURRY!
THE TRASH GETS PICKED UP AT EIGHT!
WHA—
EIGHT...?

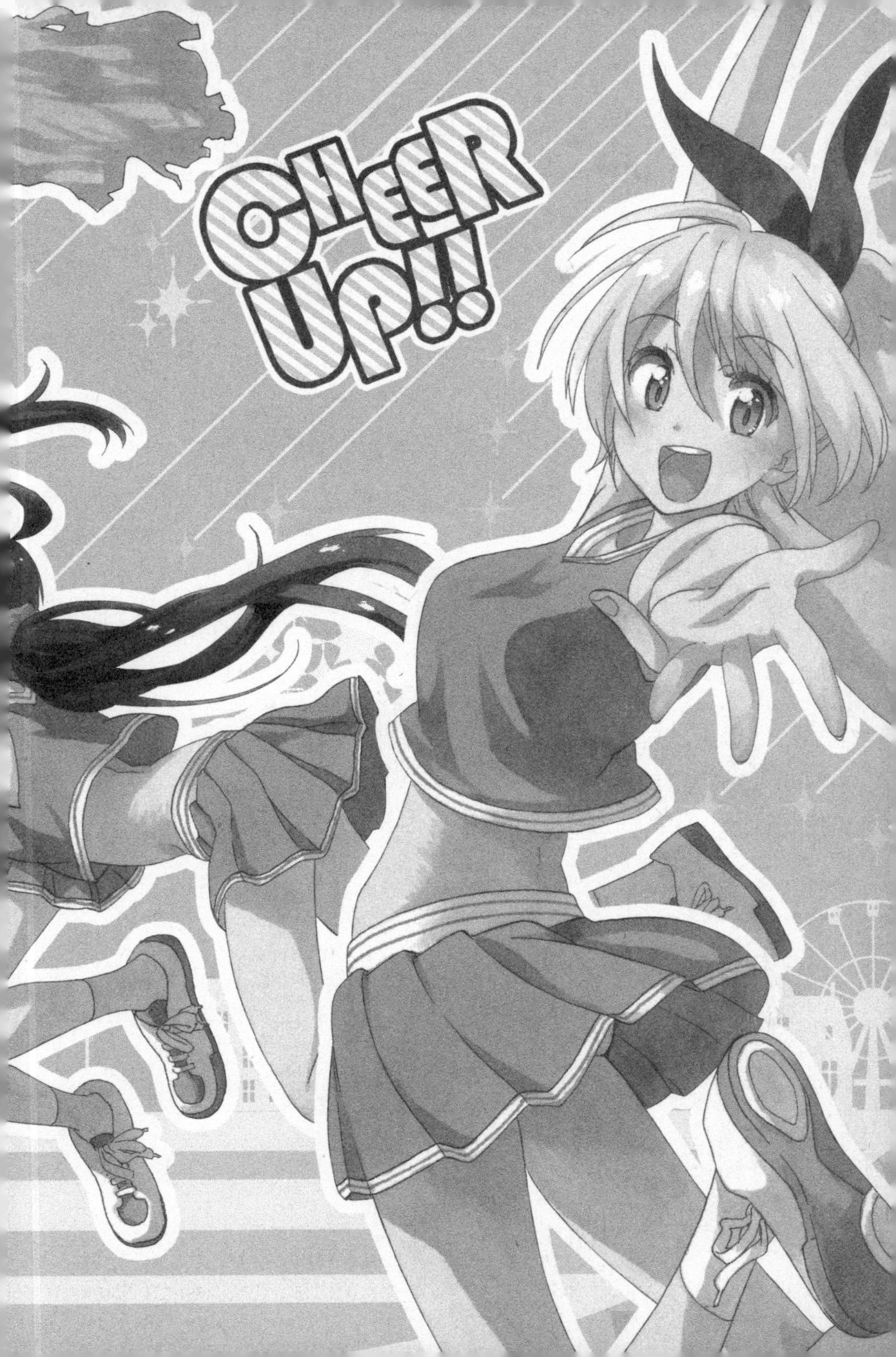
CHEER UP!!

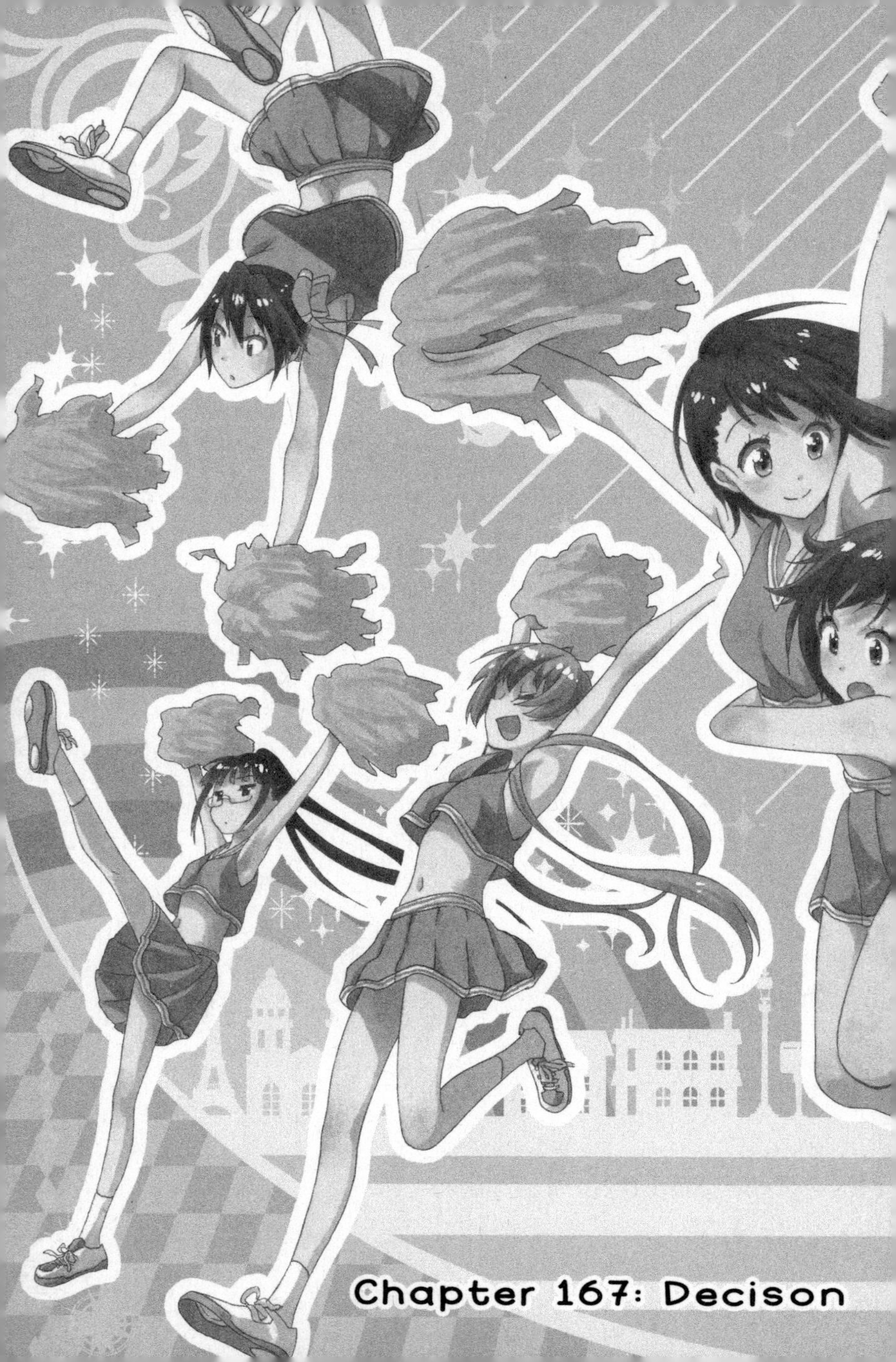

Chapter 167: Decison

NISEKOI
False Love

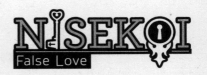

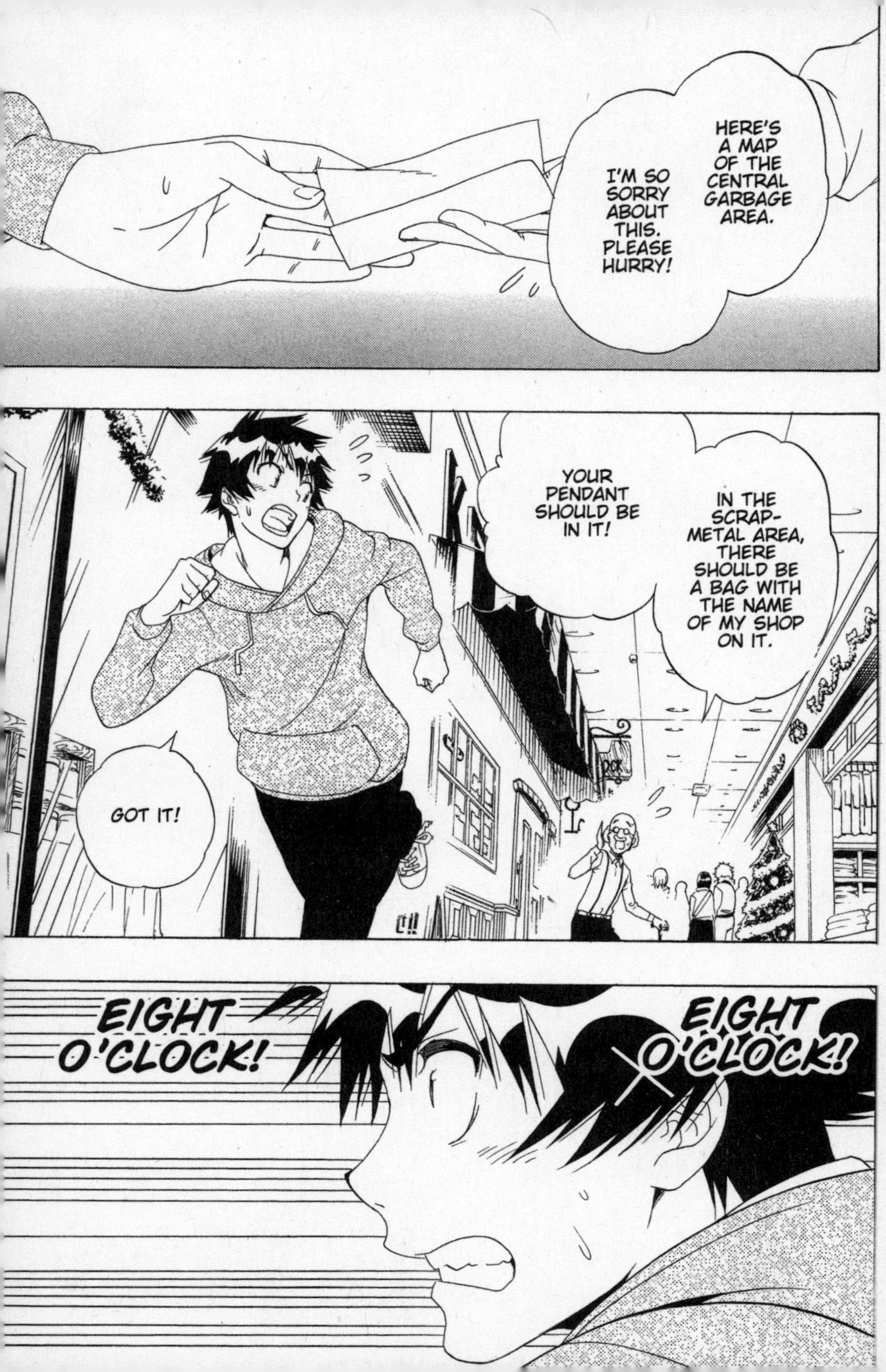
HERE'S A MAP OF THE CENTRAL GARBAGE AREA.
I'M SO SORRY ABOUT THIS. PLEASE HURRY!
IN THE SCRAP-METAL AREA, THERE SHOULD BE A BAG WITH THE NAME OF MY SHOP ON IT.
YOUR PENDANT SHOULD BE IN IT!
GOT IT!
EIGHT O'CLOCK!
EIGHT O'CLOCK!

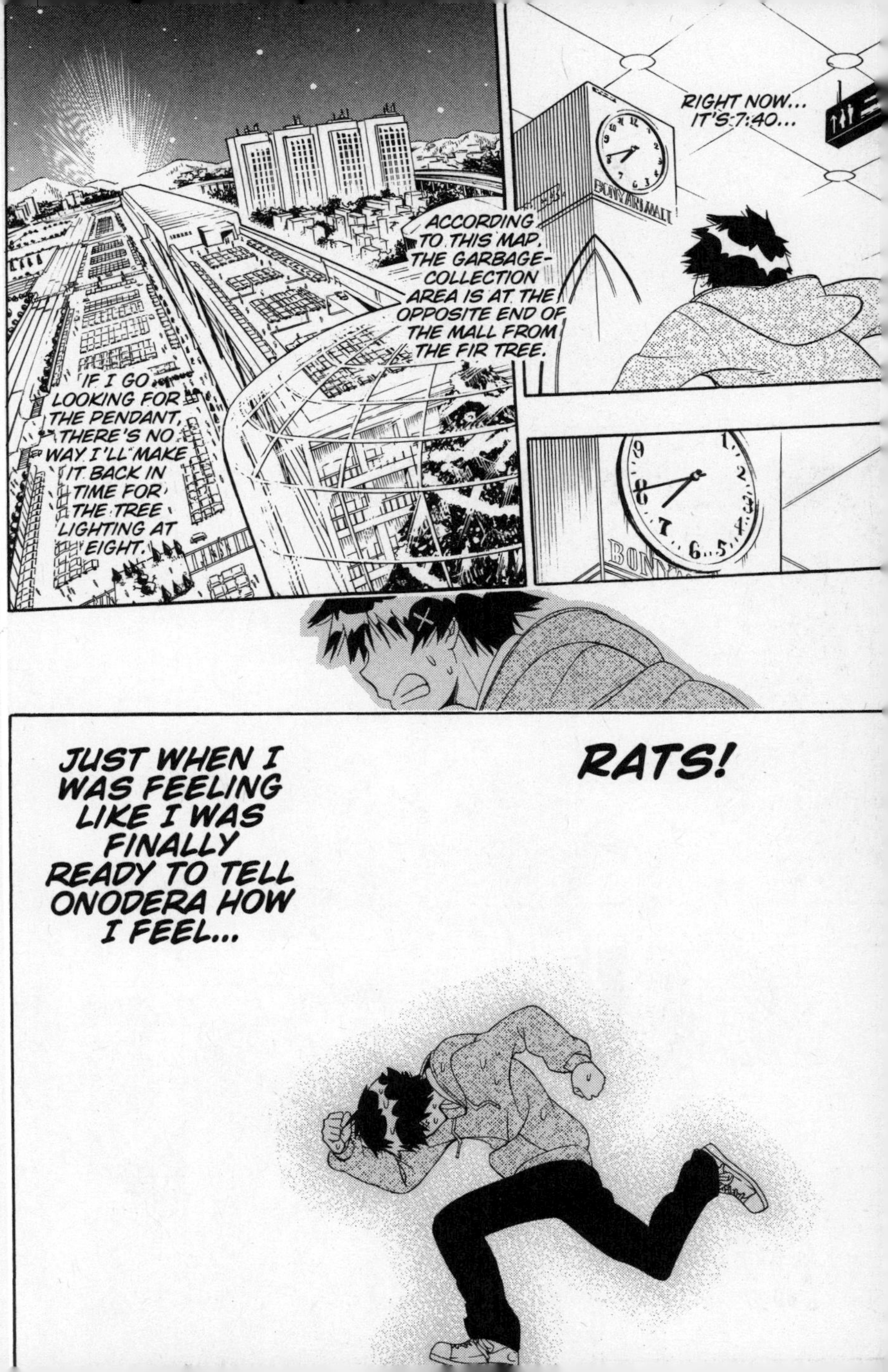
RIGHT NOW... IT'S 7:40...
ACCORDING TO THIS MAP, THE GARBAGE-COLLECTION AREA IS AT THE OPPOSITE END OF THE MALL FROM THE FIR TREE.
IF I GO LOOKING FOR THE PENDANT, THERE'S NO WAY I'LL MAKE IT BACK IN TIME FOR THE TREE LIGHTING AT EIGHT.
RATS!
JUST WHEN I WAS FEELING LIKE I WAS FINALLY READY TO TELL ONODERA HOW I FEEL...

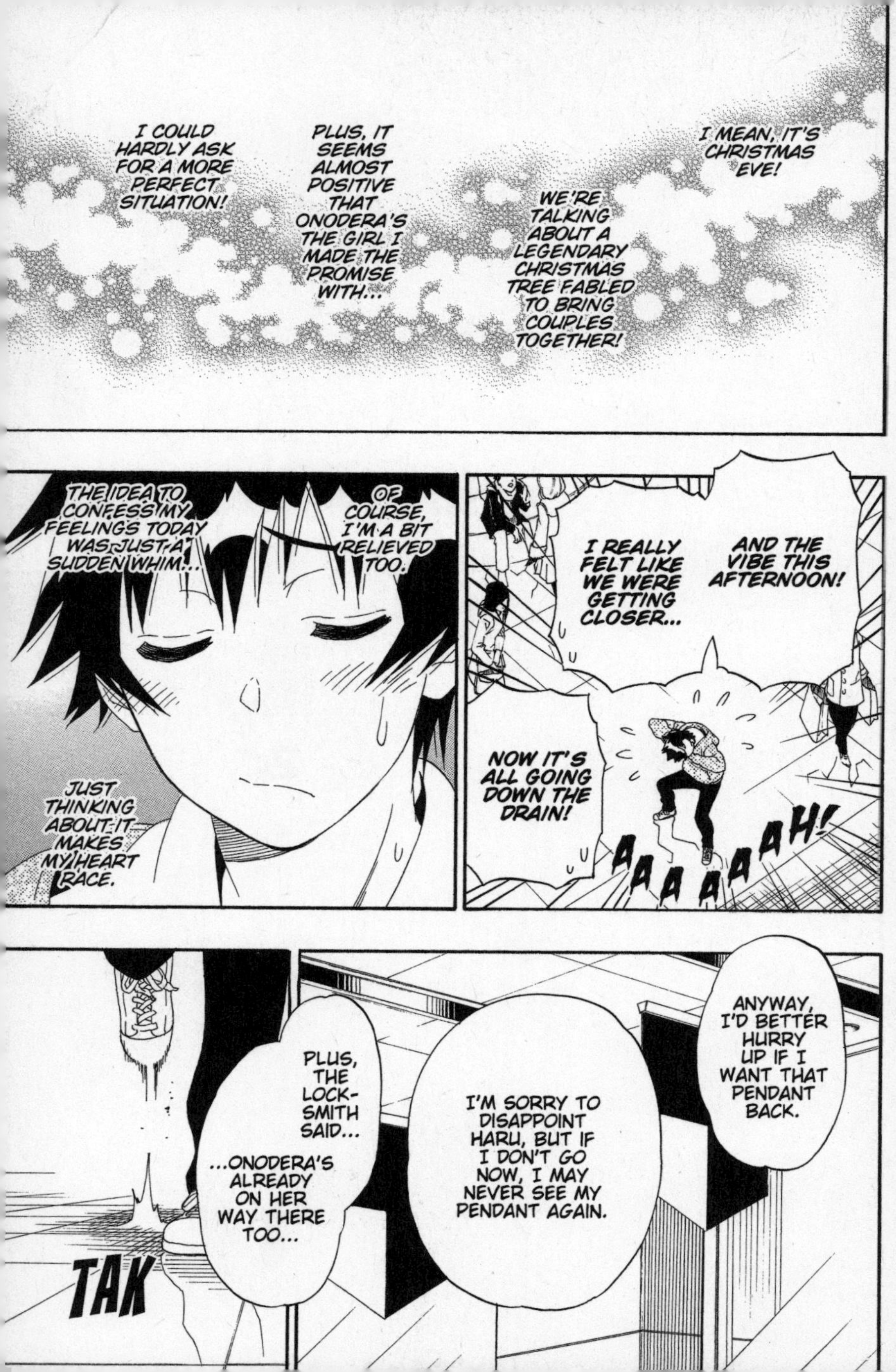
I MEAN, IT'S CHRISTMAS EVE!
WE'RE TALKING ABOUT A LEGENDARY CHRISTMAS TREE FABLED TO BRING COUPLES TOGETHER!
PLUS, IT SEEMS ALMOST POSITIVE THAT ONODERA'S THE GIRL I MADE THE PROMISE WITH...
I COULD HARDLY ASK FOR A MORE PERFECT SITUATION!
AND THE VIBE THIS AFTERNOON!
I REALLY FELT LIKE WE WERE GETTING CLOSER...
NOW IT'S ALL GOING DOWN THE DRAIN!
AAAAAAAH!
OF COURSE, I'M A BIT RELIEVED TOO.
THE IDEA TO CONFESS MY FEELINGS TODAY WAS JUST A SUDDEN WHIM...
JUST THINKING ABOUT IT MAKES MY HEART RACE.
ANYWAY, I'D BETTER HURRY UP IF I WANT THAT PENDANT BACK.
I'M SORRY TO DISAPPOINT HARU, BUT IF I DON'T GO NOW, I MAY NEVER SEE MY PENDANT AGAIN.
PLUS, THE LOCK-SMITH SAID...
...ONODERA'S ALREADY ON HER WAY THERE TOO...
TAK

FLASH

HUH...

ALL OF A SUDDEN...

...I GOT THIS STRANGE FEELING...

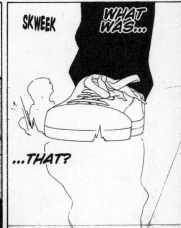

SKWEEK

WHAT WAS...

...THAT?

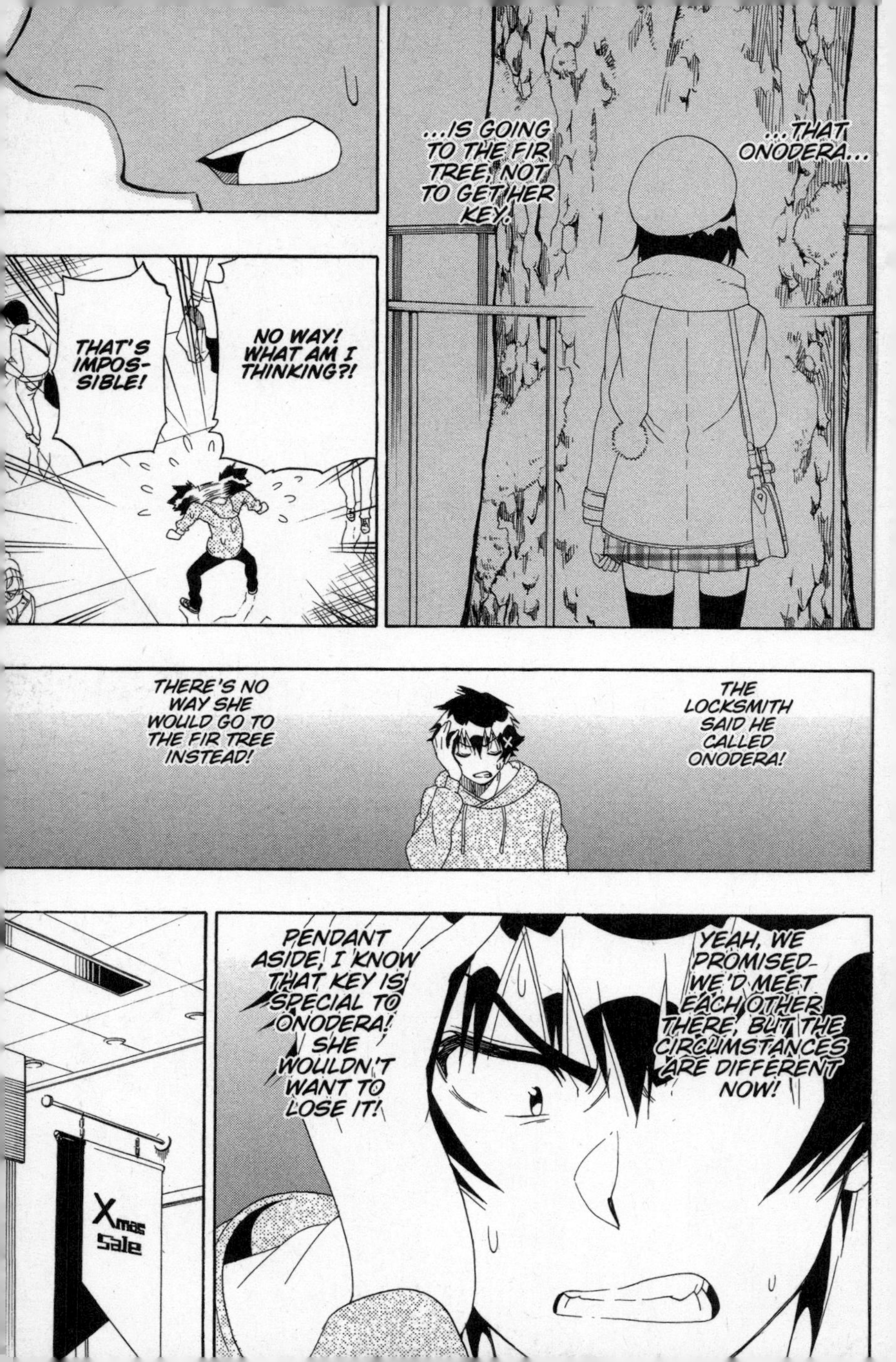
...THAT ONODERA...
...IS GOING TO THE FIR TREE, NOT TO GET HER KEY.
NO WAY! WHAT AM I THINKING?!
THAT'S IMPOSSIBLE!
THE LOCKSMITH SAID HE CALLED ONODERA!
THERE'S NO WAY SHE WOULD GO TO THE FIR TREE INSTEAD!
YEAH, WE PROMISED WE'D MEET EACH OTHER THERE, BUT THE CIRCUMSTANCES ARE DIFFERENT NOW!
PENDANT ASIDE, I KNOW THAT KEY IS SPECIAL TO ONODERA! SHE WOULDN'T WANT TO LOSE IT!
Xmas Sale

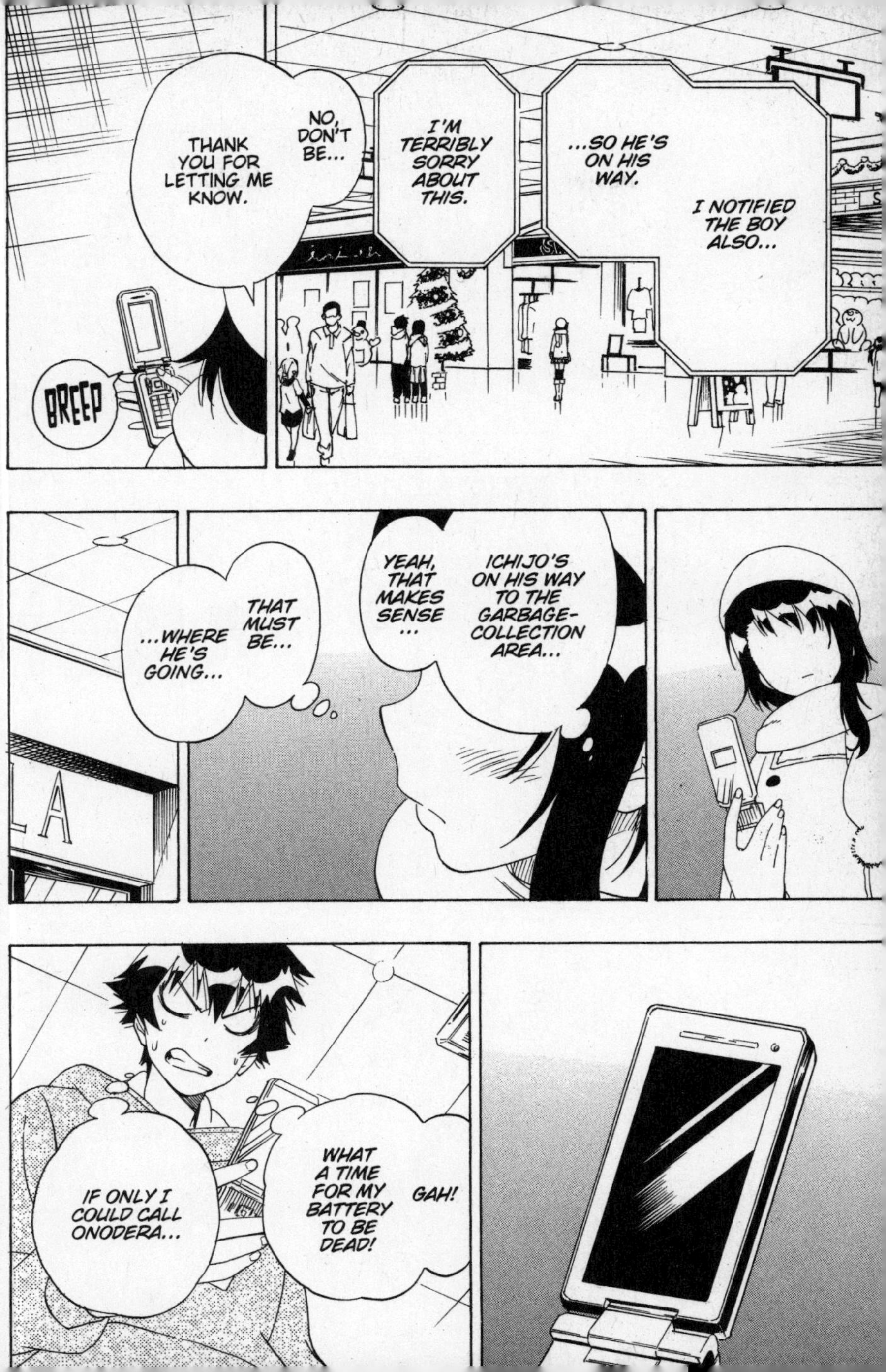
I NOTIFIED THE BOY ALSO...
...SO HE'S ON HIS WAY.
I'M TERRIBLY SORRY ABOUT THIS.
NO, DON'T BE...
THANK YOU FOR LETTING ME KNOW.
BREEP
ICHIJO'S ON HIS WAY TO THE GARBAGE-COLLECTION AREA...
YEAH, THAT MAKES SENSE...
THAT MUST BE...
...WHERE HE'S GOING...
GAH!
WHAT A TIME FOR MY BATTERY TO BE DEAD!
IF ONLY I COULD CALL ONODERA...

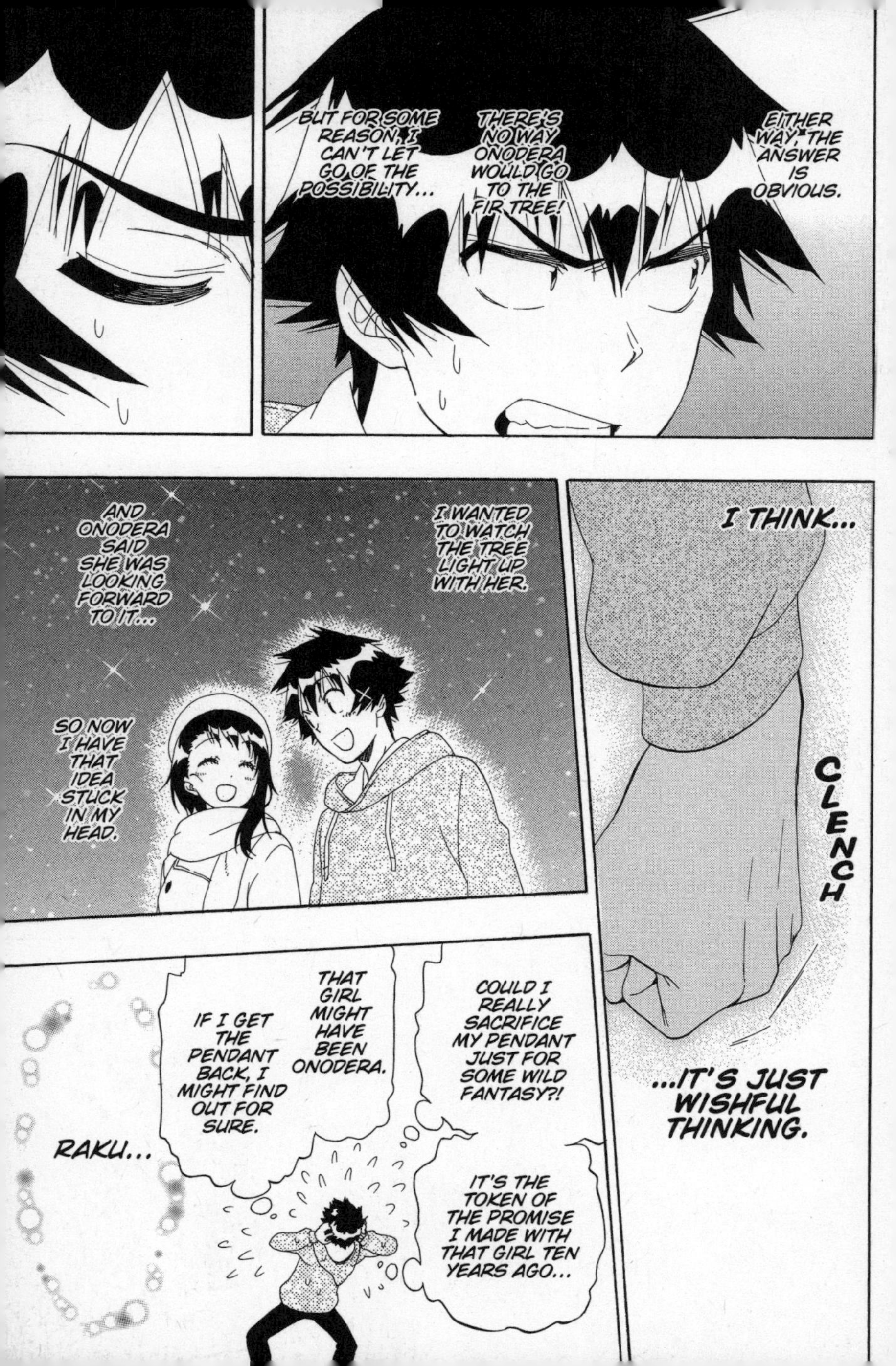
EITHER WAY, THE ANSWER IS OBVIOUS.
THERE'S NO WAY ONODERA WOULD GO TO THE FIR TREE!
BUT FOR SOME REASON, I CAN'T LET GO OF THE POSSIBILITY...
I THINK...
CLENCH
...IT'S JUST WISHFUL THINKING.
I WANTED TO WATCH THE TREE LIGHT UP WITH HER.
AND ONODERA SAID SHE WAS LOOKING FORWARD TO IT...
SO NOW I HAVE THAT IDEA STUCK IN MY HEAD.
COULD I REALLY SACRIFICE MY PENDANT JUST FOR SOME WILD FANTASY?!
IT'S THE TOKEN OF THE PROMISE I MADE WITH THAT GIRL TEN YEARS AGO...
THAT GIRL MIGHT HAVE BEEN ONODERA.
IF I GET THE PENDANT BACK, I MIGHT FIND OUT FOR SURE.
RAKU...

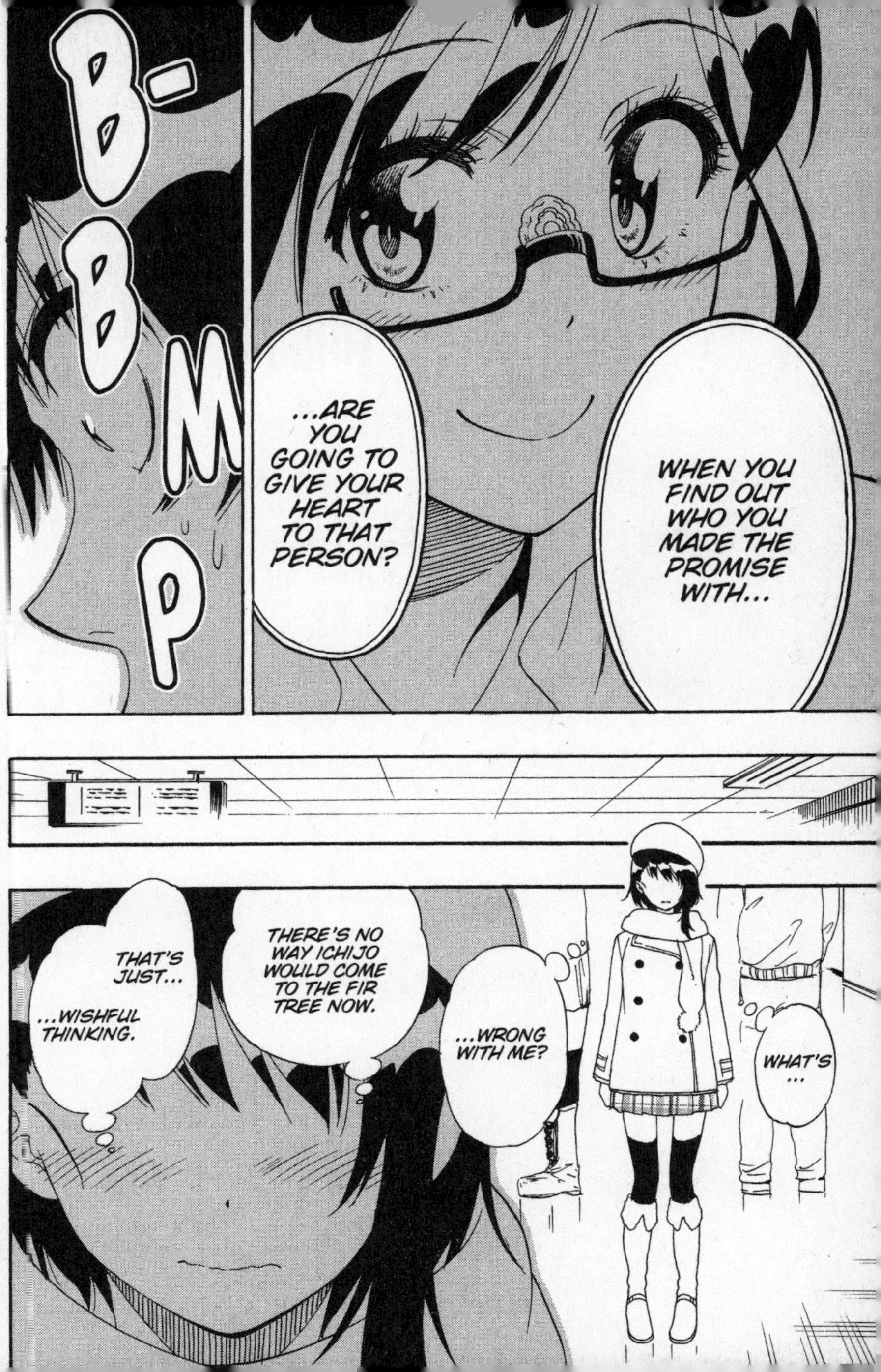

WHEN YOU FIND OUT WHO YOU MADE THE PROMISE WITH...
...ARE YOU GOING TO GIVE YOUR HEART TO THAT PERSON?
B-BMP
WHAT'S...
...WRONG WITH ME?
THERE'S NO WAY ICHIJO WOULD COME TO THE FIR TREE NOW.
THAT'S JUST...
...WISHFUL THINKING.

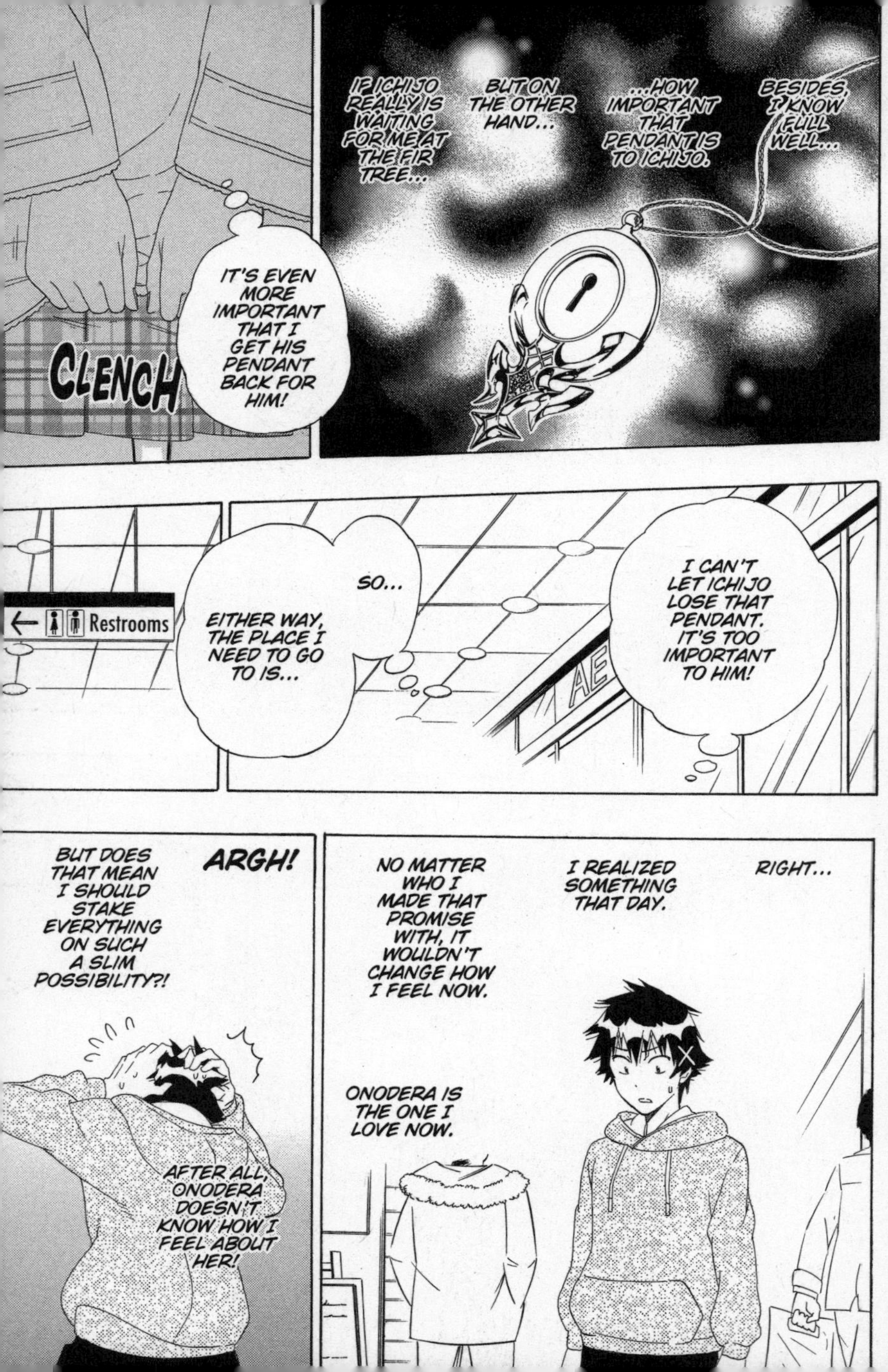

BESIDES, I KNOW FULL WELL...
...HOW IMPORTANT THAT PENDANT IS TO ICHIJO.
BUT ON THE OTHER HAND...
IF ICHIJO REALLY IS WAITING FOR ME AT THE FIR TREE...
IT'S EVEN MORE IMPORTANT THAT I GET HIS PENDANT BACK FOR HIM!
CLENCH
I CAN'T LET ICHIJO LOSE THAT PENDANT. IT'S TOO IMPORTANT TO HIM!
SO...
EITHER WAY, THE PLACE I NEED TO GO TO IS...
Restrooms
RIGHT...
I REALIZED SOMETHING THAT DAY.
NO MATTER WHO I MADE THAT PROMISE WITH, IT WOULDN'T CHANGE HOW I FEEL NOW.
ONODERA IS THE ONE I LOVE NOW.
ARGH!
BUT DOES THAT MEAN I SHOULD STAKE EVERYTHING ON SUCH A SLIM POSSIBILITY?!
AFTER ALL, ONODERA DOESN'T KNOW HOW I FEEL ABOUT HER!

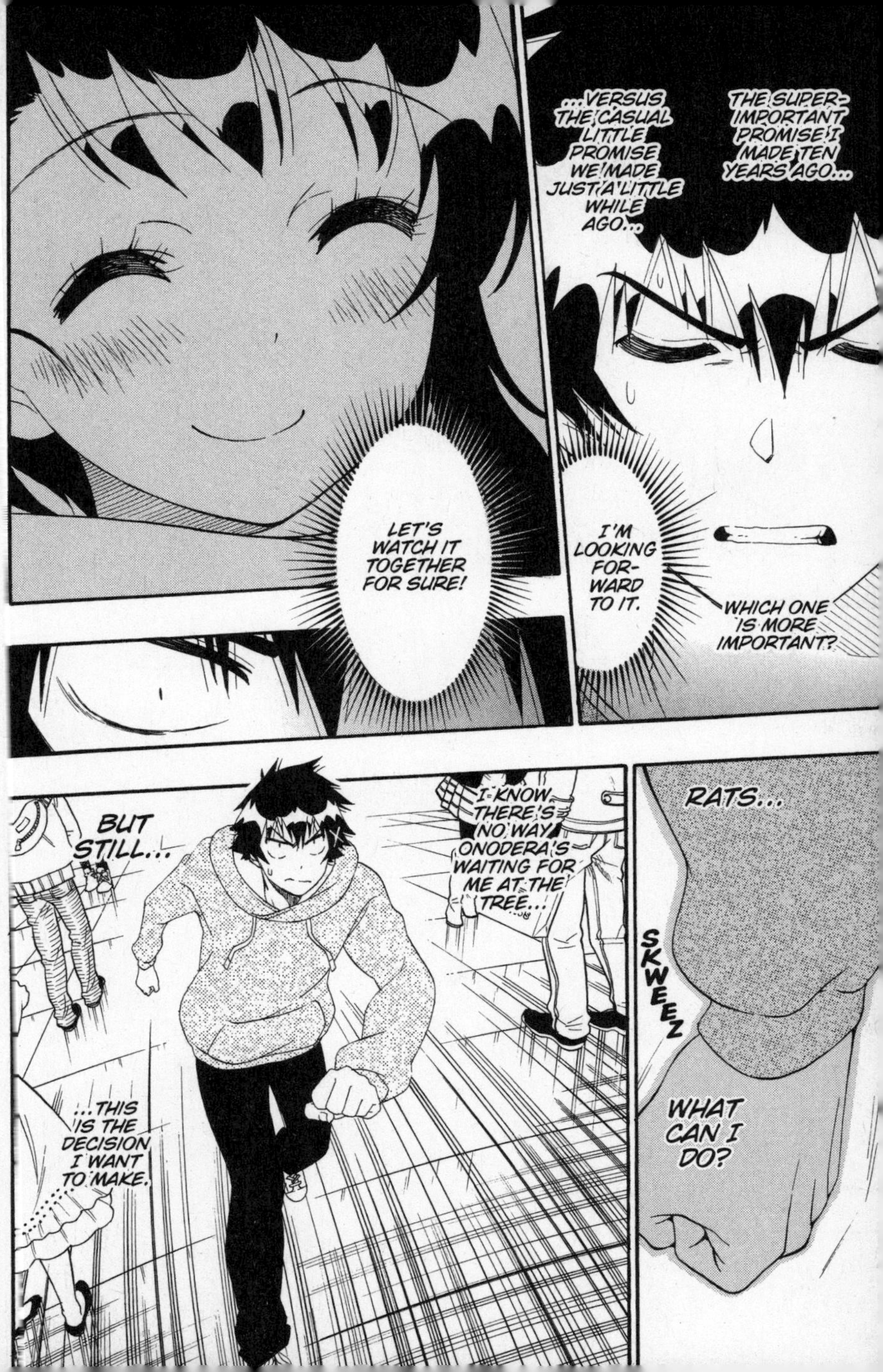
THE SUPER-IMPORTANT PROMISE I MADE TEN YEARS AGO...
...VERSUS THE CASUAL LITTLE PROMISE WE MADE JUST A LITTLE WHILE AGO...
I'M LOOKING FORWARD TO IT.
WHICH ONE IS MORE IMPORTANT?
LET'S WATCH IT TOGETHER FOR SURE!
RATS...
SKWEEZ
WHAT CAN I DO?
I KNOW THERE'S NO WAY ONODERA'S WAITING FOR ME AT THE TREE...
BUT STILL...
...THIS IS THE DECISION I WANT TO MAKE.

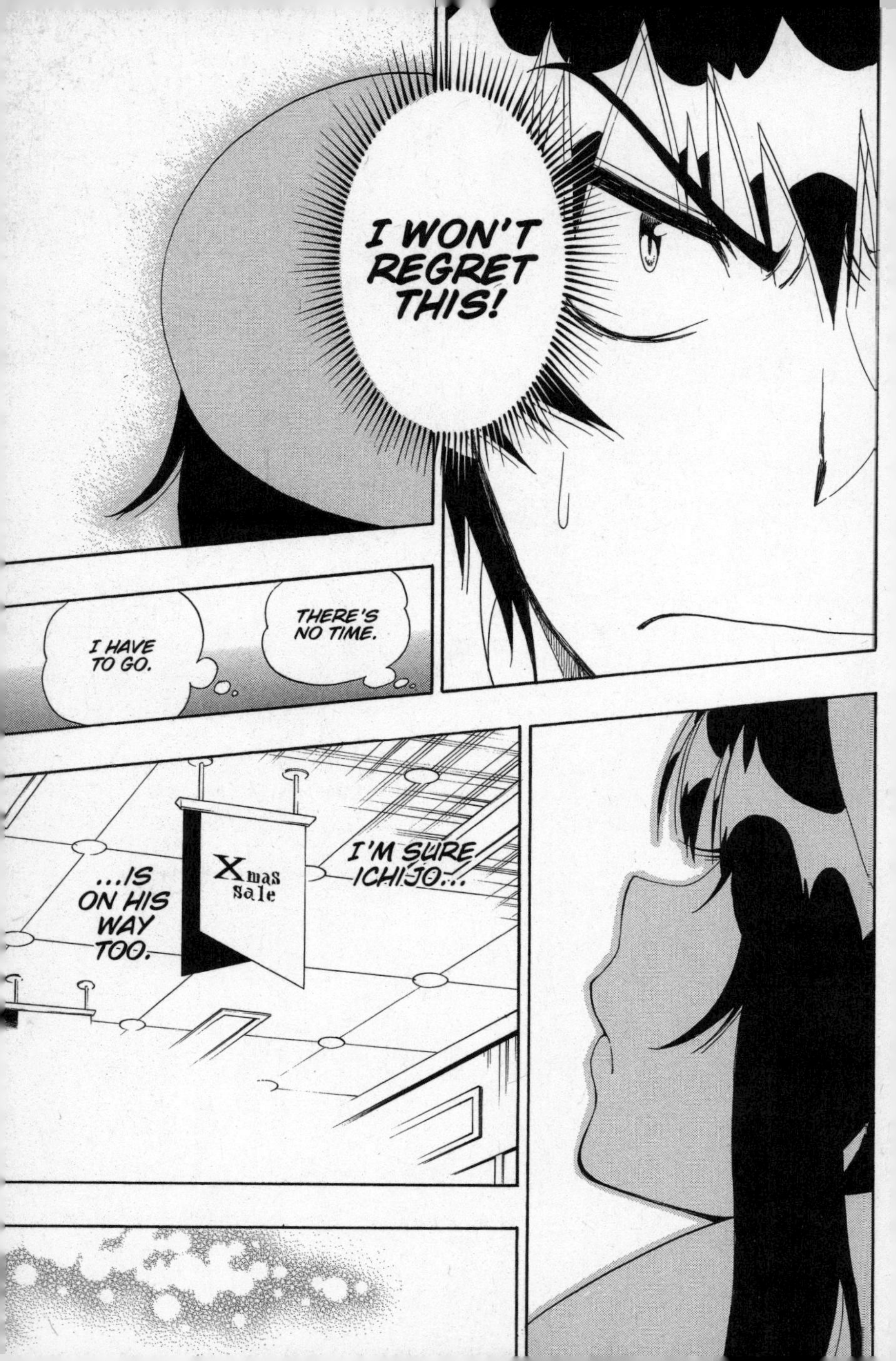
I WON'T REGRET THIS!
THERE'S NO TIME.
I HAVE TO GO.
I'M SURE ICHIJO...
Xmas sale
...IS ON HIS WAY TOO.

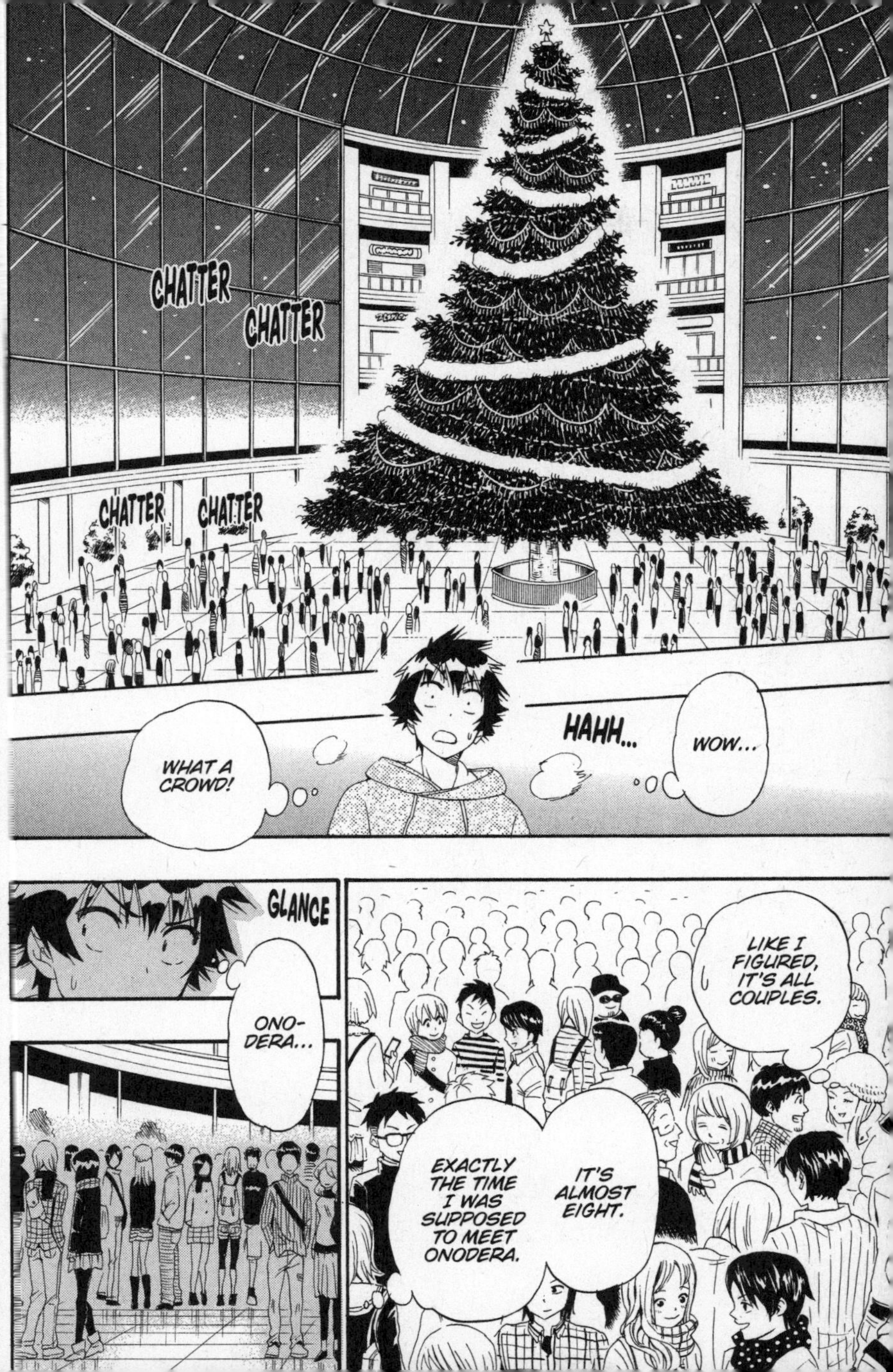
CHATTER
CHATTER
CHATTER
CHATTER
WOW...
HAHH...
WHAT A CROWD!
LIKE I FIGURED, IT'S ALL COUPLES.
IT'S ALMOST EIGHT.
EXACTLY THE TIME I WAS SUPPOSED TO MEET ONODERA.
GLANCE
ONO-DERA...

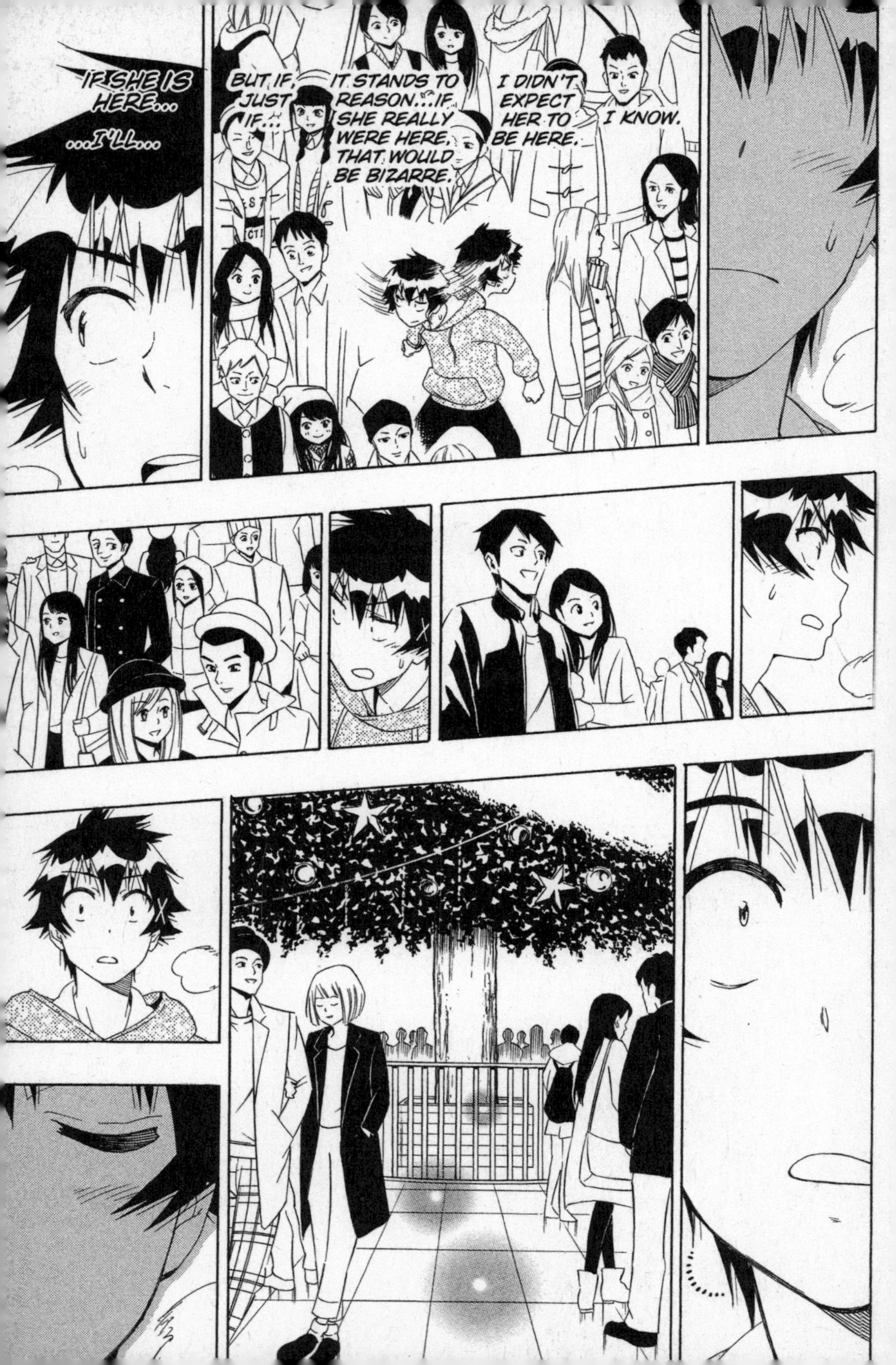
I KNOW.
I DIDN'T EXPECT HER TO BE HERE.
IT STANDS TO REASON...IF SHE REALLY WERE HERE, THAT WOULD BE BIZARRE.
BUT IF, JUST IF...
IF SHE IS HERE...
...I'LL...

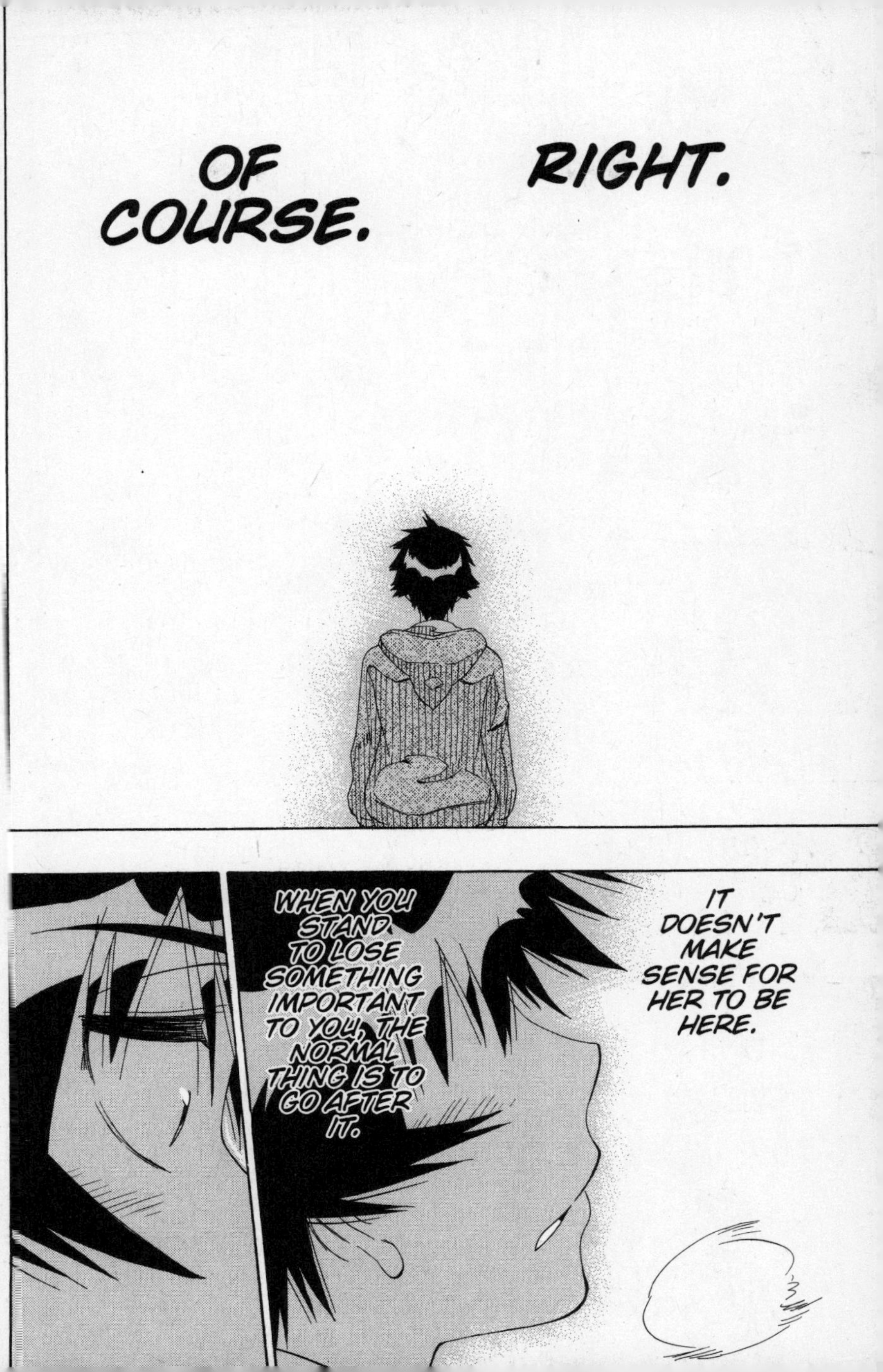
RIGHT.
OF COURSE.
IT DOESN'T MAKE SENSE FOR HER TO BE HERE.
WHEN YOU STAND TO LOSE SOMETHING IMPORTANT TO YOU, THE NORMAL THING IS TO GO AFTER IT.

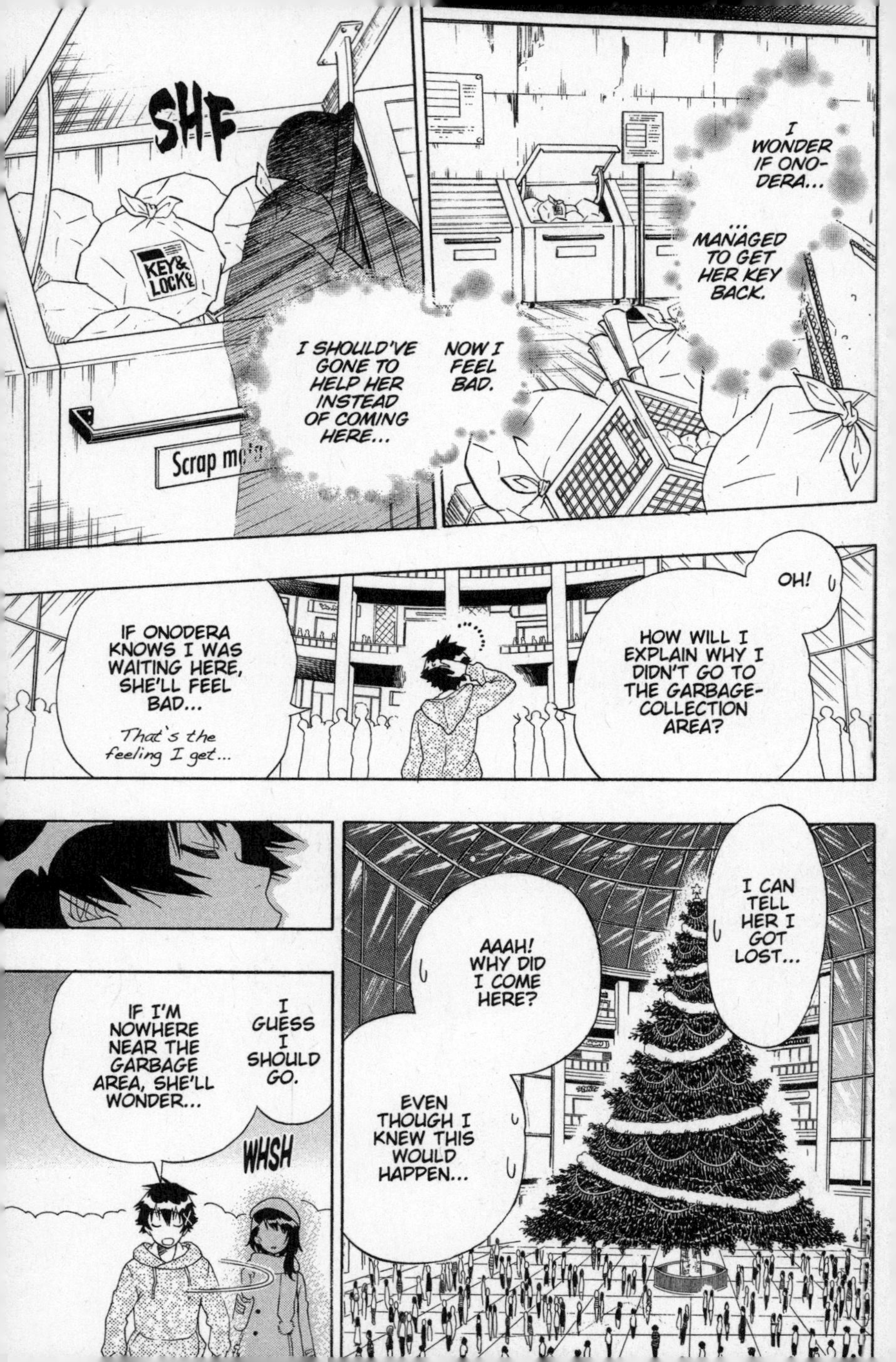
I WONDER IF ONODERA...
...MANAGED TO GET HER KEY BACK.
NOW I FEEL BAD.
I SHOULD'VE GONE TO HELP HER INSTEAD OF COMING HERE...
SHF
KEY & LOCK
Scrap me
OH!
HOW WILL I EXPLAIN WHY I DIDN'T GO TO THE GARBAGE-COLLECTION AREA?
IF ONODERA KNOWS I WAS WAITING HERE, SHE'LL FEEL BAD...
That's the feeling I get...
I CAN TELL HER I GOT LOST...
AAAH! WHY DID I COME HERE?
EVEN THOUGH I KNEW THIS WOULD HAPPEN...
I GUESS I SHOULD GO.
IF I'M NOWHERE NEAR THE GARBAGE AREA, SHE'LL WONDER...
WHSH

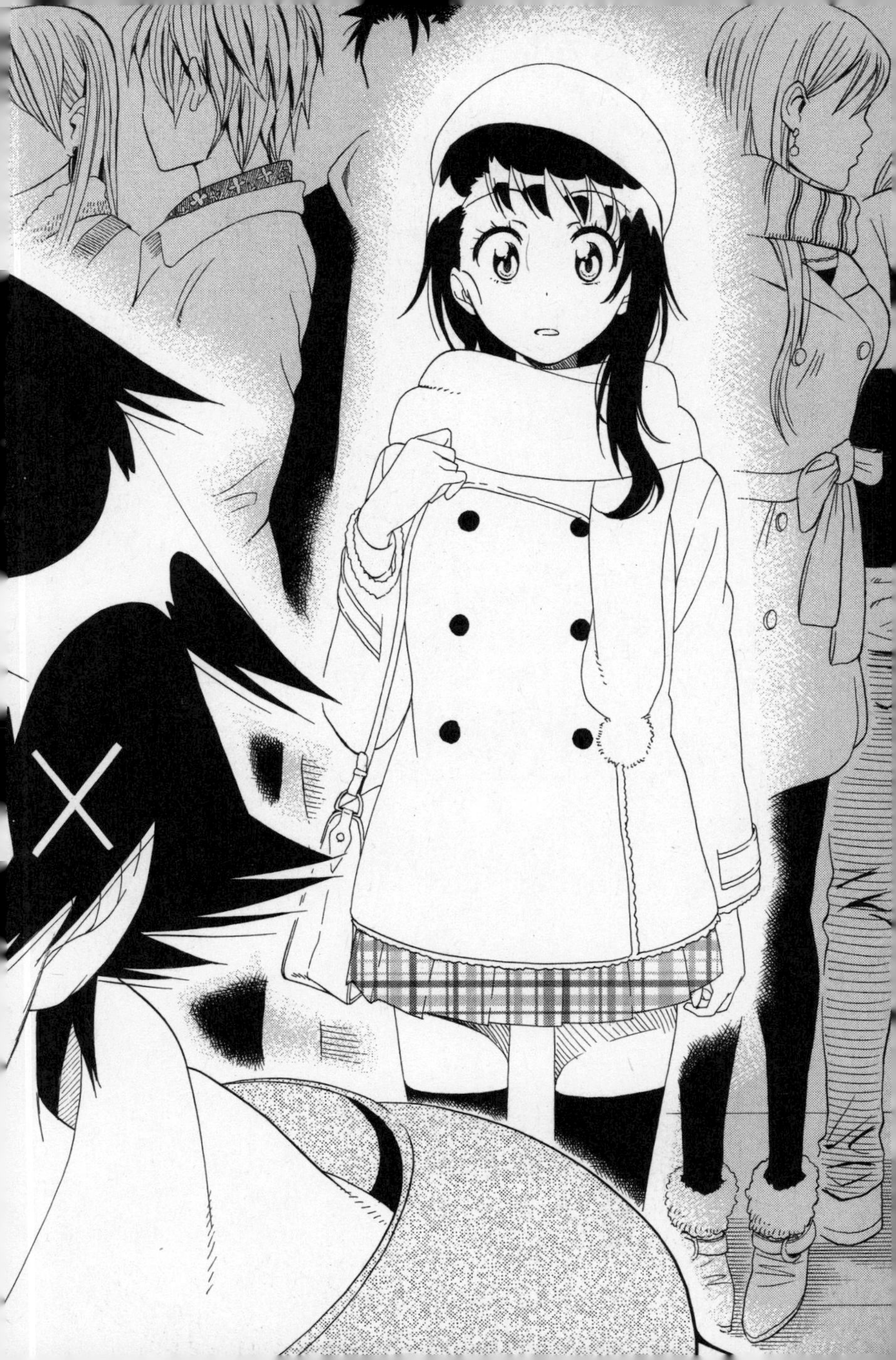

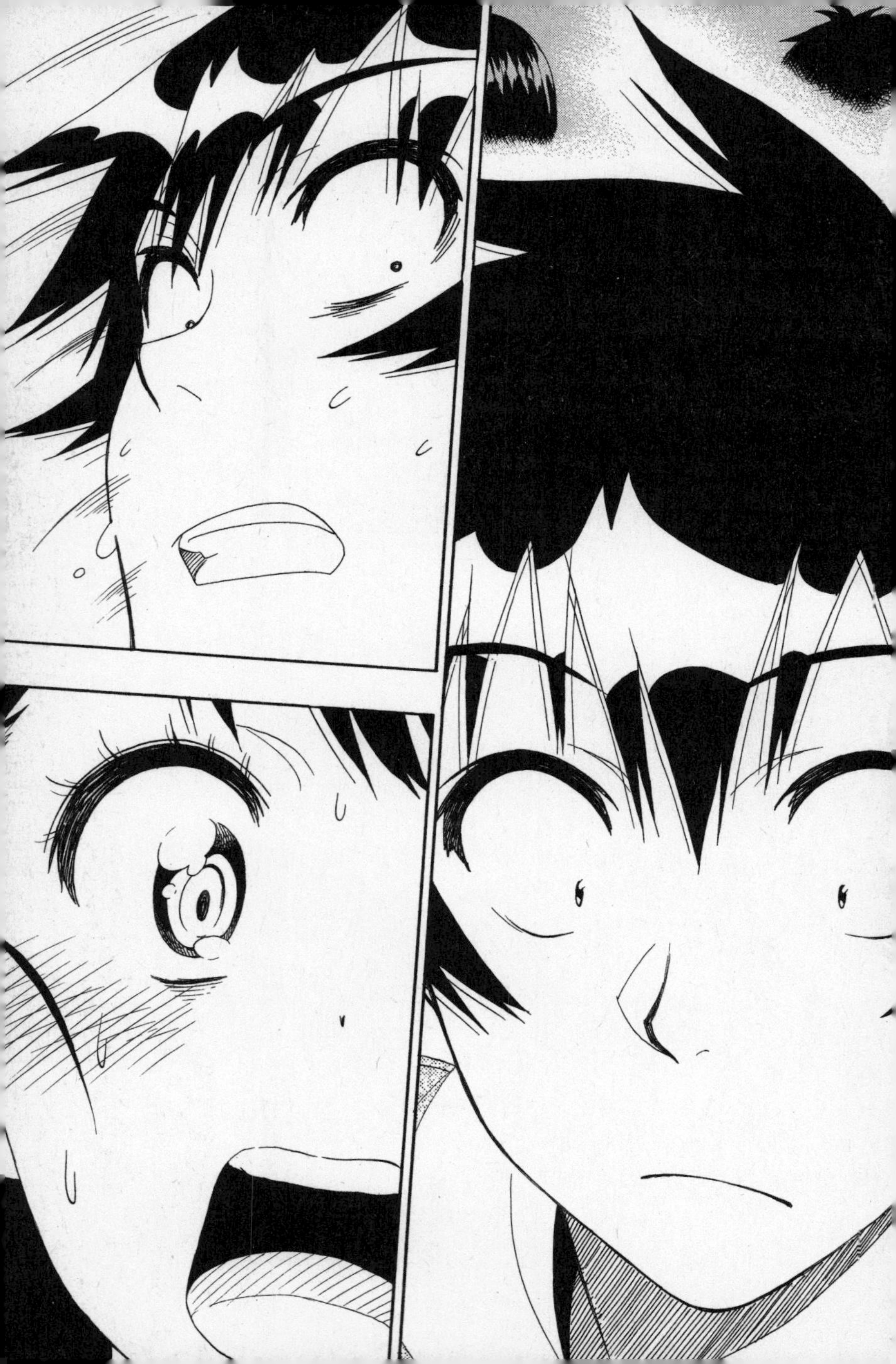

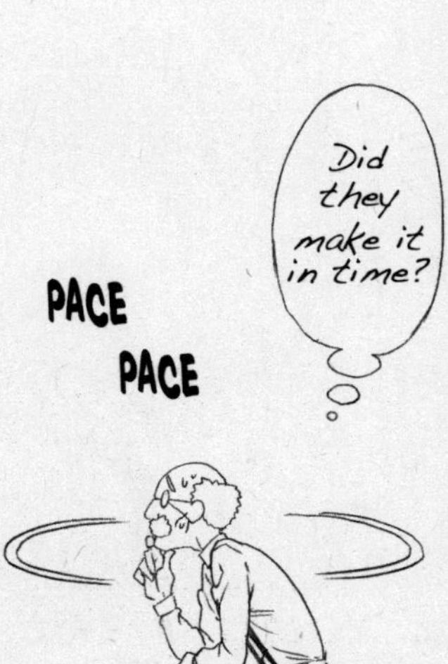
Did they make it in time?
PACE
PACE

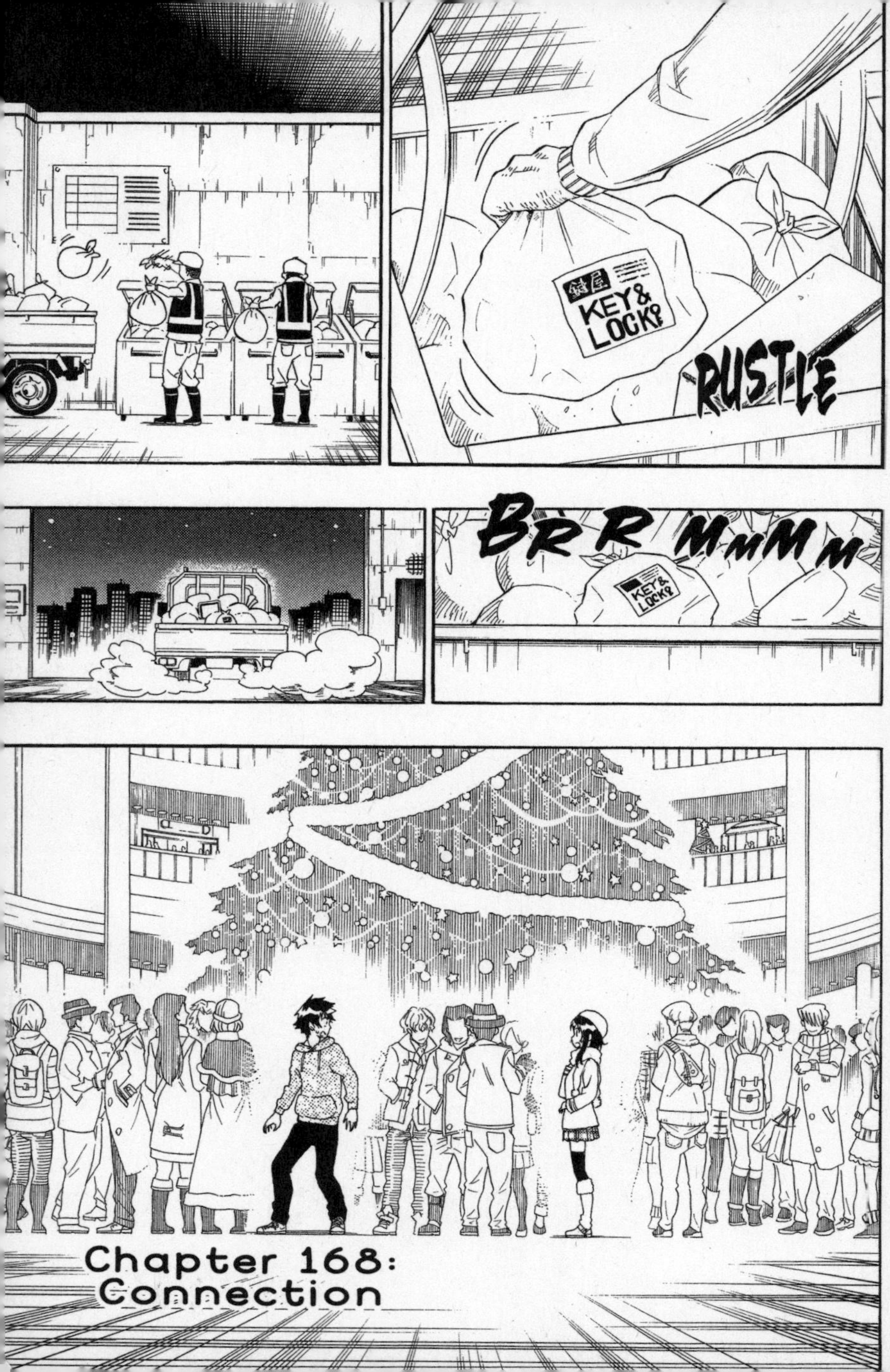
錠屋
KEY & LOCK
RUSTLE
BRRMMMM
KEY & LOCK
Chapter 168:
Connection

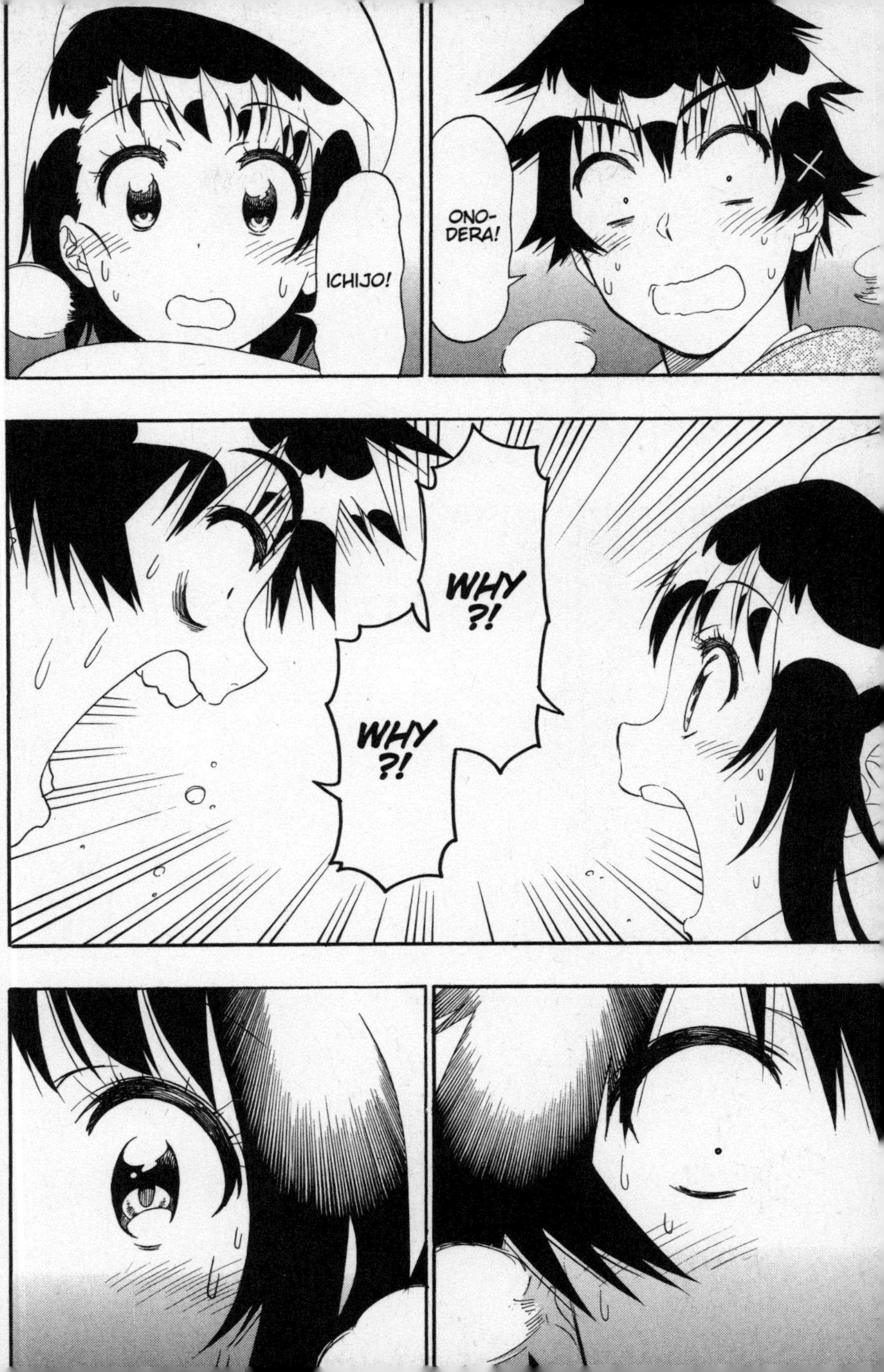
ONO-DERA!
ICHIJO!
WHY?!
WHY?!

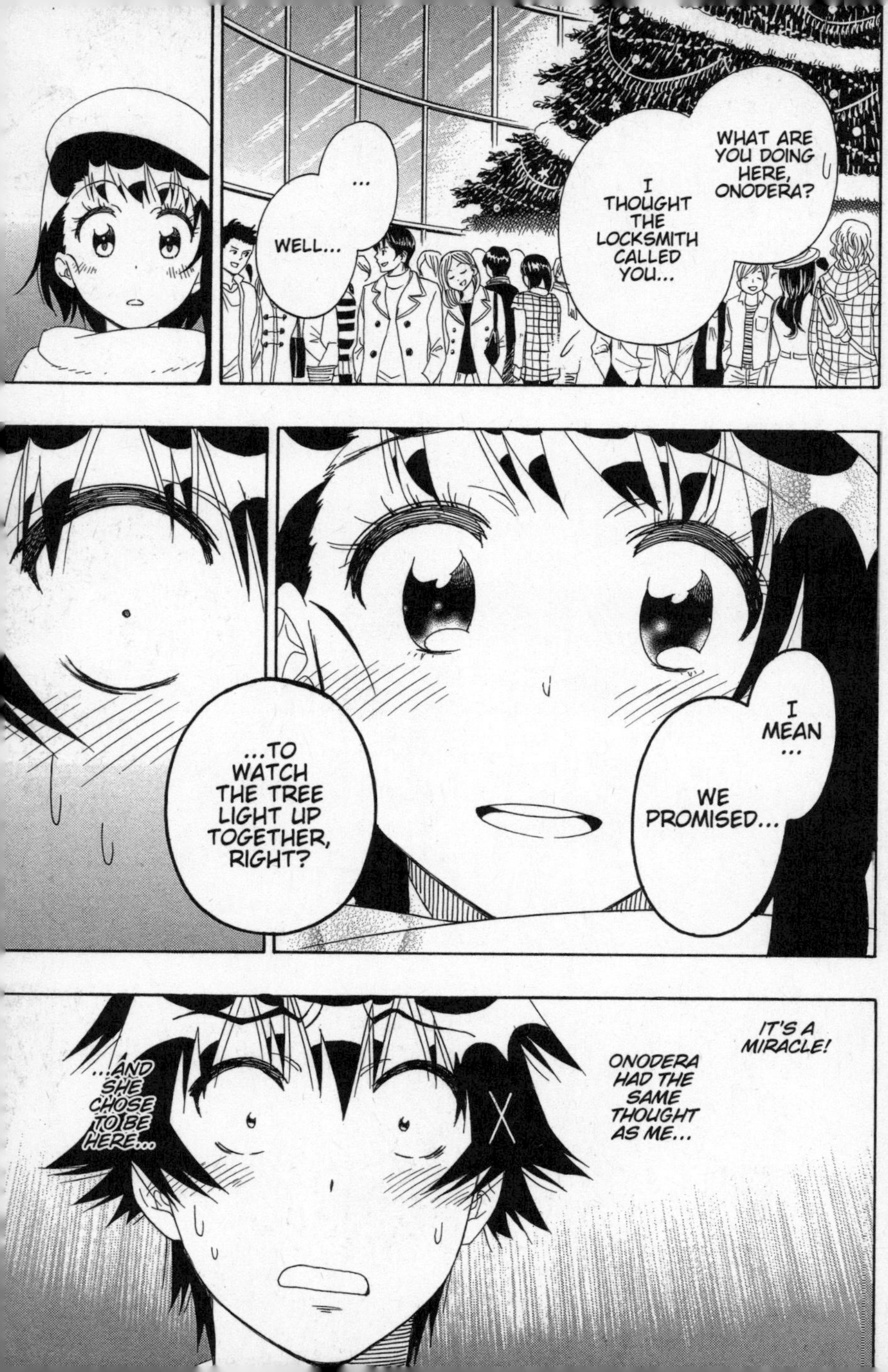
WHAT ARE YOU DOING HERE, ONODERA?
I THOUGHT THE LOCKSMITH CALLED YOU...
... WELL...
I MEAN...
WE PROMISED...
...TO WATCH THE TREE LIGHT UP TOGETHER, RIGHT?
IT'S A MIRACLE!
ONODERA HAD THE SAME THOUGHT AS ME...
...AND SHE CHOSE TO BE HERE...

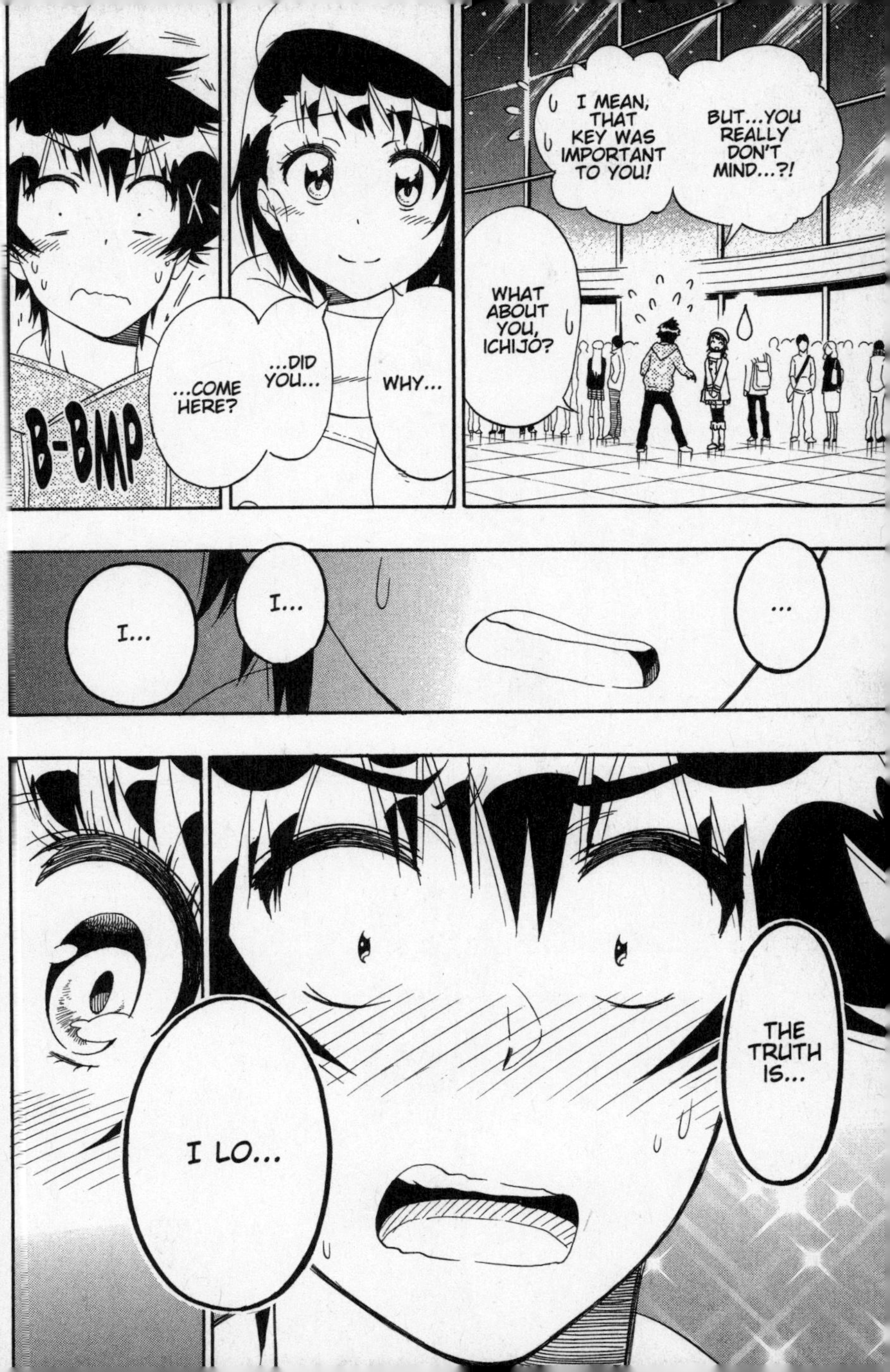
BUT...YOU REALLY DON'T MIND...?!
I MEAN, THAT KEY WAS IMPORTANT TO YOU!
WHAT ABOUT YOU, ICHIJO?
WHY...
...DID YOU...
...COME HERE?
B-BMP
...
I...
I...
THE TRUTH IS...
I LO...

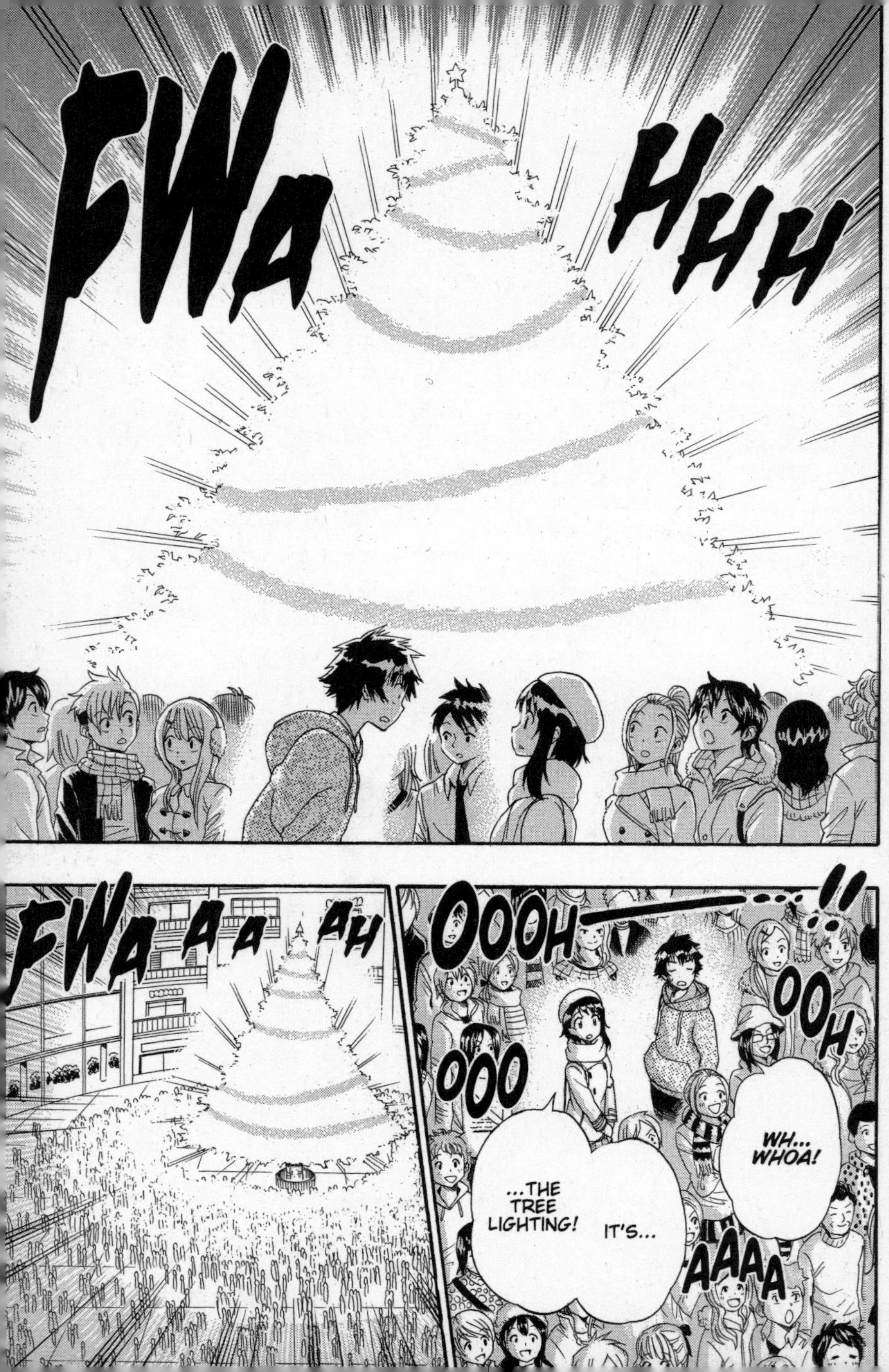
FWAHHH
OOOH———...!!
OOH
WH... WHOA!
OOO
IT'S...
...THE TREE LIGHTING!
AAAA
FWAAAAH

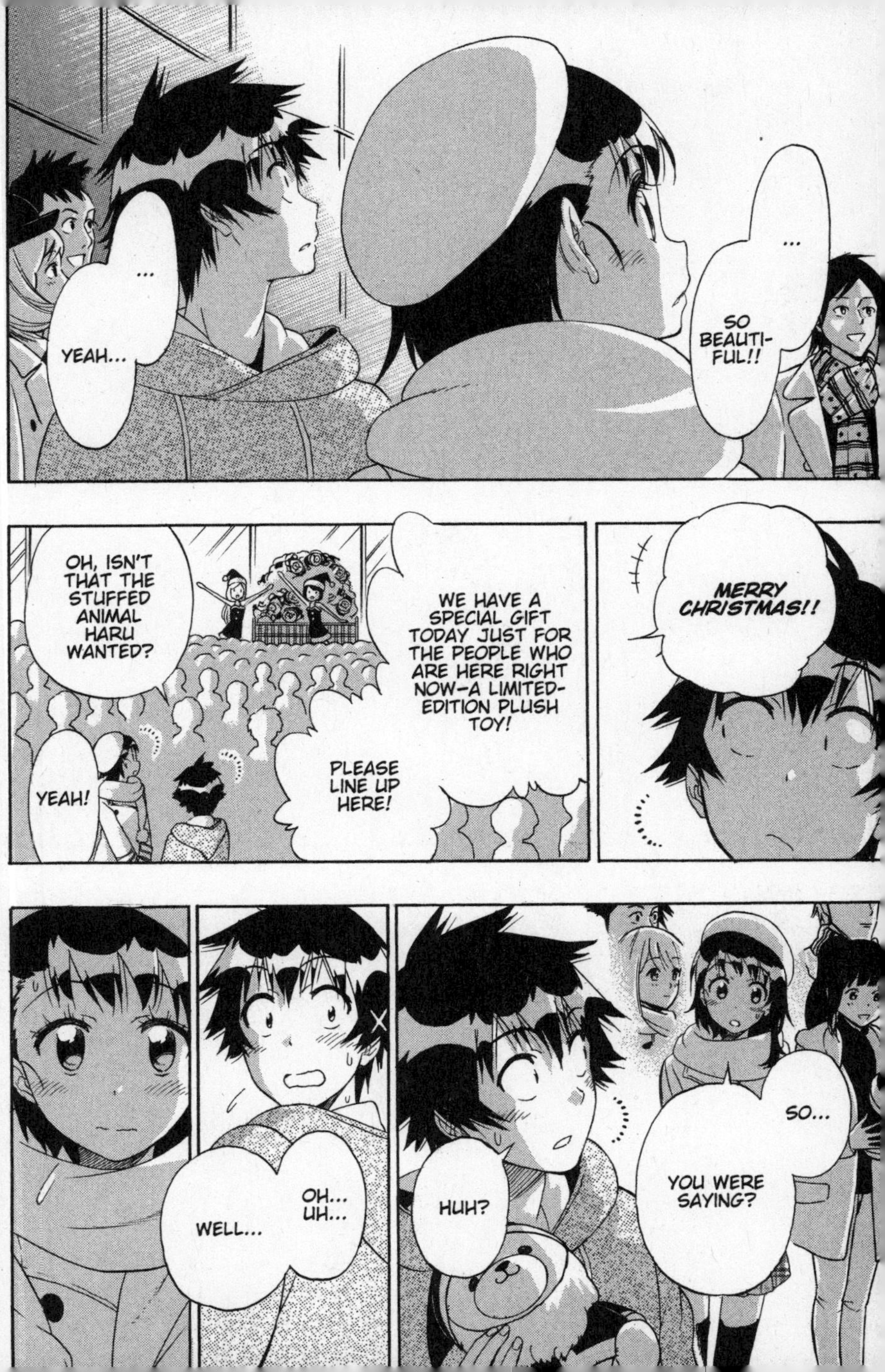
... SO BEAUTIFUL!!
... YEAH...
MERRY CHRISTMAS!!
WE HAVE A SPECIAL GIFT TODAY JUST FOR THE PEOPLE WHO ARE HERE RIGHT NOW—A LIMITED-EDITION PLUSH TOY!
PLEASE LINE UP HERE!
OH, ISN'T THAT THE STUFFED ANIMAL HARU WANTED?
YEAH!
SO... YOU WERE SAYING?
HUH?
OH... UH... WELL...

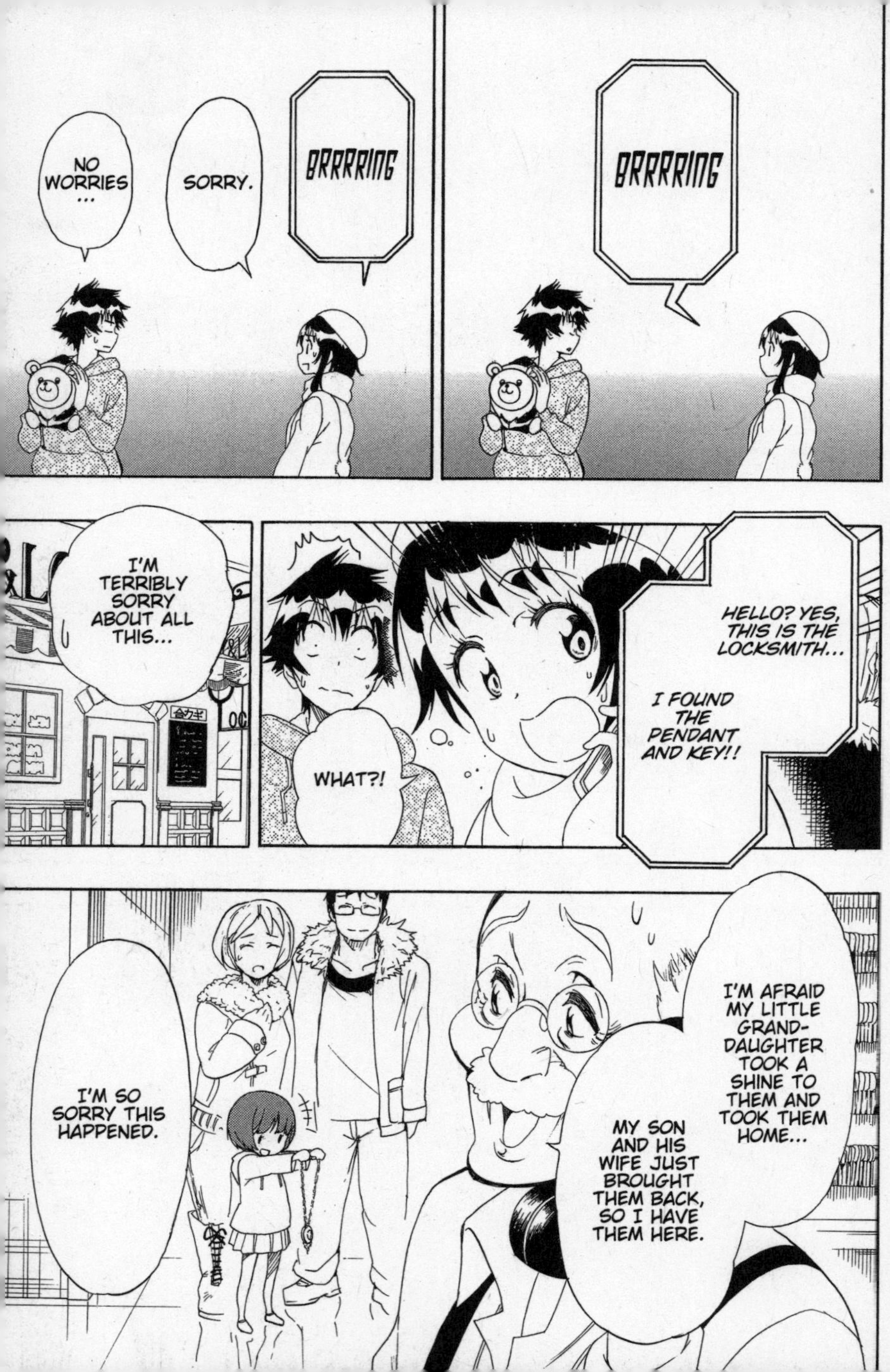
BRRRRING
BRRRRING
SORRY.
NO WORRIES...
HELLO? YES, THIS IS THE LOCKSMITH...
I FOUND THE PENDANT AND KEY!!
WHAT?!
I'M TERRIBLY SORRY ABOUT ALL THIS...
I'M AFRAID MY LITTLE GRAND-DAUGHTER TOOK A SHINE TO THEM AND TOOK THEM HOME...
MY SON AND HIS WIFE JUST BROUGHT THEM BACK, SO I HAVE THEM HERE.
I'M SO SORRY THIS HAPPENED.

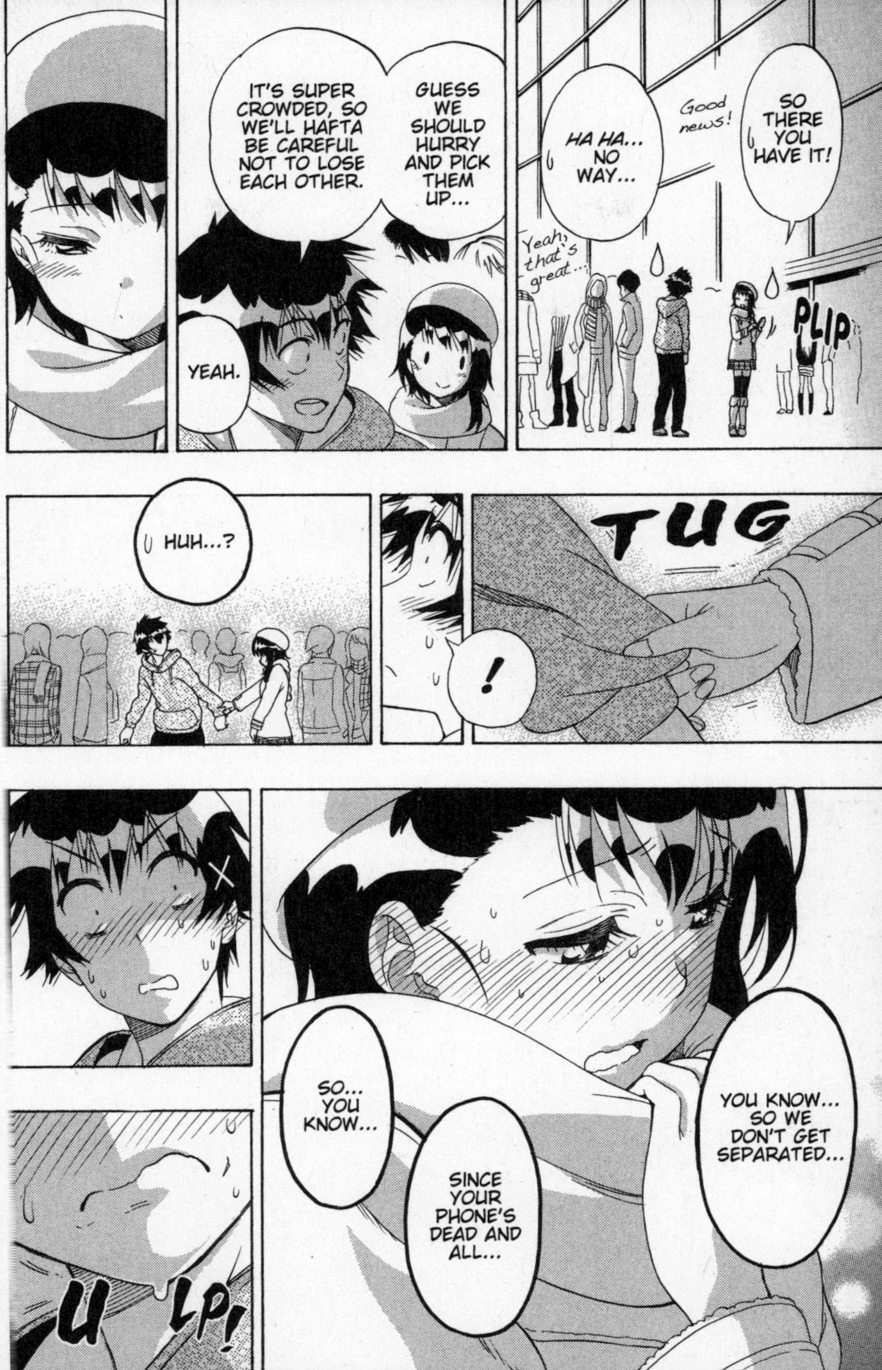
SO THERE YOU HAVE IT!
Good news!
HA HA... NO WAY...
Yeah, that's great...
PLIP
GUESS WE SHOULD HURRY AND PICK THEM UP...
IT'S SUPER CROWDED, SO WE'LL HAFTA BE CAREFUL NOT TO LOSE EACH OTHER.
YEAH.
TUG
!
HUH...?
YOU KNOW... SO WE DON'T GET SEPARATED...
SINCE YOUR PHONE'S DEAD AND ALL...
SO... YOU KNOW...
ULP!

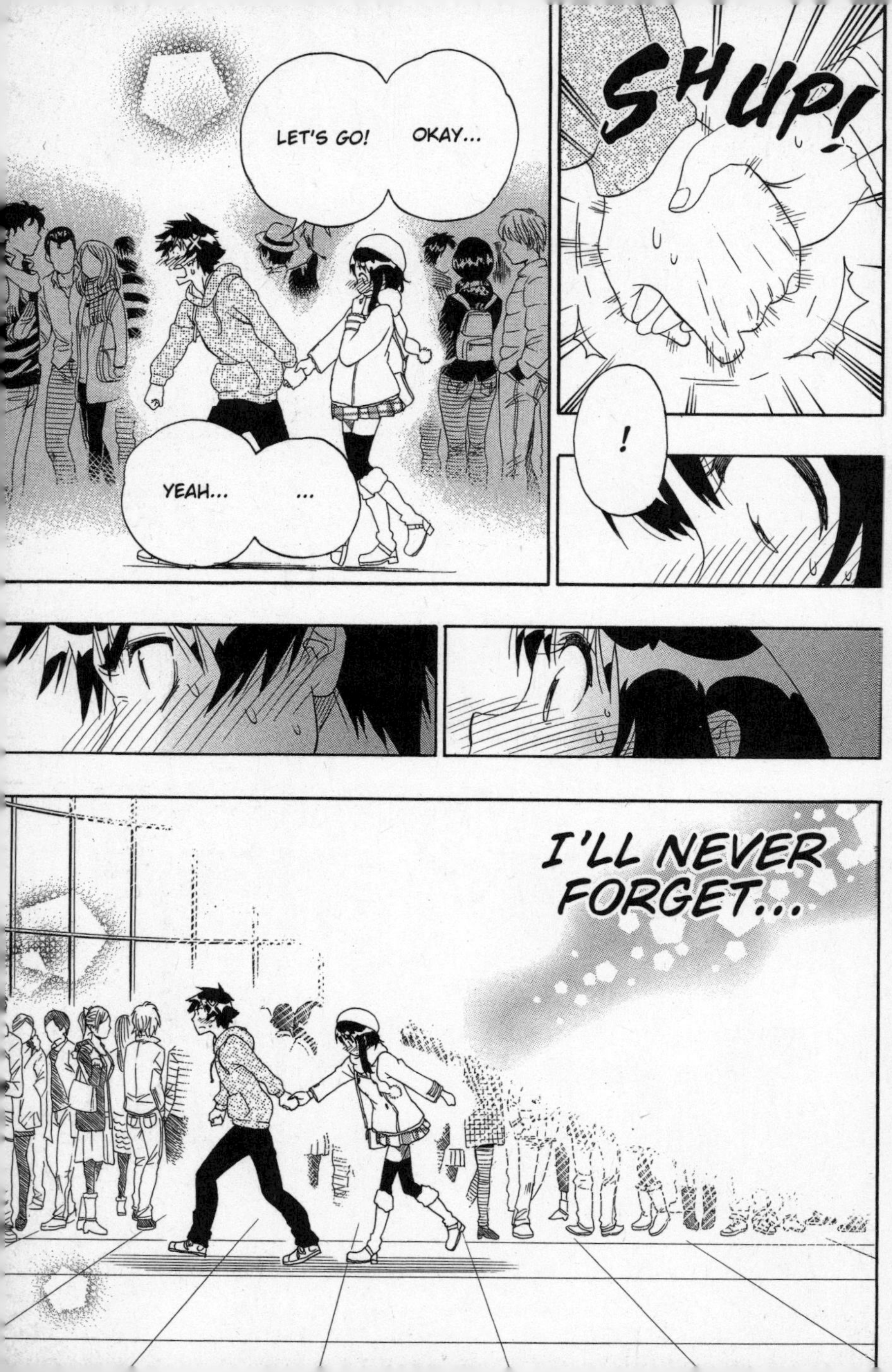
SHUP!
!
LET'S GO! OKAY...
YEAH... ...
I'LL NEVER FORGET...

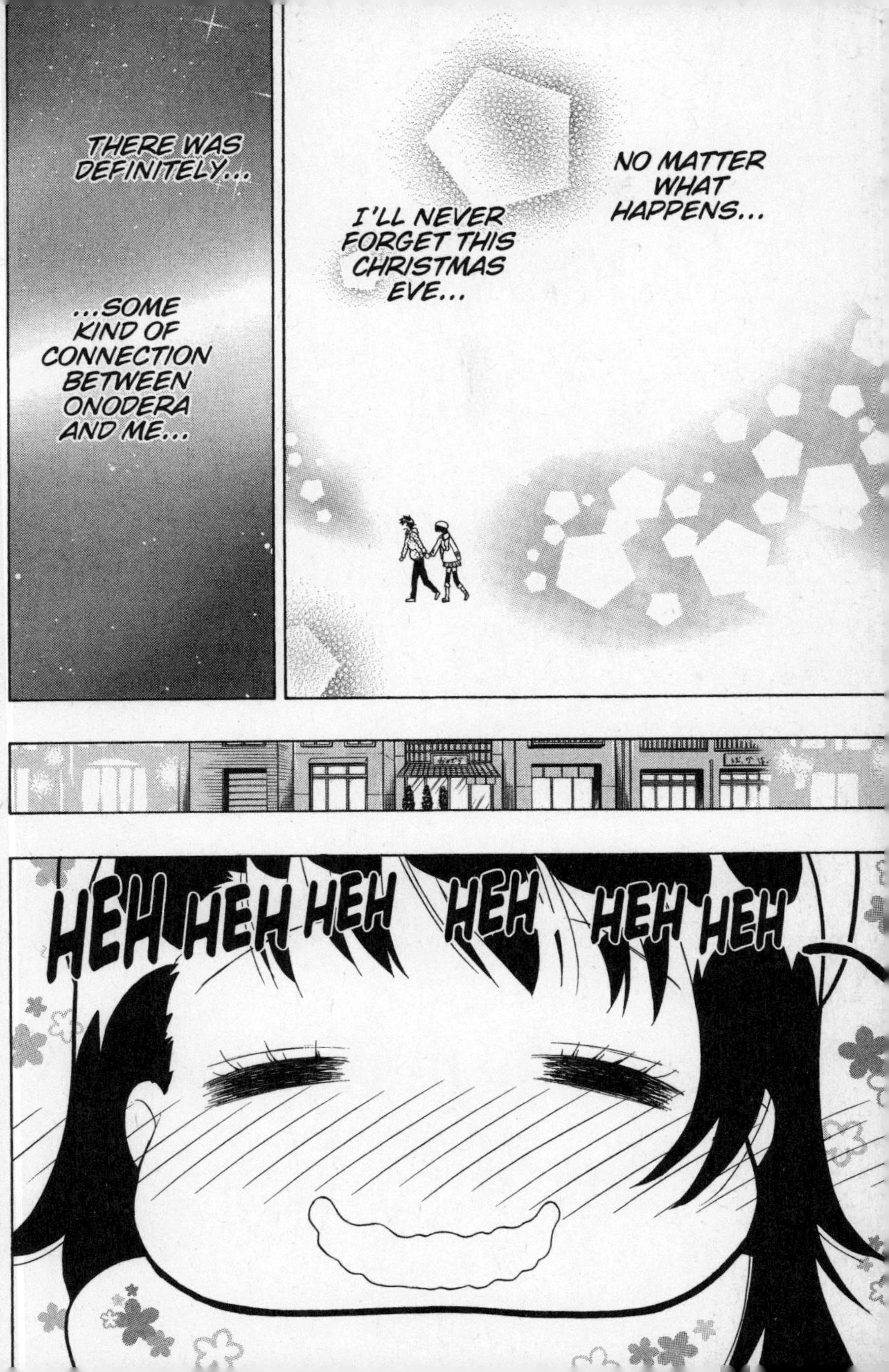
NO MATTER WHAT HAPPENS...
I'LL NEVER FORGET THIS CHRISTMAS EVE...
THERE WAS DEFINITELY...
...SOME KIND OF CONNECTION BETWEEN ONODERA AND ME...
HEH HEH HEH HEH HEH HEH

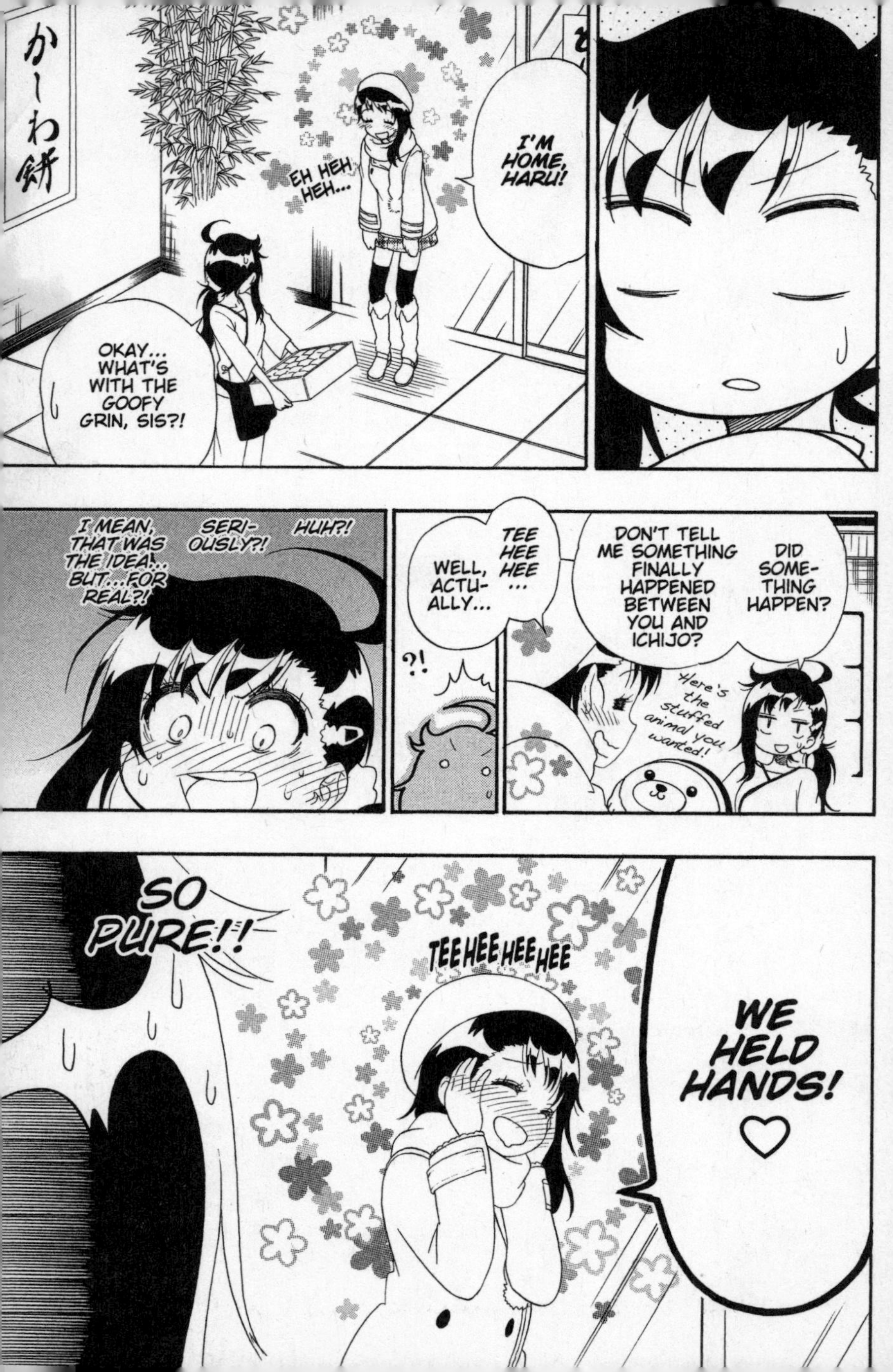
I'M HOME, HARU!
EH HEH HEH...
かしわ餅
OKAY... WHAT'S WITH THE GOOFY GRIN, SIS?!
DID SOMETHING HAPPEN?
DON'T TELL ME SOMETHING FINALLY HAPPENED BETWEEN YOU AND ICHIJO?
Here's the stuffed animal you wanted!
TEE HEE HEE...
WELL, ACTUALLY...
?!
HUH?!
SERIOUSLY?!
I MEAN, THAT WAS THE IDEA... BUT... FOR REAL?!
WE HELD HANDS! ♡
TEE HEE HEE HEE
SO PURE!!

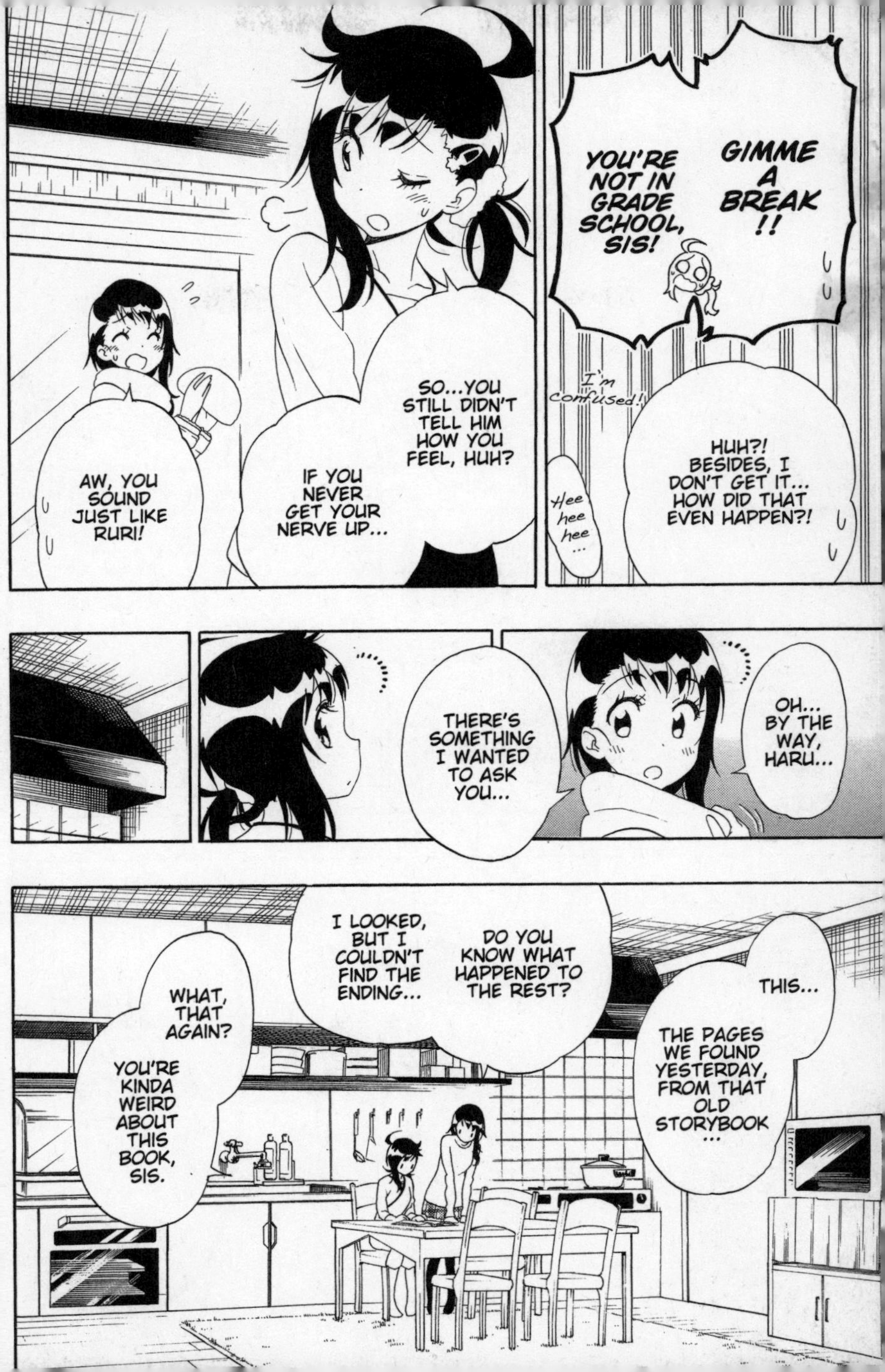
GIMME A BREAK!!
YOU'RE NOT IN GRADE SCHOOL, SIS!
I'm confused!
HUH?! BESIDES, I DON'T GET IT... HOW DID THAT EVEN HAPPEN?!
Hee hee hee...
SO...YOU STILL DIDN'T TELL HIM HOW YOU FEEL, HUH?
IF YOU NEVER GET YOUR NERVE UP...
AW, YOU SOUND JUST LIKE RURI!
OH... BY THE WAY, HARU...
THERE'S SOMETHING I WANTED TO ASK YOU...
THIS...
THE PAGES WE FOUND YESTERDAY, FROM THAT OLD STORYBOOK...
DO YOU KNOW WHAT HAPPENED TO THE REST?
I LOOKED, BUT I COULDN'T FIND THE ENDING...
WHAT, THAT AGAIN?
YOU'RE KINDA WEIRD ABOUT THIS BOOK, SIS.

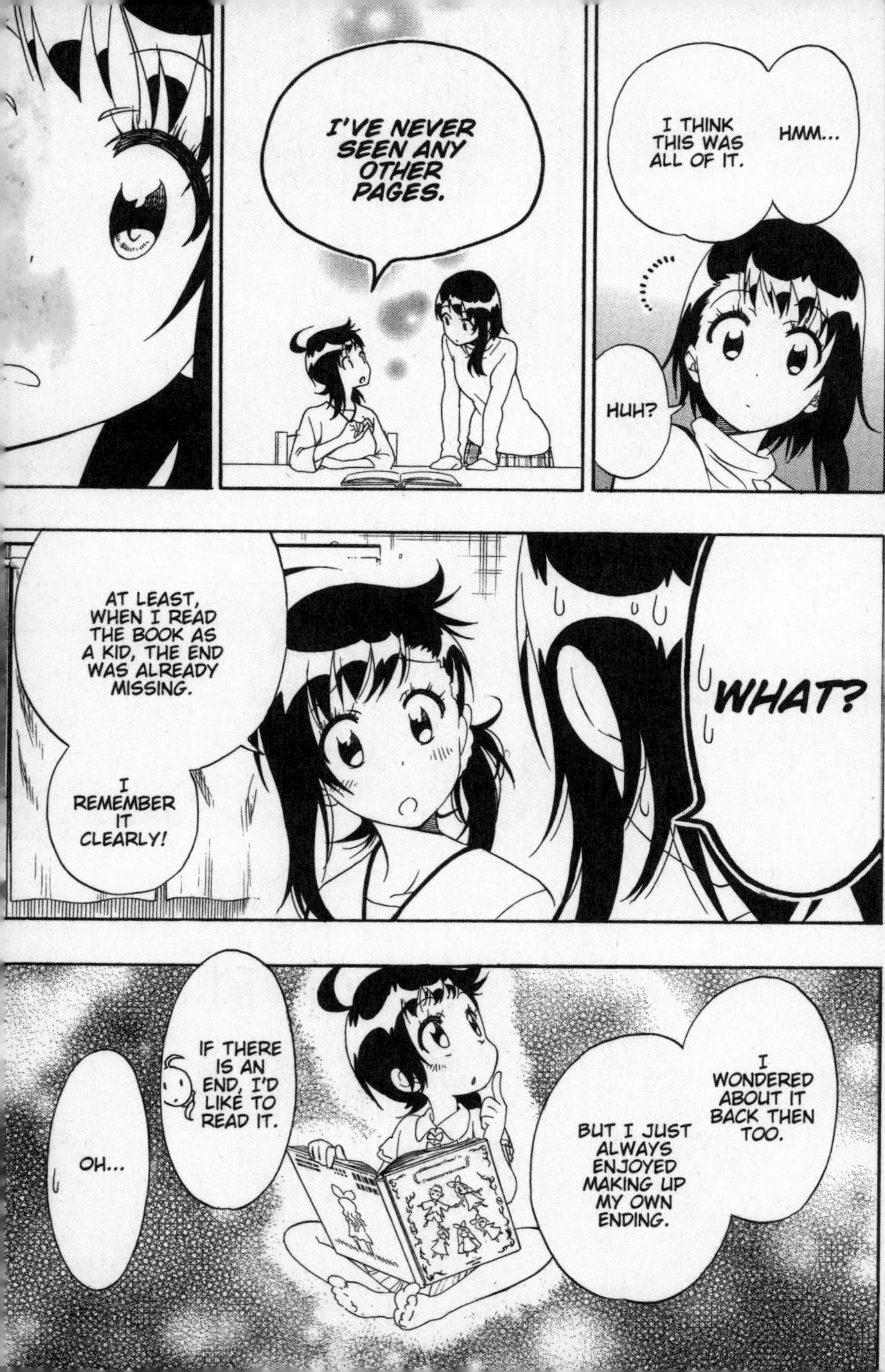
HMM...
I THINK THIS WAS ALL OF IT.
HUH?
I'VE NEVER SEEN ANY OTHER PAGES.
WHAT?
AT LEAST, WHEN I READ THE BOOK AS A KID, THE END WAS ALREADY MISSING.
I REMEMBER IT CLEARLY!
I WONDERED ABOUT IT BACK THEN TOO.
BUT I JUST ALWAYS ENJOYED MAKING UP MY OWN ENDING.
IF THERE IS AN END, I'D LIKE TO READ IT.
OH...

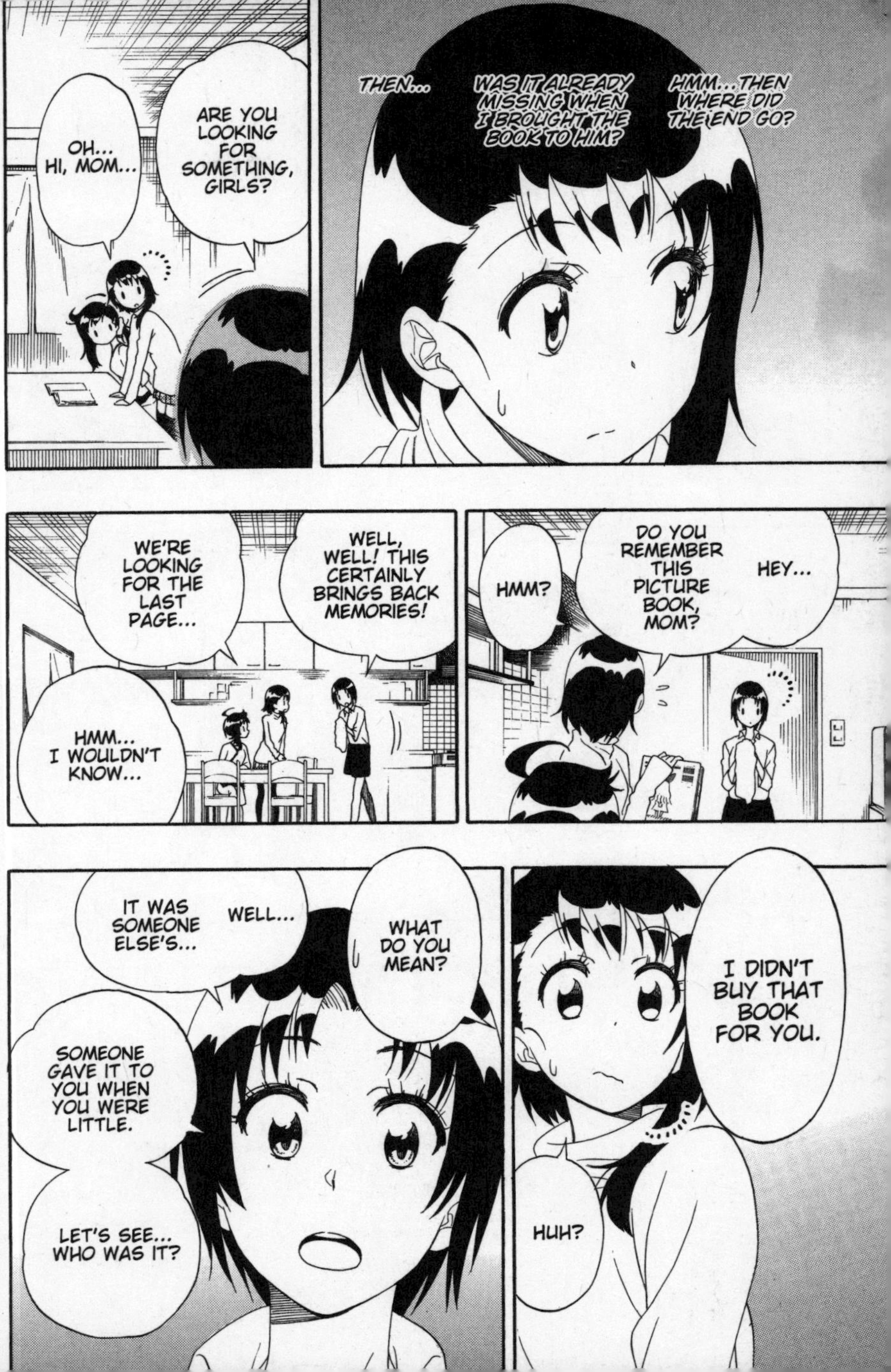
HMM... THEN WHERE DID THE END GO?
WAS IT ALREADY MISSING WHEN I BROUGHT THE BOOK TO HIM?
THEN...
ARE YOU LOOKING FOR SOMETHING, GIRLS?
OH... HI, MOM...
HEY...
DO YOU REMEMBER THIS PICTURE BOOK, MOM?
HMM?
WELL, WELL! THIS CERTAINLY BRINGS BACK MEMORIES!
WE'RE LOOKING FOR THE LAST PAGE...
HMM... I WOULDN'T KNOW...
I DIDN'T BUY THAT BOOK FOR YOU.
HUH?
WHAT DO YOU MEAN?
WELL...
IT WAS SOMEONE ELSE'S...
SOMEONE GAVE IT TO YOU WHEN YOU WERE LITTLE.
LET'S SEE... WHO WAS IT?

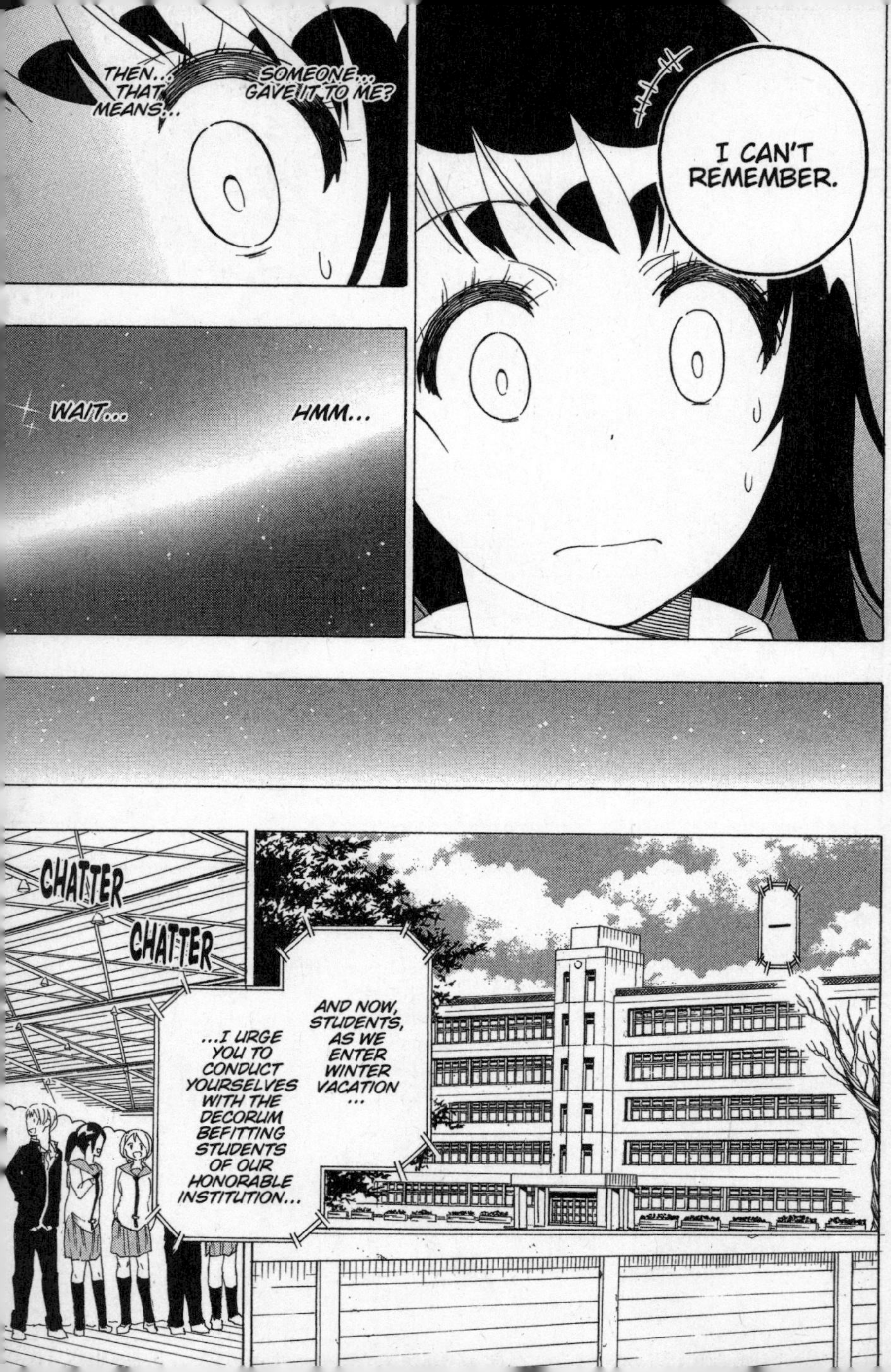
I CAN'T REMEMBER.
SOMEONE... GAVE IT TO ME?
THEN... THAT MEANS...
HMM...
WAIT...
—
AND NOW, STUDENTS, AS WE ENTER WINTER VACATION...
...I URGE YOU TO CONDUCT YOURSELVES WITH THE DECORUM BEFITTING STUDENTS OF OUR HONORABLE INSTITUTION...
CHATTER
CHATTER

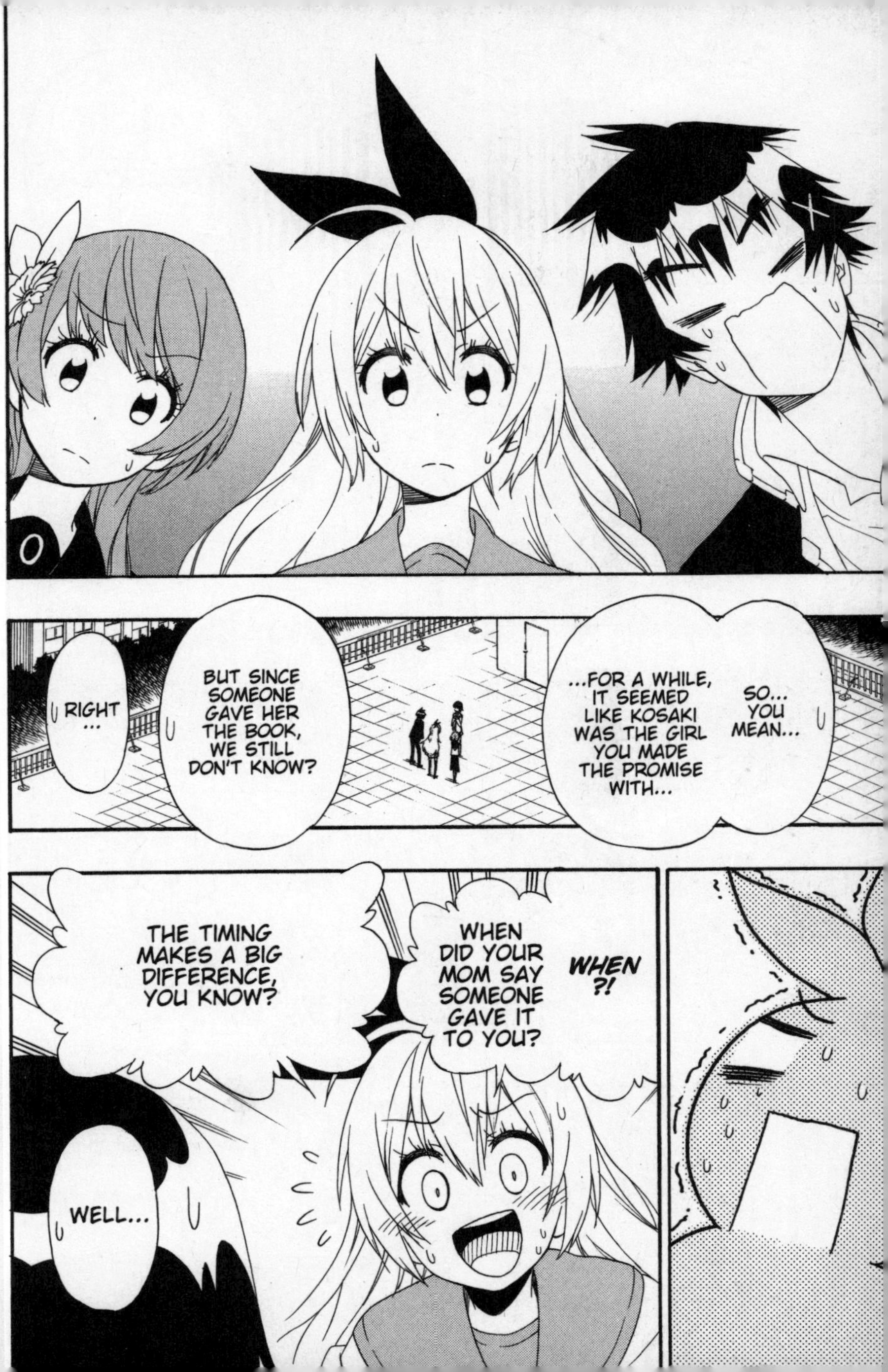
SO... YOU MEAN...
...FOR A WHILE, IT SEEMED LIKE KOSAKI WAS THE GIRL YOU MADE THE PROMISE WITH...
BUT SINCE SOMEONE GAVE HER THE BOOK, WE STILL DON'T KNOW?
RIGHT...
WHEN?!
WHEN DID YOUR MOM SAY SOMEONE GAVE IT TO YOU?
THE TIMING MAKES A BIG DIFFERENCE, YOU KNOW?
WELL...

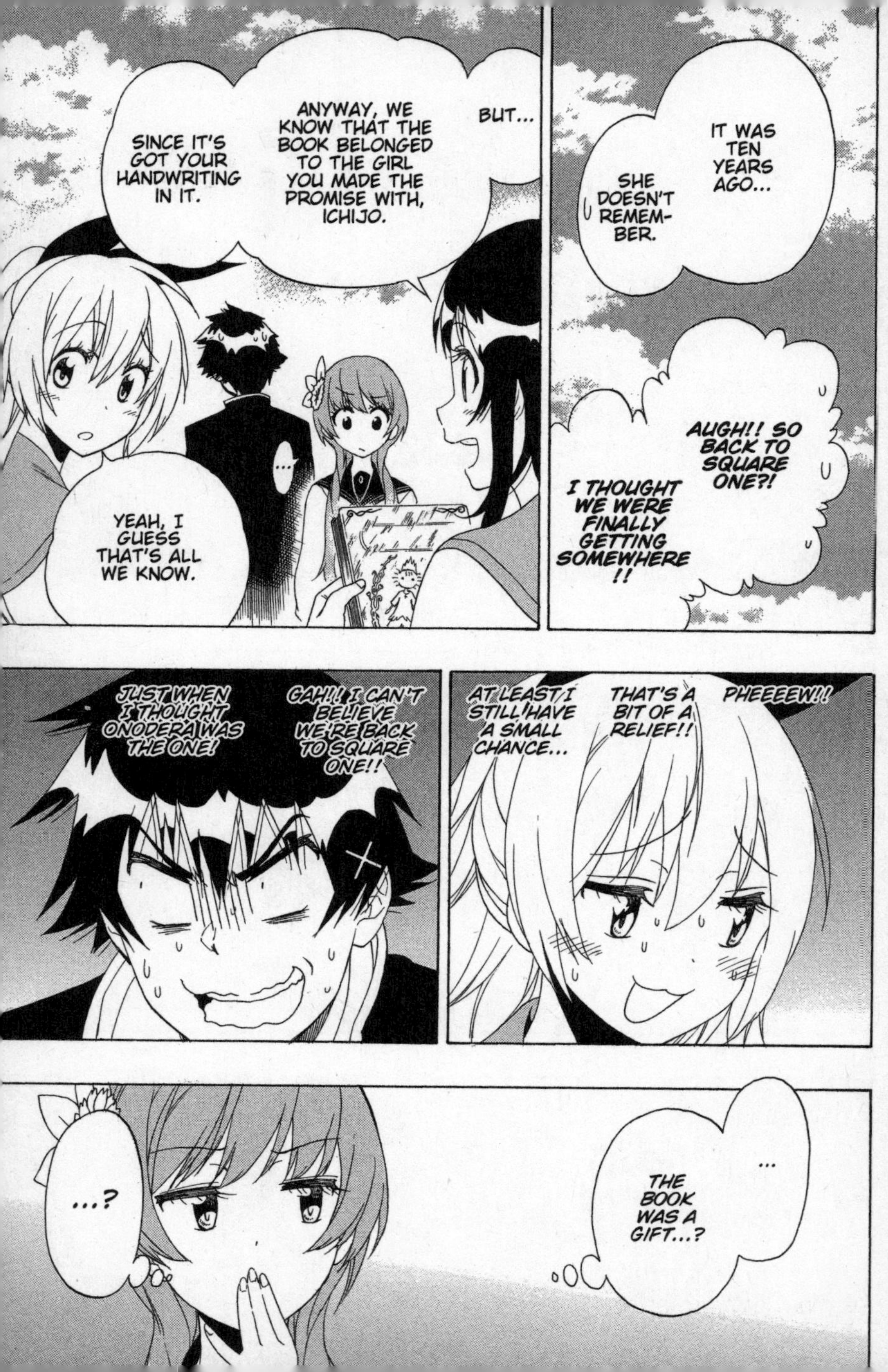
IT WAS TEN YEARS AGO...
SHE DOESN'T REMEM-BER.
AUGH!! SO BACK TO SQUARE ONE?!
I THOUGHT WE WERE FINALLY GETTING SOMEWHERE!!
BUT...
ANYWAY, WE KNOW THAT THE BOOK BELONGED TO THE GIRL YOU MADE THE PROMISE WITH, ICHIJO.
SINCE IT'S GOT YOUR HANDWRITING IN IT.
...
YEAH, I GUESS THAT'S ALL WE KNOW.
PHEEEEW!!
THAT'S A BIT OF A RELIEF!!
AT LEAST I STILL HAVE A SMALL CHANCE...
GAH!! I CAN'T BELIEVE WE'RE BACK TO SQUARE ONE!!
JUST WHEN I THOUGHT ONODERA WAS THE ONE!
...
THE BOOK WAS A GIFT...?
...?

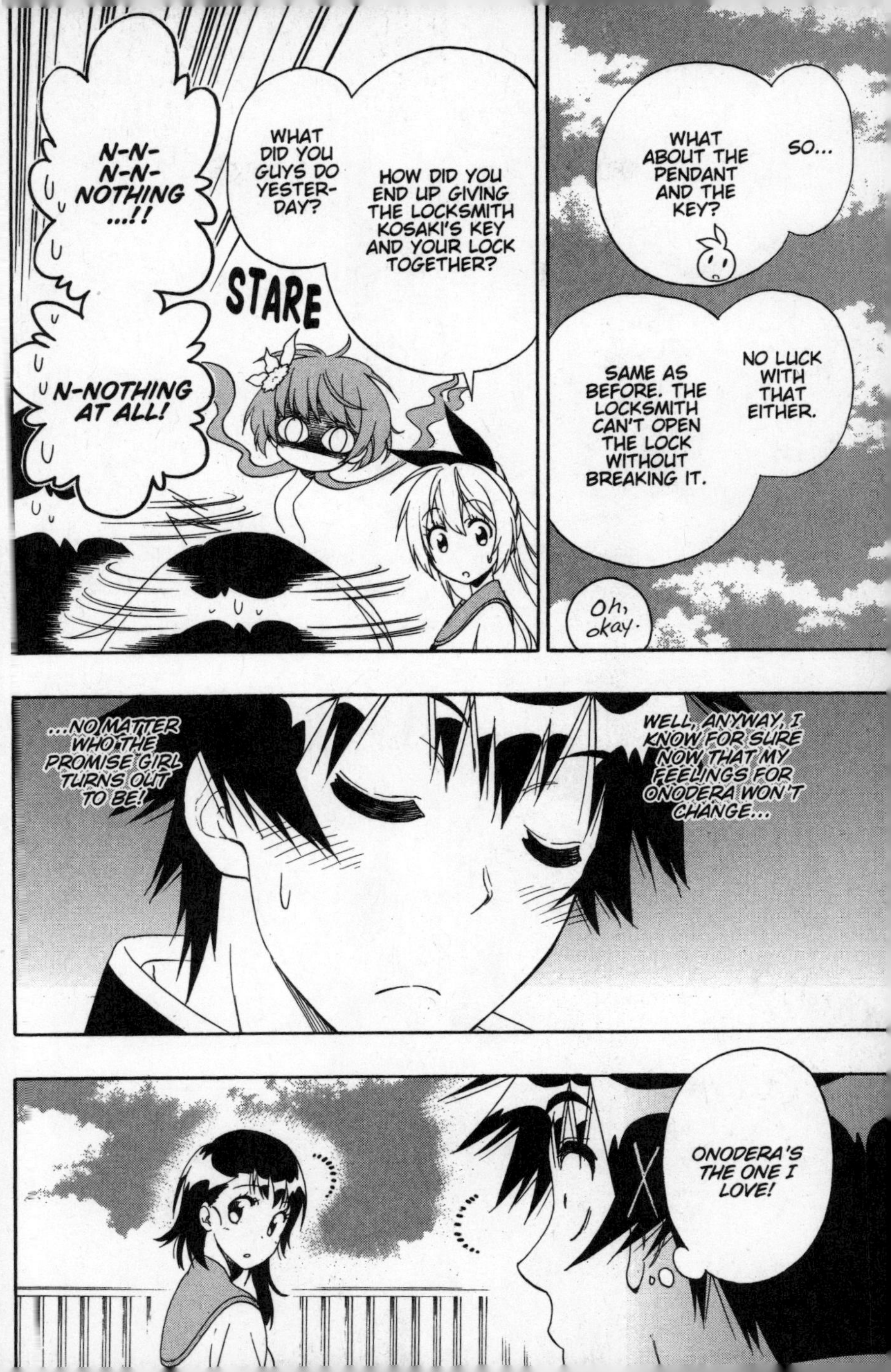
SO...
WHAT ABOUT THE PENDANT AND THE KEY?
NO LUCK WITH THAT EITHER.
SAME AS BEFORE. THE LOCKSMITH CAN'T OPEN THE LOCK WITHOUT BREAKING IT.
Oh, okay.
HOW DID YOU END UP GIVING THE LOCKSMITH KOSAKI'S KEY AND YOUR LOCK TOGETHER?
WHAT DID YOU GUYS DO YESTER-DAY?
STARE
N-N-N-N-NOTHING ...!!
N-NOTHING AT ALL!
WELL, ANYWAY, I KNOW FOR SURE NOW THAT MY FEELINGS FOR ONODERA WON'T CHANGE...
...NO MATTER WHO THE PROMISE GIRL TURNS OUT TO BE!
ONODERA'S THE ONE I LOVE!

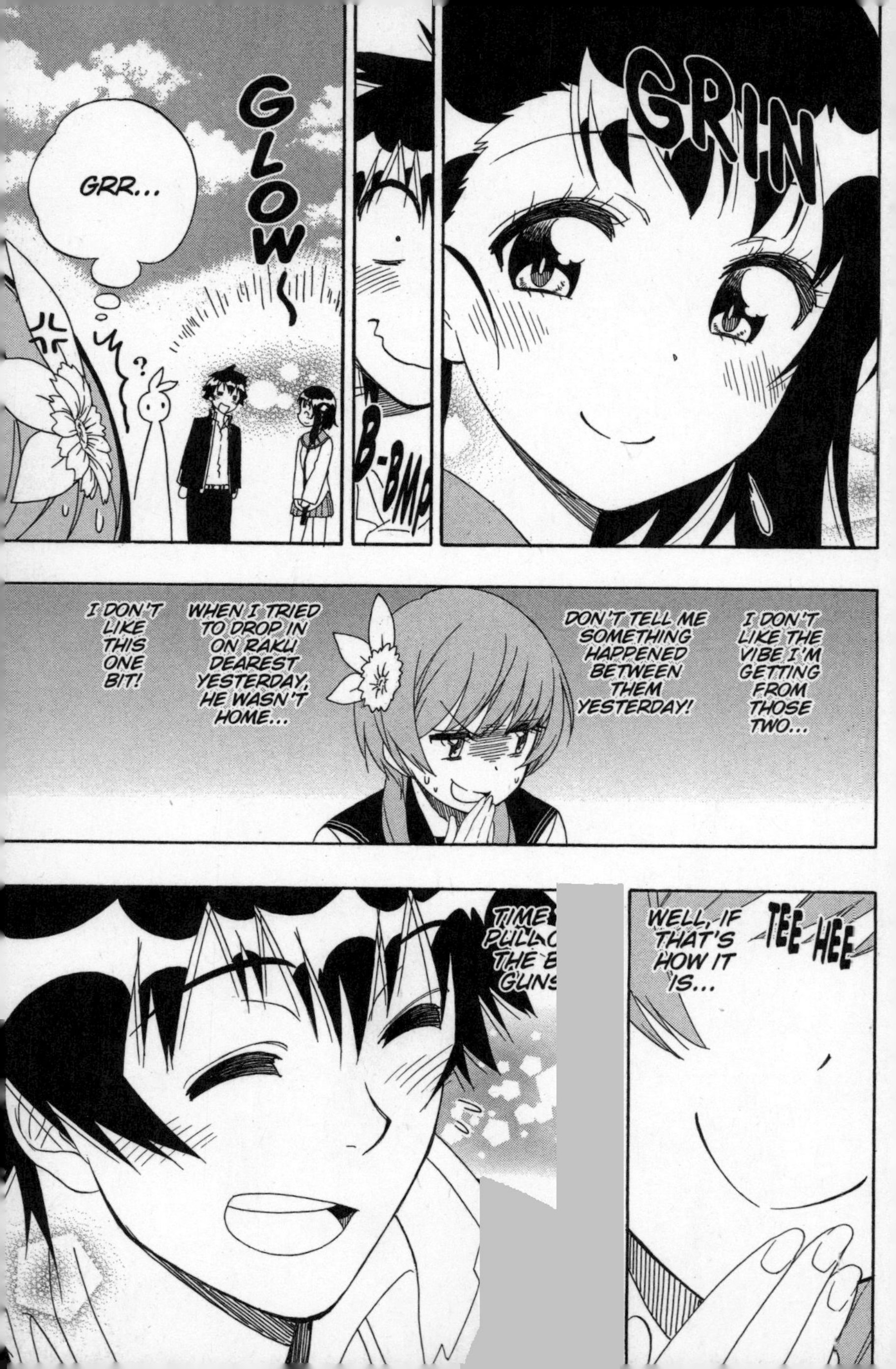
GRIN
B-BMP
GLOW
GRR...
I DON'T LIKE THE VIBE I'M GETTING FROM THOSE TWO...
DON'T TELL ME SOMETHING HAPPENED BETWEEN THEM YESTERDAY!
WHEN I TRIED TO DROP IN ON RAKU DEAREST YESTERDAY, HE WASN'T HOME...
I DON'T LIKE THIS ONE BIT!
TEE HEE
WELL, IF THAT'S HOW IT IS...
TIME
PULL
THE
GUNS

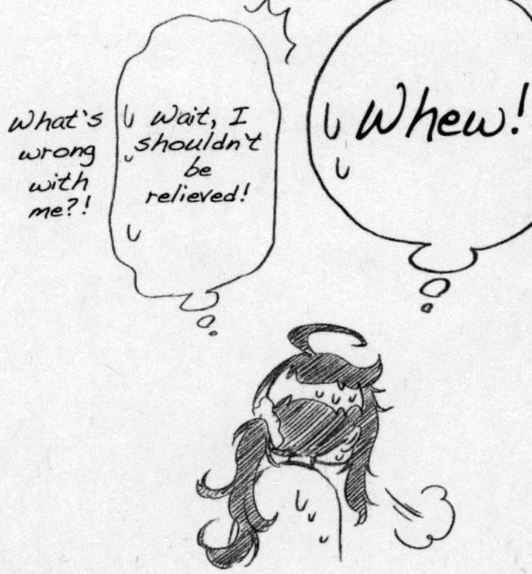
Whew!
Wait, I shouldn't be relieved!
What's wrong with me?!

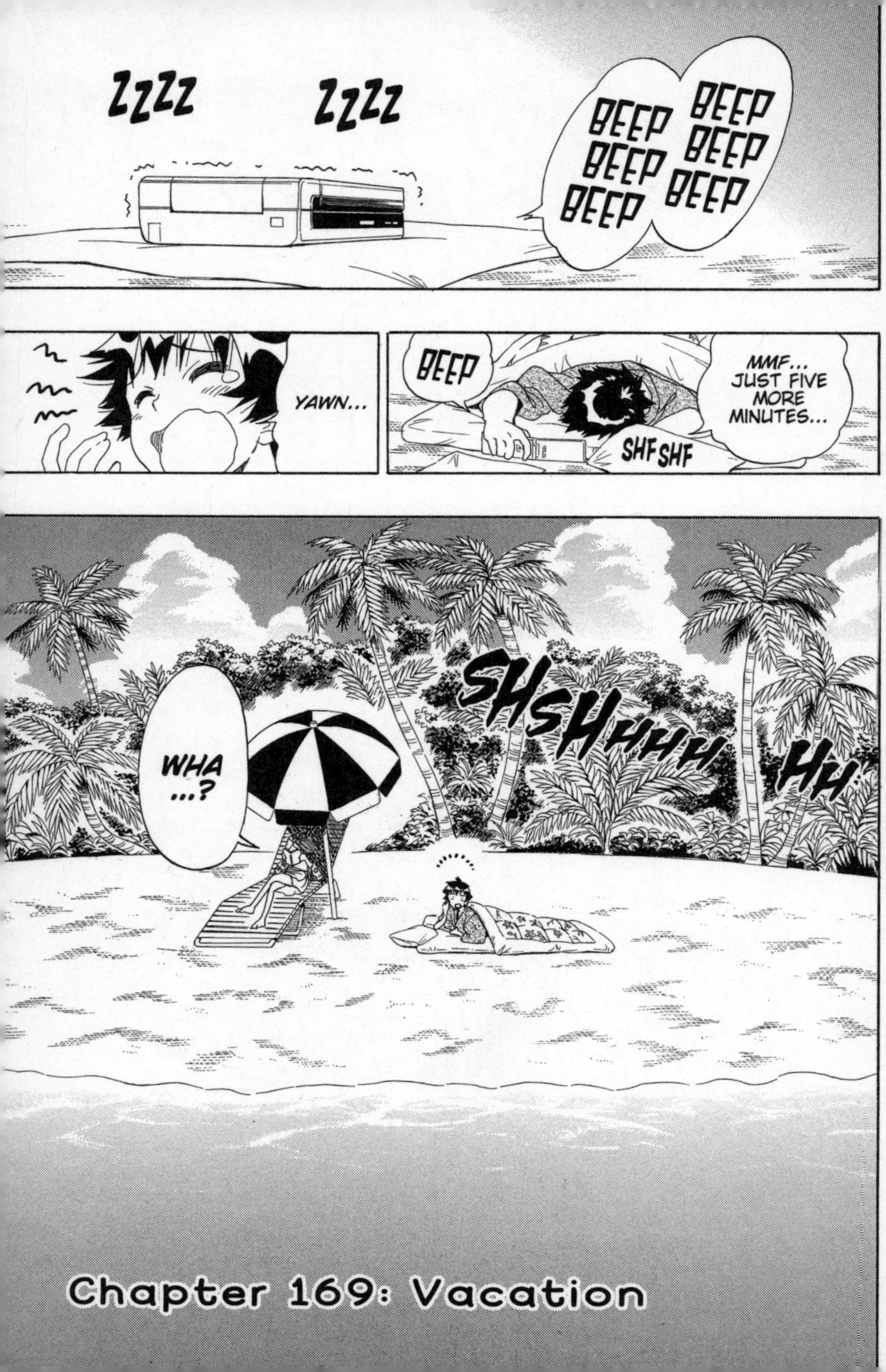
BEEP BEEP BEEP BEEP BEEP BEEP BEEP
ZZZZ
ZZZZ
MMF... JUST FIVE MORE MINUTES...
BEEP
SHF SHF
YAWN...
SHSHHHHH HH
WHA ...?

Chapter 169: Vacation

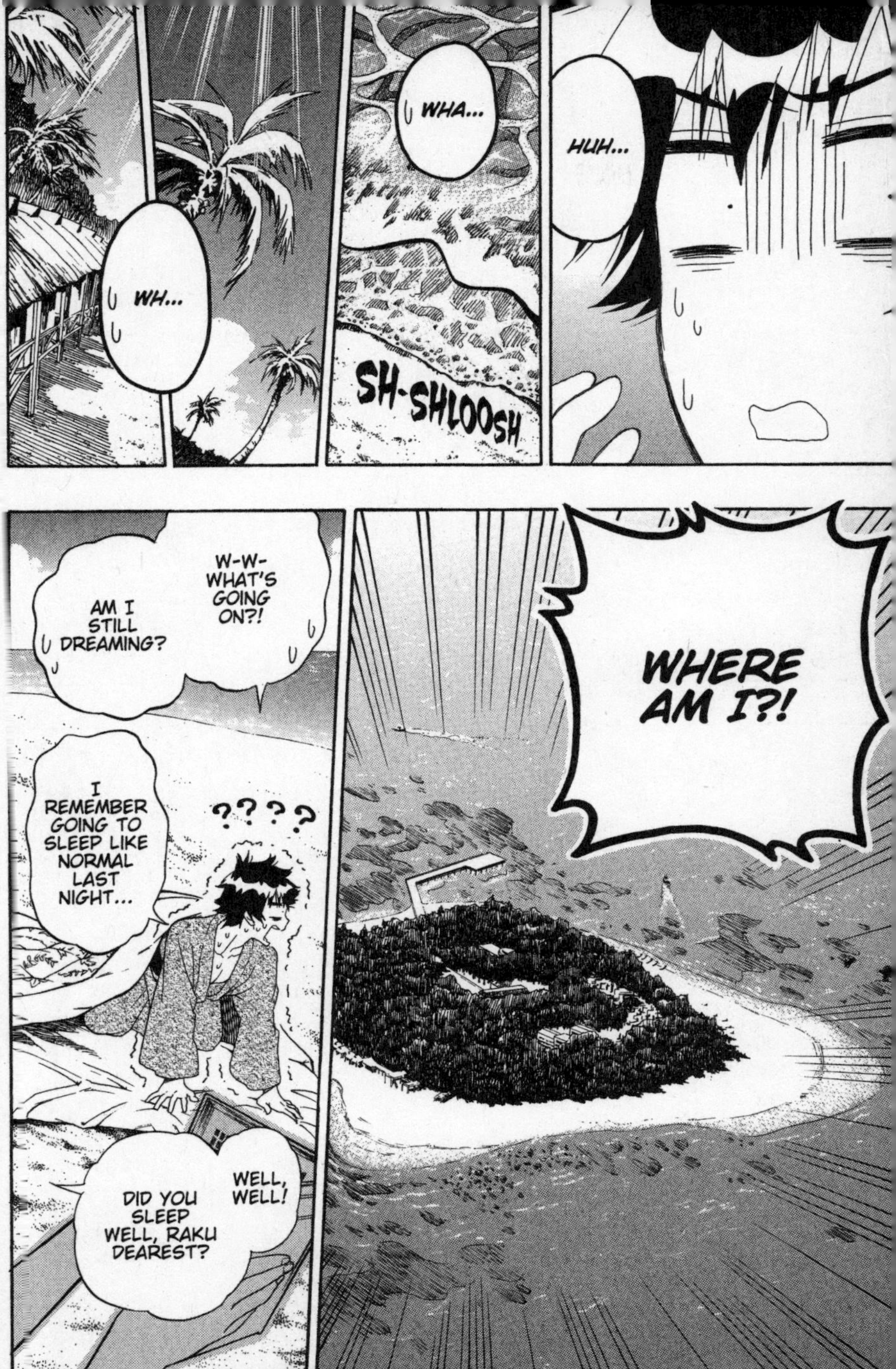
HUH...
WHA...
SH-SHLOOSH
WH...
WHERE AM I?!
W-W-WHAT'S GOING ON?!
AM I STILL DREAMING?
I REMEMBER GOING TO SLEEP LIKE NORMAL LAST NIGHT...
????
WELL, WELL!
DID YOU SLEEP WELL, RAKU DEAREST?

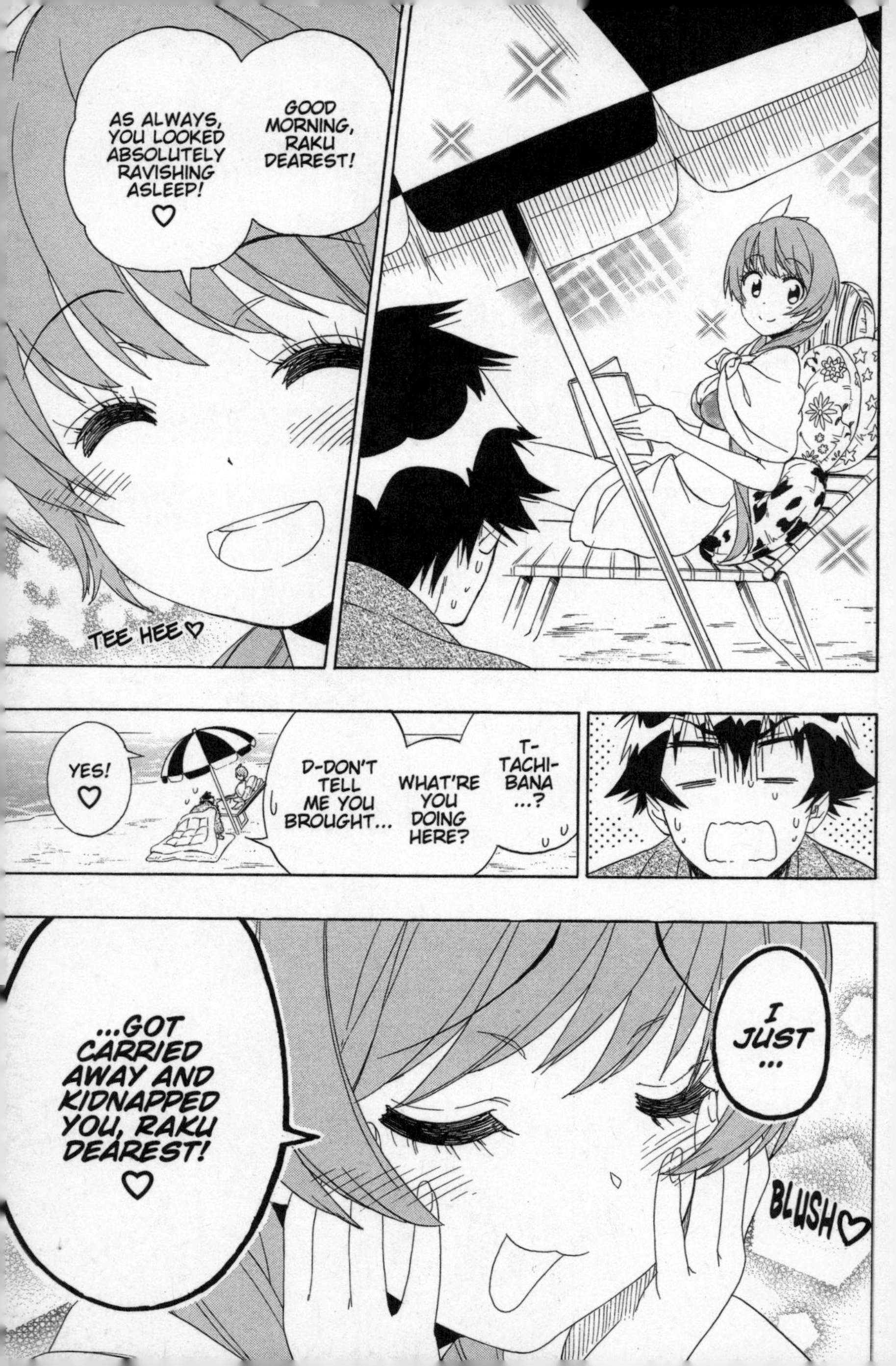
GOOD MORNING, RAKU DEAREST!
AS ALWAYS, YOU LOOKED ABSOLUTELY RAVISHING ASLEEP! ♡
TEE HEE♡
T-TACHIBANA ...?
WHAT'RE YOU DOING HERE?
D-DON'T TELL ME YOU BROUGHT...
YES! ♡
I JUST ...
...GOT CARRIED AWAY AND KIDNAPPED YOU, RAKU DEAREST! ♡
BLUSH♡

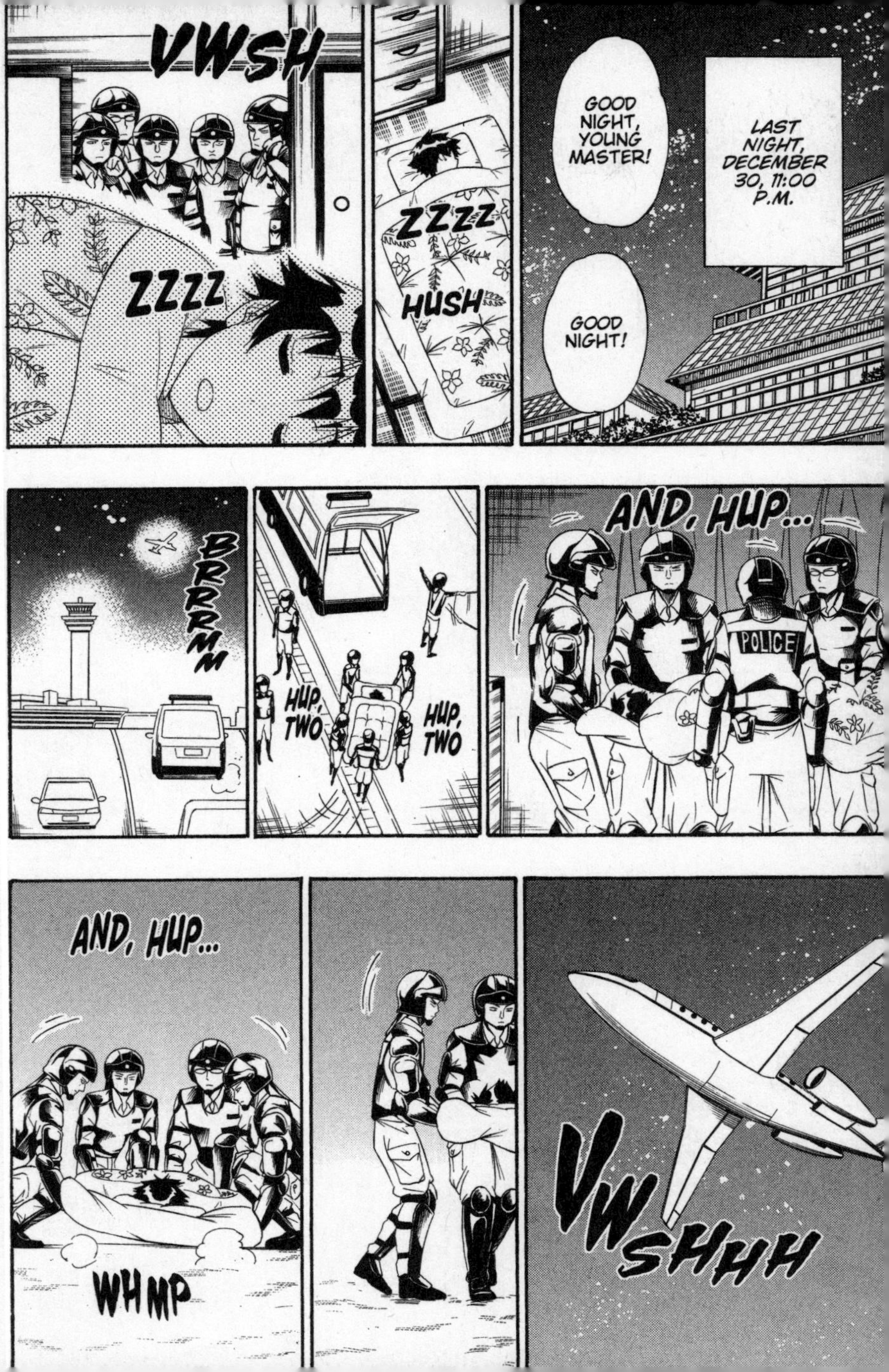

LAST NIGHT, DECEMBER 30, 11:00 P.M.
GOOD NIGHT, YOUNG MASTER!
GOOD NIGHT!
ZZZZ
HUSH
VWSH
ZZZZ
AND, HUP...
HUP, TWO
HUP, TWO
BRRRMM
VWSHHH
AND, HUP...
WHMP

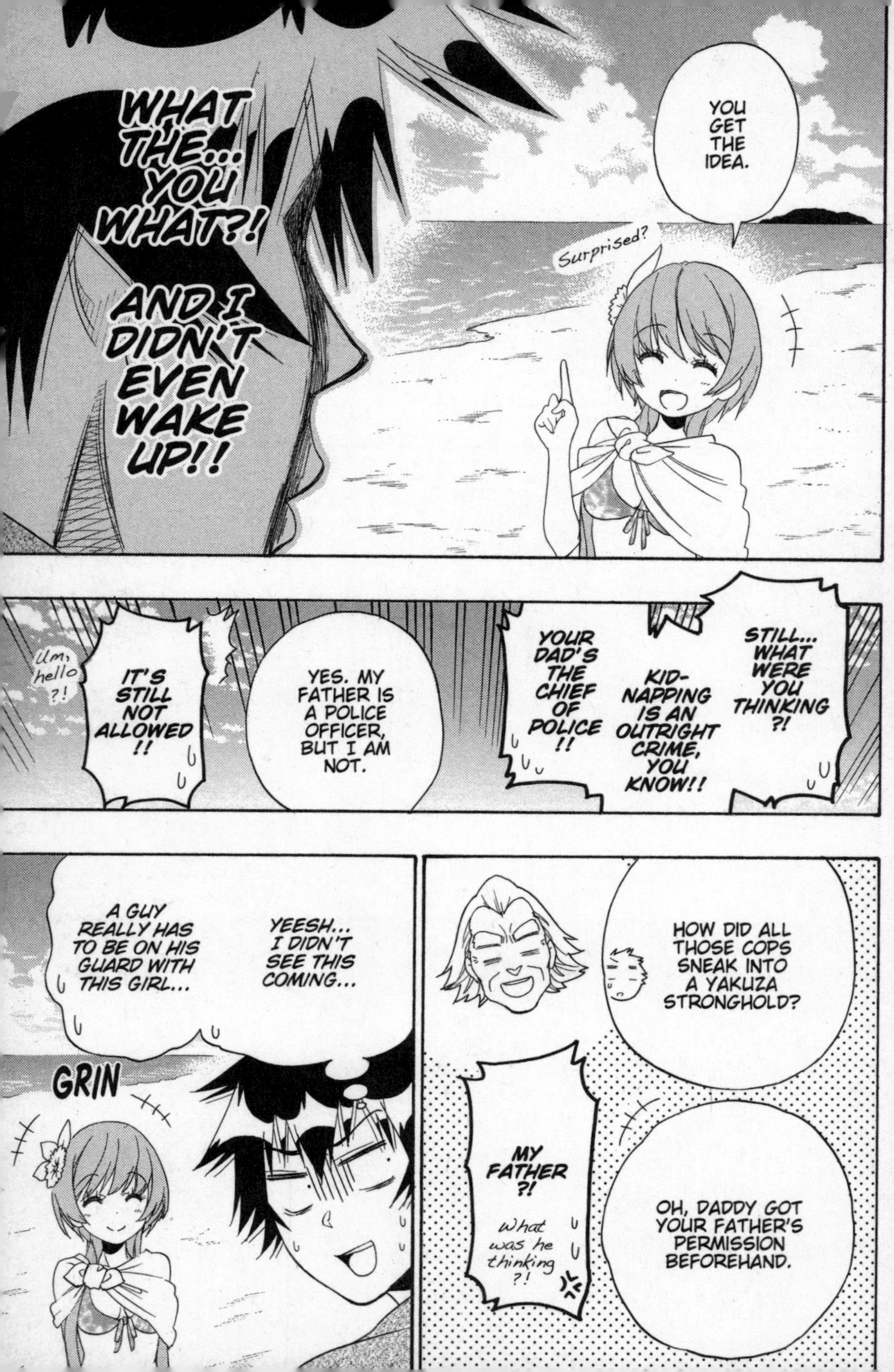
YOU GET THE IDEA.
Surprised?
WHAT THE... YOU WHAT?!
AND I DIDN'T EVEN WAKE UP!!
STILL... WHAT WERE YOU THINKING?!
KID-NAPPING IS AN OUTRIGHT CRIME, YOU KNOW!!
YOUR DAD'S THE CHIEF OF POLICE!!
YES. MY FATHER IS A POLICE OFFICER, BUT I AM NOT.
IT'S STILL NOT ALLOWED!!
Um, hello?!
HOW DID ALL THOSE COPS SNEAK INTO A YAKUZA STRONGHOLD?
OH, DADDY GOT YOUR FATHER'S PERMISSION BEFOREHAND.
MY FATHER?!
What was he thinking?!
YEESH... I DIDN'T SEE THIS COMING...
A GUY REALLY HAS TO BE ON HIS GUARD WITH THIS GIRL...
GRIN

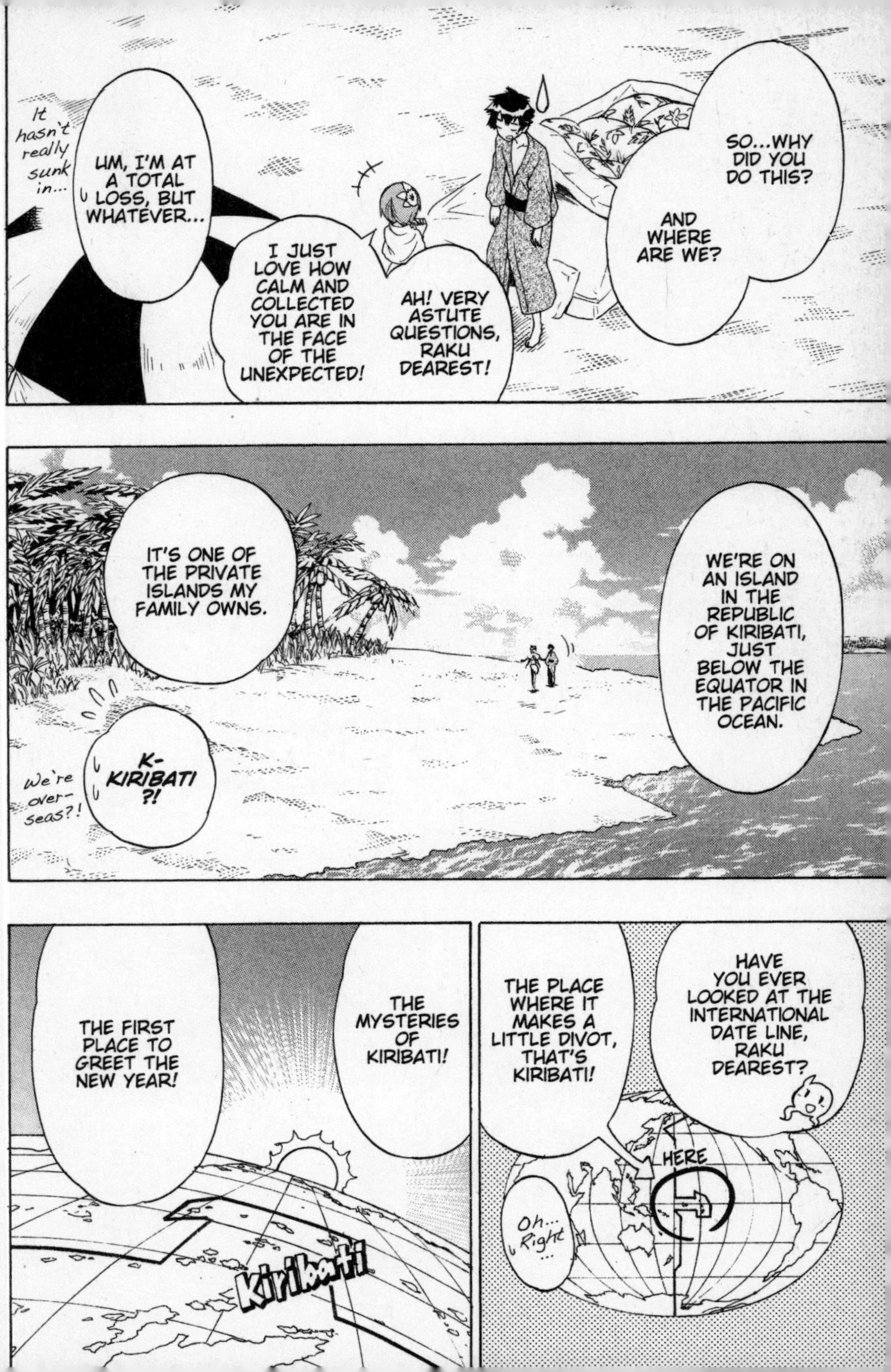
SO...WHY DID YOU DO THIS?
AND WHERE ARE WE?
AH! VERY ASTUTE QUESTIONS, RAKU DEAREST!
I JUST LOVE HOW CALM AND COLLECTED YOU ARE IN THE FACE OF THE UNEXPECTED!
UM, I'M AT A TOTAL LOSS, BUT WHATEVER...
It hasn't really sunk in...
WE'RE ON AN ISLAND IN THE REPUBLIC OF KIRIBATI, JUST BELOW THE EQUATOR IN THE PACIFIC OCEAN.
IT'S ONE OF THE PRIVATE ISLANDS MY FAMILY OWNS.
K-KIRIBATI?!
We're over-seas?!
HAVE YOU EVER LOOKED AT THE INTERNATIONAL DATE LINE, RAKU DEAREST?
THE PLACE WHERE IT MAKES A LITTLE DIVOT, THAT'S KIRIBATI!
HERE
Oh... Right...
THE MYSTERIES OF KIRIBATI!
THE FIRST PLACE TO GREET THE NEW YEAR!
Kiribati

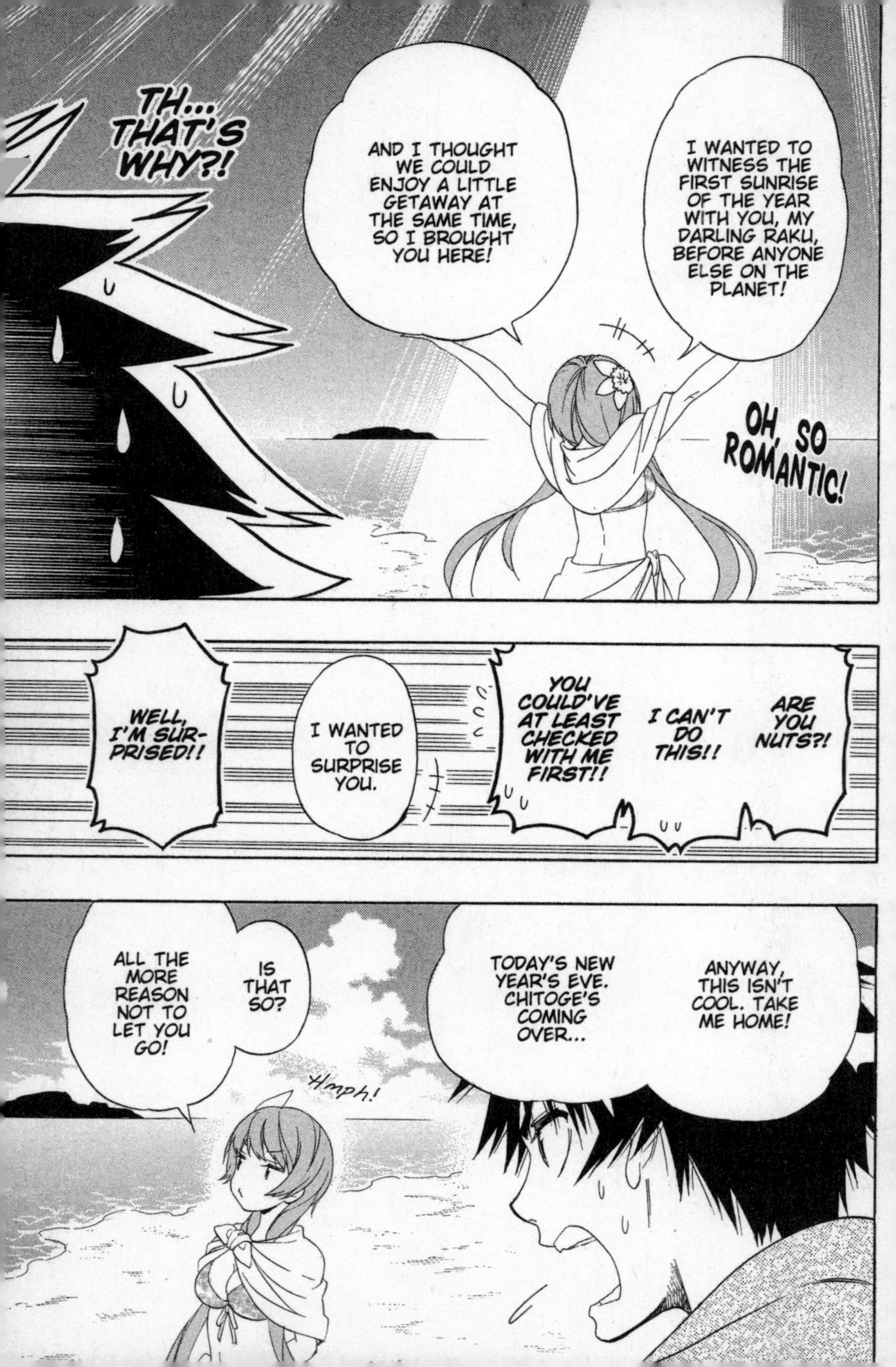
I WANTED TO WITNESS THE FIRST SUNRISE OF THE YEAR WITH YOU, MY DARLING RAKU, BEFORE ANYONE ELSE ON THE PLANET!
AND I THOUGHT WE COULD ENJOY A LITTLE GETAWAY AT THE SAME TIME, SO I BROUGHT YOU HERE!
OH, SO ROMANTIC!
TH... THAT'S WHY?!
ARE YOU NUTS?!
I CAN'T DO THIS!!
YOU COULD'VE AT LEAST CHECKED WITH ME FIRST!!
I WANTED TO SURPRISE YOU.
WELL, I'M SURPRISED!!
ANYWAY, THIS ISN'T COOL. TAKE ME HOME!
TODAY'S NEW YEAR'S EVE. CHITOGE'S COMING OVER...
IS THAT SO?
ALL THE MORE REASON NOT TO LET YOU GO!
Hmph!

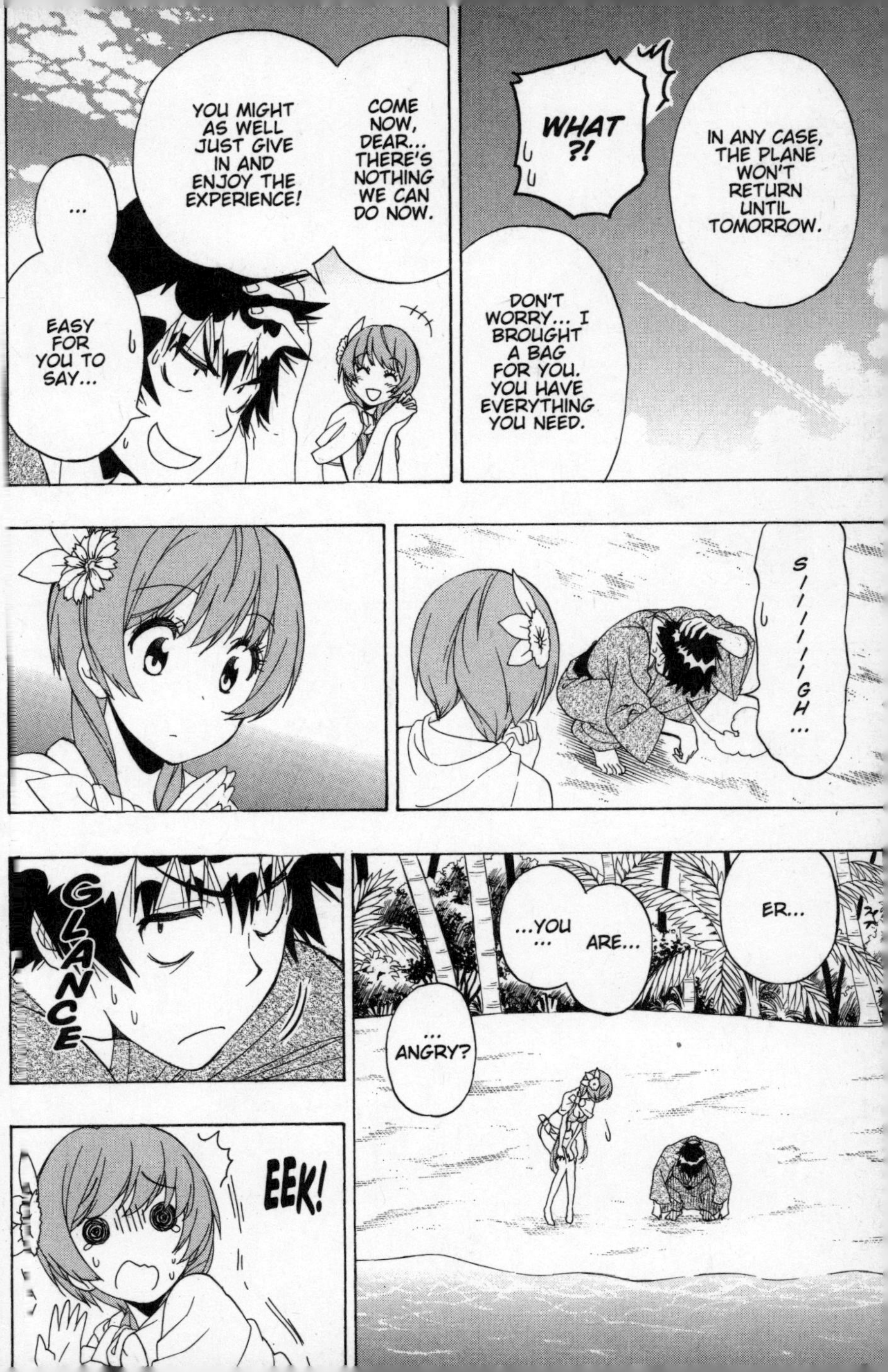
IN ANY CASE, THE PLANE WON'T RETURN UNTIL TOMORROW.
WHAT?!
DON'T WORRY... I BROUGHT A BAG FOR YOU. YOU HAVE EVERYTHING YOU NEED.
COME NOW, DEAR... THERE'S NOTHING WE CAN DO NOW.
YOU MIGHT AS WELL JUST GIVE IN AND ENJOY THE EXPERIENCE!
...
EASY FOR YOU TO SAY...
SIIIIIGH...
ER...
...YOU ... ARE...
... ANGRY?
GLANCE
EEK!

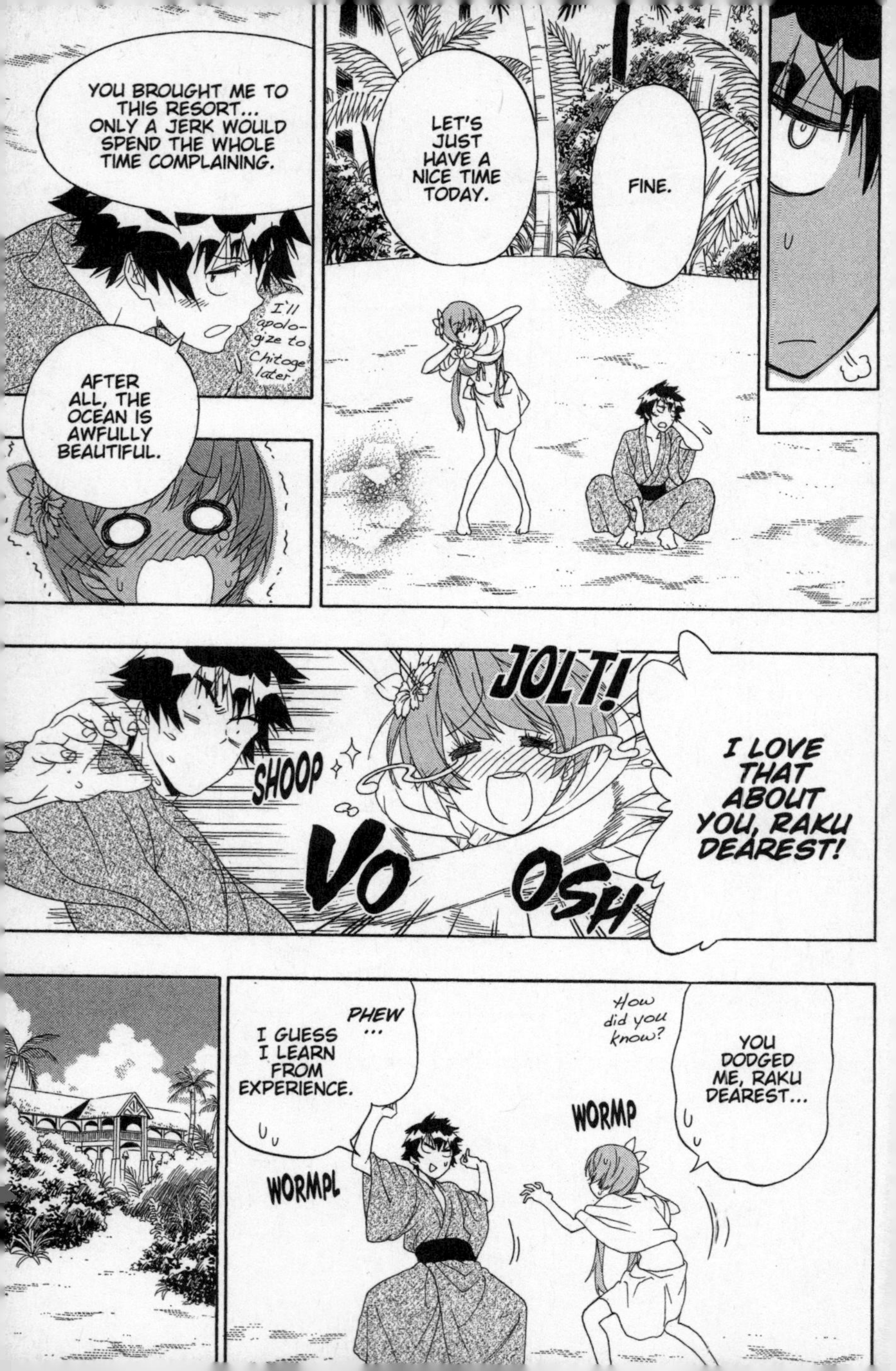
LET'S JUST HAVE A NICE TIME TODAY.
FINE.
YOU BROUGHT ME TO THIS RESORT... ONLY A JERK WOULD SPEND THE WHOLE TIME COMPLAINING.
I'll apologize to Chitoge later.
AFTER ALL, THE OCEAN IS AWFULLY BEAUTIFUL.
I LOVE THAT ABOUT YOU, RAKU DEAREST!
JOLT!
SHOOP
VOOSH
YOU DODGED ME, RAKU DEAREST...
How did you know?
WORMP
PHEW...
I GUESS I LEARN FROM EXPERIENCE.
WORMPL

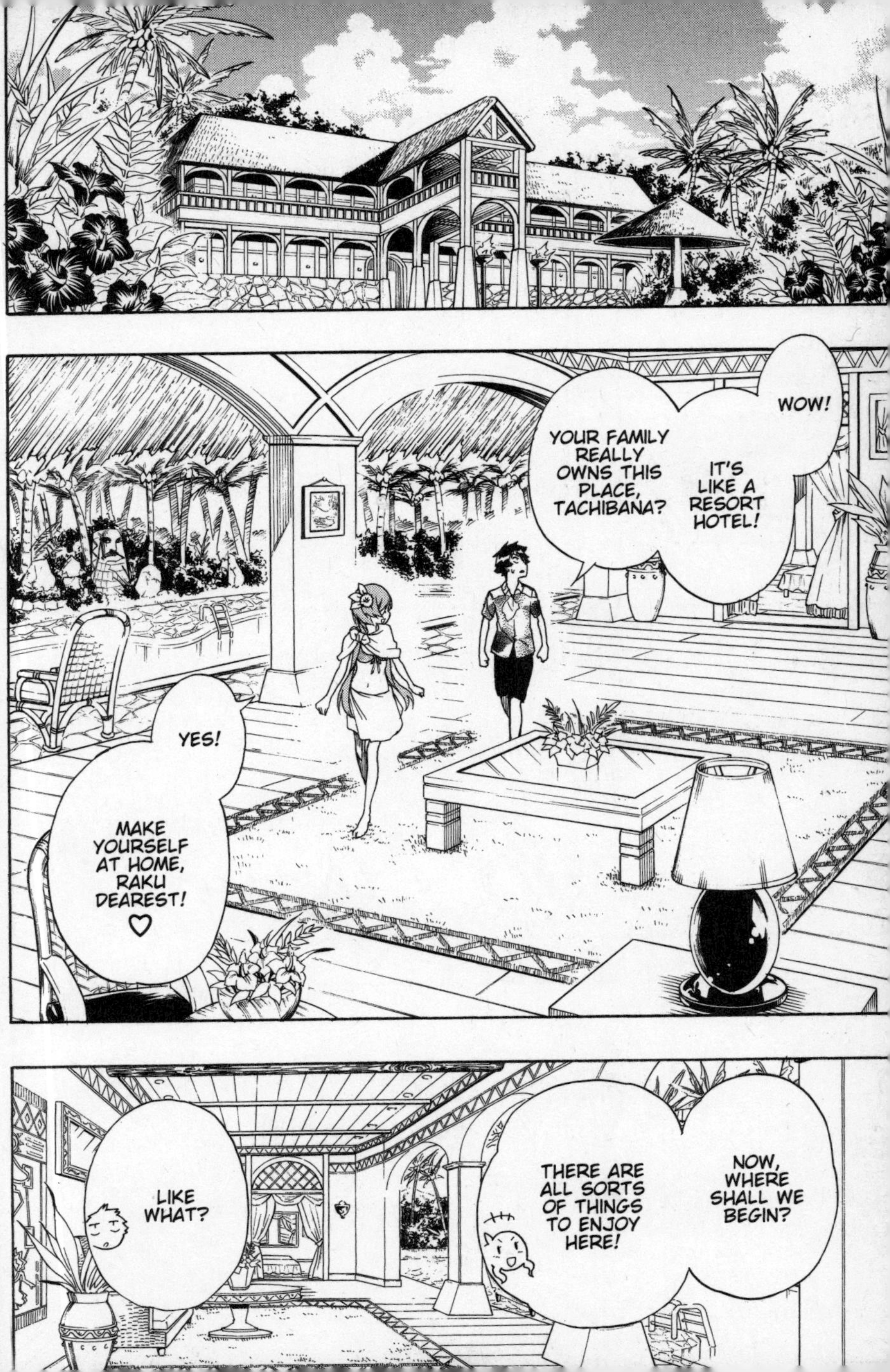
WOW! IT'S LIKE A RESORT HOTEL!
YOUR FAMILY REALLY OWNS THIS PLACE, TACHIBANA?
YES! MAKE YOURSELF AT HOME, RAKU DEAREST! ♡
NOW, WHERE SHALL WE BEGIN?
THERE ARE ALL SORTS OF THINGS TO ENJOY HERE!
LIKE WHAT?

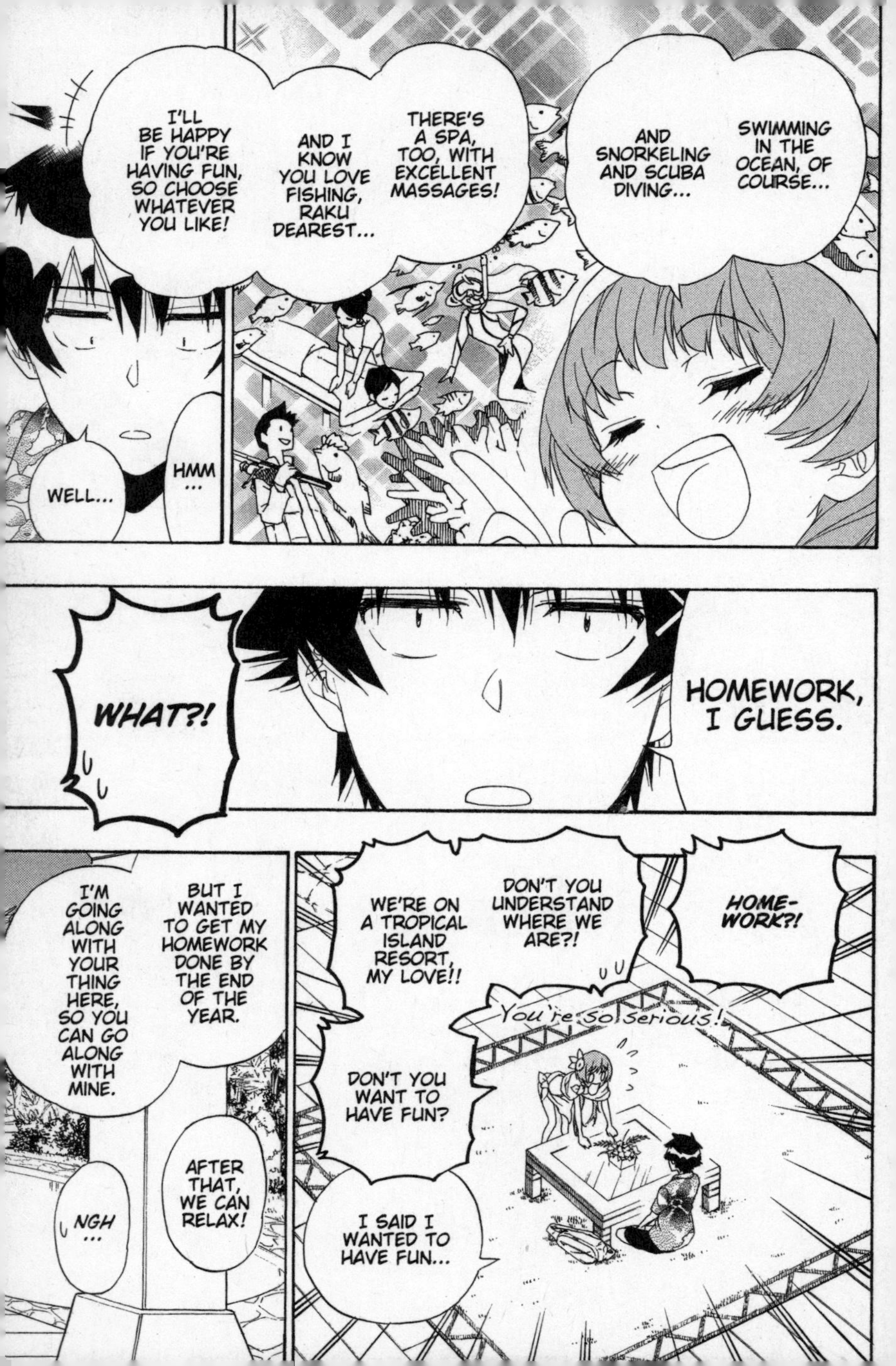
SWIMMING IN THE OCEAN, OF COURSE...
AND SNORKELING AND SCUBA DIVING...
THERE'S A SPA, TOO, WITH EXCELLENT MASSAGES!
AND I KNOW YOU LOVE FISHING, RAKU DEAREST...
I'LL BE HAPPY IF YOU'RE HAVING FUN, SO CHOOSE WHATEVER YOU LIKE!
HMM...
WELL...
HOMEWORK, I GUESS.
WHAT?!
HOME-WORK?!
DON'T YOU UNDERSTAND WHERE WE ARE?!
WE'RE ON A TROPICAL ISLAND RESORT, MY LOVE!!
You're so serious!
DON'T YOU WANT TO HAVE FUN?
I SAID I WANTED TO HAVE FUN...
BUT I WANTED TO GET MY HOMEWORK DONE BY THE END OF THE YEAR.
I'M GOING ALONG WITH YOUR THING HERE, SO YOU CAN GO ALONG WITH MINE.
AFTER THAT, WE CAN RELAX!
NGH...

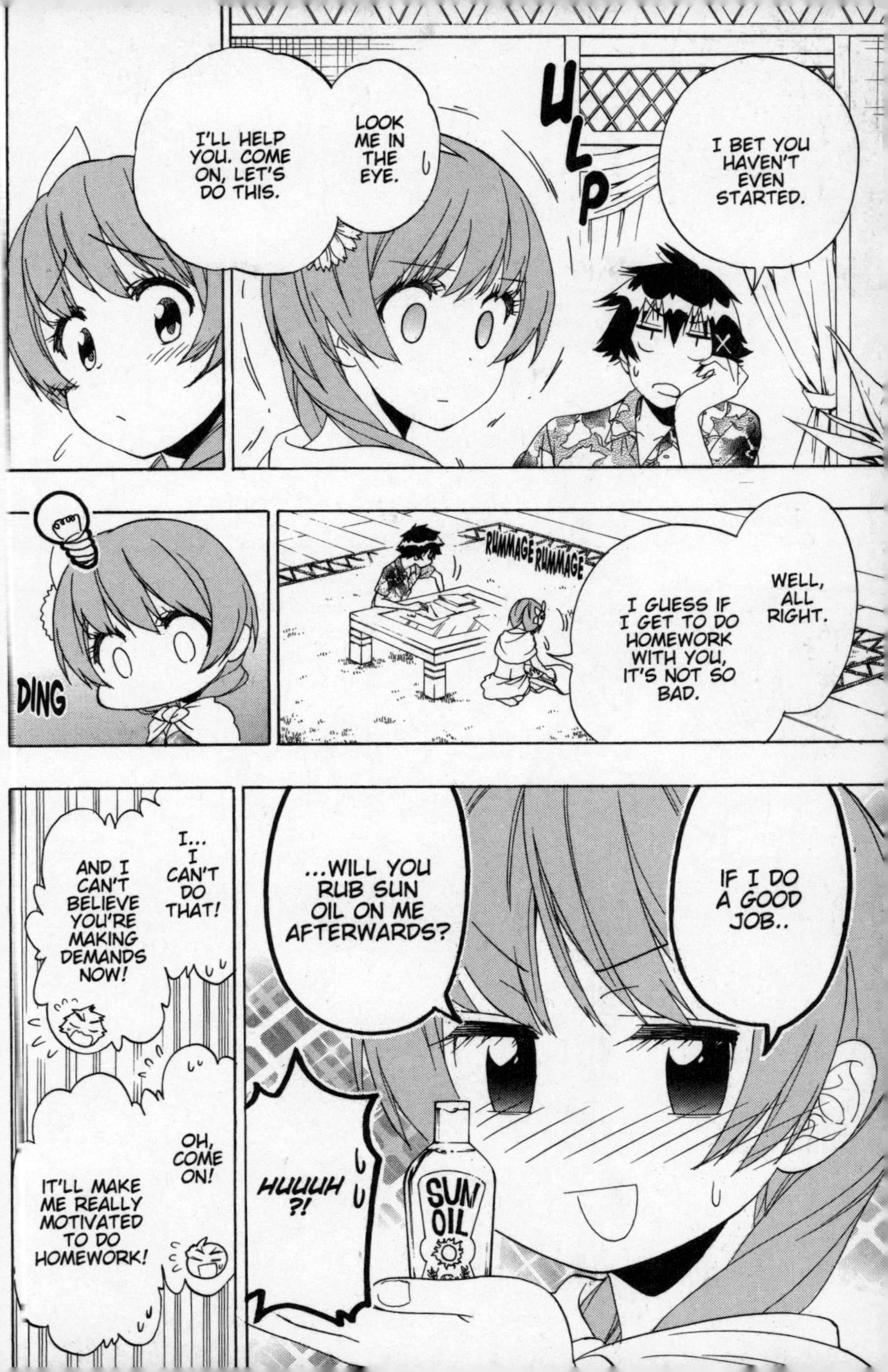

I BET YOU HAVEN'T EVEN STARTED.
ULP
LOOK ME IN THE EYE.
I'LL HELP YOU. COME ON, LET'S DO THIS.
WELL, ALL RIGHT.
I GUESS IF I GET TO DO HOMEWORK WITH YOU, IT'S NOT SO BAD.
RUMMAGE RUMMAGE
DING
IF I DO A GOOD JOB..
...WILL YOU RUB SUN OIL ON ME AFTERWARDS?
HUUUH ?!
SUN OIL
I... I CAN'T DO THAT!
AND I CAN'T BELIEVE YOU'RE MAKING DEMANDS NOW!
OH, COME ON!
IT'LL MAKE ME REALLY MOTIVATED TO DO HOMEWORK!

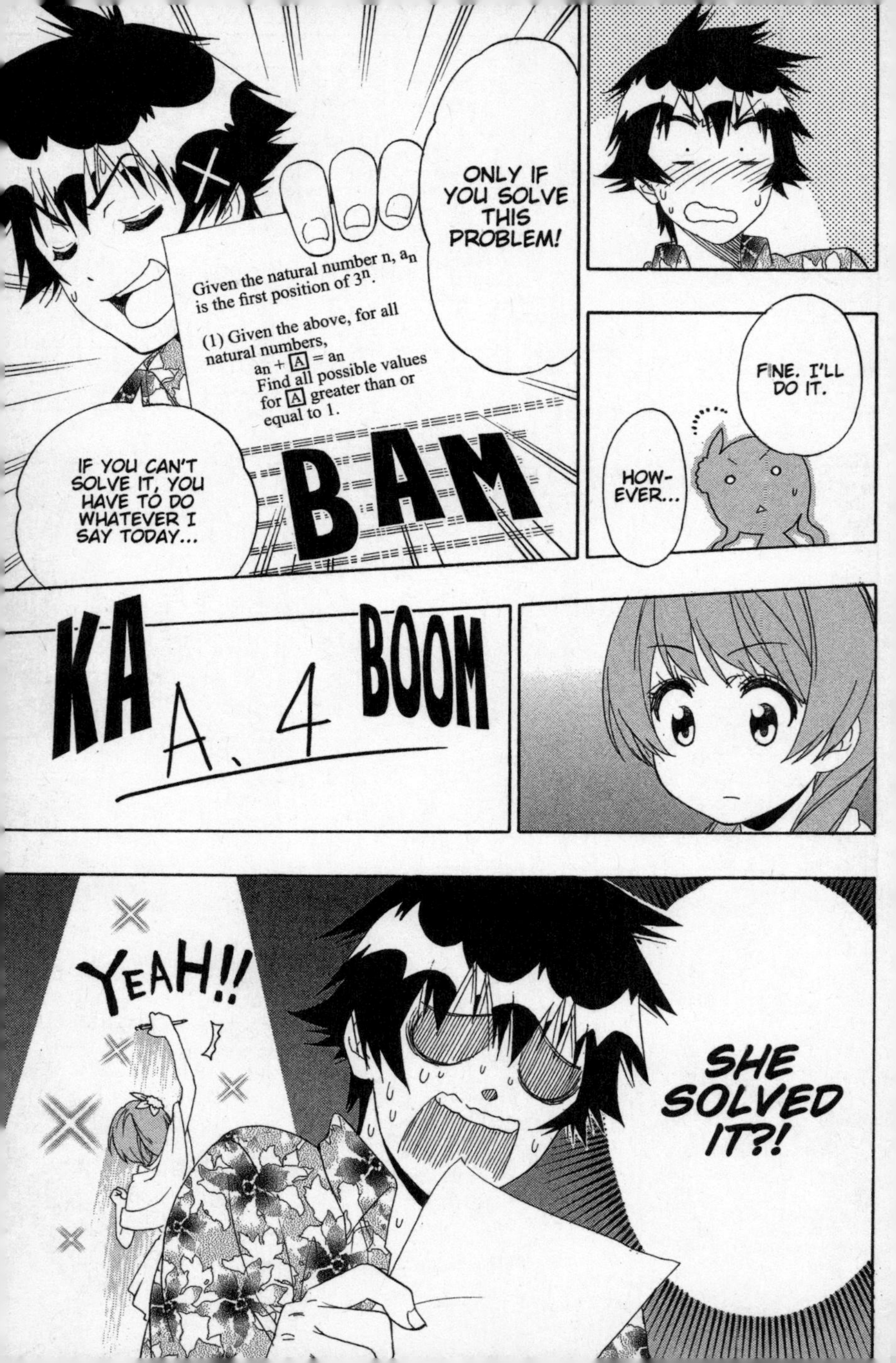
FINE. I'LL DO IT.
HOW-EVER...
ONLY IF YOU SOLVE THIS PROBLEM!
Given the natural number n, a_n is the first position of 3^n.
(1) Given the above, for all natural numbers,
an + [A] = an
Find all possible values for [A] greater than or equal to 1.
IF YOU CAN'T SOLVE IT, YOU HAVE TO DO WHATEVER I SAY TODAY...
BAM
KA BOOM
A. 4
SHE SOLVED IT?!
YEAH!!

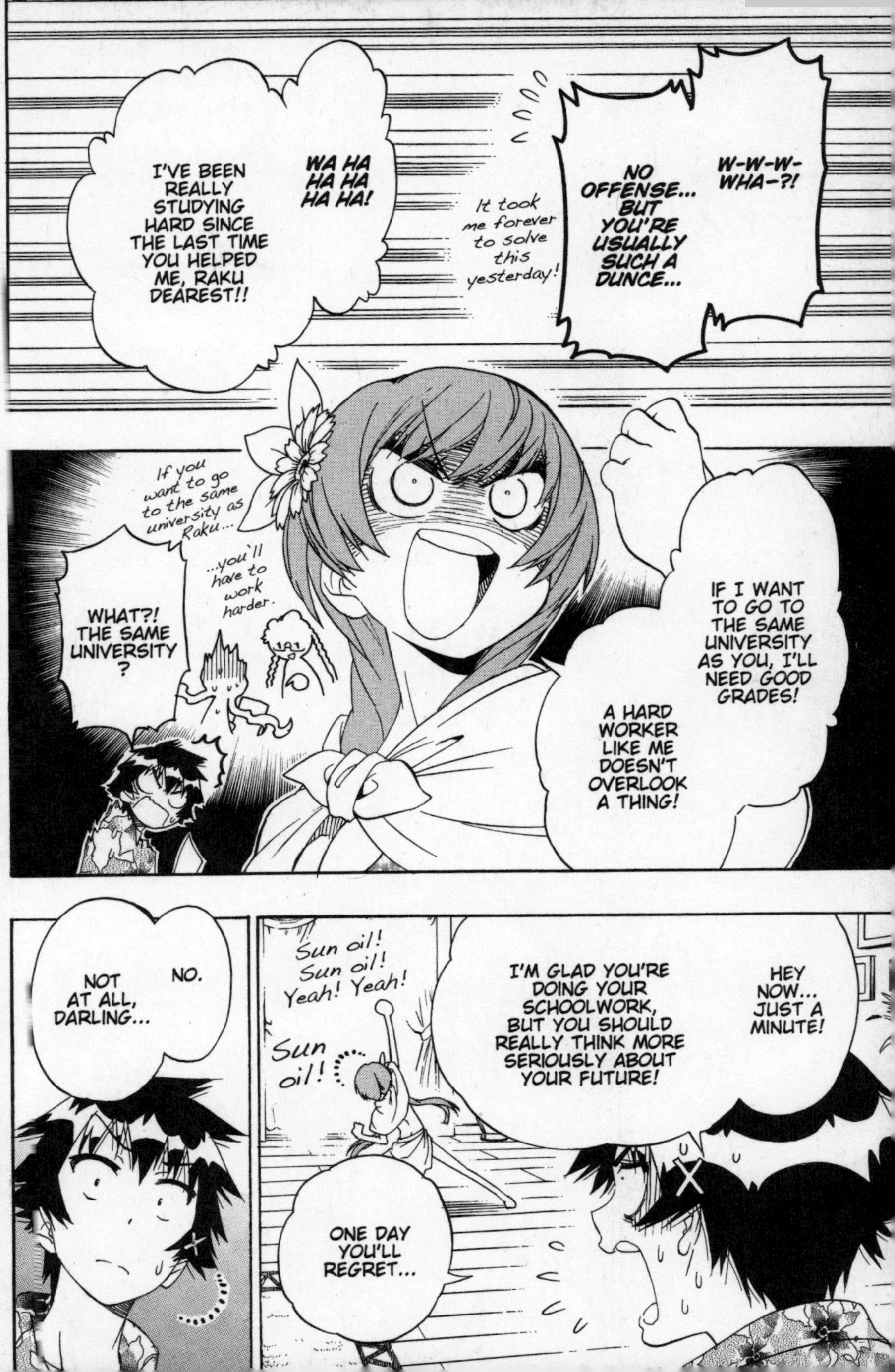
W-W-W-WHA-?!
NO OFFENSE... BUT YOU'RE USUALLY SUCH A DUNCE...
It took me forever to solve this yesterday!
WA HA HA HA HA HA!
I'VE BEEN REALLY STUDYING HARD SINCE THE LAST TIME YOU HELPED ME, RAKU DEAREST!!
IF I WANT TO GO TO THE SAME UNIVERSITY AS YOU, I'LL NEED GOOD GRADES!
A HARD WORKER LIKE ME DOESN'T OVERLOOK A THING!
If you want to go to the same university as Raku...
...you'll have to work harder.
WHAT?! THE SAME UNIVERSITY ?
HEY NOW... JUST A MINUTE!
I'M GLAD YOU'RE DOING YOUR SCHOOLWORK, BUT YOU SHOULD REALLY THINK MORE SERIOUSLY ABOUT YOUR FUTURE!
Sun oil! Sun oil! Yeah! Yeah!
Sun oil!
ONE DAY YOU'LL REGRET...
NO.
NOT AT ALL, DARLING...

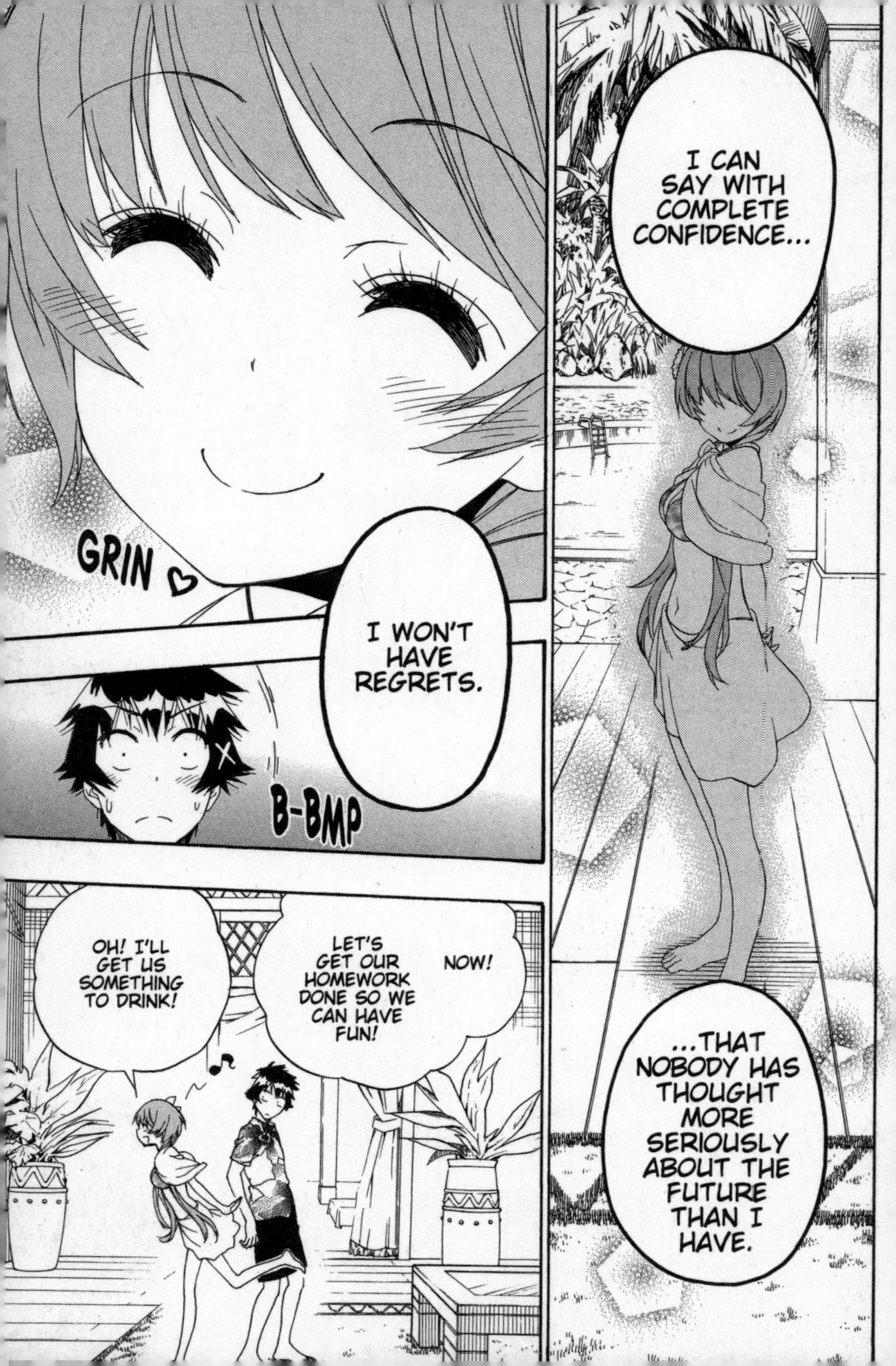
I CAN SAY WITH COMPLETE CONFIDENCE...
...THAT NOBODY HAS THOUGHT MORE SERIOUSLY ABOUT THE FUTURE THAN I HAVE.
GRIN ♡
I WON'T HAVE REGRETS.
B-BMP
LET'S GET OUR HOMEWORK DONE SO WE CAN HAVE FUN!
NOW!
OH! I'LL GET US SOMETHING TO DRINK!

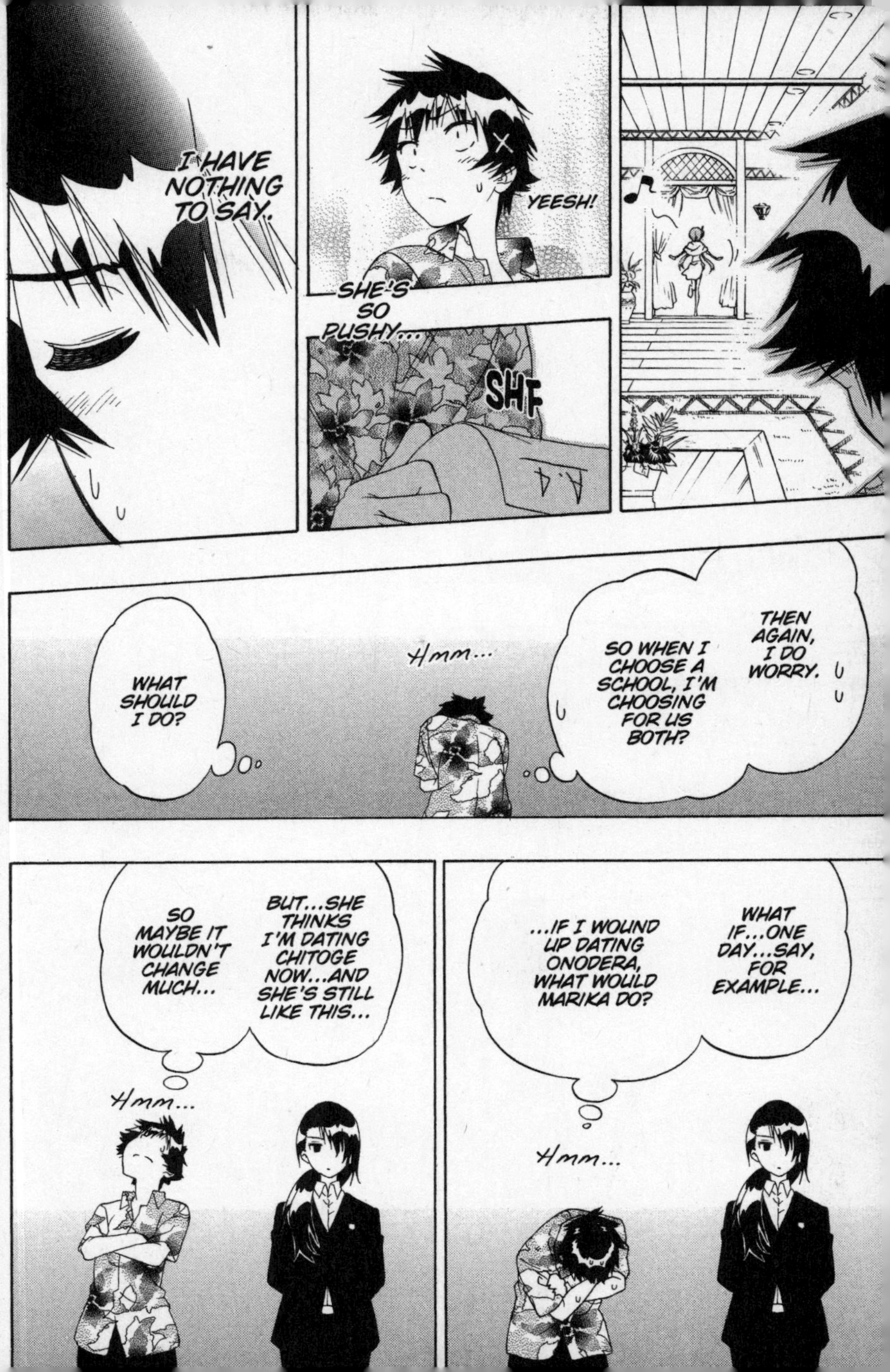
YEESH!
SHE'S SO PUSHY...
SHF
I HAVE NOTHING TO SAY.
THEN AGAIN, I DO WORRY.
SO WHEN I CHOOSE A SCHOOL, I'M CHOOSING FOR US BOTH?
Hmm...
WHAT SHOULD I DO?
WHAT IF...ONE DAY...SAY, FOR EXAMPLE...
...IF I WOUND UP DATING ONODERA, WHAT WOULD MARIKA DO?
Hmm...
BUT...SHE THINKS I'M DATING CHITOGE NOW...AND SHE'S STILL LIKE THIS...
SO MAYBE IT WOULDN'T CHANGE MUCH...
Hmm...

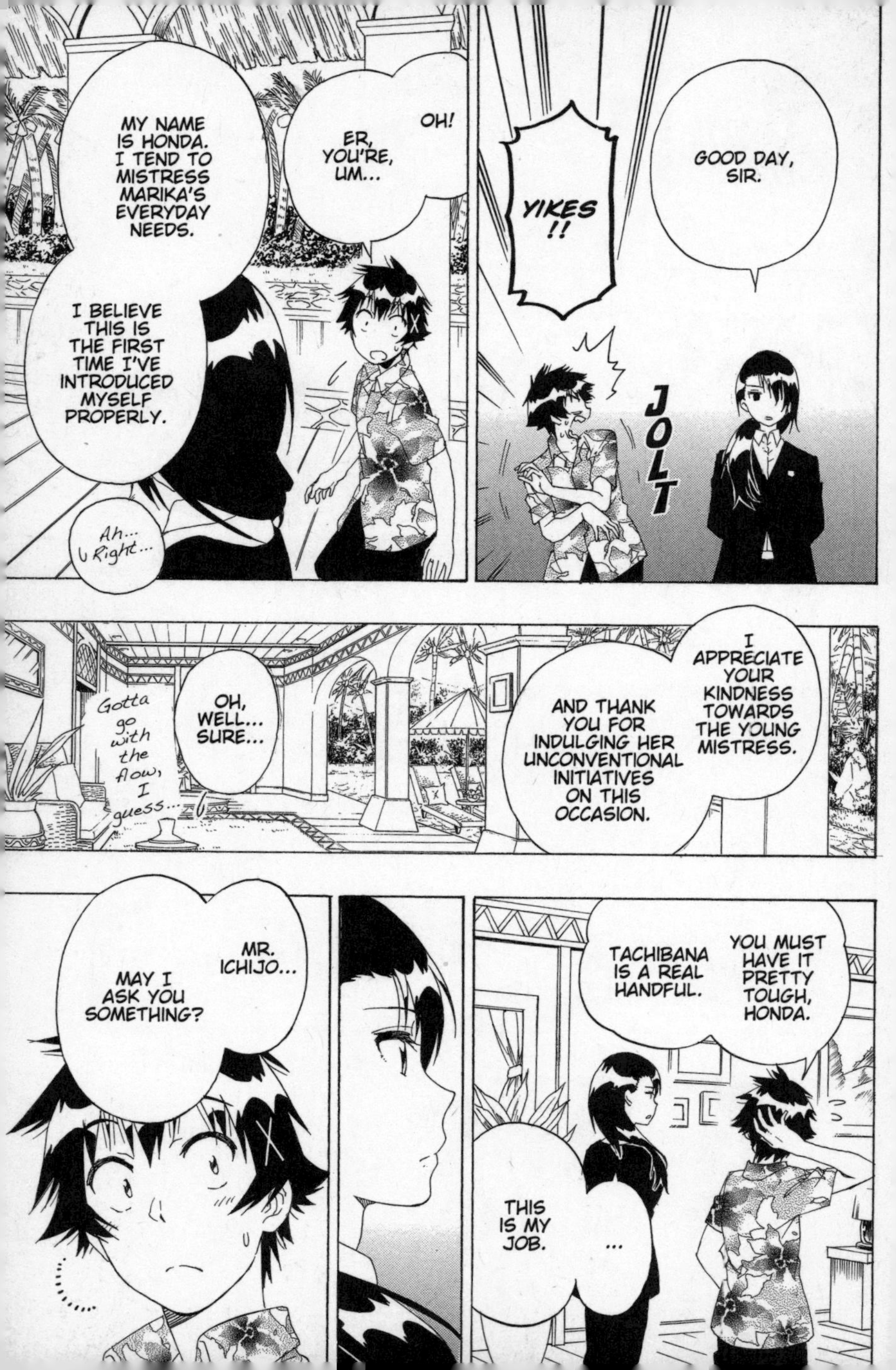
GOOD DAY, SIR.
YIKES!!
JOLT
OH!
ER, YOU'RE, UM...
MY NAME IS HONDA. I TEND TO MISTRESS MARIKA'S EVERYDAY NEEDS.
I BELIEVE THIS IS THE FIRST TIME I'VE INTRODUCED MYSELF PROPERLY.
Ah... Right...
I APPRECIATE YOUR KINDNESS TOWARDS THE YOUNG MISTRESS.
AND THANK YOU FOR INDULGING HER UNCONVENTIONAL INITIATIVES ON THIS OCCASION.
OH, WELL... SURE...
Gotta go with the flow, I guess...
YOU MUST HAVE IT PRETTY TOUGH, HONDA.
TACHIBANA IS A REAL HANDFUL.
...
THIS IS MY JOB.
MR. ICHIJO...
MAY I ASK YOU SOMETHING?
......

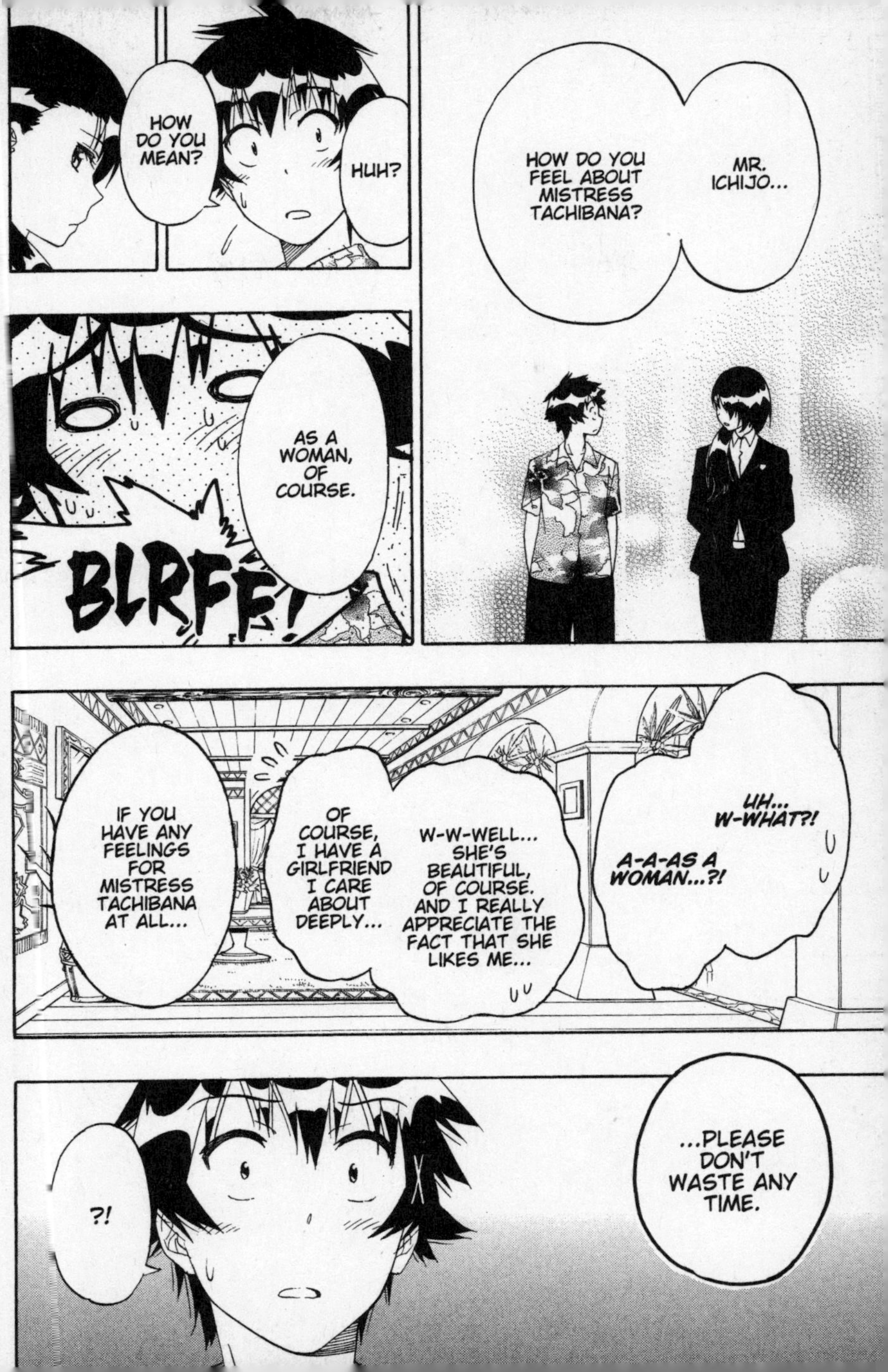

MR. ICHIJO...
HOW DO YOU FEEL ABOUT MISTRESS TACHIBANA?
HUH?
HOW DO YOU MEAN?
AS A WOMAN, OF COURSE.
BLRFF!
UH... W-WHAT?!
A-A-AS A WOMAN...?!
W-W-WELL... SHE'S BEAUTIFUL, OF COURSE. AND I REALLY APPRECIATE THE FACT THAT SHE LIKES ME...
OF COURSE, I HAVE A GIRLFRIEND I CARE ABOUT DEEPLY...
IF YOU HAVE ANY FEELINGS FOR MISTRESS TACHIBANA AT ALL...
...PLEASE DON'T WASTE ANY TIME.
?!

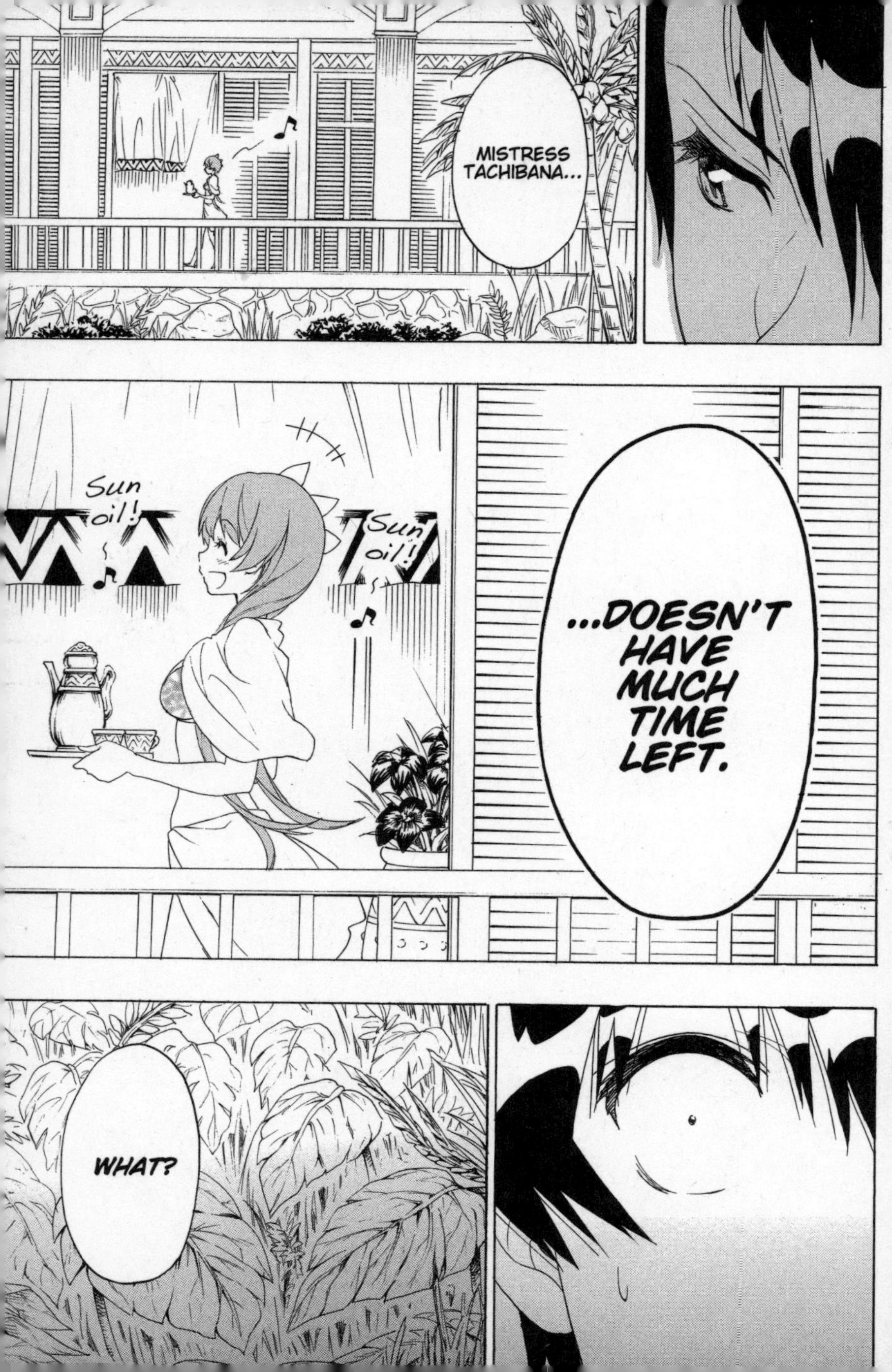
MISTRESS TACHIBANA...
...DOESN'T HAVE MUCH TIME LEFT.
Sun oil!
Sun oil!
WHAT?

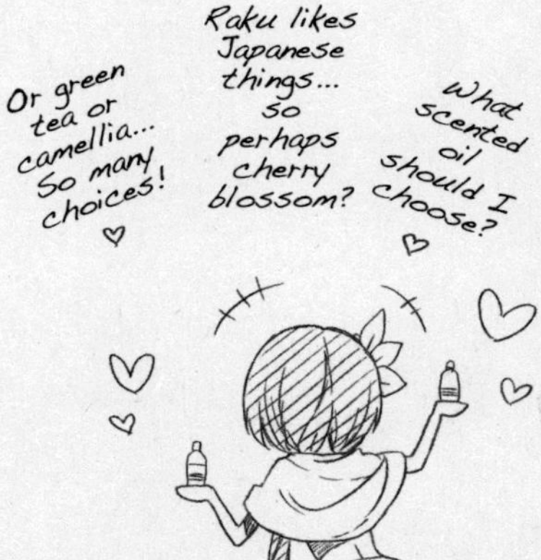
What scented oil should I choose?
Raku likes Japanese things... so perhaps cherry blossom?
Or green tea or camellia... So many choices!

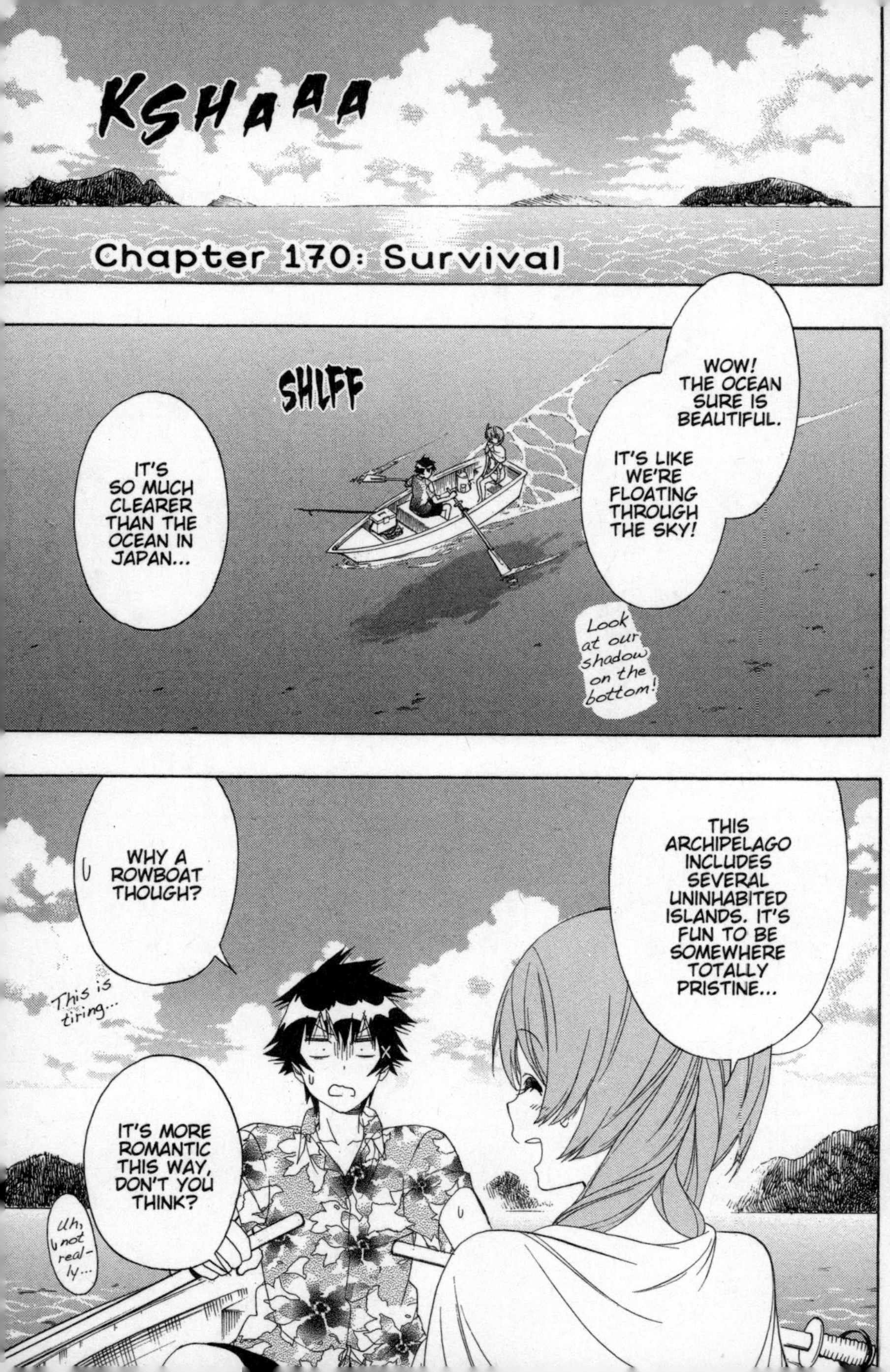
KSHAAA
Chapter 170: Survival
WOW! THE OCEAN SURE IS BEAUTIFUL.
IT'S LIKE WE'RE FLOATING THROUGH THE SKY!
Look at our shadow on the bottom!
SHLFF
IT'S SO MUCH CLEARER THAN THE OCEAN IN JAPAN...
THIS ARCHIPELAGO INCLUDES SEVERAL UNINHABITED ISLANDS. IT'S FUN TO BE SOMEWHERE TOTALLY PRISTINE...
WHY A ROWBOAT THOUGH?
This is tiring...
IT'S MORE ROMANTIC THIS WAY, DON'T YOU THINK?
Uh, not real-ly...

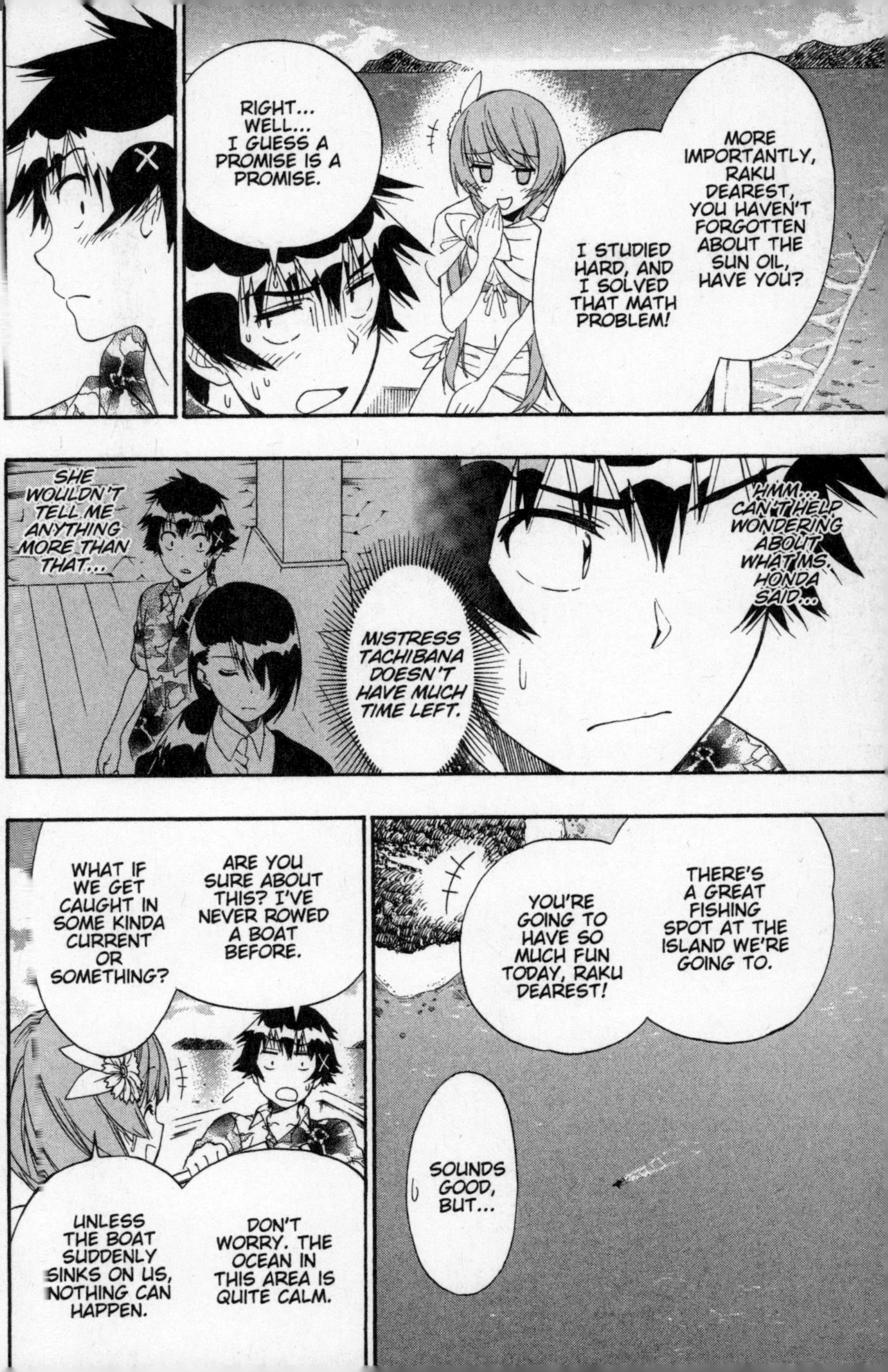
MORE IMPORTANTLY, RAKU DEAREST, YOU HAVEN'T FORGOTTEN ABOUT THE SUN OIL, HAVE YOU?
I STUDIED HARD, AND I SOLVED THAT MATH PROBLEM!
RIGHT... WELL... I GUESS A PROMISE IS A PROMISE.
HMM... CAN'T HELP WONDERING ABOUT WHAT MS. HONDA SAID...
MISTRESS TACHIBANA DOESN'T HAVE MUCH TIME LEFT.
SHE WOULDN'T TELL ME ANYTHING MORE THAN THAT...
THERE'S A GREAT FISHING SPOT AT THE ISLAND WE'RE GOING TO.
YOU'RE GOING TO HAVE SO MUCH FUN TODAY, RAKU DEAREST!
SOUNDS GOOD, BUT...
ARE YOU SURE ABOUT THIS? I'VE NEVER ROWED A BOAT BEFORE.
WHAT IF WE GET CAUGHT IN SOME KINDA CURRENT OR SOMETHING?
DON'T WORRY. THE OCEAN IN THIS AREA IS QUITE CALM.
UNLESS THE BOAT SUDDENLY SINKS ON US, NOTHING CAN HAPPEN.

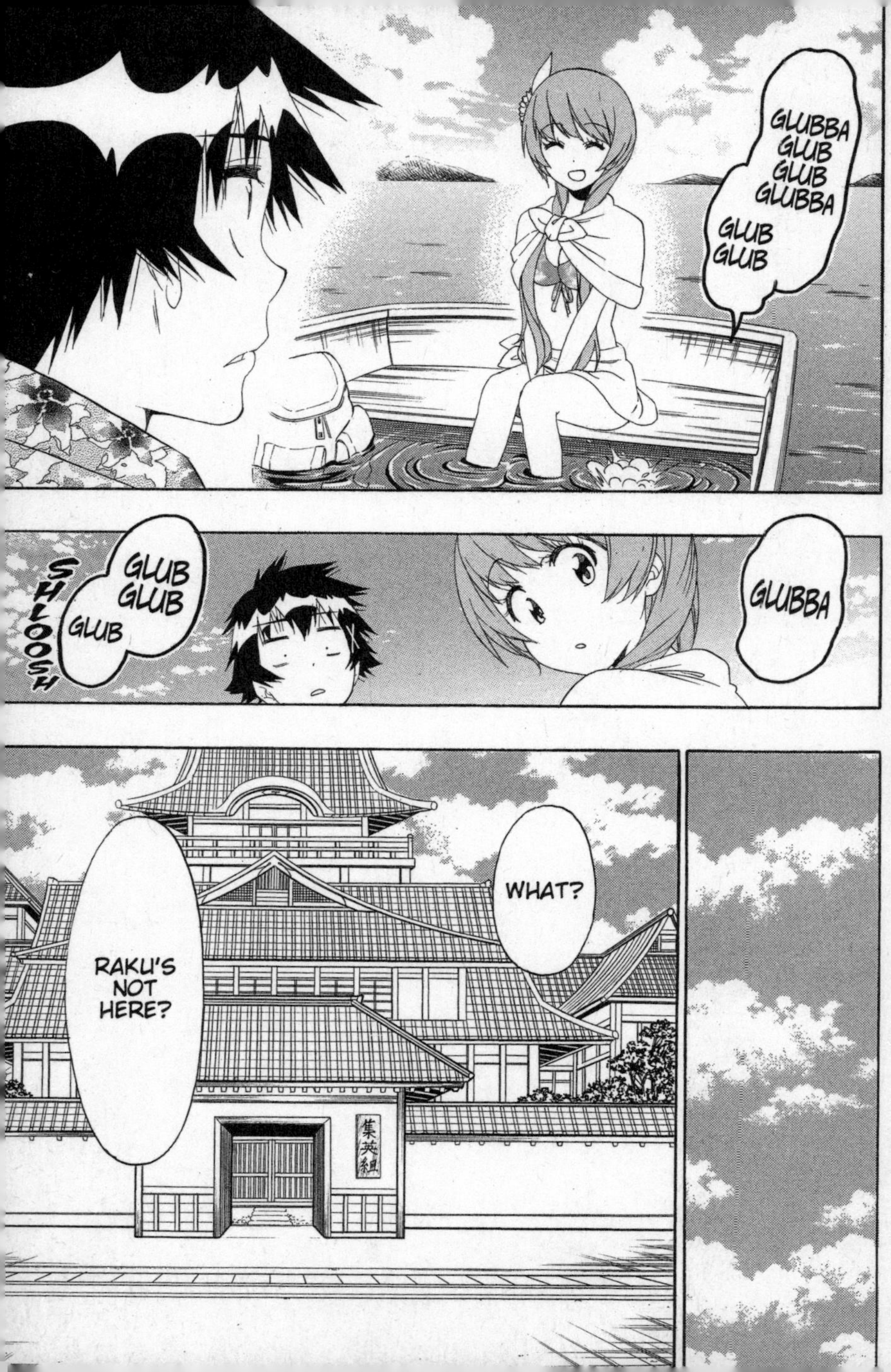
GLUBBA GLUB GLUB GLUBBA
GLUB GLUB
GLUBBA
GLUB GLUB
GLUB
SHLOOSH
WHAT?
RAKU'S NOT HERE?
集英組

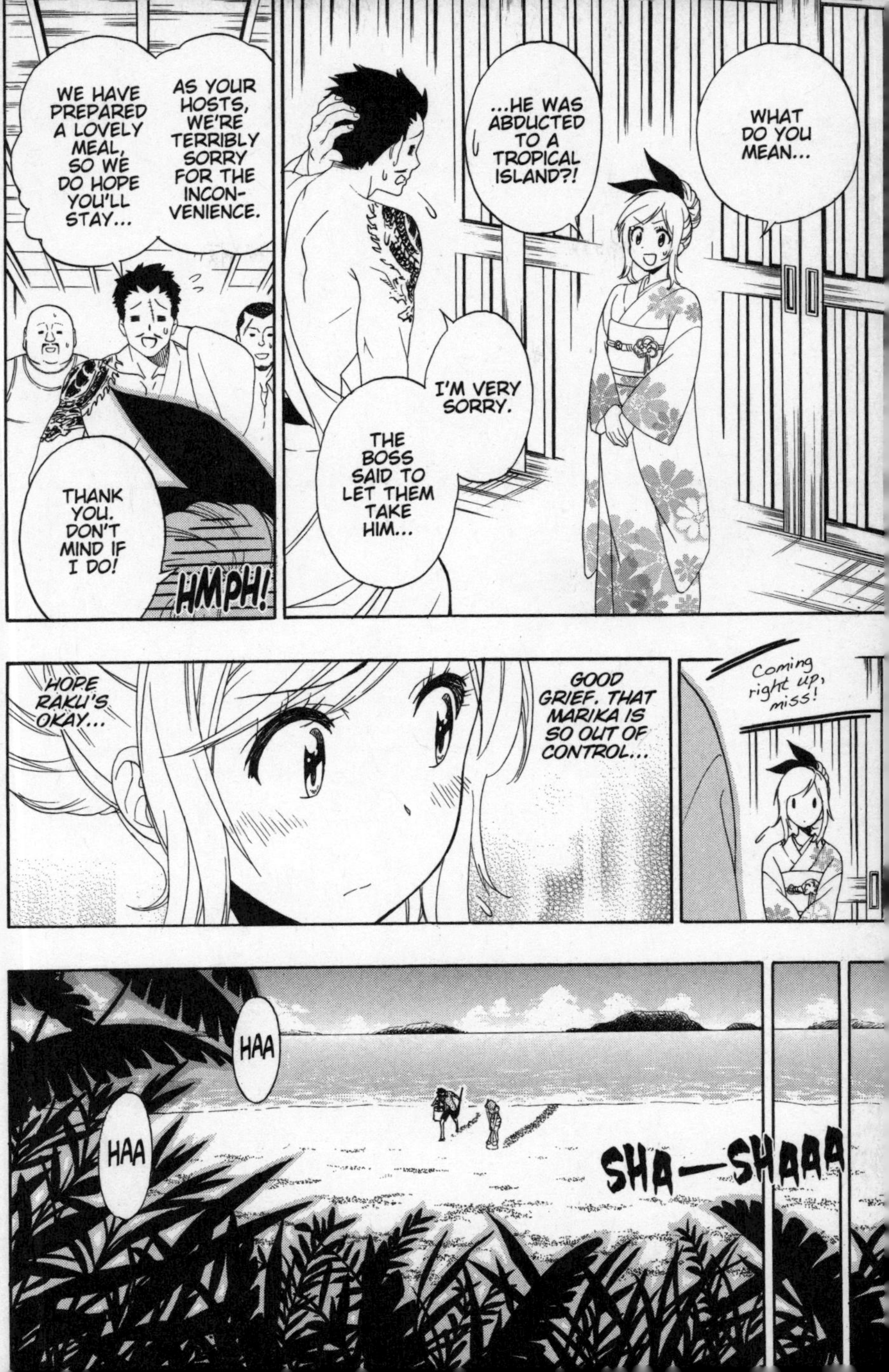
WHAT DO YOU MEAN...
...HE WAS ABDUCTED TO A TROPICAL ISLAND?!
I'M VERY SORRY.
THE BOSS SAID TO LET THEM TAKE HIM...
AS YOUR HOSTS, WE'RE TERRIBLY SORRY FOR THE INCON-VENIENCE.
WE HAVE PREPARED A LOVELY MEAL, SO WE DO HOPE YOU'LL STAY...
THANK YOU. DON'T MIND IF I DO!
HMPH!
Coming right up, miss!
GOOD GRIEF. THAT MARIKA IS SO OUT OF CONTROL...
HOPE RAKU'S OKAY...
HAA
HAA
SHA—SHAAA

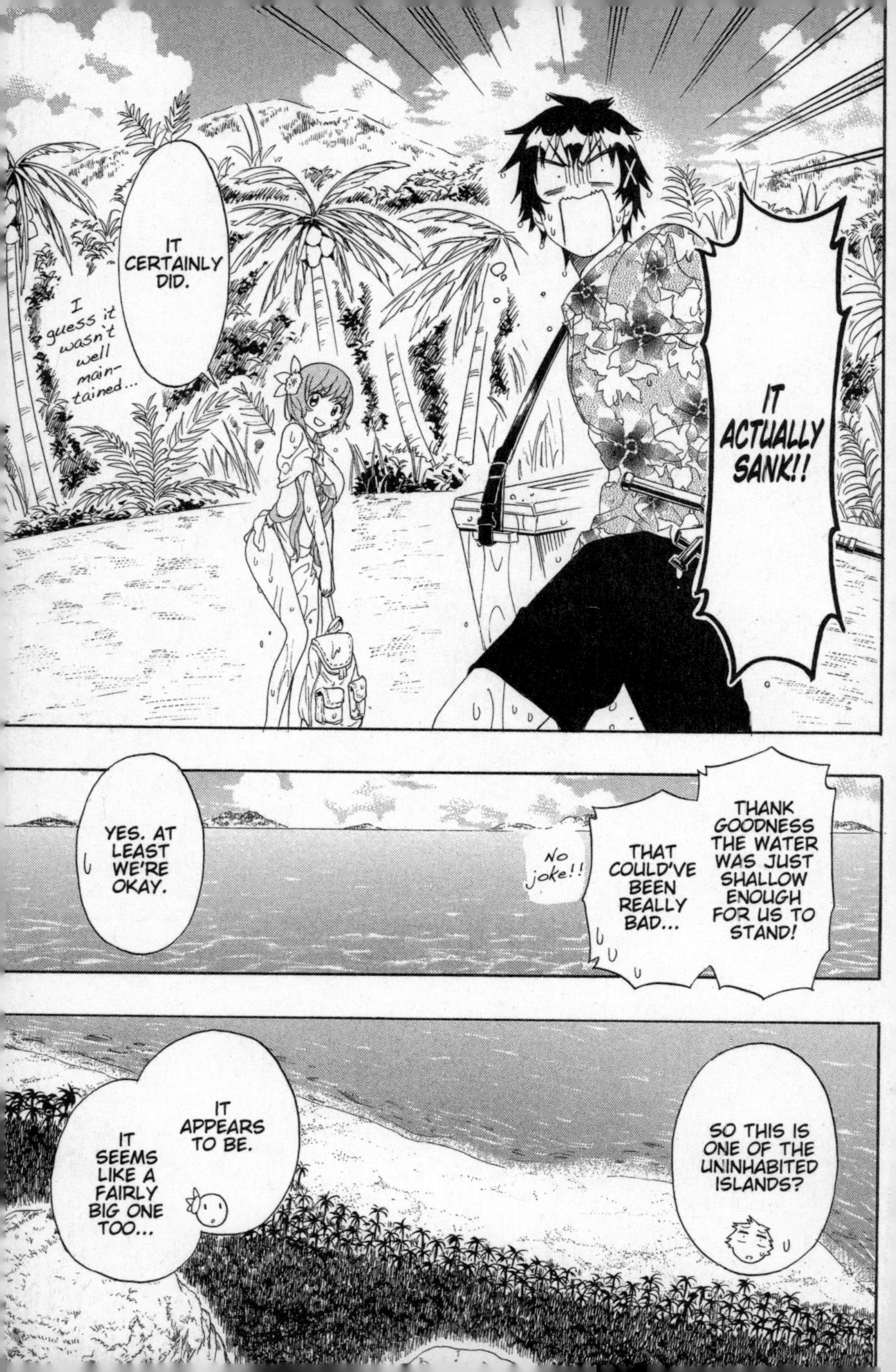
IT ACTUALLY SANK!!
IT CERTAINLY DID.
I guess it wasn't well maintained...
THANK GOODNESS THE WATER WAS JUST SHALLOW ENOUGH FOR US TO STAND!
THAT COULD'VE BEEN REALLY BAD...
No joke!!
YES. AT LEAST WE'RE OKAY.
SO THIS IS ONE OF THE UNINHABITED ISLANDS?
IT APPEARS TO BE.
IT SEEMS LIKE A FAIRLY BIG ONE TOO...

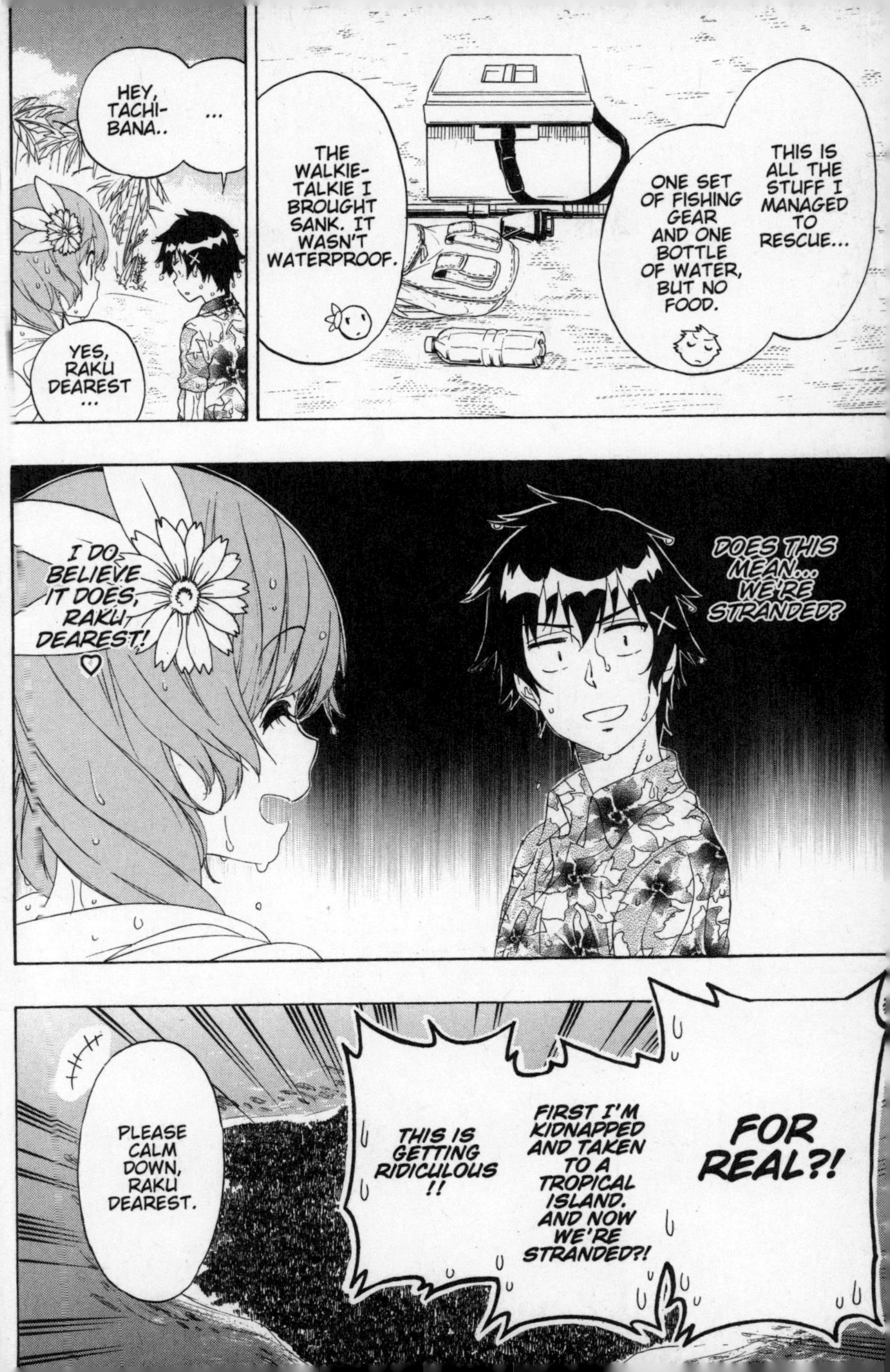
THIS IS ALL THE STUFF I MANAGED TO RESCUE...
ONE SET OF FISHING GEAR AND ONE BOTTLE OF WATER, BUT NO FOOD.
THE WALKIE-TALKIE I BROUGHT SANK. IT WASN'T WATERPROOF.
HEY, TACHIBANA..
...
YES, RAKU DEAREST ...
DOES THIS MEAN... WE'RE STRANDED?
I DO BELIEVE IT DOES, RAKU DEAREST! ♡
FOR REAL?!
FIRST I'M KIDNAPPED AND TAKEN TO A TROPICAL ISLAND. AND NOW WE'RE STRANDED?!
THIS IS GETTING RIDICULOUS!!
PLEASE CALM DOWN, RAKU DEAREST.

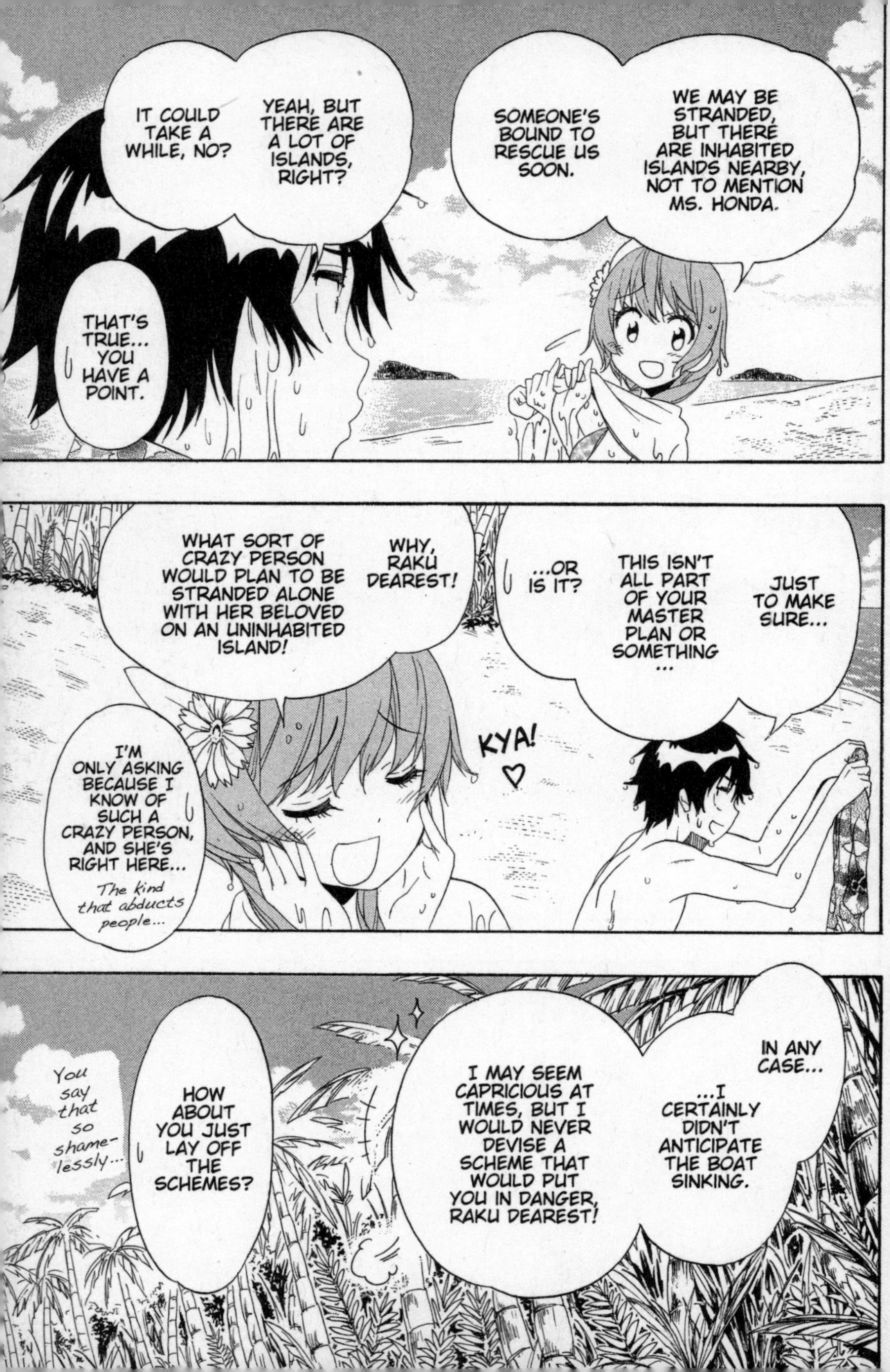
WE MAY BE STRANDED, BUT THERE ARE INHABITED ISLANDS NEARBY, NOT TO MENTION MS. HONDA.
SOMEONE'S BOUND TO RESCUE US SOON.
YEAH, BUT THERE ARE A LOT OF ISLANDS, RIGHT?
IT COULD TAKE A WHILE, NO?
THAT'S TRUE... YOU HAVE A POINT.
JUST TO MAKE SURE...
THIS ISN'T ALL PART OF YOUR MASTER PLAN OR SOMETHING...
...OR IS IT?
WHY, RAKU DEAREST!
WHAT SORT OF CRAZY PERSON WOULD PLAN TO BE STRANDED ALONE WITH HER BELOVED ON AN UNINHABITED ISLAND!
KYA! ♡
I'M ONLY ASKING BECAUSE I KNOW OF SUCH A CRAZY PERSON, AND SHE'S RIGHT HERE...
The kind that abducts people...
IN ANY CASE...
...I CERTAINLY DIDN'T ANTICIPATE THE BOAT SINKING.
I MAY SEEM CAPRICIOUS AT TIMES, BUT I WOULD NEVER DEVISE A SCHEME THAT WOULD PUT YOU IN DANGER, RAKU DEAREST!
HOW ABOUT YOU JUST LAY OFF THE SCHEMES?
You say that so shame-lessly...

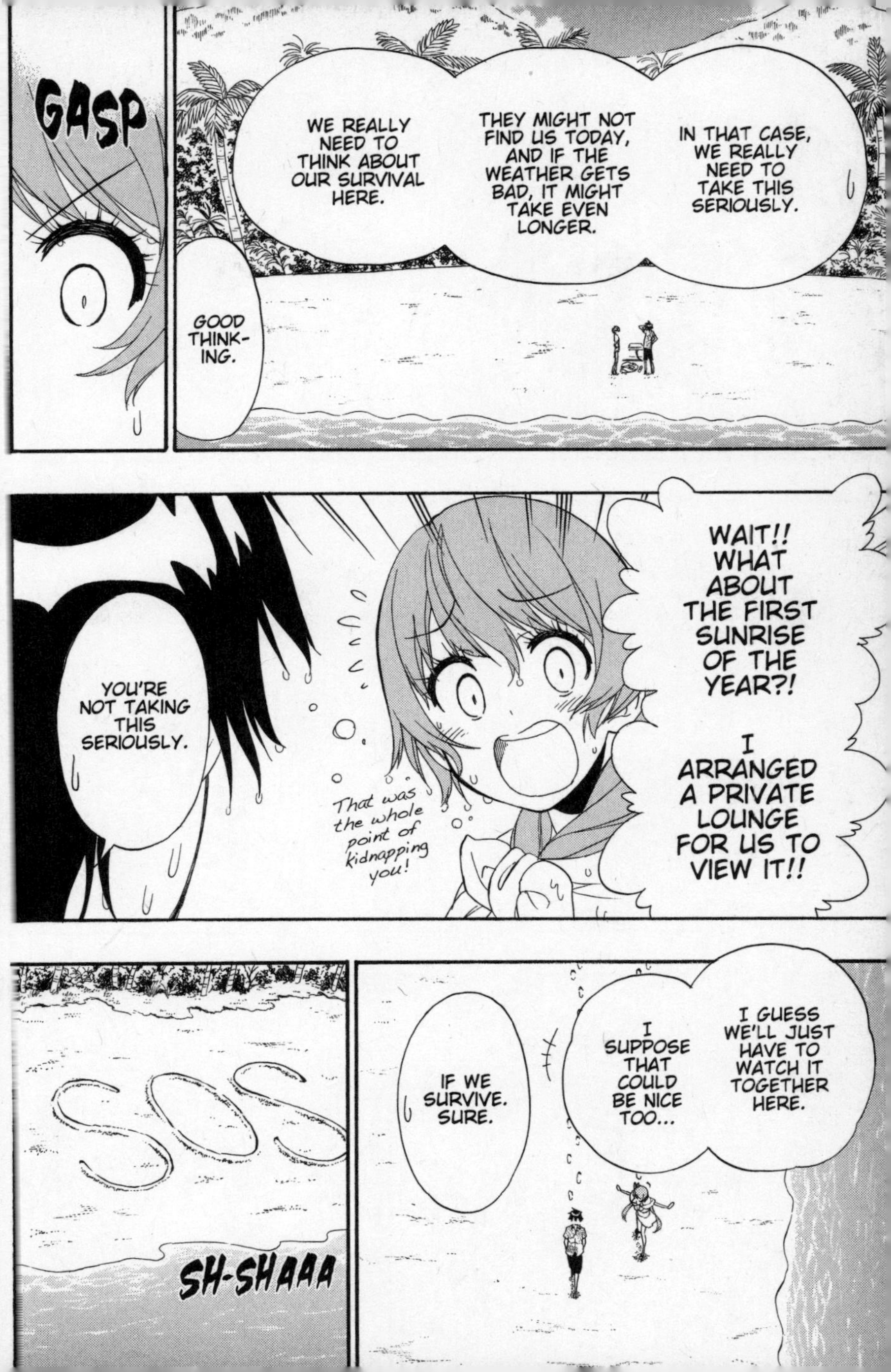
WE REALLY NEED TO THINK ABOUT OUR SURVIVAL HERE. THEY MIGHT NOT FIND US TODAY, AND IF THE WEATHER GETS BAD, IT MIGHT TAKE EVEN LONGER. IN THAT CASE, WE REALLY NEED TO TAKE THIS SERIOUSLY.
GOOD THINK-ING.
GASP
WAIT!! WHAT ABOUT THE FIRST SUNRISE OF THE YEAR?!
I ARRANGED A PRIVATE LOUNGE FOR US TO VIEW IT!!
That was the whole point of kidnapping you!
YOU'RE NOT TAKING THIS SERIOUSLY.
I GUESS WE'LL JUST HAVE TO WATCH IT TOGETHER HERE.
I SUPPOSE THAT COULD BE NICE TOO...
IF WE SURVIVE. SURE.
SH-SHAAA

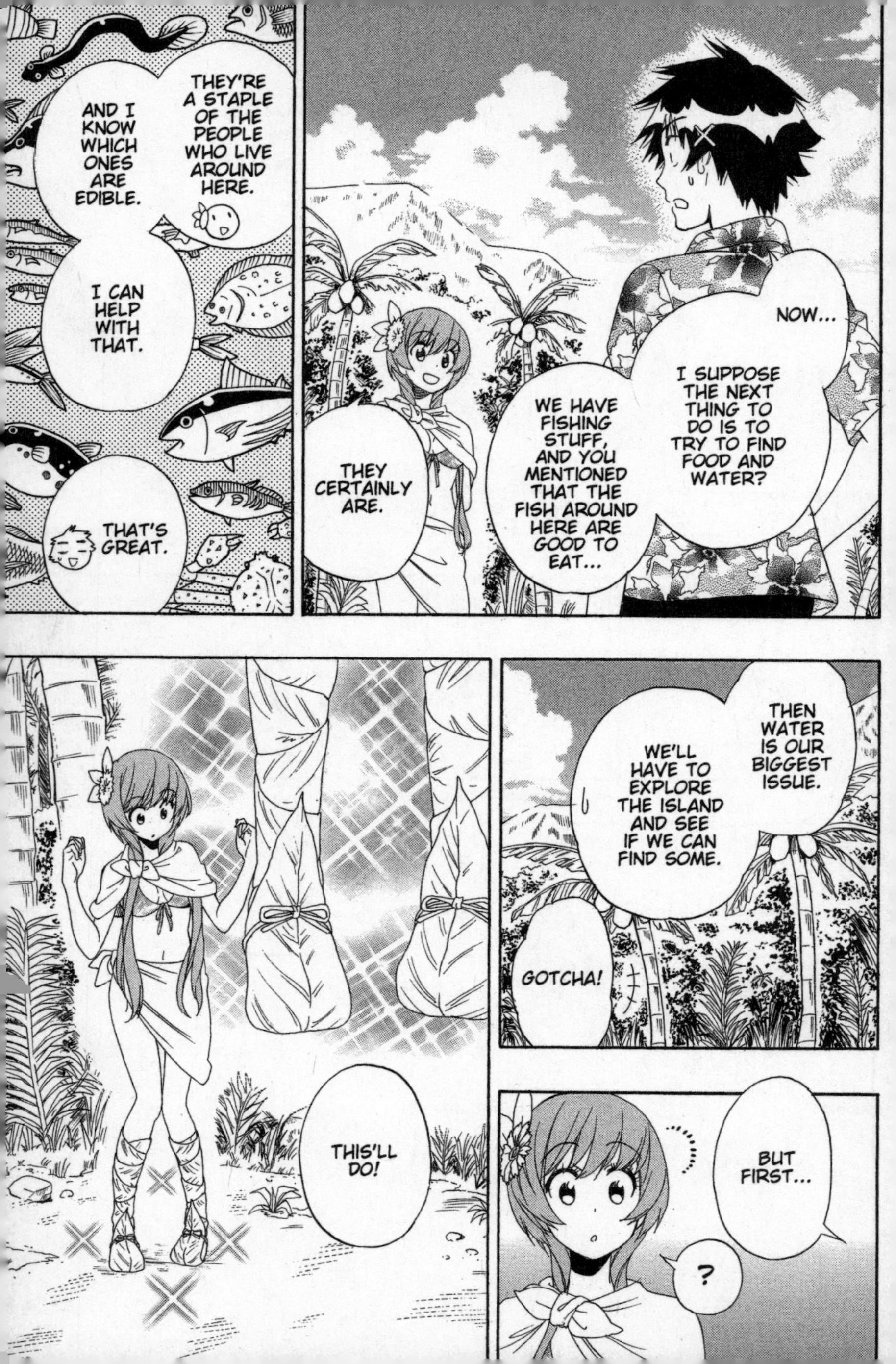
NOW...
I SUPPOSE THE NEXT THING TO DO IS TO TRY TO FIND FOOD AND WATER?
WE HAVE FISHING STUFF, AND YOU MENTIONED THAT THE FISH AROUND HERE ARE GOOD TO EAT...
THEY CERTAINLY ARE.
THEY'RE A STAPLE OF THE PEOPLE WHO LIVE AROUND HERE.
AND I KNOW WHICH ONES ARE EDIBLE.
I CAN HELP WITH THAT.
THAT'S GREAT.
THEN WATER IS OUR BIGGEST ISSUE.
WE'LL HAVE TO EXPLORE THE ISLAND AND SEE IF WE CAN FIND SOME.
GOTCHA!
BUT FIRST...
?
THIS'LL DO!

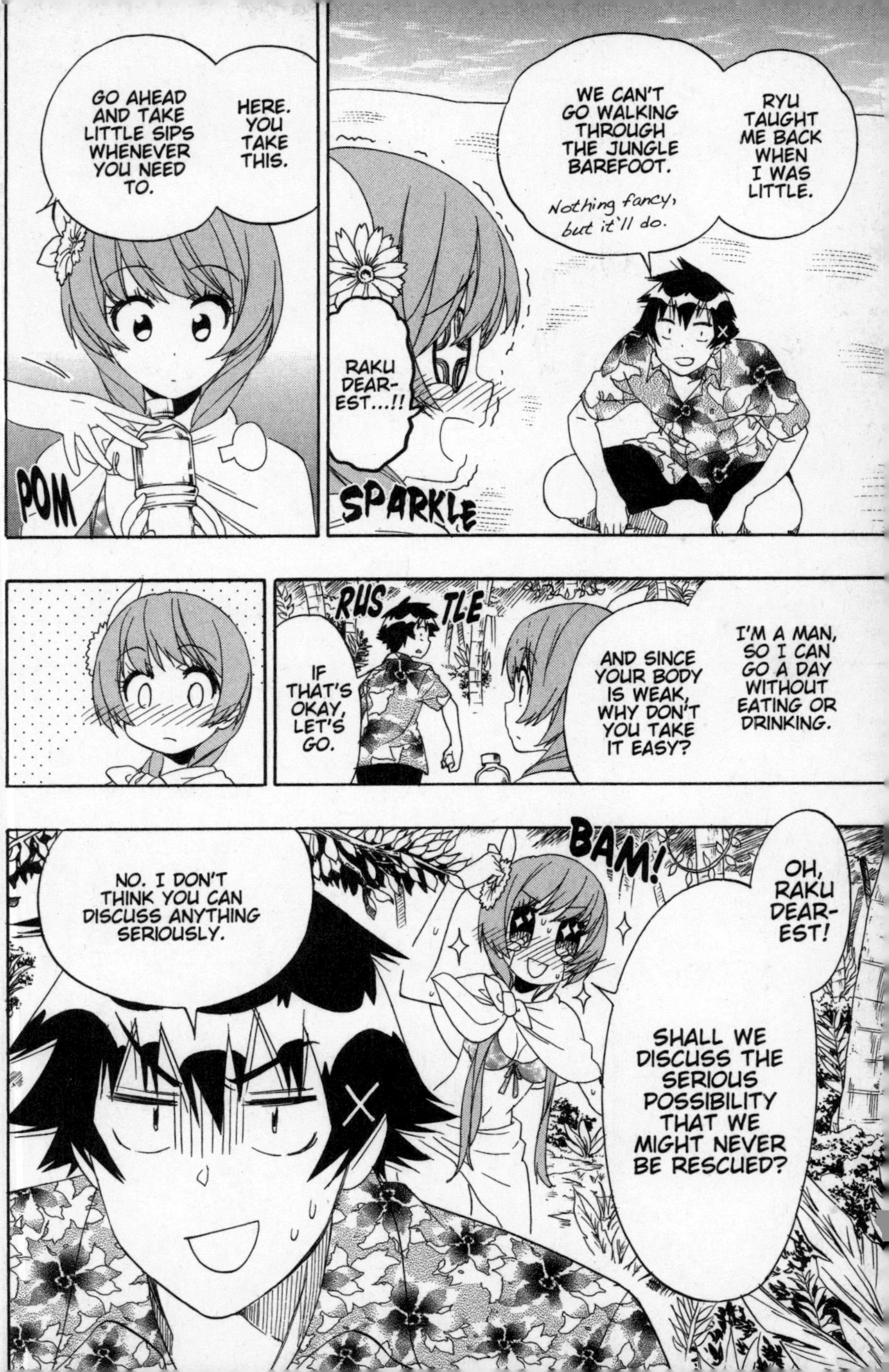
RYU TAUGHT ME BACK WHEN I WAS LITTLE.
WE CAN'T GO WALKING THROUGH THE JUNGLE BAREFOOT.
Nothing fancy, but it'll do.
RAKU DEAR-EST...!!
SPARKLE
HERE. YOU TAKE THIS.
GO AHEAD AND TAKE LITTLE SIPS WHENEVER YOU NEED TO.
POM
I'M A MAN, SO I CAN GO A DAY WITHOUT EATING OR DRINKING.
AND SINCE YOUR BODY IS WEAK, WHY DON'T YOU TAKE IT EASY?
RUS TLE
IF THAT'S OKAY, LET'S GO.
OH, RAKU DEAR-EST!
SHALL WE DISCUSS THE SERIOUS POSSIBILITY THAT WE MIGHT NEVER BE RESCUED?
BAM!
NO. I DON'T THINK YOU CAN DISCUSS ANYTHING SERIOUSLY.

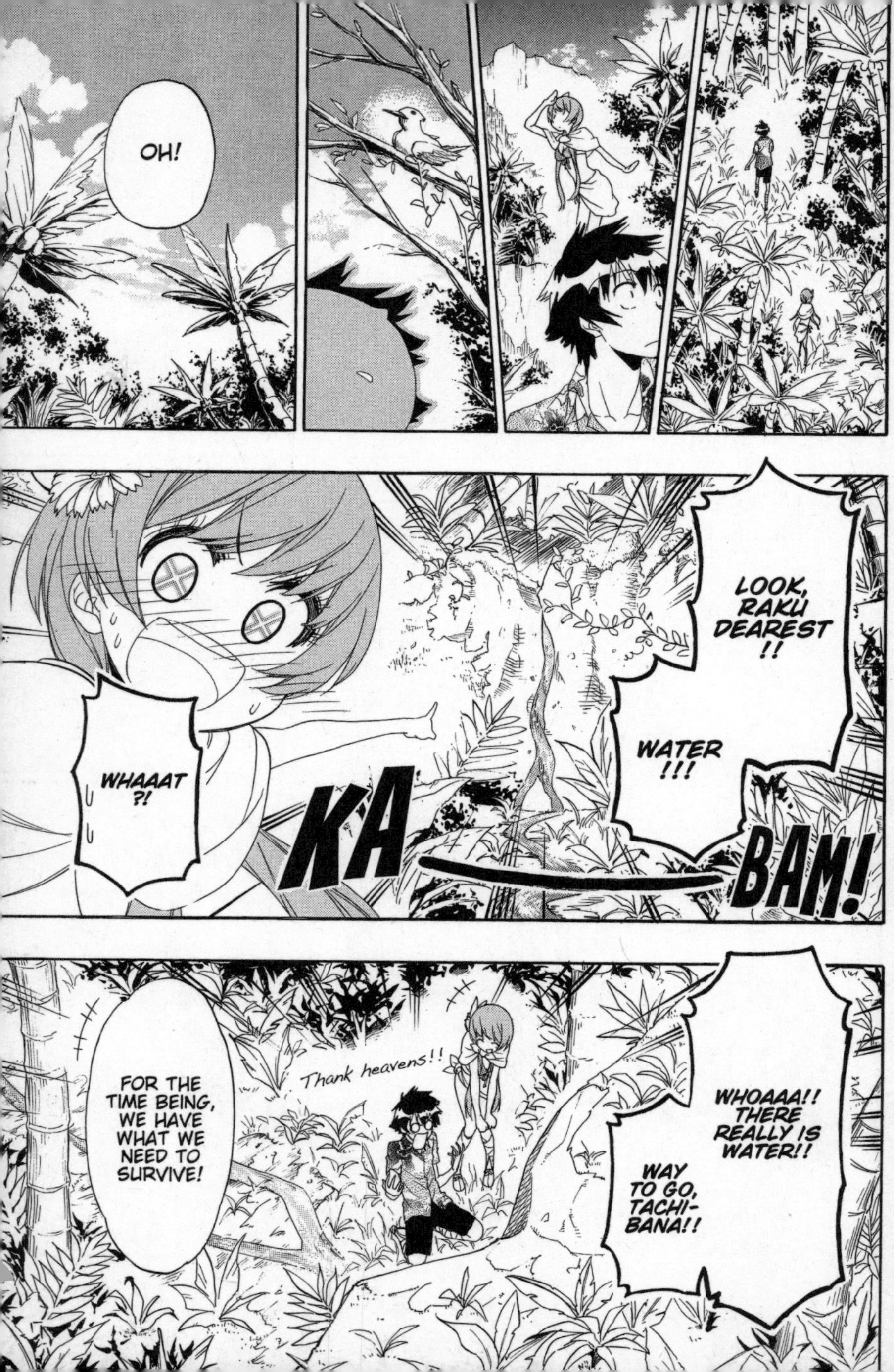
OH!
LOOK, RAKU DEAREST!!
WATER!!!
KA—BAM!
WHAAAT?!
WHOAAA!! THERE REALLY IS WATER!!
WAY TO GO, TACHIBANA!!
Thank heavens!!
FOR THE TIME BEING, WE HAVE WHAT WE NEED TO SURVIVE!

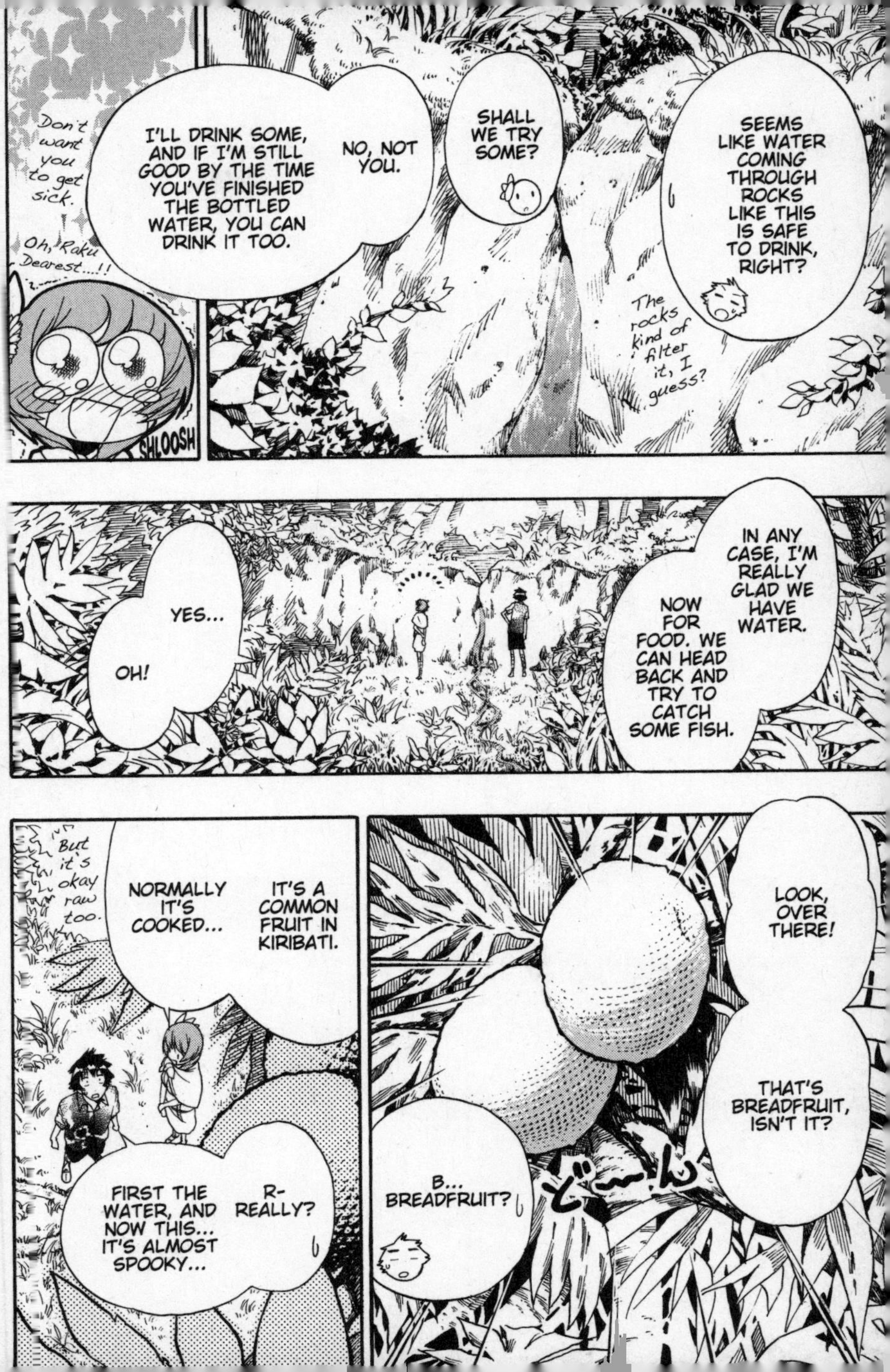
SEEMS LIKE WATER COMING THROUGH ROCKS LIKE THIS IS SAFE TO DRINK, RIGHT?
The rocks kind of filter it, I guess?
SHALL WE TRY SOME?
NO, NOT YOU.
I'LL DRINK SOME, AND IF I'M STILL GOOD BY THE TIME YOU'VE FINISHED THE BOTTLED WATER, YOU CAN DRINK IT TOO.
Don't want you to get sick.
Oh, Raku Dearest...!!
SHLOOSH
IN ANY CASE, I'M REALLY GLAD WE HAVE WATER.
NOW FOR FOOD. WE CAN HEAD BACK AND TRY TO CATCH SOME FISH.
YES...
OH!
LOOK, OVER THERE!
THAT'S BREADFRUIT, ISN'T IT?
B... BREADFRUIT?
IT'S A COMMON FRUIT IN KIRIBATI.
NORMALLY IT'S COOKED...
But it's okay raw too.
R-REALLY?
FIRST THE WATER, AND NOW THIS... IT'S ALMOST SPOOKY...

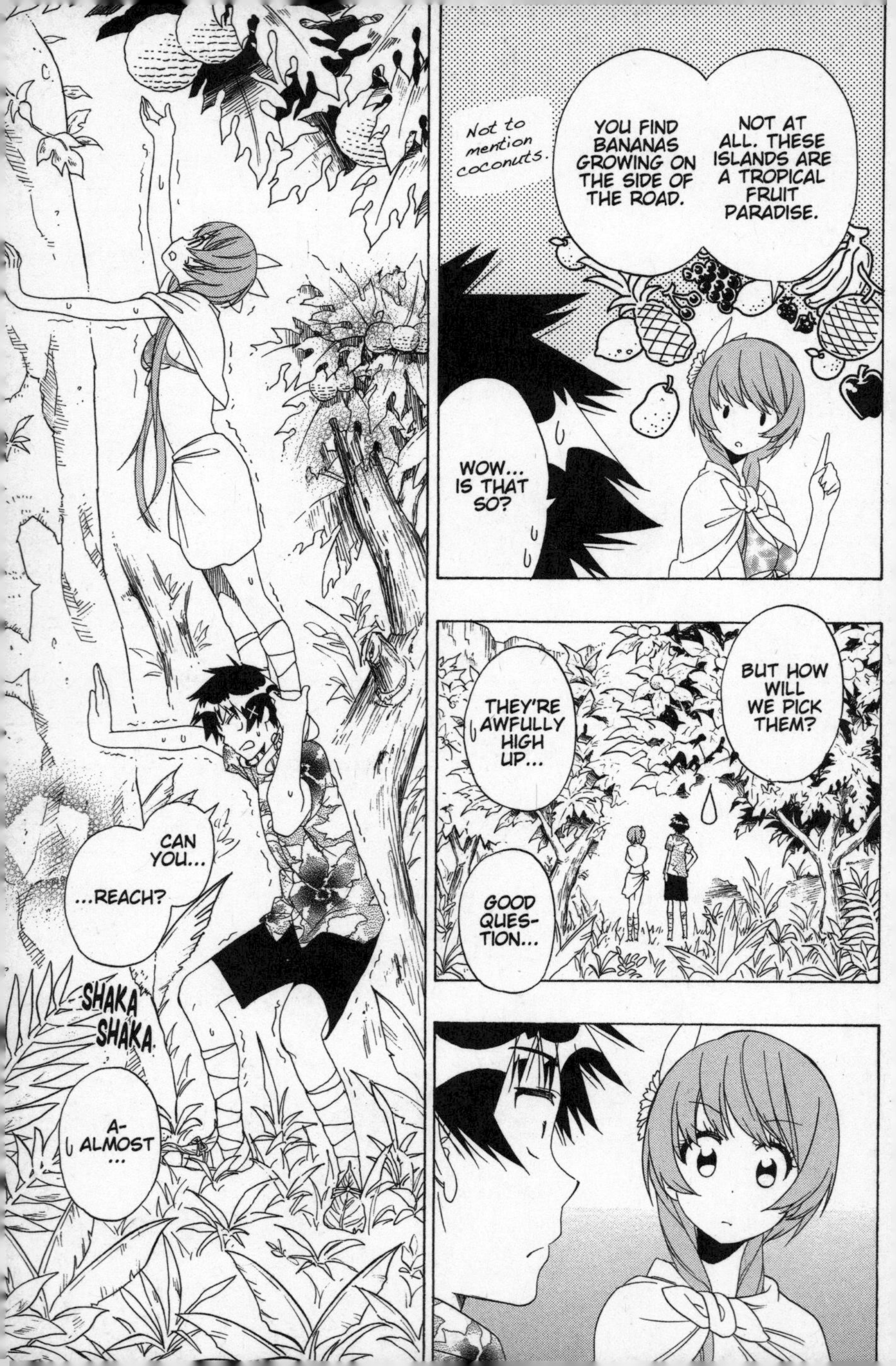
NOT AT ALL. THESE ISLANDS ARE A TROPICAL FRUIT PARADISE.
YOU FIND BANANAS GROWING ON THE SIDE OF THE ROAD.
Not to mention coconuts.
WOW... IS THAT SO?
BUT HOW WILL WE PICK THEM?
THEY'RE AWFULLY HIGH UP...
GOOD QUES-TION...
CAN YOU...
...REACH?
SHAKA SHAKA
A-ALMOST ...

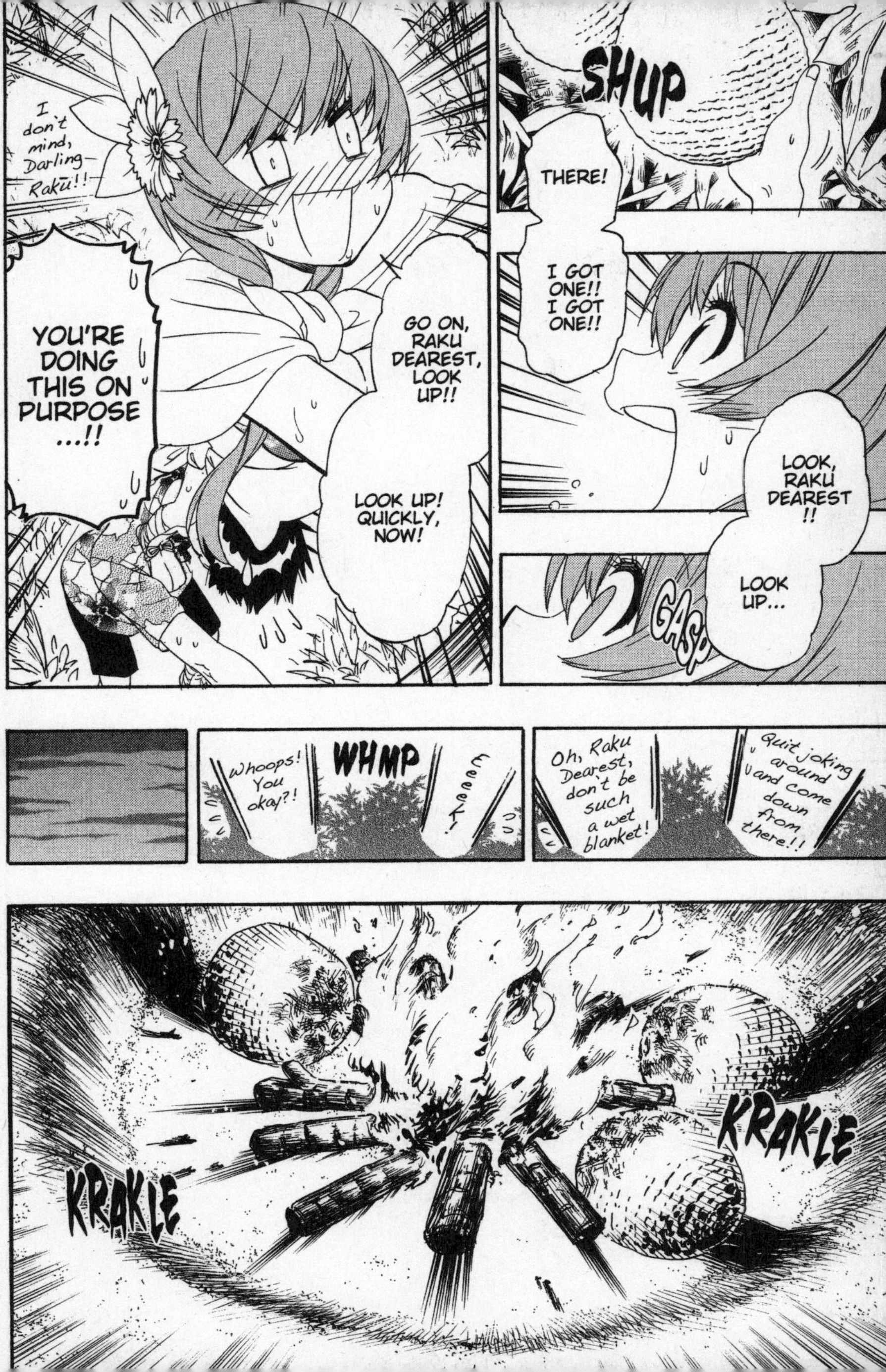
SHUP
THERE!
I GOT ONE!! I GOT ONE!!
LOOK, RAKU DEAREST!!
LOOK UP...
GASP
GO ON, RAKU DEAREST, LOOK UP!!
LOOK UP! QUICKLY, NOW!
I don't mind, Darling-Rakū!!
YOU'RE DOING THIS ON PURPOSE...!!
Quit joking around and come down from there!!
Oh, Raku Dearest, don't be such a wet blanket!
Eeeek!
WHMP
Whoops! You okay?!
KRAKLE
KRAKLE

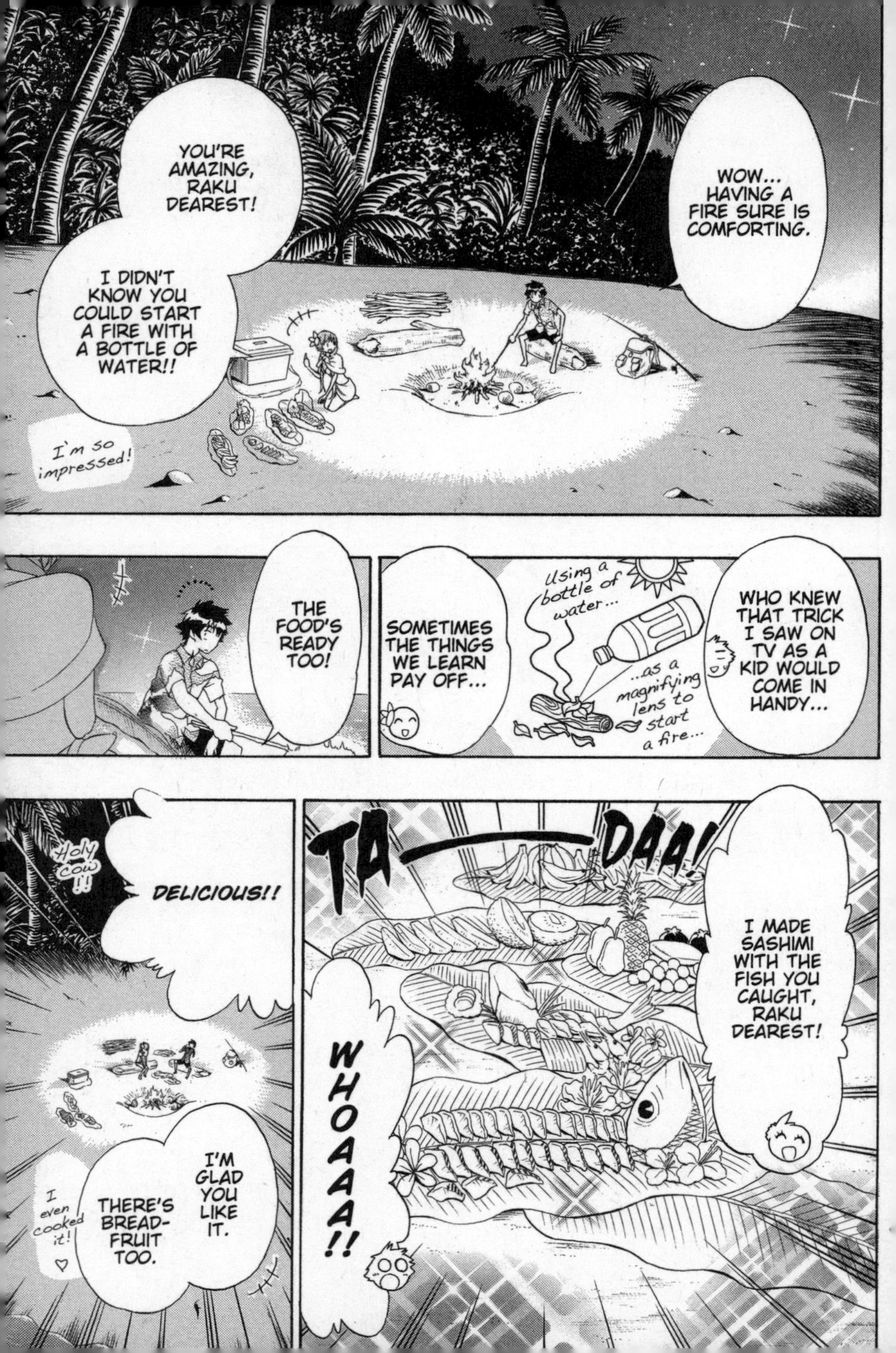
WOW... HAVING A FIRE SURE IS COMFORTING.
YOU'RE AMAZING, RAKU DEAREST!
I DIDN'T KNOW YOU COULD START A FIRE WITH A BOTTLE OF WATER!!
I'm so impressed!
WHO KNEW THAT TRICK I SAW ON TV AS A KID WOULD COME IN HANDY...
Using a bottle of water...
...as a magnifying lens to start a fire...
SOMETIMES THE THINGS WE LEARN PAY OFF...
THE FOOD'S READY TOO!
TA—DAA!
I MADE SASHIMI WITH THE FISH YOU CAUGHT, RAKU DEAREST!
WHOAAAA!!
DELICIOUS!!
Holy cow!!
I'M GLAD YOU LIKE IT.
THERE'S BREAD-FRUIT TOO.
I even cooked it! ♡

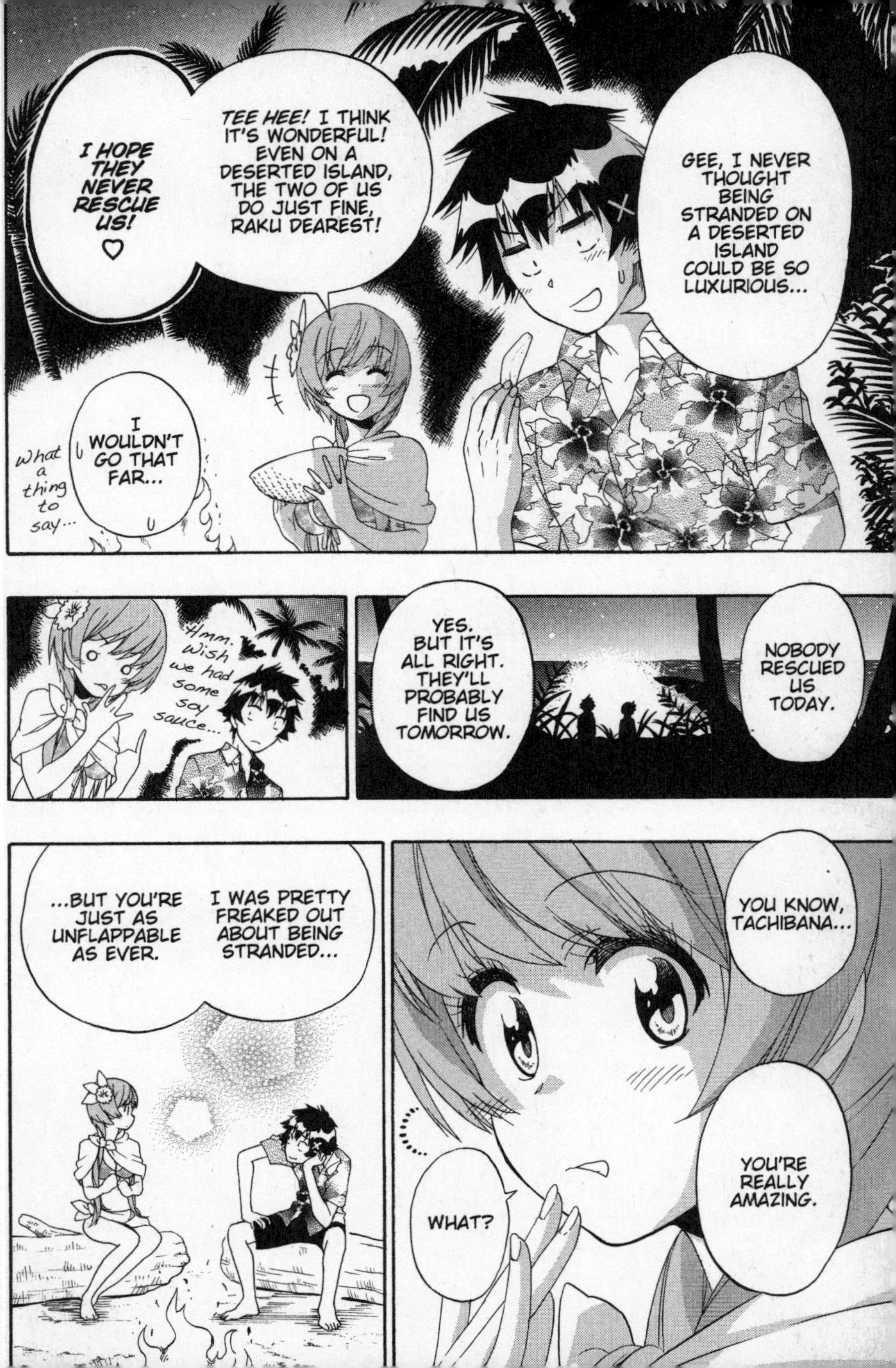
GEE, I NEVER THOUGHT BEING STRANDED ON A DESERTED ISLAND COULD BE SO LUXURIOUS...
TEE HEE! I THINK IT'S WONDERFUL! EVEN ON A DESERTED ISLAND, THE TWO OF US DO JUST FINE, RAKU DEAREST!
I HOPE THEY NEVER RESCUE US! ♡
I WOULDN'T GO THAT FAR...
What a thing to say...
NOBODY RESCUED US TODAY.
YES. BUT IT'S ALL RIGHT. THEY'LL PROBABLY FIND US TOMORROW.
Hmm. Wish we had some soy sauce...
YOU KNOW, TACHIBANA...
YOU'RE REALLY AMAZING.
WHAT?
I WAS PRETTY FREAKED OUT ABOUT BEING STRANDED...
...BUT YOU'RE JUST AS UNFLAPPABLE AS EVER.

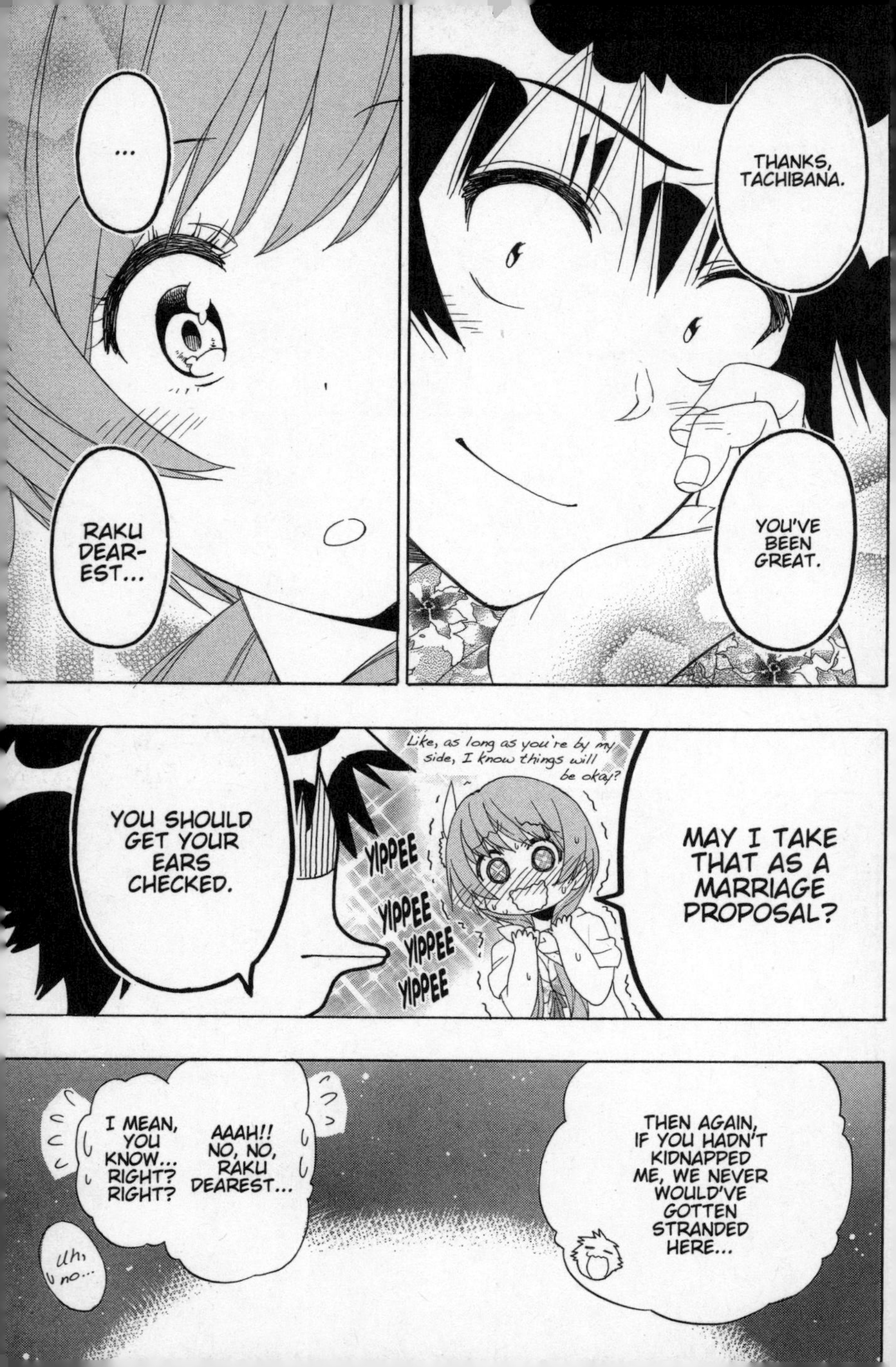
THANKS, TACHIBANA.
YOU'VE BEEN GREAT.
...
RAKU DEAREST...
MAY I TAKE THAT AS A MARRIAGE PROPOSAL?
Like, as long as you're by my side, I know things will be okay?
YIPPEE YIPPEE YIPPEE YIPPEE
YOU SHOULD GET YOUR EARS CHECKED.
THEN AGAIN, IF YOU HADN'T KIDNAPPED ME, WE NEVER WOULD'VE GOTTEN STRANDED HERE...
AAAH!! NO, NO, RAKU DEAREST...
I MEAN, YOU KNOW... RIGHT? RIGHT?
Uh, no...

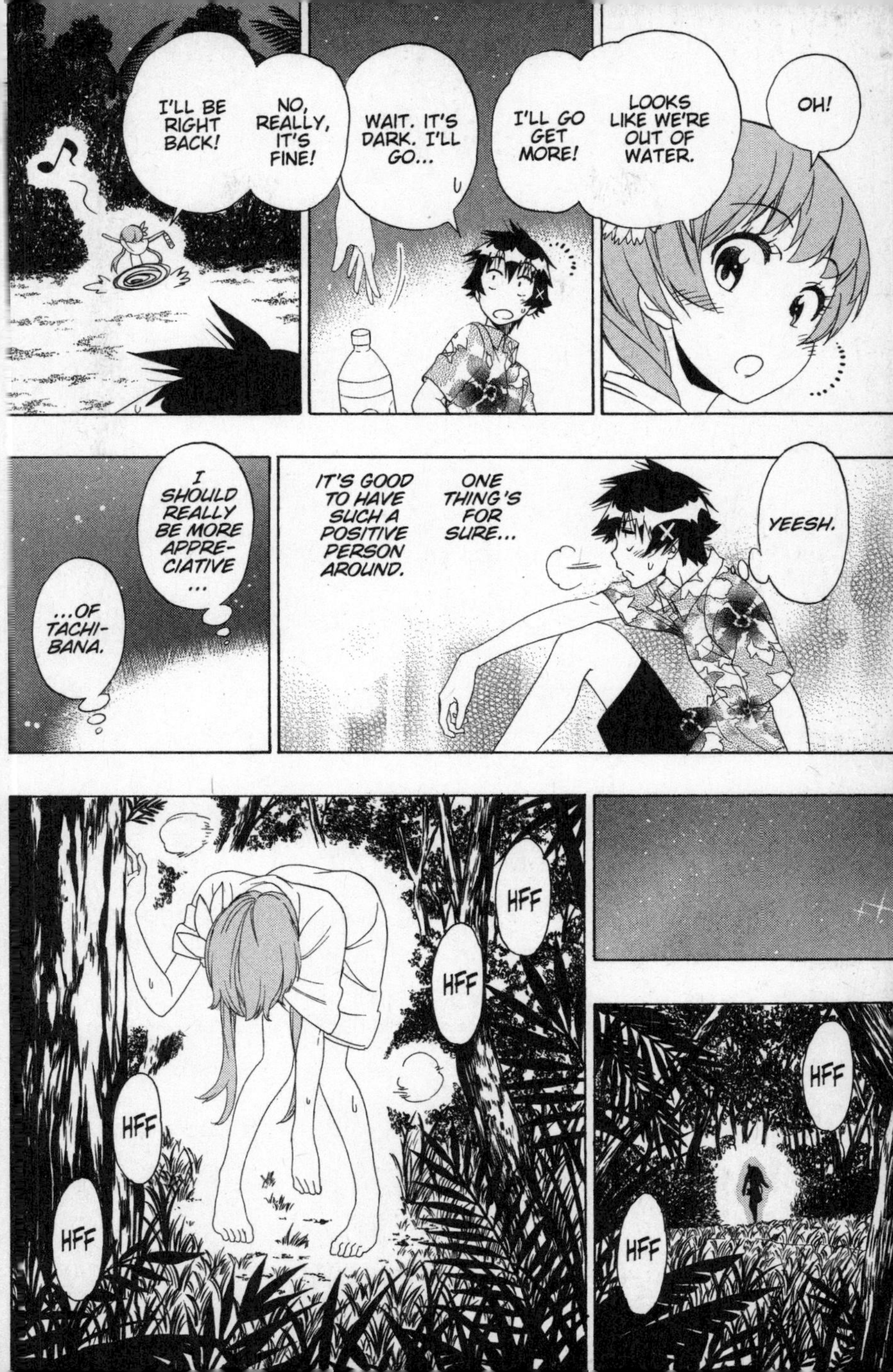
OH!
LOOKS LIKE WE'RE OUT OF WATER.
I'LL GO GET MORE!
WAIT. IT'S DARK. I'LL GO...
NO, REALLY, IT'S FINE!
I'LL BE RIGHT BACK!
YEESH.
ONE THING'S FOR SURE...
IT'S GOOD TO HAVE SUCH A POSITIVE PERSON AROUND.
I SHOULD REALLY BE MORE APPRECIATIVE ...
...OF TACHIBANA.
HFF
HFF
HFF
HFF
HFF
HFF

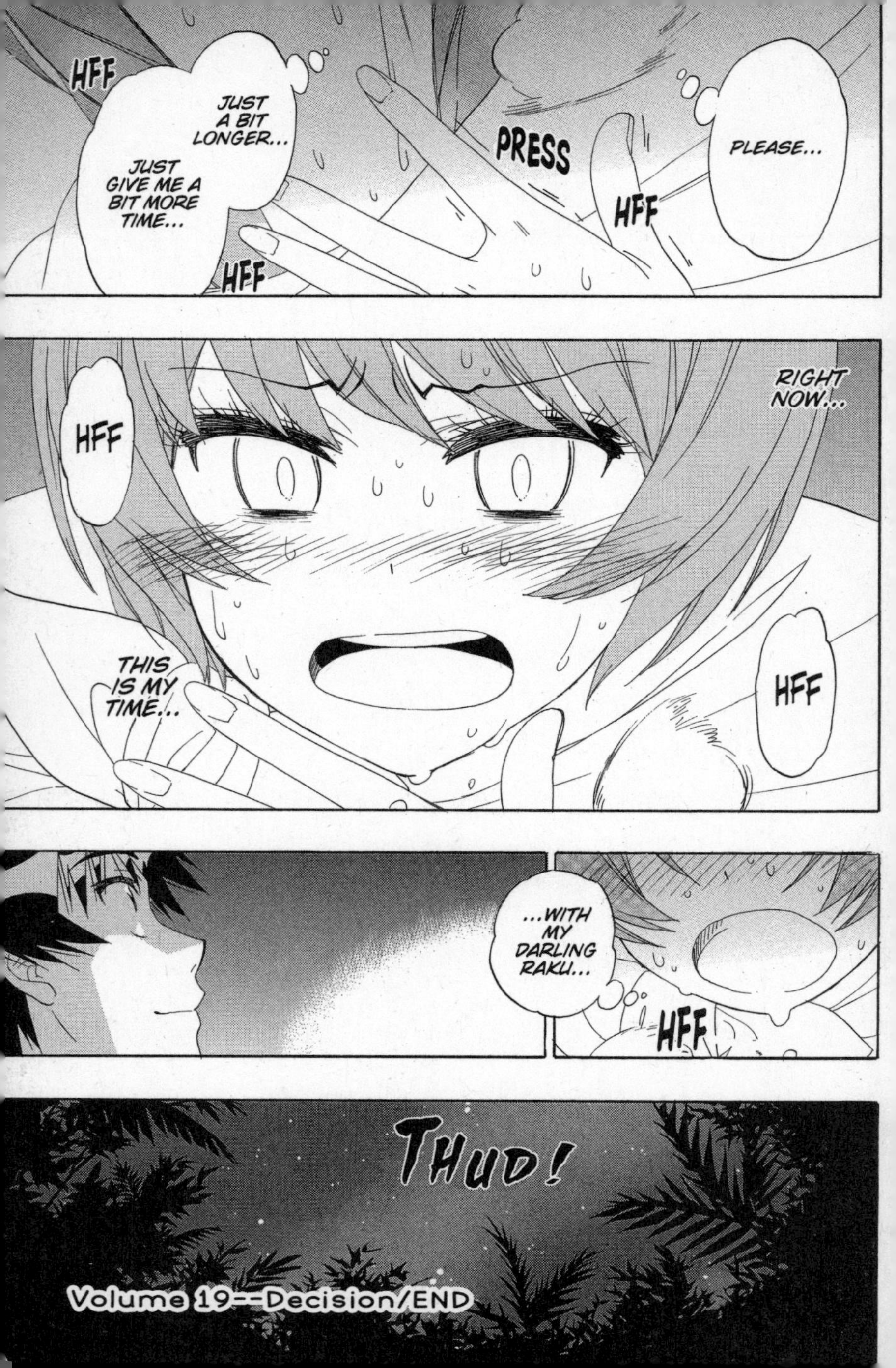
PLEASE...
HFF
PRESS
HFF
JUST A BIT LONGER...
JUST GIVE ME A BIT MORE TIME...
HFF
RIGHT NOW...
HFF
HFF
THIS IS MY TIME...
...WITH MY DARLING RAKU...
HFF
THUD!

Volume 19--Decision/END

It took about an hour.

Oh man... The sun's starting to go down!!
FWOO! FWOO!
You can do it, Raku Dearest!! It's starting to smoke!

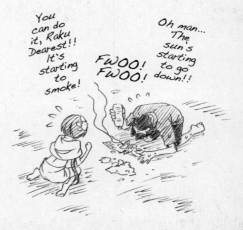

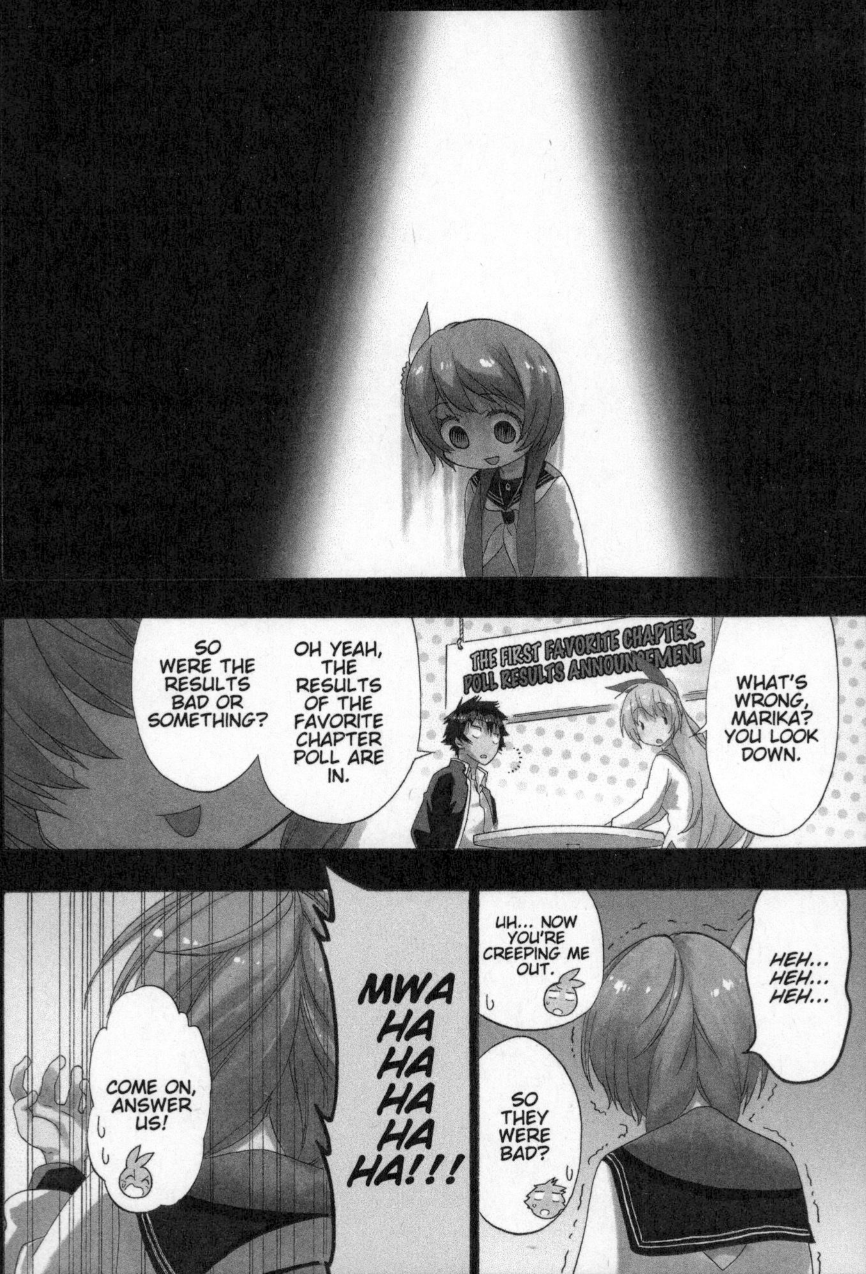
WHAT'S WRONG, MARIKA? YOU LOOK DOWN.
THE FIRST FAVORITE CHAPTER POLL RESULTS ANNOUNCEMENT
OH YEAH, THE RESULTS OF THE FAVORITE CHAPTER POLL ARE IN.
SO WERE THE RESULTS BAD OR SOMETHING?
HEH... HEH... HEH...
UH... NOW YOU'RE CREEPING ME OUT.
SO THEY WERE BAD?
MWA HA HA HA HA HA HA!!!
COME ON, ANSWER US!

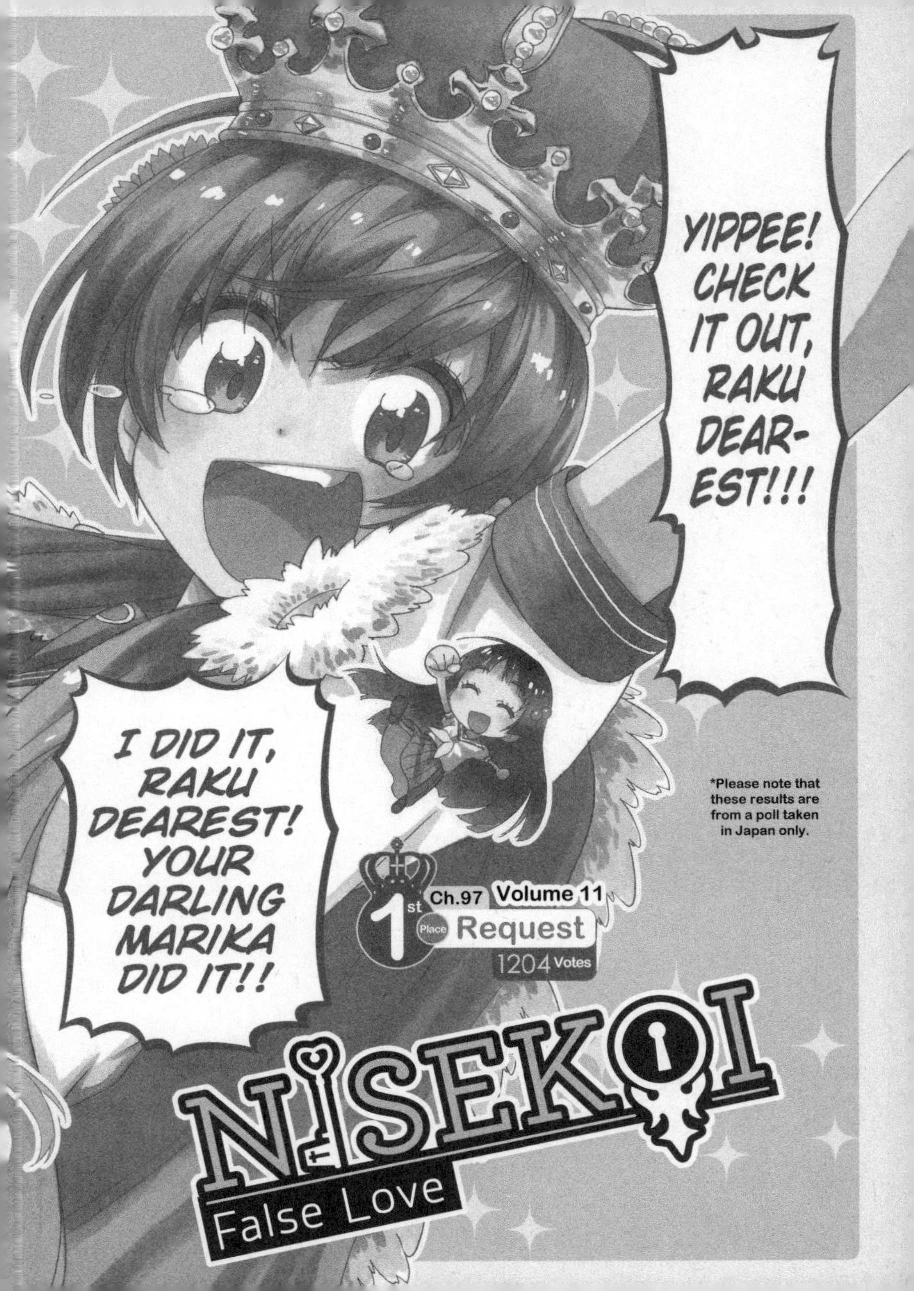
YIPPEE! CHECK IT OUT, RAKU DEAR-EST!!!
I DID IT, RAKU DEAREST! YOUR DARLING MARIKA DID IT!!
*Please note that these results are from a poll taken in Japan only.
1st Place
Ch.97 Volume 11
Request
1204 Votes
NISEKOI
False Love

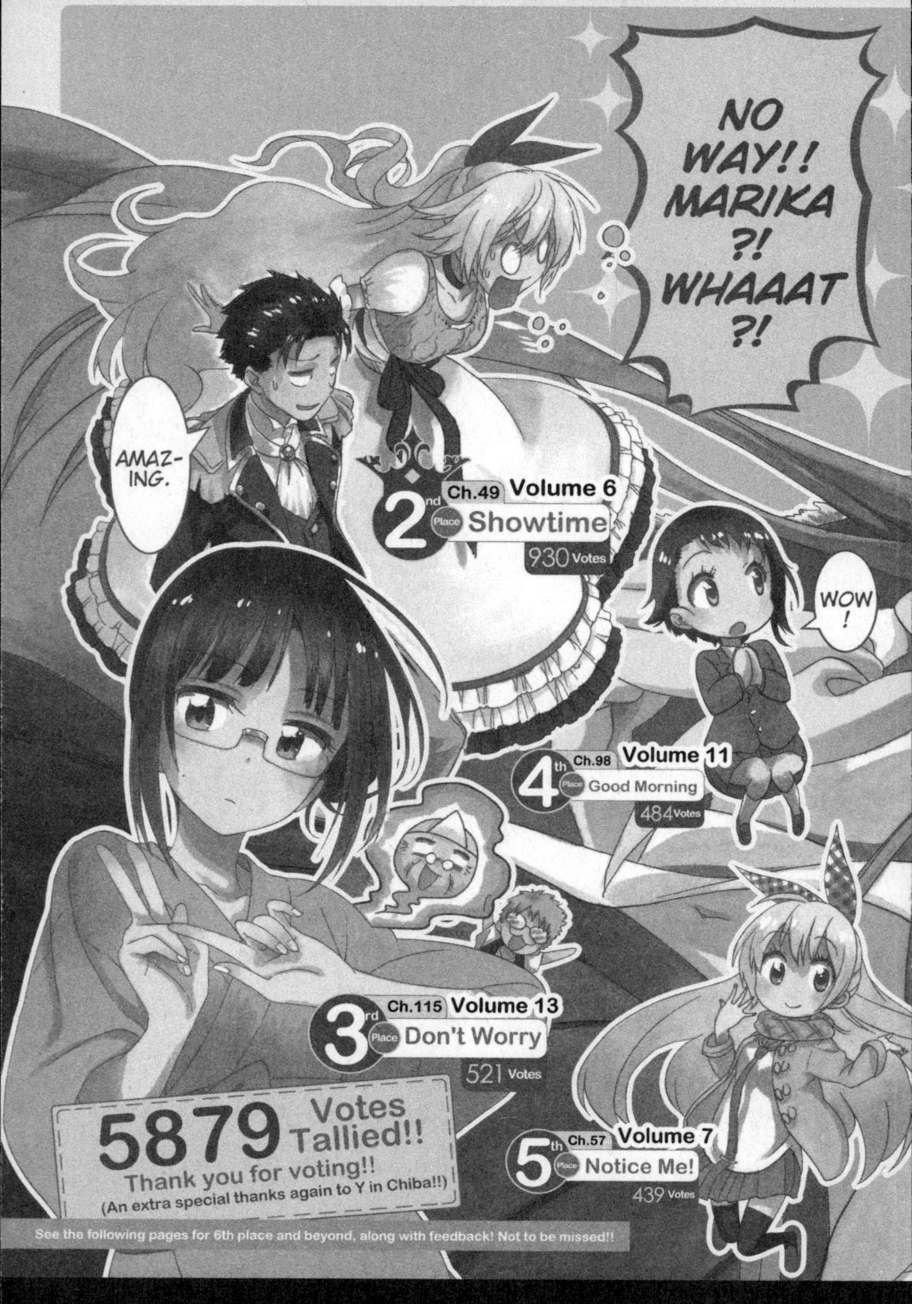
NO WAY!! MARIKA ?! WHAAAT ?!
AMAZ-ING.
2nd Place Ch.49 Volume 6 Showtime 930 Votes
WOW !
4th Place Ch.98 Volume 11 Good Morning 484 Votes
3rd Place Ch.115 Volume 13 Don't Worry 521 Votes
5th Place Ch.57 Volume 7 Notice Me! 439 Votes
5879 Votes Tallied!!
Thank you for voting!!
(An extra special thanks again to Y in Chiba!!)
See the following pages for 6th place and beyond, along with feedback! Not to be missed!!

1st

Favorite Chapter Poll Results

5th Place
rd beyond!

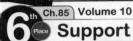

Revealed: Readers' favorite episodes! And comments from our enthusiastic fans!

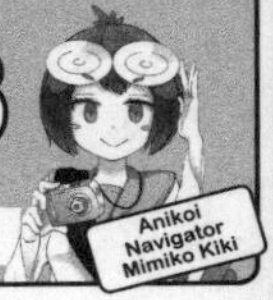

Anikoi Navigator Mimiko Kiki

6th Place — Ch.85 Volume 10 — Support

202 Votes

EPISODE

Shu normally plays the joker, but in this chapter he reveals his sincere side! When Kyoko Sensei quits teaching to get married, Shu intends to let her go without revealing his feelings for her, but Raku isn't willing to let his good friend ignore his heart. Ah, young love!

Love declaration in the rain!

Shu runs after Kyoko Sensei, even knowing that his feelings won't be returned. After his confession, his face is peaceful and serene.

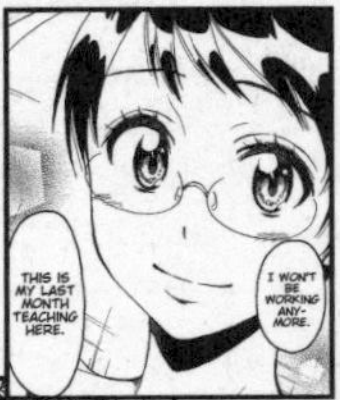

I WON'T BE WORKING ANY-MORE.
THIS IS MY LAST MONTH TEACHING HERE.

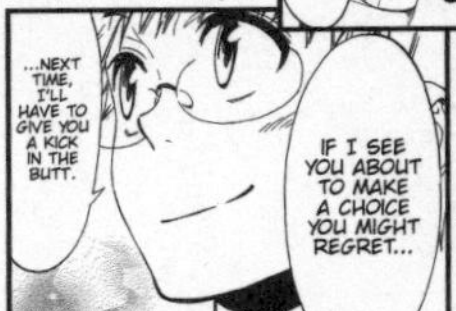

IF I SEE YOU ABOUT TO MAKE A CHOICE YOU MIGHT REGRET...
...NEXT TIME, I'LL HAVE TO GIVE YOU A KICK IN THE BUTT.

Raku and Shu are bros!

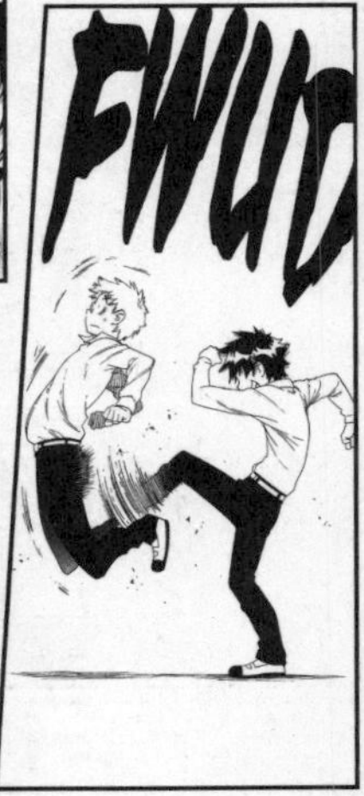

FWUD

Seishiro plays a supporting role too!

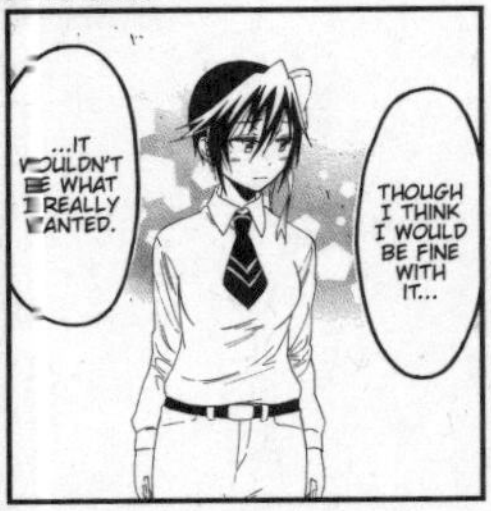

THOUGH I THINK I WOULD BE FINE WITH IT...
...IT WOULDN'T BE WHAT I REALLY WANTED.

Voters' Comments

- I was totally moved by seeing a new side of Shu and by his friendship with Raku! (male, 27)
- A super cool episode depicting sincere friendship between two boys! (female, 22)
- My heart was most struck by the scene where Shu sprints through the rain to reach Kyoko Sensei! (male,16)

7th Place — Ch.147 Volume 17 — Big Sis Yui

132 Votes

EPISODE

When Yui lost her parents as a young girl, Raku was like family to her, and served as her greatest support. A poignant portrayal of her powerful devotion to Raku, and her constant yearning to be reunited with him!

Yui's tragic past revealed!

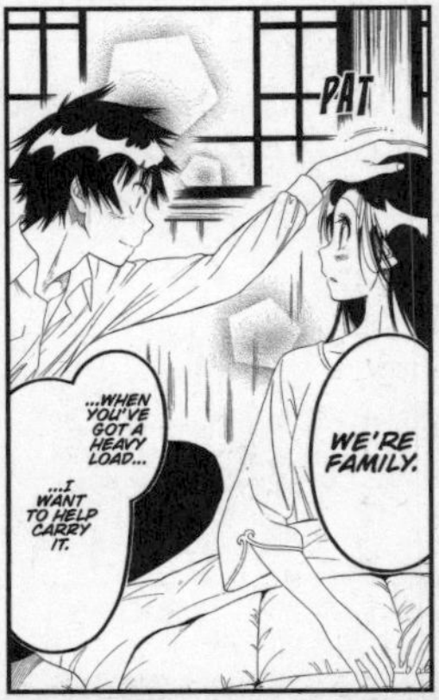

PAT
...WHEN YOU'VE GOT A HEAVY LOAD...
...I WANT TO HELP CARRY IT.
WE'RE FAMILY.

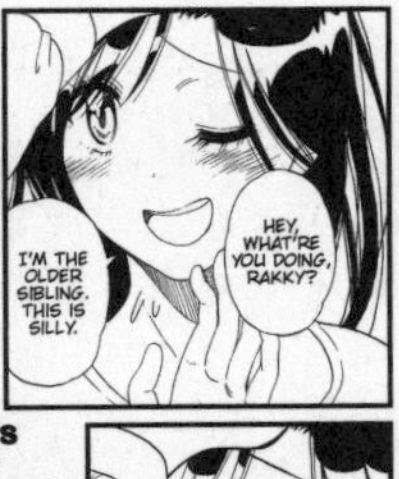

HEY, WHAT'RE YOU DOING, RAKKY?
I'M THE OLDER SIBLING. THIS IS SILLY.

Yui always hides her weaknesses... but then the tears come...

Yui tells Raku that it relaxes her when he pats her head. But when she remembers him patting her head as a child, the tears start to flow...

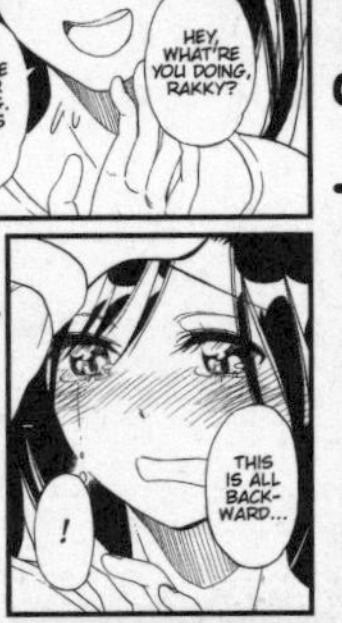

THIS IS ALL BACK-WARD...
!

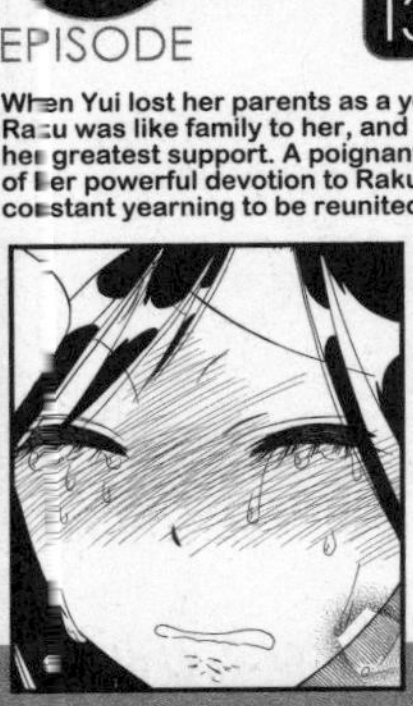

8th Place — Ch.144 Volume 17

Sleepover

114 Votes

EPISODE

Raku and Kosaki go to work at an inn... and wind up sleeping over! Plus, the bath is co-ed! With its heart-pounding thrills, this chapter came in 8th place!

Raku takes a bath with Kosaki?!

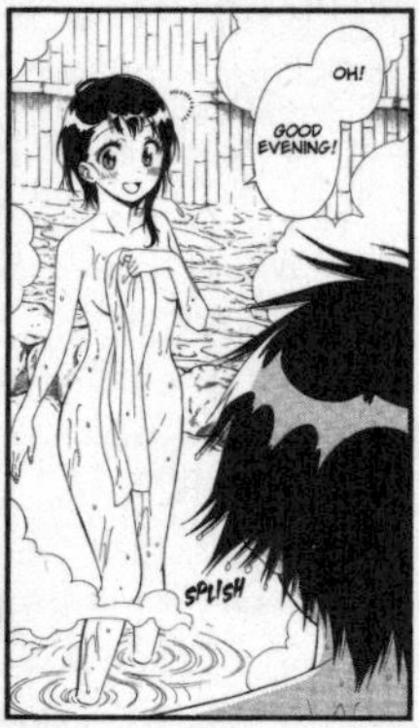
OH!
GOOD EVENING!
SPLISH

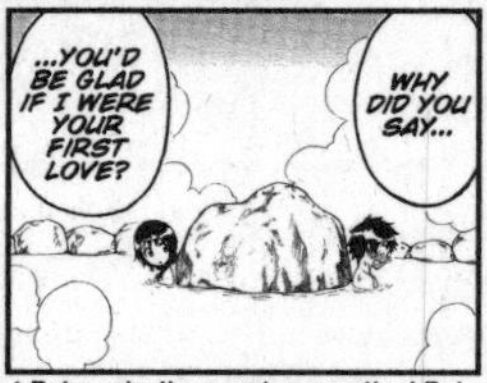
WHY DID YOU SAY...
...YOU'D BE GLAD IF I WERE YOUR FIRST LOVE?

⬆ Raku asks the nagging question! But Kosaki gets overheated and passes out, and Raku never gets an answer!

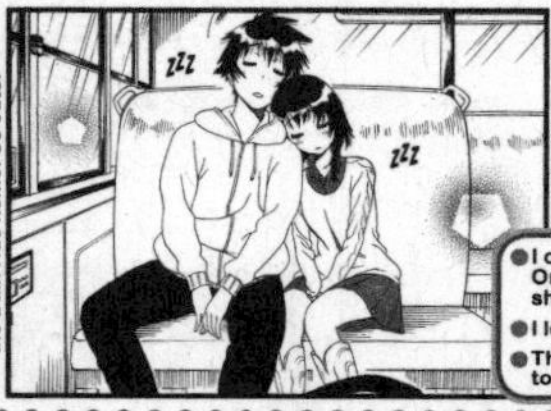
ZZZ
ZZZ

Raku and Onodera fall asleep on the train ride home. So cute!

Voters' Comments

- I can't help rooting for Onodera. She's so sweet and she tries so hard! (male, 30)
- I love Raku and Onodera! (female)
- The best is at the end, when they fall asleep together! (female, 15)

9th Place — Ch.39 Volume 5

Typhoon

97 Votes

EPISODE

When Raku is over at Kosaki's house helping out at the shop, a sudden typhoon prevents him from leaving. He ends up hanging out in her bedroom! Lots of readers loved Kosaki's move at the end!

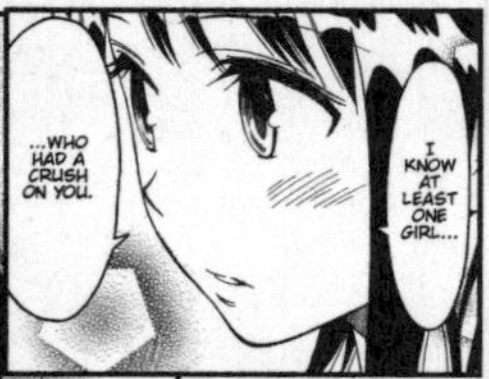
I KNOW AT LEAST ONE GIRL...
...WHO HAD A CRUSH ON YOU.

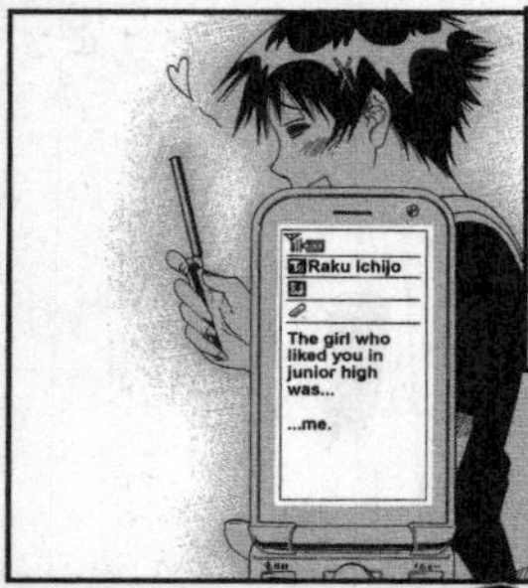
Raku Ichijo
The girl who liked you in junior high was...
...me.

Raku sets foot in Kosaki's bedroom!

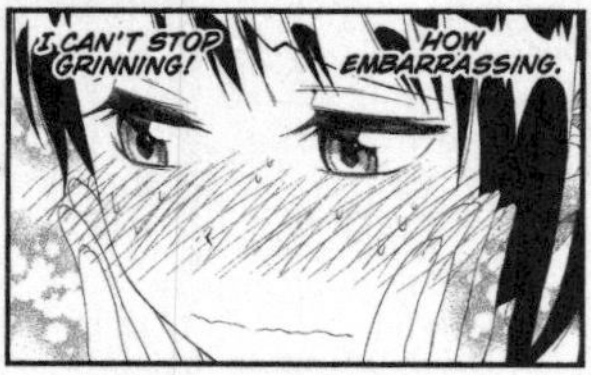
HOW EMBARRASSING.
I CAN'T STOP GRINNING!

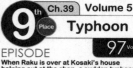

Kosaki ➡ was too cute, sprucing up her room, primping, and grinning like a fool in anticipation of Raku's visit.

Voters' Comments

- When Onodera wrote her message at the end and then deleted it, my heart skipped a beat! (male, 19)
- This chapter made me a NISEKOI fan! (male,17)

10th Place — Ch.109 Volume 13

Awkward

83 Votes

EPISODE

It's summer break, and Haru figures out that her Prince Charming is Raku. But Raku is Kosaki's crush... In this moving episode, Haru realizes her feelings... and decides she has to let go.

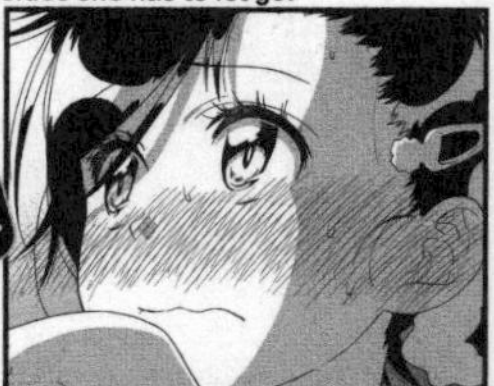

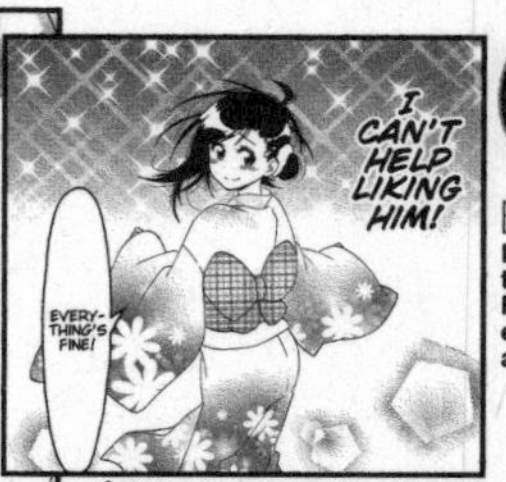
I CAN'T HELP LIKING HIM!
EVERYTHING'S FINE!

⬆ Haru realizes her feelings for Raku! But she decides to give up and support her sister instead. Her solitary tears ⬅ touched readers' hearts...

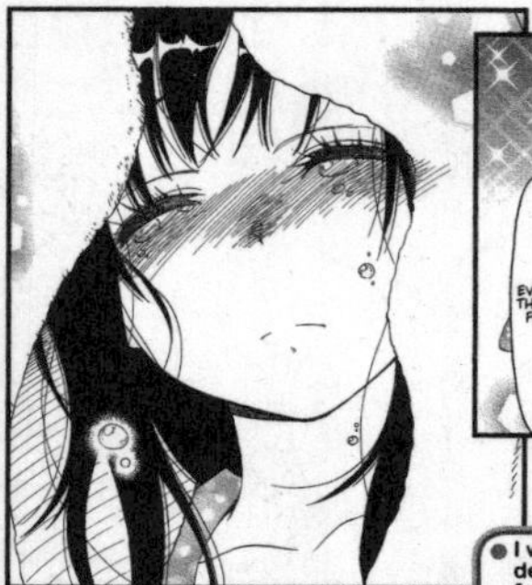

Haru weeps alone for lost love

Voters' Comments

- I was so moved when Haru decided to sacrifice her own feelings for her sister! (male, 20)
- When Haru gave up on her crush and decided to support her sister, it moved me to tears. (male, 22)

See the next page for 11th Place and beyond!

11th Place and beyond!

Place	Volume	Chapter	
11th Place	Volume 6	Ch. 50: The Stars	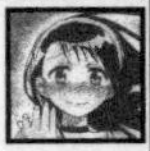
12th Place	Volume 15	Ch. 134: Choice	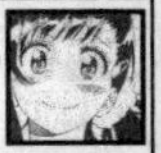
13th Place	Volume 1	Ch. 1: The Promise	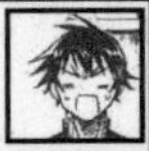
13th Place	Volume 15	Ch. 129: Cold	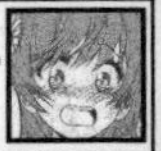
15th Place	Volume 14	Ch. 125: Girls Are...	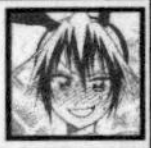
16th Place	Volume 4	Ch. 27: Detour	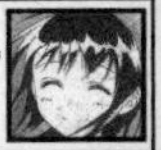
17th Place	Volume 12	Ch. 106: Search	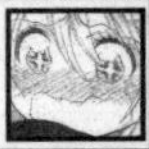
18th Place	Volume 8	Ch. 69: Last Minute	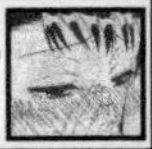
19th Place	Volume 7	Ch. 62: The Reason	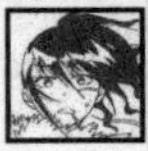
20th Place	Volume 13	Ch. 110: Outing	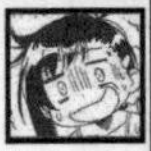

Rank	Chapter	Title	Rank	Chapter	Title	Rank	Chapter	Title
21st Place	38	Work	41st Place	71	Work		101	Cake Shop
	122	Conference		143	Let's Work		116	Lunchbox
23rd Place	91	Chagrin	43rd Place	25	What's in a Name?		126	Declaration
24th Place	81	Public Bath	44th Place	37	Greeting		132	Beauty Contest
	130	Interview	45th Place	51	From Now On	65th Place	41	Stray Dog
26th Place	149	Mistress		58	Lost		61	Mother
27th Place	18	Happiness	47th Place	55	Contest		74	Big Lie
28th Place	65	Transformation		142	Animals		105	Tanabata
	84	Friends	49th Place	16	Showdown		112	Steps
30th Place	141	Sincere		40	Liar		123	Suitable
31st Place	13	Zawsze in Love		44	At the Beach		139	Speech
32nd Place	10	Swimming		104	Raku Dearest	72nd Place	23	Women's Bath
	99	Delicate		111	Head Over Heels		43	Blessings
34th Place	26	Love Letter		148	Successor		45	Turmoil
	33	Showdown		150	Groups		56	Teach Me!
36th Place	64	Shrine Maidens	56th Place	3	The First Time		127	The King
	131	Plot		15	Rival	77th Place	32	Umbrella Buddies
38th Place	100	Test		75	Kamikaze		36	Three Keys
	107	Festival		88	Loss		53	Horoscope
	133	One-on-One		93	Slimming Down		94	Costume

Rank	Chapter	Title	Rank	Chapter	Title	Rank	Chapter	Title
	114	A Smidge		24	Luck of the Draw		87	Special Day
	128	Together		28	Celebration		90	Blue
	138	Daikichi		34	Pursuit		96	Imagine
84th Place	19	Visiting the Sick		117	Stomach Pain		140	Sleep
	35	Explosion		118	Big Sister	127th Place	4	The Encounter
	86	Caregiver		119	Teacher		52	Measurements
	102	Cheer		137	Glad		63	Afterwards
	103	Overcoming		145	Sports		66	Changing Seats
	108	Question	110th Place	6	Birds of a Feather		72	Race Day
	136	Look-Alike		7	Homemade		82	Pool Cleanup
91st Place	14	We're Even		9	Up Close	133rd Place	8	The Visit
	70	Handcuffs		11	The Keyhole		12	Out of the Bag
	77	Get to Work!		20	Dense		54	Destiny
	83	Shu's Crush		42	Festival		73	Indirect
	92	Bouquet		46	The Play		89	Recreation
	113	Great-Grandpa		48	The Show		95	Dirty Old Man
	124	Lady		59	Long Time No See		120	Need to Know
	135	Singing Voice		68	Could it Be?		146	Perfect
99th Place	2	Questions		76	Younger Sister		152	Sound Asleep
	17	Cute		79	Peace of Mind			
	22	Hot Spring		80	Suspension Bridge			

Conclusions

Our first-ever Favorite Chapter Poll resulted in a white-hot battle. Marika took 2nd place in the last character ranking, but she stole first in the Favorite Chapter Poll!! Since we changed the voting system, we didn't expect the results to be skewed by heavy hitters again, but Y of Chiba Prefecture once again astonished us by voting more than 800 times! Talk about unprecedented love! Congratulations, Marika...!!

Weekly Shonen Jump 2015 Issue 18 Special Insert

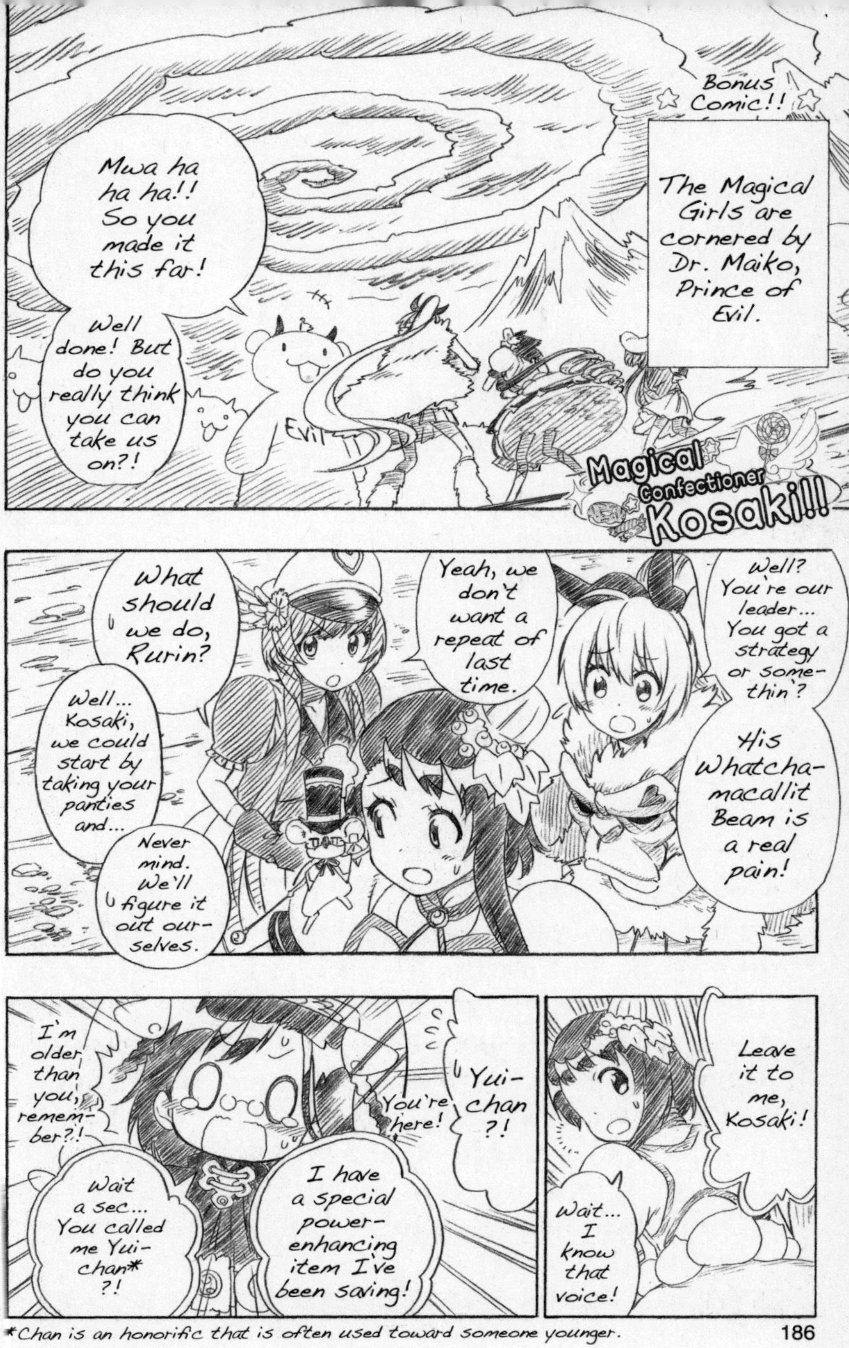
Bonus Comic!!
The Magical Girls are cornered by Dr. Maiko, Prince of Evil.
Mwa ha ha ha!! So you made it this far!
Well done! But do you really think you can take us on?!
Evil
Magical Confectioner Kosaki!!
Well? You're our leader... You got a strategy or somethin'?
His Whatchamacallit Beam is a real pain!
Yeah, we don't want a repeat of last time.
What should we do, Rurin?
Well... Kosaki, we could start by taking your panties and...
Never mind. We'll figure it out ourselves.
Leave it to me, Kosaki!
Wait... I know that voice!
Yui-chan?!
You're here!
I have a special power-enhancing item I've been saving!
I'm older than you, remember?!
Wait a sec... You called me Yui-chan* ?!

*Chan is an honorific that is often used toward someone younger.

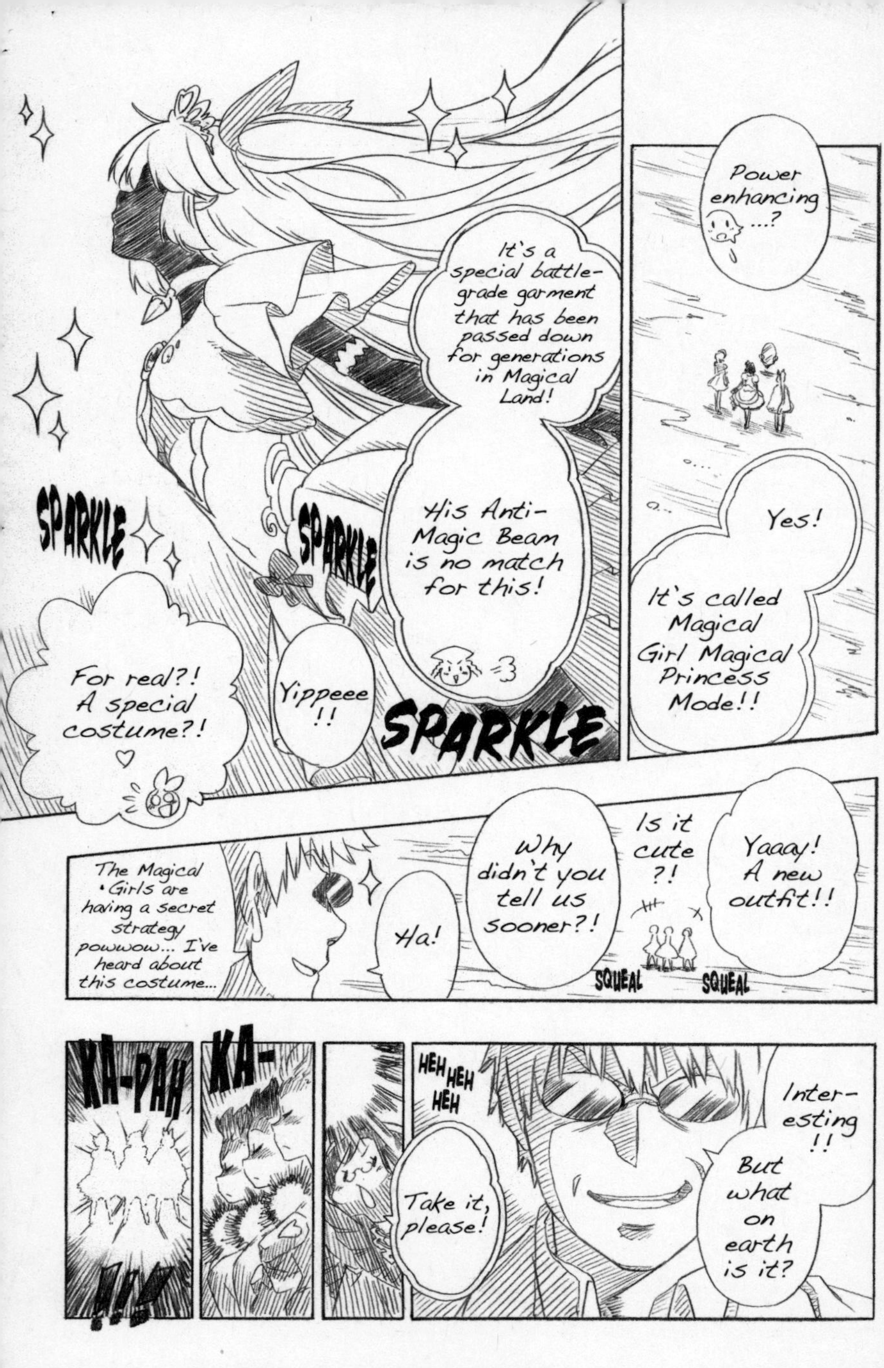
Power enhancing ...?
...
Yes!
It's called Magical Girl Magical Princess Mode!!
It's a special battle-grade garment that has been passed down for generations in Magical Land!
His Anti-Magic Beam is no match for this!
SPARKLE
SPARKLE
SPARKLE
Yippeee!!
For real?! A special costume?!
Yaaay! A new outfit!!
Is it cute?!
Why didn't you tell us sooner?!
SQUEAL
SQUEAL
Ha!
The Magical Girls are having a secret strategy powwow... I've heard about this costume...
Interesting!!
But what on earth is it?
HEH HEH HEH
Take it, please!
KA-
KA-PAH
!!!

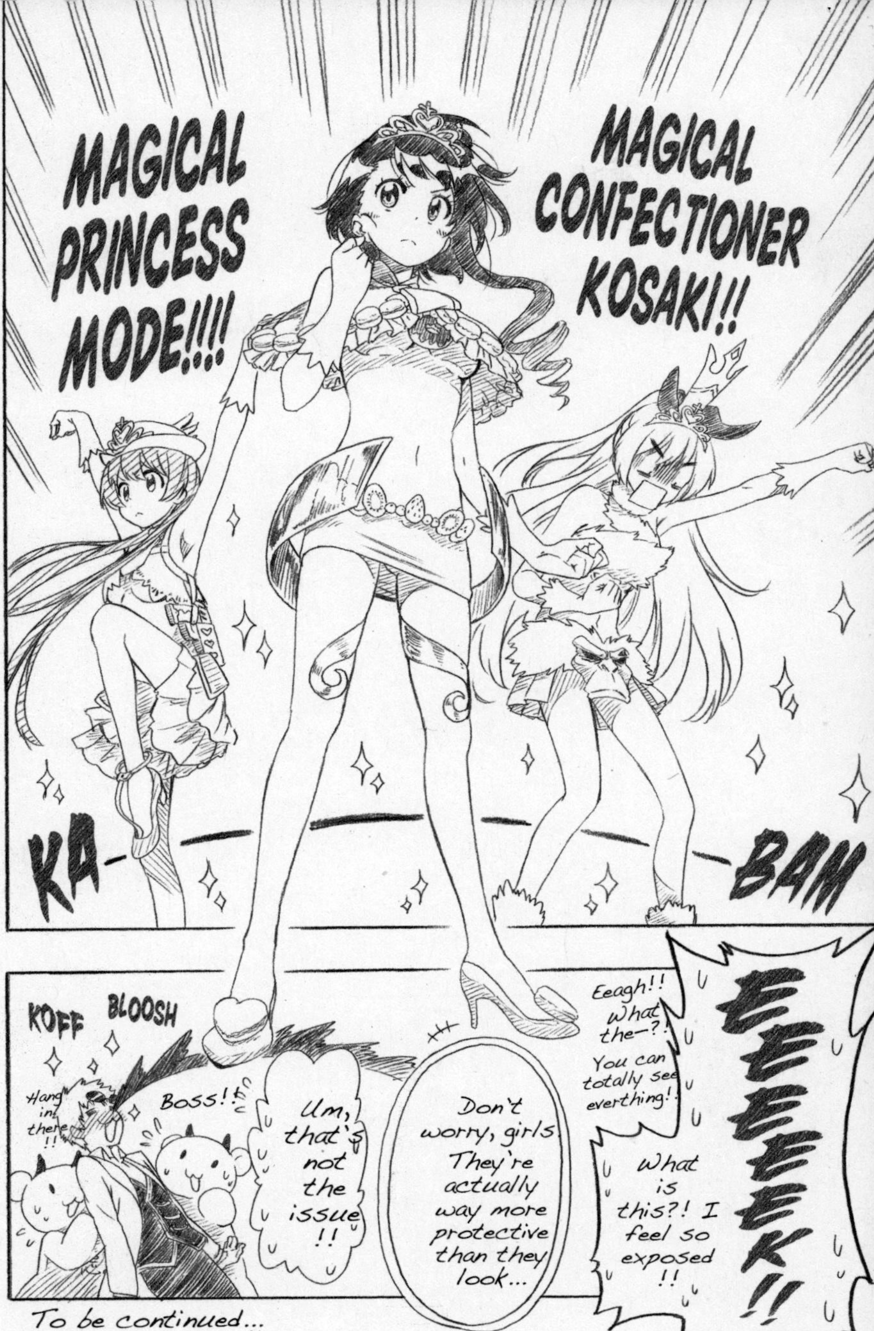
MAGICAL CONFECTIONER KOSAKI!!
MAGICAL PRINCESS MODE!!!!
KA————BAM
EEEEEK!!
Eeagh!! What the–?! You can totally see everthing!!
What is this?! I feel so exposed!!
Don't worry, girls. They're actually way more protective than they look...
Um, that's not the issue!!
Boss!!
Hang in there!!
KOFF
BLOOSH

To be continued...

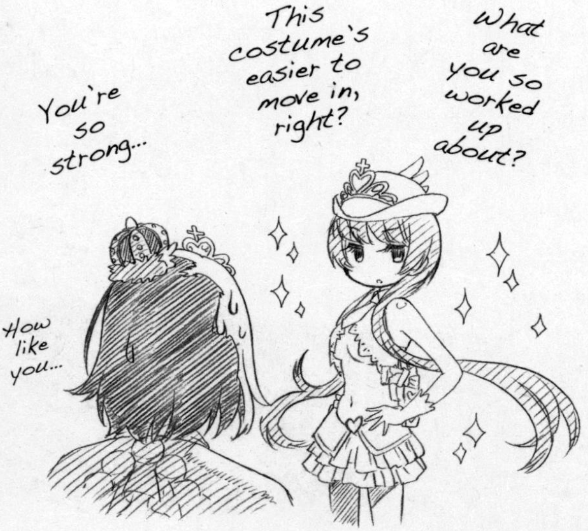
What are you so worked up about?
This costume's easier to move in, right?
You're so strong...
How like you...

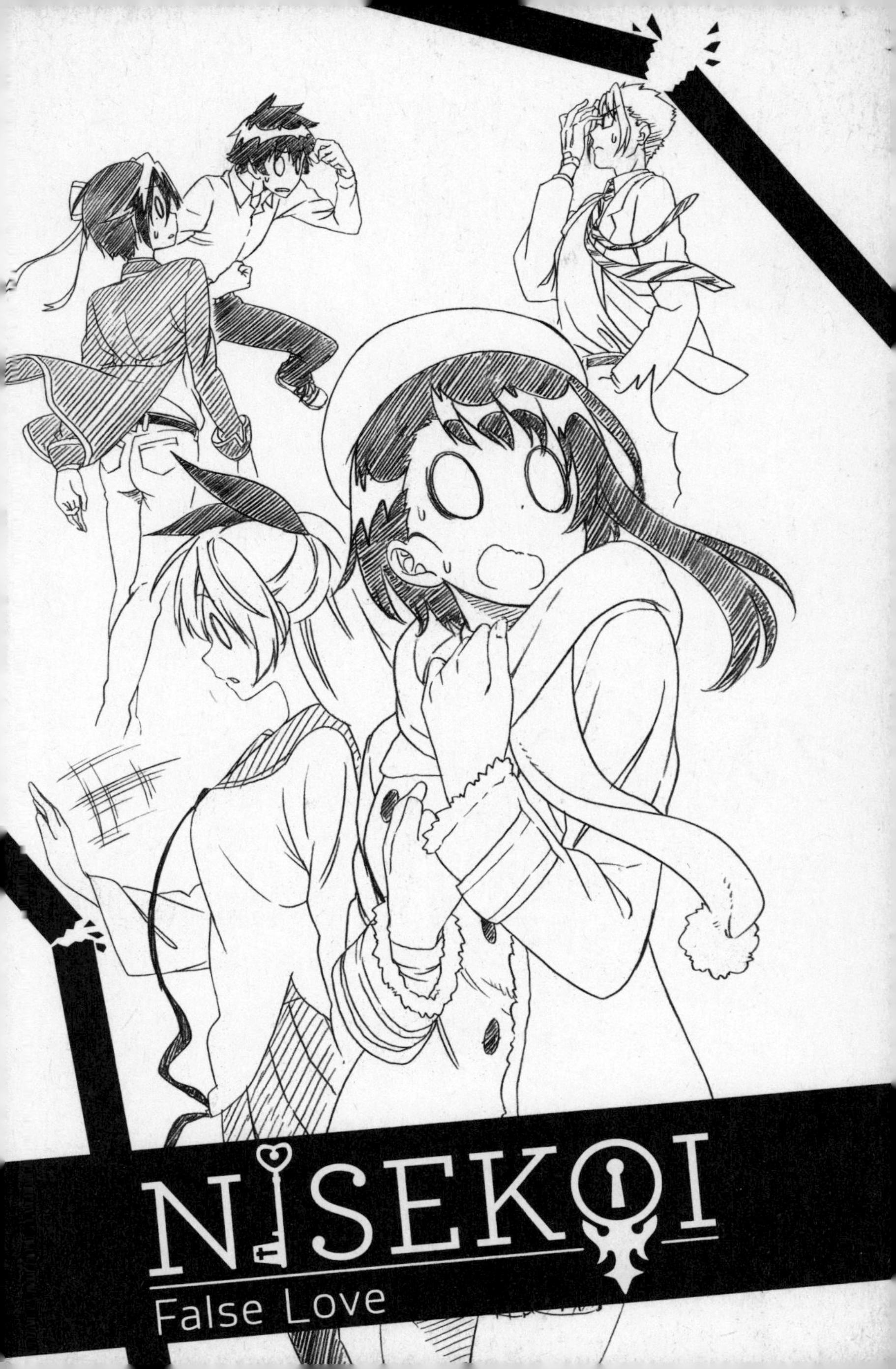
NISEKOI
False Love